SEV7EN
INTERACTIVE

Revelation: The Fifth Gospel
with Translation and Commentary

David M. Spencer, DMin, MD

Revelation: The Fifth Gospel

Copyright © 2024 by D. M. Spencer, DMin, MD

First Edition
Published by Seven Interactive Academic
1702 Villa Circle
Lebanon, TN 37090

All rights reserved. No part of this book may be reproduced or published by any means whatsoever without written permission. Brief quotations may be used with appropriate attribution.

For information, contact Admin@SevenInteractive.com.

Cover painting by Patti Sheets.
ISBN: 9798870228037

You can scan this QR code to access free slides that support your study of Revelation: The Fifth Gospel.

Scripture translation is by the author. The Greek text is the Textus Receptus.

Scripture quotations marked (NIV) are taken from the Holy Bible, New International Version®, NIV®. Copyright ©1973, 1978, 1984, 2011 by Biblica, Inc.™ Used by permission of Zondervan. All rights reserved worldwide. www.zondervan.com The "NIV" and "New International Version" are trademarks registered in the United States Patent and Trademark Office by Biblica, Inc.™

Scriptures quotations marked (KJV) are from the King James Version of the Bible.

Dedication

I dedicate this work to my mother who is an incessant student of Revelation and the Word in her later years. She exemplifies the faithfulness that Jesus expected of the members of the seven Lycus Valley Churches. She is the example for me of encouragement and wisdom in the Lord. She has an insatiable appetite to witness to the lost about Jesus. She will likely be a "pillar in the Temple of My God and will never go out from it" (Rev. 3:12).

Acknowledgments

I am indebted to my mother and stepfather who had curiosity and appetite for the future of Revelation and the hope of taking part in the activities of the New Jerusalem. My mother was a nurse who took great pride in teaching other nurses in the local nursing school in Danville, Illinois. But she had wonderful discussions about the Lord with her father, my grandfather, a cardiologist and internist in Danville. My grandfather raised her in the Presbyterian church where she learned and memorized Scripture. She married Dr. William Hensold, a retired family physician, after my father Malcolm Spencer, M.D., a dermatologist, died who both encouraged her relationship with the Lord. Both had insatiable appetites for the Book of Revelation and encouraged my curiosity for the same. I also acknowledge the input of the many students I taught Revelation to at the Harvest Bible Institute, Bridges Christian College, and my Sunday School class at Winston Salem First Assembly of God, Winston-Salem, North Carolina. I would usually learn much from them and from the Holy Spirit while teaching these classes. I look forward to seeing my grandfather, father, stepfather, and brother John in the New Jerusalem, as well as my other loved ones who have already passed through the veil of death into His marvelous light.

Preface

I never had much interest in the Book of Revelation until *after* attending seminary. But once my appetite for it was piqued by my mother Jane, stepfather Bill, and students wanting to know more about it, I began reading, thinking, and meditating on it. After reading the Gospels, memorizing, and writing about them (*The Chronological Gospel of Jesus Christ with Translation and Commentary*), I began memorizing The Revelation about seven years ago when I was teaching students at Bridges Christian College and my adult Sunday school class. For the latter, I realized that too much time was spent looking up the Scriptures and then having each student or class member read from his/her Bible the appropriate passages. So much variation existed between translations for the Book of Revelation, particularly the idiomatic translation versions (like *The Message translation*), that I decided to decrease variability and time to read from classmate to classmate or student to student. I began translating from the Greek into English, memorizing the Book, and then reciting before and teaching my classes the appropriate passages of Revelation. I was surprised that the memorization process came so easily. Over time, instead of taking a month to memorize a chapter, within six months it only took about five to seven days and another week to write the commentary on each chapter. It also became clear to me that the commentaries written on Revelation were usually done so by nonscientists and nonmedical people who had no interest in understanding the practical applications of John's vision of a future much closer to our age than John's several millennia ago. These commentaries usually interpret John's Apocalypse as simply symbolic allegories with little factual significance for the future and allusions based on Old Testament apocalyptic prophecies. I think it best to interpret *John's Revelation* literally as a first century Jewish Christian receiving glimpses of future events and describing these with first century language. The members of my classes received their commentary notes a few days before each session and were usually quite prepared to share their own meditations on Revelation. Their comments were inculcated into this my second book, *Revelation: The Fifth Gospel with Translation and Commentary*. As this work goes to the publisher, I am once again engaged by the Holy Spirit and my students in memorizing and writing about the Acts of the Apostles which should be ready for publishing by summer, 2024.

Foreword

Interest in end-time events is at an all-time high! As history continues to unfold, Christians need to prayerfully study the Scriptures to see what they reveal about the last days.

Dr. David Spencer provides a scholarly, insightful, and practical guide to the Book of Revelation. Any serious student of Revelation will benefit from the unique perspectives he presents, offering insights on the book that you won't find in other commentaries.

Dr. Spencer combines his scholarly theological training and his scientific and medical knowledge to bring unique insights and applications to eschatological passages of Scripture.

Preaching and teaching on Revelation are often neglected, in part because many lack confidence to apply the texts to Christian life. Yet Revelation is extremely relevant and practical. It was given to us to build our faith, grant us peace that the future is in God's hands, and motivate us to live rightly as we prepare for eternity. As the apostle Peter wrote, "What sort of people ought you to be in holy conduct and godliness, looking for and hastening the coming of the day of God" (2 Peter 3:11-12, NASB).

Dr. Spencer's commentary translates powerfully into how we live—so we're ready to stand before our Savior and can practice daily what the apostle John exhorted—to "abide in Him, so that when He appears, we may have confidence and not shrink away from Him in shame at His coming" (1 John 2:28, NASB).

Randy Hurst
Special Consultant to the Executive Director
Assemblies of God World Missions

CONTENTS

Introduction 11

REVELATION 1
John introduced to the Conquering Messiah 25

REVELATION 2
Messages to the Churches at Ephesus, Smyrna, Pergamum, & Thyatira 35

REVELATION 3
Messages to the Churches at Sardis, Philadelphia, and Laodicea 59

REVELATION 4
The Throne Room 75

REVELATION 5
The Scroll 87

REVELATION 6
The First through the Sixth Seal Judgments 95

REVELATION 7
Sealing & Commissioning of the Christian Jewish Evangelists 115

REVELATION 8
Wormwood 127

Revelation: The Fifth Gospel

REVELATION 9
The Fifth and Sixth Trumpet Judgments 139

REVELATION 10
John and the Mighty Angel 151

REVELATION 11
Two Jerusalem Prophets...159

REVELATION 12
Satan's Fall and Expulsion from Heaven 173

REVELATION 13
Rise of the Antichrist Beast 185

REVELATION 14
Jewish Christian Martyrs..199

REVELATION 15
Seven Angels with the Seven Last Plagues 209

REVELATION 16
The Seven Bowl Judgments 215

REVELATION 17
Destruction of Religious Babylon 231

REVELATION 18

Destruction of Economic Babylon 241

REVELATION 19

The Wedding of the Lamb with His Church 253

REVELATION 20

Millennial Reign 263

REVELATION 21

New Jerusalem 279

REVELATION 22

The River of the Water of Life 297

Summary 313

Index 321

Introduction

The Apostle John was quite busy with epistle, gospel and apocalyptic writing in the last two decades of his life. He was the closest to Jesus of the Twelve, as far as can be ascertained. In fact, John refers to himself five times in his Gospel as "Jesus' beloved disciple" (τον μαθητην ον ηγαπα ο Ιησους; Jn. 21:20; see also 13:23; 19:26; 20:2; 21:7). His close connection with the Lord is evident in his letters and Gospel. Not only is there a strong tradition that he was Jesus' first cousin, his mother, Salome, was very likely Mary's younger sister, making her Jesus' aunt (Mt. 27:1; 28:1; Mk. 15:40; 16:1; Jn. 19:25; 20:20). John likely was introduced to Jesus in his childhood through his mother and her close relationship with her sister Mary. She would take her family with Mary's to Jerusalem at least one time each year during the Spring for the Passover in Jerusalem. John and Jesus would have grown up together through these and through other family gatherings. He was obviously the closest to Jesus emotionally throughout Jesus' last three years. At His crucifixion, it was no surprise that John was the only disciple at the cross. In Jesus' last few hours, Jesus told John to add His mother Mary to his household since at the time of His crucifixion His four half-brothers were not a part of His *yeshiva*. It is therefore fitting that Jesus chose John to receive the visions associated with the End Times—the Book of the Apocalypse (Revelation). Its twenty-two chapters are full of references to this genuine communication privilege which even allowed John to experience and receive information about the End Times without being permitted to write down some of these episodes in Revelation (vis-à-vis Rev. 10:4).

Revelation: The Fifth Gospel

After John's post-Pentecost experiences in Jerusalem building the Church with Peter and the other Apostles, Deacon Stephen confronted the Sanhedrin suggesting that Jesus and His message marked a new covenant that God was offering to His people. His words resulted in his unjust and cruel stoning and marked a several year persecution against the Church under Saul's direction (Acts 6-7). The Church and its Hellenistic deacons were largely forced to leave Jerusalem during this time (cf. Acts 8:1-4). John helped Peter evangelize the Judean and Samaritan regions and then eventually migrated to Ephesus where he became head pastor succeeding Timothy's stint there in the late 70s. As we can ascertain by his three epistles, John led the Ephesus church with great wisdom, patience, and love. It would appear that he also had the privilege of mentoring the Lycus Valley pastors after his Ephesus head pastorship ended. His walk with Jesus was so compelling and the demonstration of the charismata so convincing that Emperor Domitian sent Praetorian guards to apprehend him and bring him to Rome. Little is known about the Emperor's interaction with Apostle John except that he felt threatened by John and gave orders for his execution.

Bust of Roman Emperor Domitian

According to the church historian Tertullian, John was boiled in hot oil by Emperor Domitian in Rome around AD 95.[1] John miraculously survived and then for two years was banished to Patmos, an island for political prisoners in the Aegean Sea.[2] Because he had such a great responsibility to receive and accurately report the

---

1   Tertullian (Latin: Quintus Septimius Florens Tertullianus), *The Prescription Against Heretics*, chapter 36., the Rev. Peter Holmes, DD, trans., (Cambridge, England: Cambridge University Press, 1845, pd), https://carm.org/tertullian/tertullian-the-prescription-against-heretics/ Accessed May 30, 2023).

2   Adela Collins. "Patmos." *Harper's Bible Dictionary*. Paul J. Achtemeier, gen. ed. (San Francisco: Harper & Row, 1985), 755

Introduction

words and visions of the Book of Revelation, I believe God allowed him to be on this island so that nothing would interrupt this spiritual task. Some scholars throughout the Church Age have questioned the Johannine authorship of Revelation including such notables as Martin Luther and Heinrich Zwingli.[3] But most, including the early patristic fathers Irenaeus (130-202), Clement of Alexandria (150-215), Tertullian (160-220), Bishop Victorinus (≈220-304), and Eusebius (265-339) thought that the beloved Apostle John wrote the work at the end of his life during the last two years of Emperor Domitian's reign.[4]

The Book is written in rougher Greek than John's previous works because he likely did not have access to skilled amanuenses as he did for the writing of his Gospel and the three Epistles. Revelation is apocalyptic because it reveals or unveils the End Times and second Parousia events hidden from the Church until this book was delivered to John. Scholars disagree on how to interpret Revelation; I think the simple approach is best. John explains what needs to be explained and doesn't offer explanation when he is directed by the Holy Spirit not to explain. Apocalyptic symbolism and imagery can be very confusing; of course, the Apostle knew this. So, John gives very adequate and cogent explanations of the events he witnesses when necessary. I think John receives his visions through time travel and/or through "heavenly video." He receives and faithfully records the events of Revelation in "linear fashion" and not in a "circular" manner. To think as the third century Victorinus from Pettau, Slovenia,[5] suggested that John wrote Revelation in cyclical fashion with the seal judgments taking place at the same time as the trumpet and bowl judgments is preposterous.[6] Each of the twenty-one judgments is distinctive despite some similarity for the sixth and seventh seal, trumpet, and bowl judgments. Some well-meaning modern Revelation commentators and scholars have suggested that the seven seal events of Revelation 6 and 8 are superimposed on the seven trumpet events of Revelation 8, 9, and 11 and the seven bowl episodes of Revelation 16 in a somewhat circular time frame. This circular understanding of these catastrophic events makes chapters 6-16 appear far too complicated, confusing, and uncharacteristic of the linear, direct, and straightforward style of

---

[3] David E. Aune, David A. Hubbard, Glenn W. Barker, John D. W. Watts, and Ralph P. Martin, *Revelation 1-5*, Vol. 52A, Word Biblical Commentary (Nashville, TN: Thomas Nelson, Inc., 1997), vi.
[4] Robert L. Thomas, "Theonomy and the Dating of Revelation," *Evangelical Hermeneutics: The New Versus the Old* (Grand Rapids, MI: Kregel Publications, 2002), 451-471.
[5] Robert H. Mounce, *The Book of Revelation*, 2nd Edition, The New International Commentary on the New Testament (Grand Rapids, MI: Wm. B. Eerdmans Publishing Company, 1998), 39, 45.
[6] LeRoy Froom, *The Prophetic Faith of our Fathers*, vol. 1 (Hagerstown, MD: Review and Herald Publishing 1950), 338-339.

the Bible. True, the Book of Revelation is apocalyptic and mysterious. However, it is unlikely that the Lord utilizes linear time for all Scripture and then switches the rules about time and uses circular time parameters for Revelation. The linear time frame is evident in several key Revelation passages describing the *last* plagues, inferring that the others come before in a temporal order:

- In Revelation 15:1, John saw seven angels coming out of the Temple carrying "the seven *last* plagues." (πληγας επτα τας εσχατος; 15:1)
- In *Revelation* 21:9, John and the angel revealing the events to John made it clear that the Revelation is linear and not circular: "And one of the seven angels having the seven bowls filled with the seven *last* plagues . . ." (των επτα πληγων των εσχατων; 21:9)

The Revelation and the Old Testament

Other Biblical apocalyptic literature includes passages from Daniel and Ezekiel of the Old Testament and from the Gospels of the New Testament. These passages are not nearly as complete about the Tribulation Period as is John's Revelation. The End Times is composed of seven years and is divided into two, three and a half year periods; the first is called the "Time of Sorrows" and the second period is called the "Great Tribulation Period." Much of the calculation and many of the critical events of these seven years are found in Daniel 7–9 and Matthew 24. The prophet Daniel enumerates what he referred to as "seventy sevens" (Dan. 9:24) and explains to some degree what this means:

> *"Seventy 'sevens' are decreed for your people and your holy city to finish transgression, to put an end to sin, to atone for wickedness, to bring in everlasting righteousness, to seal up vision and prophecy and to anoint the Most Holy Place.*
>
> *Know and understand this: from the time the word goes out to restore and rebuild Jerusalem until the Anointed One, the ruler, comes, there will be seven 'sevens,' and sixty-two 'sevens.' It will be rebuilt with streets and a trench, but in times of trouble. After the sixty-two 'sevens,' the Anointed One will be put to death and will have nothing. The people of the ruler who will come will destroy the city and the*

sanctuary. The end will come like a flood: war will continue until the end, and desolations have been decreed. He will confirm a covenant with many for one 'seven.' In the middle of the seven he will put an end to sacrifice and offering. And at the Temple he will set up an abomination that causes desolation, until the end that is decreed is poured out on him." (Dan. 9:24-27, NIV)

Daniel 9 discusses the seventy weeks of years of the End Times with sixty-nine weeks being fulfilled in the 483 years from the announcement to rebuild the city of Jerusalem (456 BC) to Jesus' death there (AD 27). The passages in Daniel 9 and in Matthew 24 discuss the last "week" or seven years of the Tribulation Period which is also mentioned in Revelation 6-16.

Ezekiel 1:1-28 also deals with some visions of heaven supported by John's vision of heaven but with some differences:

- Ezekiel saw the four living beings like John records in Revelation 4, but Ezekiel's living beings only had two pair of wings and John's had three pair of wings.
- Ezekiel's beings each had the four faces contained within each being whereas John's beings were distinctly different: one was a lion, another was a baby ox, another demonstrated the face of a man, and another looked like a flying eagle.
- Ezekiel's living beings were powered by "wheels" whereas John's were not.

The Revelation Interpretation Camps

At least four major camps or groups of Revelation scholars exist:

- **Preterists:** Various scholars are convinced that John simply received information from his Lord concerning the first century church and its future with the Roman Empire either during the apostolic age or throughout the history of the Empire until its demise around AD 476 when Odoacer (433-493) from the Celts conquered the last Roman Emperor Romulus

Augustus and his armies.[7] The weakness with this perspective is that the events of Revelation do not parallel the events of the first century church as recorded in the New Testament or by the Roman or Jewish historians of the times (i.e., Tacitus, Suetonius, Josephus). Nor does this perspective follow the developments of the decay and fall of the Roman Empire no matter how the events of the Apocalypse are interpreted.

▸▸ **Symbolic/Allegorists/Idealists:** Some well-meaning scholars feel that as apocalyptic literature, Revelation represents the Christian journey from birth to death in metaphorical, symbolic terms without relationship to actual physical events on earth or in heaven. In their opinion, John's Apocalypse was an attempt by deluded Christian apologists during periods of Roman persecution to encourage faithfulness and trust despite the hardships of their lives.[8]

▸▸ **Historicists:** These scholars believe that each major church-age dispensation is depicted by the chapters and the seven churches in John's bishopric. For example, they suggest that:

- Ephesus (Rev. 2:1–7) represents the first century church before Nero's persecution.

- Smyrna (Rev. 2:8–11) represents the persecuted church during Emperor Decius' and Emperor Diocletian's reigns of terror of the third and fourth centuries.

- Pergamum (Rev. 2:12–17) depicts the extravagant, excessive Roman Catholic Golden Age preceding the Reformation (1300–1500s).

- Thyatira (Rev. 2:18–29) may represent the New Thought Mysticism movement/Universalist Movement and subsequent development of the American Cults Era of the mid-1800s to present.

- Sardis (Rev. 3:1–6) may symbolize the Era of Modern American Liberalism and the world-wide Ecumenical Movement period of the 1900s to present: the so called "sleeping giant."

---

[7] Kenneth L. Gentry, Jr., *The Book of Revelation Made Easy: You Can Understand Bible Prophecy* (Powder Springs, GA: American Vision, 2008), 1–25.

[8] Gregory K. Beale, *The Book of Revelation* (Grand Rapids, MI: Wm. B. Eerdmans, 1999), 5–60.

- Philadelphia (Rev. 3:7-13) possibly refers to the "Modern Underground Church Era" in Arabic, Chinese, Russian, and Iranian dominated countries who are experiencing much persecution and martyrdom each year for their faith.
- Laodicea (Rev. 3:14-22) may refer to the Modern Evangelical American Church with its penchant for ambivalence and tolerance (lukewarmness/indifference).[9]

▸ **Literal futurists:** The majority of evangelical scholars believe for many good reasons that John's Apocalypse represents future events describing the Parousia, Rapture, judgments, millennial reign, Armageddon I and II, the Great White Throne Judgment, and The New Jerusalem. They believe that history is always linear and was described by John with the vernacular of John's times without the language or experiences to adequately depict the events of the future. These theologians believe, however, that John did his best to characterize a different future world and really did an admirable job at doing so.[10]

The Revelation Angel

The Revelation of Jesus Christ was delivered to the Apostle John through an angel who is never identified throughout the work. (Rev. 1:1) As God's vessel for the dissemination of the most important vision ever afforded humans, the angel takes his task very seriously. Often, apocalyptic literature in ancient times were introduced to the world through angels or "phantoms." Even Old Testament prophecies about the End Times were sometimes delivered to the prophets through an intermediary angel (vis-à-vis Daniel chapters 8 and 10). Remember that angels are beings created to minister/to serve us humans, as we see throughout Scripture and from Hebrews 1:14.

The angel was very familiar with John's strengths of outstanding intelligence and memory. He knew of John's tendency to rely on his intellect which was likely

---

[9] Francis Nigel Lee, *John's Revelation Unveiled* (Brisbane, New Zealand: Queensland Presbyterian Theological College, 2000), 1-15.
[10] Grant R. Osborne, *Revelation* (Grand Rapids, MI: Baker Academic, 2002), 21.

somewhat compromised as a nonagenarian. The angel reminds John to write down the vision on several different occasions throughout the course of the vision (vis-à-vis Rev. 1:11,19; 14:13; 21:5). The angel released and revealed the vision of the End Times to John in a logical and sequential fashion from past, to present, to future events. The Book of Revelation is divided into the following sections:

- Section 1: Past (chapter 1)
- Section 2: Present (chapters 2–3)
- Section 3: Future (chapters 4–22)

The Apostle John's Background

The Apostle John (A.D 6–100) was born the second son of Zebedee and his wife Salome who was likely the sister of Mary, Jesus' mother, as previously mentioned. His early life as Jesus' first cousin was spent going to family gatherings in Capernaum and to Jesus' boyhood home in Nazareth about 25 miles away. John was about ten to eleven years younger than Jesus and about five years younger than his brother James. As indicated by the Gospels, the two brothers always did things together; in fact, Jesus paired them as apostles (Lk. 6:14) and sent them on their first missionary tour around Galilee and Judea together (Mt. 10). John had an insatiable appetite for the spiritual and began to follow John the Baptist during the year before Jesus called him to become one of His *yeshiva* members.

During the Maccabean and first century, "holy men" or rabbis from the Pharisee, Zealot, Essene, and Sadducee parties would give free lectures during the evenings and during the winter-early spring months when workers and tradesmen had no or little work. The *yeshiva* rabbi would expound on the Talmud and Mishnah and then through the Socratic method pose a question and expect an answer from his *yeshiva* members when they gathered as a *yeshiva* at the end of the day.[11] Sometimes the answers would come from the groups within the *yeshiva*-two members per group designated by the *yeshiva* leader called "*chavrutas*."[12]

---

11   A Messianic *Yeshiva*, *Netivyah Bible Instruction Ministry*, accessed April 16, 2021, https://netivyah.org/a-messianic-yeshiva/.
12   Arye Forta, *Judaism (Examining Religions)*. (Portsmouth, NH: Heinemann Educational Publishers, 1989), 89.

Introduction

I believe that Jesus intentionally paired the twelve disciples in six groups of two so that His morning questions could be thought about and discussed together before answering Jesus, their *yeshiva* leader, at night. Jesus made sure that John was nurtured by Himself and his older brother James and Peter throughout the three years of ministry. I believe that the Gospels clearly indicate that Jesus invited His core group of six disciples (Peter, Andrew, James, John, Philip, and Nathaniel; Jn. 1) two times before they joined Him on a full-time basis. Immediately after the miracle catch of fish recorded in Luke 5 and after Jesus asked them a third time to become "fishers of men," they joined Him as full-time *yeshiva* members. They could do this because the catch of fish was so lucrative that their families could live off the proceeds from the catch for several years. John and his brother James were known to be impetuous and at times emotional. They were known as the "sons of thunder" ("υιοι Βροντης," Mk. 3:17) due to their desire to judge the Samaritans who didn't want to offer their *yeshiva* hospitality or accept the gospel when the *yeshiva* was passing through Samaria on their way to Jerusalem (cf. Lk. 9:54). True to his nature, John reported the more emotionally charged episodes of Jesus confronting the Sanhedrin and religious authorities in the Temple during the Feasts more than any other of the evangelists. By the end of the Gospel accounts, he was known to be *the disciple whom Jesus loved* ("τον μαθητην ον ηγαπα ο Ιησους," Jn. 13:23; 19:26; 20:2; 21:7, 20) as previously mentioned. John obviously was transformed into one of the key Kingdom personalities even before he received the Holy Spirit baptism and release in his life on the Day of Pentecost. Jesus told Peter in the presence of John and the other disciples that if He wanted John to stay alive until His return, what was that to Peter? Jesus' point to Peter was "mind your own business concerning the future" (Jn. 21:22). However, the inference was made by the disciples as a group that John would not die. John corrected this thought in John 21:23 telling his readers that Jesus did not indicate by His conversation with Peter that John would not die. Indeed, he did not die a martyr's death as did all of the disciples and most of the 120 people in the Upper Room. Jesus had another idea concerning John. He directed John and (according to a weak tradition) possibly His mother Mary to emigrate to Ephesus to avoid the death and destruction at the hand of General Titus and his Roman legions in AD 70.[13] John settled there and then helped pastor the burgeoning Ephesus church. He was instrumental in establishing the

---

13   Iza, "House of the Virgin Mary in Ephesus" *Turkish Archeological News*, December 9, 2019, accessed September 11, 2021, https://turkisharchaeonews.net/object/house-virgin-mary-ephesus#:~:text=These%20written%20pieces%20of%20evidence%20are%20also%20very,testified%20by%20Juvenal%2C%20Bishop%20of%20Jerusalem%2C%20in%20451.

Revelation: The Fifth Gospel

six churches of the Lycus Valley as the Bishop of the six pastors of this district which along with Ephesus were the seven churches that Jesus had messages for in Revelation 2-3. He allowed John to be banished to the relatively deserted island of Patmos in the Aegean Sea to allow for a fully engaged and undisturbed John to receive Jesus' critical map of the future of the Church and His Parousia.

Central to John's banishment to Patmos was his insistence on the worship of only one God—the Triune God of Father, Son, and Holy Spirit. As previously mentioned, the Roman Emperor of John's later years was Domitian from the Flavian Family which included his father, Emperor Vespasian (AD 68-79), and his brother, General

The Colosseum in Rome

Titus, who succeeded his father Emperor for just two years before his untimely death of a fever of unknown origin (AD 79-81). Domitian was one of three emperors claiming to be deity and demanding worship in the first century: the other two were Caligula (AD 37-41) and Nero (AD 54-68). After the three "deity" emperors died, the Roman Senate blocked their families' requests to honor them with posthumous deity status. Emperor Domitian required all to consider him "dominus et deus" (master and god).[14] Historians considered him a benevolent despot whom the army and the public revered, but the Senate hated. Domitian built many buildings in Rome, repaired its walls, expanded its borders, and bolstered its economy.

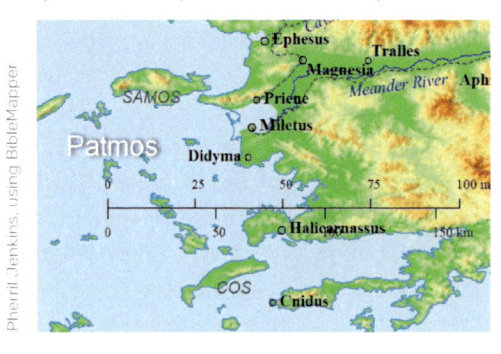

The map shows Patmos in relation to cities of Asia Minor.

---

14 C. Suetonius Transquillus, *Domitianus: The Lives of the Twelve Caesars: An English Translation*, chap. 2, J. Eugene Reed and Alexander Thomson, eds. (Philadelphia, PA: Gebbie & Co., 1889), accessed May 20, 2023, https://www.perseus.tufts.edu/hopper/text?doc=Perseus%3Atext%3A1999.02.0132%3Alife%3Ddom.%3Achapter%3D2.

Introduction

Domitian was tolerant of other religions but not Christianity and was suspicious of the Jews.[15] Emperor worship was expected of all Roman subjects except for the Jews; Jewish Christians could seek "sanction" from emperor worship unless they were excluded from the synagogues which occurred in Smyrna and Philadelphia. This exclusion from the synagogue caused their persecution and deaths at the hand of Domitian which the Lord Jesus was upset about as we see in Revelation 2–3. Domitian wanted to put an end to the Apostle John's influence in Christendom and his ability to lead Roman citizens away from emperor worship to Christ. He ordered his Praetorian guard to arrest John and bring him to Rome for hot oil boiling in the Roman Coliseum. So, by tradition, when the crowd saw that John survived the boiling oil unscathed, many people turned to the Lord Jesus Christ. After John's escape from sure death, Domitian thought that maybe he should not try to kill John again because "the gods were protecting him." He decided to send John to Patmos for several years as a religious exile.[16] Patmos was a nearly deserted 17 square mile island in the Aegean Sea about 50 miles from Ephesus in the Sporades chain of islands[17] often used by the emperor to banish political-religious prisoners.[18] In the previous century, it was a thriving Roman colony and a shipping center. The island had a gymnasium and was the home of a cult of Diana worshippers. As a nonagenarian, John would have been stressed by the banishment, although his needs were supplied. He could receive visitors and obviously a person to deliver his circular letter, Revelation, to the seven churches of the Lycus Valley.

The Island of Patmos

---

15   Cassius Dio Cocceianus, *Dio's Roman History*, 67:4:7, Herbert Baldwin Foster, trans., (nd, pd), accessed May 30, 2023, https://www.gutenberg.org/files/10890/10890-h/10890-h.htm#a67_4.
16   Tertullian, *The Prescription Against Heretics*, chapt. 26, Peter Holmes, D.D., et.al, trans. (nd, pd), accessed May 30, 2023, https://www.tertullian.org/anf/anf03/anf03-24.htm#P3482_1195909.
17   Gaius Plinus Secundus, *Pliny's Natural History in Thirty-Nine Books*, Book 4, chap. 12, Jonathan Couch, trans. (nd, pd) 22–23, accessed May 30, 2023, https://archive.org/details/plinysnaturalhis00plinrich/page/n233/mode/2up?q=sporades.
18   Tacitus, *The Annals of Tacitus*, iv.30, Alfred John Church and William Jackson Brodribb, trans. (New York: Macmillan, 1906, PD), accessed May 29, 2023, http://classics.mit.edu/Tacitus/annals.4.iv.html.

Revelation: The Fifth Gospel

John received the Revelation over several hours or days starting on a Sunday on this island. Interestingly, the Lord thought ninety-year-old John capable of receiving the most important revelation ever given to a human. Despite the intricacies and hundreds of details, John was intellectually capable of capturing God's End-Time message of over twelve thousand words in the twenty-two chapters of Revelation! Never mind the usual cognitive impairment that normally nonagenarians demonstrate. God trusted the Apostle of Love to deliver His "Battle Manual to Christendom" without hesitation.

John was a nonagenaraian (at least ninety years old) and was far more vulnerable to "senility" and the effects of Alzheimer's and fragility than in his previous decades. Like most elderly adults, he probably needed assistance with his basic needs. I am sure the church at Ephesus supplied these with attendants and monetary support particularly on the minimum security island of Patmos. In America, the nonagenarian population has exploded; at present, over two million people are ninety years old or above and by the year 2050, this number will quadruple. Nearly 90 percent of nonagenarians are white, 3:1 are female, and most live in poverty; 30 percent of nonagenarians live in assisted living facilities but interestingly, most still live independently or live with family members.[19] Most nonagenarians have multiple health issues the most common of which is Alzheimer's disease (AD). About 50 percent of all nonagenarins have AD in this country caused by genetic factors (three genes identified causing amyloid plaques and tau protein neurofibrillary tangle abnormalities in the thinking centers of the brain) and some suggestion of environmental factors such as heavy metals (aluminum, lead, and copper), smoking history, and head trauma (closed head injuries and concussions).[20]

Jesus took a great risk involving John in His Revelation because of the normal age-related weaknesses; but of course He knew every cell in John's body. The Holy Spirit also knew that John would *not be as vulnerable to radiation* seeing and in close proximity to the resurrected and empowered Christ who reintroduced Himself to John after seventy-five years of physical absence. Because of his advanced years, *if* exposed to radiation from Jesus' eyes, skin, hair, and mouth (Rev. 1:14–17)

---

19 Jon Lapook, "More and more Americans living past 90," AFP CBS News, August.5, 2013, accessed May 29, 2023, https://www.cbsnews.com/news/more-and-more-americans-living-past-90/.

20 Xu H, David I. Finkelstein and Paul A. Adlard, "Interactions of metals and Apolipoprotein E in Alzheimer's disease," *Frontiers in Aging Neuroscience*, June 12, 2014, accessed May 3, 2023, https://www.ncbi.nlm.nih.gov/pmc/articles/PMC4054654/.

and from the throne room (Rev. 4–5), the radiation effects on his bone marrow (i.e. platelets, red blood cells, and white blood cells) would not be expressed until many years later. Presumably his passing just a few years after receiving this Apocalypse would have prevented John from experiencing leukemia, lymphoma, and other radiation effects. A younger disciple receiving this vision of the future would have been vulnerable to chronic radiation effects if the radiation emanating from Jesus' body and or the throne room was more than just the visible light spectrum.[21] Of course it is obvious that the radiation emanating from Jesus' mouth-laser in Rev. 19:21 is far more destructive than what John was exposed to in his meeting with Jesus in Revelaton 1. Jesus knew that John could be trusted to attentively watch, listen, and write down the Revelation without error, bias, or distraction. What a privilege to receive the Revelation. But what a responsibility too.

---

21 Luke D. Spencer, MD, conversation on October 7, 2022.

REVELATION 1

John introduced to the Conquering Messiah

1 "This is the revelation of Jesus Christ that God gave to Him to show his servants what must soon take place. And He made it clear by sending it through His angel to His servant John [2] who testified to the Word of God and the testimony of Jesus Christ, as much as he saw. [3] Blessed is the one reading it, as well as the ones hearing the words of this prophecy, and obeying the things written in it, for the time is near.

[4] "John, to the seven churches in Asia, grace and peace to you from the One who was, and is, and is to come and from the seven spirits before His throne [5] and from Jesus Christ, the faithful witness, the firstborn from the dead, and the ruler of the Kings of the earth, to the One loving us and loosing us from our sins by His blood, [6] and making us into a kingdom of priests for His God and Father, to Him be glory and power, forever and ever, Amen. [7] Behold, He is coming in the clouds, and every eye will see Him, and whoever pierced Him, and all the nations of the earth will mourn because of Him, yes, Amen. [8] I am the Alpha and the Omega says the Lord God, the One who was and is and is to come, The Almighty.

Revelation: The Fifth Gospel

> [9] "I, John, your brother and partner in suffering, in the Kingdom, and in patient endurance with Jesus, I was on the island of Patmos because of the Word of God and the testimony of Jesus, [10] and on the Lord's Day I was in the Spirit when I heard a loud voice like a trumpet behind me [11] saying, 'Write what you see in a scroll and send it to the seven churches: to Ephesus, to Smyrna, to Pergamum, to Thyatira, to Sardis, to Philadelphia, and to Laodicea.' [12] Then I turned around to see the voice that spoke with me and having turned, I saw seven golden lampstands [13] and One like the Son of Man standing in the middle of the lampstands dressed in a long robe with a golden sash around His chest [14] and His face, including His hair was like white wool like snow, and His eyes like a flame of fire, [15] and His feet like fine bronze as in a fiery hot furnace and His voice was like the voice of many waters; [16] And He held seven stars in His right hand and out of His mouth projects a double edged sharp sword and His face shines like the sun in its power. [17] Upon seeing Him, I fell at His feet as if dead. But He put His right hand on me saying, 'Do not be afraid, for I am the first and the last, [18] the living One; I was once dead, but look! I am alive forever and ever and I hold the keys of Death and Hades. [19] Now write down what you saw: both what happens and what takes place after these things.' [20] 'The mystery of the seven stars that you saw in My right hand and the seven golden lampstands: the seven stars are the messengers (pastors) of the seven churches and the seven lampstands are the seven churches.'"

Apocalyptic literature writers of the first and second centuries often used Old Testament pseudonyms to establish believability with their audiences and to validate their writings. But John did not. His audience recognized who he was and knew about his impeccable reputation and character which were without reproach. He probably was head bishop of Ephesus and leader of the association of the seven churches mentioned in chapters 2 and 3. According to Erikson's psychosocial stages, those over sixty-five years old experience "ego integrity versus despair." They learn to be comfortable with their past, can forgive themselves when necessary, and can say "I lived my life well" or they end up perseverating on their failures, live in regret

John introduced to the Conquering Messiah

and disappointment, and eventually slip into despair and depression.[22] The Apostle John obviously learned to work through the failures of life, had few regrets that we know about, and probably felt very good about his life—so good that he was praying as was his custom on a Sunday on a lonely island and not feeling sorry for himself when he received the Revelation. We are not told what time of the day John began his encounter with Jesus, but when it began, the world and its future would never be the same.

The Apostle John received the Revelation through "an angel" not identified by name throughout the book. One wonders if Gabriel was the angel of record since Gabriel was known to be very verbal; God would often use him to announce important events or give significant messages. John tells his audience that the angel was responsible for the "making it clear" (εσημανεν, v.1) since, by its very nature, the Revelation (αποκαλυψις, v.1) would contain information difficult to understand and not yet revealed to humans. John stated that he is a "servant" (δουλω, v.1), not surprising, since he had lived a life of servant-leadership to his flock in Ephesus and dutifully took care of Mary and others in his household. He was noted earlier to be the disciple of "love" as the closest emotionally to Jesus. His love for the world and the lost of the Roman Empire was effortless; but being the servant of Jesus was his life's mission. Remember that up to 40 percent of the population in and around Rome and in its expansive Empire were of the slave class which amounted to nearly eighteen million slaves throughout the Empire.[23] These and those from the lower classes would have understood the significance of John's identity as δουλος. John explains in verse 1 that he faithfully reported the reception and recording of the Revelation and everything that he saw and heard. He also stated that the future events in the Revelation "must very soon take place" (α δει γενεσθαι εν ταχει, v. 1). This phrase suggests a difference between human time and heaven/divine time. Those humans who have experienced heaven in near death experiences have reported that spending a few days or weeks there was like a few seconds here. At the very least, their reports indicate that heaven time is very different from earth time. In Revelation 5:6, John saw Jesus as the lamb recently slaughtered. If John received this vision at the end of his life around AD 95 or AD 96, then even though Jesus experienced death by crucifixion seventy years before, it was as if He had just been crucified when John sees Him.

---

22 Divya Tiwari, *Ego Integrity vs. Despair*: (A Comprehensive Guide), accessed April 24, 2021, https://optimistminds.com/ego-integrity-vs-despair/.
23 "Slaves of Ancient Rome," Legends and Chronicles, accessed May 4, 2023, https://www.legendsandchronicles.com/ancient-civilizations/ancient-rome/slaves-of-ancient-rome/.

Revelation: The Fifth Gospel

This is the only book in the Bible where blessing is conferred on those "reading" (αναγινωσκων, v. 3) and "hearing" (ακουοντες, v. 3) its words/revelation. Of course, both terms connote more than just the physical acts. They both indicate heartfelt, intellectual assent of cherishing the Revelation of John and the promises of the Lord to those who are obedient servants of His Word and Christ. Indeed, the next phrase after reading and hearing is, "and obeying the things having been written in it" (και τηρουντες τα εν αυτη γεγραμενα, v. 3). There are five other "blessings" reported to the readers/doers of Revelation (14:13, 16:15, 19:9, 22:7, 22:14). No other book in the Bible has so much promise of blessing—with the exception of Proverbs.

John continued reporting the Revelation of Jesus Christ by mentioning the origin of the vision—the Triune God who sends this apocalypse to the seven churches of the Lycus Valley region. From the beginning of the book, the immediate purpose of the Revelation is clear. The recipients of the vision are the seven churches who will be reading what Jesus thinks about them shortly. John established one of the major proof texts in Scripture for the Triune God by describing the Trinity and each of their main functions: "from the One who was, and is, and is to come" (απο ο ων και ο ην και ο ερχομενος, v. 4), "and from the seven Spirits before His throne" (και απο των επτα πνευματων α ενωπιον του θρονου αυτου, v. 4), "and from Jesus Christ, the faithful witness, the firstborn from the dead, and the ruler of the kings of the earth." (και απο Ιησου Χριστου ο μαρτυς ο πιστος ο πρωτοτοκος των νεκρον και ο αρκων των βασιλεων της γης, v. 4). Several American cults and the "Oneness" group within the Charismatic Movement would do well to note John's descriptors of the Triune God. Indeed, the Father heads the Trinity—John mentioned Him first with no beginning or end. Then the Holy Spirit is mentioned second as the Being composed of seven spirits located before God and His throne where also He is mentioned being in Revelation 4:5 and 5:6. It is interesting that the Holy Spirit is described as composed of *seven* spirits. The integer "seven" has always been considered a perfect number representing God. One wonders if the seven spirits described by John in John 5:6 as going out "to the whole world" refers to the work of the Holy Spirit in each one of the seven continents of the world.

John continued his introduction stating that Jesus was the faithful, steady witness to the world of the Godhead. His sinless and loving life filled with great teaching and healing moments for the people of Israel and the Gentiles allowed humans to see what the Father and the Spirit were all about. In effect, as the writer of Hebrews stated, "The Son [Jesus] . . . is the exact representation of His being" (Heb. 1:3). John also mentioned that Jesus was the first human to be fully resurrected from the dead, although the widow of Nain's son (Lk. 7:15), Jairus' daughter (Lk. 8:55), Lazarus (Jn. 11:43-44) were resuscitated. I believe Jesus' body at the resurrection was restored to His pre-incarnation form which He had from before the beginning of time and creation. John also stated that Jesus was the ruler over the kings of the earth confirming multiple Old Testament passages of His dominant Kingship. (see Deut. 10:17; Ps. 136:3; Is.9:6-7).

In the next sentence, John captured the raison d'être of Christ on the earth and the purpose of all Christ-followers. John continued elaborating on the person and identity of Jesus by telling his audience that Jesus "unconditionally loved us" (αγαπωντι ημας, v. 5) and because of that love "loosed us from our sins by His blood" (λυσαντι ημας εκ των αμαρτιων ημων εν τω αιματι αυτου, v. 5) and "made us into a kingdom of priests to His God and Father" (εποιησεν ημας βασιλειαν ιερεις τω θεω και πατρι αυτου, v. 5). In one sentence, John summarized the whole of Pauline systematic theology and the mission of Jesus' life and our lives after our conversions. I would say that Revelation 1:5 summarizes Christianity as succinctly as any passage in the New Testament. The Passion and crucifixion of Jesus would not go unpunished as John indicated in the next sentence. Jesus as the Judge will return with every eye watching Him including those who "pierced Him" (αυτον εξεκεντησεν, v. 7). John did not mention their punishment but inferred consequences for their actions because he stated that the nations "will mourn because of Him" (κοψονται επ αυτον, v. 7). Indeed, from the beginning of this book, the Godhead represents Jesus as the Conquering Messiah who mediates judgment against those who opposed Him while He ministered on the earth as a Rabbi from Nazareth and as the Savior of the world. As the reader of the middle and later chapters of Revelation sees throughout the twenty-one judgments on the earth, Jesus truly is the Conquering Messiah and Judge of the nations and of the unholy trinity—the dragon (the devil), the Beast (the Antichrist), and the false prophet. In the next verse, John confirms the identity of the originator of the vision—Father God who was and is and is to come the "alpha and the omega" (το αλφα και το ω, v. 8).

John then continued with his suggestion that he was a brother to the recipients of the Revelation and was a partner in the "suffering" (θλιψει, v. 9) and Kingdom living which included "patient endurance" (υπομονη, v. 9). After completing the introduction, John began the Revelation with the story of his encounter with the resurrected Christ. But first and appropriately, he set up his life-changing vision by mentioning the setting: The Romans placed John on the Island of Patmos due

Revelation: The Fifth Gospel

to his outspoken faith and dedication to Jesus Christ. As previously discussed, Domitian banished John because he was not killed as he should have been in the hot oil bath he was plunged into in the Colosseum at Rome. John found himself alone on the island except for a skeleton crew who took care of his basic needs and the other prisoners there who were political-ideological "criminals" in the eyes of Rome. Surely John was a fellow sufferer with the members of the seven churches in Asia Minor who were also experiencing hardship and outright opposition (cf. Smyrna and Philadelphia). John identified himself with the sufferings of his fellow church members at the hand of Emperor Domitian due to his uncompromising Christian walk and for spreading the Gospel to the Roman Empire. The Wesleyan Quadrilateral identifies four aspects to our Christian walk/faith critical in spiritual formation: Scripture, tradition, reason, and experience.[24] Our experience in Christ of necessity involves "suffering because of Him" (Phil. 1:29); without suffering we have no perseverance (endurance), character, or hope (Rom. 5:3-5). John's life reflected the high value the Spirit places on His followers who experience suffering and recognize the value that persecution brings to their lives. The Spirit values this so much that He even directs our lives *into* suffering when it is necessary as we see throughout Revelation.

John described a normal Sunday for him—he was praying and meditating "in the Spirit" (εν πνευματι, v. 10) when he heard a "loud trumpet-like voice" (φωνην μεγαλην ως σαλπιγγος, v. 10) behind him directing him to write down what he is about to see in a book/scroll and send this to the seven churches beginning with his home church Ephesus and then to the others associated with it. In the first century, people wrote on papyrus (παπυρος) made from papyrus plant pith and on parchments/vellum (μεμβρανος, 2 Tim. 4:13) which were specially prepared goat, sheep, or calf skins.[25] These were either connected and rolled together in scrolls or later in the first century were cut into rectangles and bound together in codex (book) form. John would not have had the materials to write the vision down in a book since books were very rare in the first century. He likely had scrolls of vellum or parchment material processed from the hides of young animals.[26] John could have gotten his vellum writing material from the hides of one year old lambs possibly supplied by his attendants on the island or maybe even from his Ephesus

---

24   Alan K. Waltz, *A Dictionary for United Methodists* (Nashville, TN: Abingdon Press, 1991).

25   Marion Kite and Roy Thomson, eds., *Conservation of Leather and Related Materials* (Oxford, United Kingdom: Elsevier Butterworth-Heinemann, 2006), 201-203.

26   The cover of this commentary was painted by my local artist friend Patti Hricinak Sheets onto vellum sent to her by David Bianco of the Flying B Bar Ranch, Selma, Oregon who slaughtered a one-year-old lamb and processed the hide into a thin vellum sheet; the symbology is striking.

John introduced to the Conquering Messiah

congregation some 50 miles away who were involved in raising sheep and goats for a living.

A word about the chapters and verses of the Book of Revelation, and for that matter, the whole Bible. The scrolls of parchment (skins of sheep, calves or goats), vellum (lambs or calves), or papyrus of the original writings of the evangelists and authors of the rest of the New Testament never had chapter or verse markings.[27] In fact, not until the Archbishop of Canterbury, Stephen Langton, designated the chapters of the New Testament in AD 1227 in his Bible, did Christendom have any reference points for the Word. The Wycliffe Bible of 1382 adopted Archbishop Langton's suggestion for the chapters.[28] The verses were designated several hundred years later in 1555 when the French printer Robert Estienne (known as Robertus Stephanus, his Latin name) printed the Vulgate using the Rabbi Nathan's verses designations of the Old Testament and himself compiled the New Testament verses.[29] The Geneva Bible, the first English translation to adopt both chapter divisions and verses, was released to the public in 1560.[30]

In Revelation 1:10, the loud voice surely frightened John, but he suppressed his surprise and fear response enough to listen to the voice's command that he write down his experience and send to the seven churches under his influence. John didn't even need to have the voice tell him which seven churches he was to send the message to: Ephesus, Smyrna, Pergamum, Thyatira, Sardis, Philadelphia, and Laodicea. The enumeration of each of the churches was more for the readers than for him. He then turned around to identify the voice and saw seven golden lampstands (επτα λυχνιας χρυσας, v. 12) and a Being standing in the middle of these candelabra "like the Son of Man" (ομοιον υιον ανθρωπου, v. 13). The menorah (lampstand) signified true Israel throughout the Old Testament and during the intertestamental periods. Indeed, the two prophets appearing in Revelation 11 in Jerusalem were described as "two lampstands" because they both were truly dedicated to God and to the task of protecting the Holy City from the Beast and

---

27   The Bible Illuminated: How Art Brought the Bible to an Illiterate World. Edited by Karen York. (Franklin, TN: Museum of the Bible Books. 2017), 5.
28   Compelling Truth, "When were the books of the Bible divided into chapters and verses? Who did the dividing?" accessed May 4, 2023, https://www.compellingtruth.org/divided-Bible-chapters-verses.html.
29   Matthew Crutchmer, "Robert Estiennce: 1503–1559" Desiring God, accessed May 4, 2023, https://www.desiringgod.org/articles/the-ink.
30   Arthur Sumner Herbert, *Historical Catalogue of Printed Editions of the English Bible 1525-1961*, (London: United Bible Societies, 1968).

his minions. The human figure that John saw standing near the lampstands of course *had* to be Jesus. But John, at that moment, was understandably startled and terrified. Jesus chose to appear to John in His gloried form like John had seen Jesus on Mt. Herman with his brother James and Peter at the Transfiguration (Mk. 9, Mt. 17, Lk.9). As in the Transfiguration, Jesus appeared to him as a very bright figure. But on this close encounter of the third (seeing Jesus), fourth (Jesus touched John), and fifth (Jesus communicated with John) kinds[31], John saw more detail. He observed that Jesus was clothed in the long robe of a priest with a golden sash around His chest (v. 13). This was the same garb of the seven angels with the seven bowls of God's wrath that John saw as he described in Revelation 15:6. John then noticed Jesus' head, particularly His hair which was "like white wool, like snow" (ως εριον λευκον ως χιων, v. 14). Jesus' hair reflected the solar-like radiation of His heavenly environment and from His brain which the three disciples were acutely aware of when Jesus appeared with Moses and Elijah. John described Jesus' eyes as "flame of fire" (φλοξ πυρος, v. 14), again indicative of the tremendous power coursing throughout His body and through His brain and through His feet, which John describes as being like molten bronze treated in a "fiery hot furnace" (καμινω πεπυρωμενης, v. 15). Neuroscientists have long researched the human brain and have revealed that the average adult brain can produce up to 15 watts of energy which could power a light bulb. They also suggest that the entire human body can produce as much as 2,000 watts of energy during an athletic event.[32] The description of Jesus here is remindful of John's vision of the New Jerusalem and how Jesus appeared in this celestial city after it came to earth in Revelation 21:23: John saw Jesus as the moon giving light to the residents inside it walls and by this, replacing the moon's light which John states is not needed in the city.

John then discussed Jesus' voice which he first heard *before* actually seeing Jesus. Jesus' amplified voice, "like a trumpet," was easier for John to deal with

---

[31] Encounters with aliens has been classified into seven distinct "close encounter" entities: first kind=five hundred ft. from the UFO showing great detail of it; second kind=physical effect experienced from the UFO such as heat, discomfort, chemical tastes, burnt vegetation; third kind=observation of a humanoid, robot, or other form as occupants or pilots of the UFO; fourth kind=actual contact with extraterrestrial, including hallucinatory or altered reality states during and/or after the contact; fifth kind=direct communication between humans and aliens through "conscious, voluntary and proactive human-initiated cooperative communication."; sixth kind=death of a human or animal associated with UFO or alien; seventh kind=creation of a human or alien hybrid by sexual or other scientific means

[32] Julia Layton, "How does the body make electricity–and how does it use it?" How Stuff Works, accessed September 22, 2021, https://health.howstuffworks.com/human-body/systems/nervous-system/human-body-make-electricity.htm.

John introduced to the Conquering Messiah

than Jesus' physical glorified appearance. John is not overwhelmed with Jesus' voice because as a nonagenarian he had lost some of his hearing. However, when John turned around to *see* who was speaking, Jesus' physical appearance actually *was* overwhelming to him. John states that Jesus' voice sounded like a cataract or "many waters" (υδατων πολλων, v. 15). Before John passed out, he saw two more details—somewhat shocking to a first century Israelite. Jesus held seven stars in His hand and a "double-edged sharp sword comes out of His mouth" (εκ του στοματος αυτου ρομφαια διστομος οξεια εκπορευομενα, v. 16). John could not describe this "sword" phenomenon in any other way than with the vernacular of his times. His description of an actual sword going out of Jesus' mouth may actually have been a thick beam of laser-like light which was "sharp" or well defined on both of its edges. John uses this same descriptor of the "sword" in Revelation 19:15, 21 coming out of Jesus' mouth and destroying the armies of the Beast and his kings. The sword is likely therefore a type of weaponized laser which even now is part of America's space defense system.[33] Since 2020, a weaponized laser beam system has been operational in Israel called "Iron Beam" to shoot down short-range rockets and mortar bombs targeted against Israel with a maximum effective range of up to 17 kilometers (about 10 miles) away.[34]

 The seven stars in Jesus' right hand indicate that Jesus possesses the well-being and the future of His seven Lycus Valley churches that we see from John's own explanation of the seven stars and the seven lampstands at the end of this chapter. As the Apostle John took in the scene of the glorified Jesus, the last thing he noticed, before blacking out, was Jesus' face reflecting the radiant energy of His inner being as if he were looking at the sun at midday; John states that Jesus' face "shines like the sun in its power" (ως ο ηλιος φαινει εν τη δυναμει αυτου, v. 16). John's central nervous system had enough: his stress hormones norepinephrine and epinephrine from his adrenal glands poured into his vascular system eventually making it to his brain causing vasoconstriction and lack of blood flow into the brain's wake center and made him black out. He fell down at Jesus' bronze-like feet. We don't know how long he stayed on the ground during this syncopal event. But Jesus made him "come to" by placing His right hand on John's head or back and with soothing

---

33   Kris Osborn, "Laser Weapons Are Headed to Space to Shoot Down Missiles," *The National Interest*, September 18, 2020, accessed April 22, 2021, htpps://nationalinterest.org/blog/buzz/laser-weapons-are-headed-space-shoot-down-missiles-169176.

34   Mark Episkopos, "The 'Iron Beam': Israel's Anti-Missile Laser," *The National Interest*, September 8, 2020, accessed May 5, 2023, https://nationalinterest.org/blog/reboot/iron-beam-israels-anti-missile-laser-168570.

words told him not to fear and that He was the resurrected Christ whom John had seen about seventy years before, who had been dead but now is very much alive and living forever. Jesus also mentioned that He has "the keys of death and Hades" (τας κλεις του θανατου και του αδου, v. 18). By this time, John knew that this "Son of Man" figure was certainly his first cousin[35] in His resurrected, death-defying form who was engaging John for the very important task of informing all interested about the End Times. Jesus' angel again reminded John to write down the details of the vision that he just received and the coming events of the Apocalypse. Then the angel revealed the symbolism of the seven stars and golden lampstands.

Jesus told John that the sevens stars were the (αγγελοι, v. 20) messengers or pastors of the seven Lycus Valley churches and that the seven lampstands stood for the seven churches (εκκλησιαι, v. 20). The seven stars in Jesus' right hand ("angels"/"messengers") were either the head pastors of the seven churches or the protective angels of the churches. It makes more sense to consider the messengers of the churches as the *pastors* due to the warnings against sinful practices going on in five of the seven Lycus Valley churches which holy angels *would not* commit or be responsible for. I don't think that angels are ever put in charge of churches. The New Testament never suggests this. Jesus had much to tell John and the readers and hearers of the vision about the seven churches that he had once overseen. The seven churches mentioned in Revelation 2 and 3 experienced some of what the American churches face today and are an excellent example of good and bad behavior.

---

35 Jay Rogers, "Jesus' cousins were the Apostle James and John" The Forerunner, August 28, 2007, accessed May 5, 2023, https://www.forerunner.com/blog/jesus-cousins-were-the-apostles-james-and-john.

REVELATION 2

Messages to the Churches at Ephesus, Smyrna, Pergamum, & Thyatira

Ephesus

1 "To the pastor of the church in Ephesus write, the one holding the seven stars in his right hand and standing in the middle of the seven golden lampstands says these things: ² 'I know your works, your labor, your patient endurance, and that you cannot accept evil ones; you have examined those who say they are apostles but are not, indeed you found them to be liars. ³ You have patient endurance and have endured on behalf of My Name and you have not given up. ⁴ But I have against you that you gave up your first love. ⁵ Remember then from where you have fallen, repent and do the first works; but if not, I am coming to you and will remove your lampstand from its place, if you would not repent. ⁶ But you have this: you hate the work of the Nicolaitans which I also hate. ⁷ The one with

an ear to hear, let him hear what the Spirit is saying to the churches. To the victorious one I will allow him to eat from the Tree of Life which is in the Paradise of God.'"

Smyrna:

[8] "And to the pastor of the church in Smyrna write, the One who is the first and the last who became dead but is now alive again says this: [9] 'I know your suffering and your poverty yet you are rich and the blasphemy from those saying they are Jews yet they are not, but are from the Synagogue of Satan. [10] Do not fear what you are about to suffer. Indeed, the devil is about to throw some of you into prison that you might be tested; you will have suffering for 10 days but be faithful even to death and I will give you the crown of life. [11] The one with an ear to hear, let him hear what the Spirit is saying to the churches. The victorious one will not at all be hurt by the second death.'"

Pergamum:

[12] "And to the pastor of the church in Pergamum write, 'The One with the double-edged sharp sword says these things, [13] 'I know where you live, where Satan's throne is; and you have held on to My Name and have not denied your faith in Me even in the days of Antipas, My faithful witness, who was killed among you where Satan dwells. [14] But I have a few things against you, namely, you have some there who hold on to the teaching of Balaam who taught Balak to put a trap before the people of Israel to eat idol meat and to fornicate. [15] In addition, there are some there holding on to the teaching of the Nicolaitans. [16] Repent then, but if not, I am coming to you soon, I will make war against them with the sword from My mouth. [17] The one with an ear to hear, let him hear what the Spirit is saying to the Churches. To the victorious one I will give the hidden manna and I will give him a white pebble and a new name written on the pebble that no one knows except the one receiving it.'"

Thyatira:

[18] "And to the pastor of the church in Thyatira write: The Son of God with eyes like a flame of fire and feet like fine bronze says these things: [19] 'I know your works, your love, your ministry, your faith, and your patient endurance and your latter works are more complete than your former works. [20] But I have against you that you allowed the woman Jezebel who calls herself a prophetess to teach and deceive my servants to fornicate and to eat idol meat. [21] I even gave her time to repent, but she is not willing to repent from her fornication. [22] Therefore, I am making her sick and those who fornicate with her resulting in great affliction unless they would repent from her deeds. [23] I will kill her children with death. Then all the churches will know that I am the One searching hearts and desires and I will give to each of you according to your works. [24] And I speak to the rest of you in Thyatira as many as do not hold on to this teaching and who do not know the so called "deep secrets" of Satan, I will not lay on you another burden, [25] except hold on to what you have until I arrive. [26] In addition, the victorious one and the one who guards My works until the end, I will give him authority over the nations; [27] and he will rule them with a rod of iron and will crush them like clay pottery. [28] Just as I received from My Father, I will also give him the morning star. [29] The one with an ear to hear, let him hear what the Spirit is saying to the churches.'"

I think it important to develop the dispensational perspective of some conservative evangelical scholars that Jesus may have actually been describing future church periods in John's Revelation. The eclectic approach to Revelation would allow for this as well as the fact that the Word of God possesses many levels and depths of meaning, particularly as the most astounding apocalyptic book of the Bible. I believe that whether dispensational or not, Revelation was written at a time during the first century when persecution and philosophical/Gnostic influences caused identity crisis of sorts in some churches. We see from Jesus' comments to the Ephesians in Revelation 2:1-7 that Gnostic philosophers threatened the church there.[36] But Jesus could see all of time and all the struggles of His church over the

---

[36] Arthur Patzia, "Colossians," *Ephesians, Colossians, Philemon, New International Biblical Commentary* (Peabody, MA: Hendrickson. 1999).

years and may have decided to let His church know of different challenges to them through John in this last book of the Bible.

Ephesian Christians had been warned on many occasions about the Gnostics and their penchant for slanting the truth about the gospel. The Gnostics taught that Jesus only swooned on the cross, that Jesus was not true God and not true man, and that Jesus was not actually part of the Godhead. All these thoughts were due to their perspective that humans had no real right or claim to eternity because they were unworthy, including their Savior Jesus Christ. The Greek Gnostics influenced many countries in these thoughts about Jesus; Paul, Apollos and Timothy were aware of them. In fact, Paul warned the Ephesian elders, "fierce wolves will come in among you not sparing the flock" (Acts 20:29). I think that so much energy went into monitoring the religious climate and filtering out the negative pagan influences, that the Ephesian and other Christian communities forgot about the most important Christian duty: their first responsibility to love God, themselves, and their neighbors (Mt. 22:37-39; Mark 12:31-31; Luke 10:27). The first century Ephesian Christian church majored in technical Christianity but unfortunately minored in the relational. Despite persecution against Christians by emperors Caligula (AD 37-41), Nero (AD 54-68), and Domitian (AD 81-96), the Church on the whole throughout the first century enjoyed comfort and evangelical success in the larger population centers. However, it still remained a sect of Judaism and did not gain Empire prominence until the beginning of the fourth century after Emperor Constantine converted and protected Christianity (AD 313-Edict of Milan) and Theodosius I made Christianity the state religion (AD 380-Edict of Thessalonica).[37]

The Dispensational crowd feels that Jesus' comments to Smyrna really represent the struggles of Christianity at large throughout the Roman Empire during Decius' and Diocletian's emperorships. During the second century, Christianity survived the derision and hardships of a *religio illicita* (illegal sect) through the steady guidance and protection of the Holy Spirit and the teaching and defense of the church leaders/patristic fathers. The first century and early second century Roman Emperors such as Nero (AD 54-68), Domitian (AD 81-96), Trajan (AD 98-117), and Marcus Aurelius (AD 161-180), killed Christians in small number compared to Decius

---

[37] Kat Cendana, "Christianity Became the State Religion," Amazing Bible Timeline with World History, September 13, 2016; accessed April 25, 2021. @ https://amazingbibletimeline.com/blog/christianity-became-the-state-religion/#:~:text=After%20many%20years%20of%20persecution%20at%20the%20hands,Bible%20Timeline%20with%20World%20History%20at%20380%20AD.

(AD 250-251) and Diocletian (AD 303-305) who martyred thousands during their evil but short reigns. Despite the threat to their lives, these gifted Christian leaders defended the faith against Roman and other pagan outsiders and from government officials bent on the destruction and annihilation of Christianity. Lucian of Samosata (*De Peregrinus*), Marcus Cornelius Fronto (*Octavius 9*), and Celsus (*True Discourse*), the most noted of Roman thinkers during this time, attacked Christians and their belief system through their writings. But brave Christians with excellent literary skills answered these challenges with apologetic writings. The Holy Spirit moved these "apologists" to encourage the church during this frightful time including Justin Martyr (AD 100-165), Tatian (AD 120-180), Athenagoras (AD 133-190), and Tertullian (AD 155-220).

For the dispensationalists, the church at Pergamum, known for its wealth and apostacy, represents the decadent Roman Catholic Church during its "Golden Age" from 1300–1500. During this period, the Catholic popes became more concerned about power, prestige, and money than ever before in their history. They had little regard for true relationship with the Lord or His people and did little to really lead their flocks in meaningful ways. On top of spiritual decadence was their insatiable appetite for property and property improvements, including the building of St. Peter's Basilica (1506-1626) and other churches, universities, and monasteries. These projects placed a huge financial burden on the general public and parishes of the Catholic Church. This and the rising influence of scholastic nominalism (anthropocentricism, man is the center of reality and his experience is the way to gain knowledge) caused a spiritual vacuum in the Catholic Church making many uncomfortable with their faith and willing to search for the Truth outside the Church and its doctrine. Other crises negatively impacted the Catholic Church and caused the public to question their allegiance to it including the "Babylonian Captivity" (the transference of the papal residence from Rome to Avignon, France from 1309-1379 with eight popes located in France and not in Rome) and the Western Schism (1378-1417), a period during the Catholic papacy when three popes competed for dominance (Popes John XXIII [Konstanz], Benedict XIII [Avignon], Gregory XII [Rome]). During the late 1400s and early 1500s, St Peter's Basilica in Rome was only partially completed. In order to create momentum and reverse the financial slump for building, Pope Leo X (AD 1475-1521) started a money campaign by requiring Roman Catholic Church members to pay for a paper copy of the "indulgence" abolishing or decreasing a relative's time in purgatory for sin committed while on earth. This became one of the causes of the Protestant Reformation as Martin Luther objected by forcefully protesting with his Ninety-five Theses.

The next church era represented by the church at Thyatira in Revelation 2:18–29 is the rise of American/European worldliness and religious liberalism, which began with a few church goers and theologians who should have known better than to write from their universities and church posts what they did. Their influence was extensive and did great harm to the church just like the Jezebel prophetess in the church at Thyatira. Some of the more influential rebellious leaders were the following:

- Immanuel Kant (1724–1804): Kant concluded that time is not a thing derived from experience, objects, motion, and change, but rather an unavoidable framework of the human mind that predetermines experience. Kant asserted that, because of the limitations of rational argument in the absence of irrefutable evidence, no one could really know whether there is a God and an afterlife or not. For the sake of society and morality, Kant asserted people are reasonably justified in believing in them, even though they could never know for sure whether society and morality are real or not. He believed that reason and experience must be engaged together to find the truth; but that religious truth cannot be objectively known. He stated that God and Christ are only the product of our conscience.
- Ludwig Feuerbach (1804–1872) stated that the concept of God is really a god-myth created by man to explain the unexplainable and the "supernatural."
- Auguste Comte (1798–1857) believed that God was an irrelevant superstition created by man during his early (theological/superstitious) development to explain all phenomena by immediate intervention of the "divine." He explained that man became more sophisticated and developed into the second/metaphysical stage which explains the unknown through abstract ideas. Comte stated that the third level of human development employs the scientific method of deductive and inductive reasoning and applies these concepts to man's world without need for God and other "superstitions."
- Jean-Paul Sartre (1905–1981), the most popular existential thinker of the twentieth century, believed and taught that man was the center of the universe and creates his own destiny and is solely responsible for it. He believed that man exists only in reference to himself, not others and "existence precedes essence." He believed that God does not exist—just in our minds.

Message to Church at Ephesus: No First Love

Revelation 2:1-7

Ancient Ephesus was the largest city of Asia (150,000–200,000 people) and 6 miles from the Aegean sea with a port which often silted up.[38] Eventually Ephesus was destroyed by an earthquake in AD 614 and was moved from its original site at the mouth of the Cayster River to a more advantageous site 1.5 miles farther up the river. The silting up of its harbor every springtime was eventually avoided by this move. It became the gateway to Rome from traffic through Asia and its three main roads which converged outside Ephesus. Emperor Augustus Caesar allowed the Ephesians to build two temples in his honor around 27 BC. Emperor Domitian made Ephesus the guardian of the emperor cult ten years before John wrote Revelation. The Temple of Artemis was built for the third and last time after first being destroyed by a flood and then by a fire. Its third construction began in 323 BC and continued for 120 years.[39] By the first century, the Temple of Artemis was considered one of the seven wonders of the ancient world and boasted a lucrative temple economy centered around the worship of Diana/

The Amphitheater at Ephesus

---

38   O'Conner, Jerome Murphy (2008). *St. Paul's Ephesus*. p. 130.
39   Pausanias, *Description of Greece*, 10.38.6, W.H.S Jones, trans., accessed May 29, 2023, https://www.theoi.com/Text/Pausanias10C.html.

Revelation: The Fifth Gospel

Artemis during Paul's day (Acts 19:23-40) and the worship of the Roman Emperor during John's latter years.

The Temple of Artemis (Diana) painted in 1886 by Ferdinand Knab as part of his "Seven Wonders of the Ancient World Series

The temple was impressive in size and architecture. It was 450 feet long and 150 feet wide. It was 77 feet high and was supported by 127 pillars each 60 feet tall. No wonder that the Christian community centered their efforts at negating the activities and worship of Artemis/Diana and the other Greek and Roman gods of the pantheon of false gods. But in their conscientious desire to root out sin and uncover imposters in their midst, they forgot how to love and left behind their emotional attraction to the Triune God.

The Ephesian church also became so focused on confronting the Gnostic philosophers who attempted to infiltrate and mislead their church members that they forgot the basics of maintaining Kingdom relationships. Indeed, in Jesus' letter to the Ephesian pastor and his members, He confirmed their well-meaning deeds/works (εργα, v. 2), their tireless energy (κοπον, v. 2) to promote Jesus' message, and their patient endurance (υπομονην, v. 2) in the face of public opposition to Christianity (v. 2). But by the end of the first century, the Ephesus church lacked love for its members, its community, and even for the Lord. Paul, Timothy, and John who taught, preached, and mentored this great church, were very influential in developing the church's ability to avoid, identify, and insulate themselves from the philosophical influences of the travelling Gnostic teachers of the first century.

But despite the great influence of John, the expert on love and how to love, the church became technocrats of the gospel not disseminators of Christ's love to each other or to the Ephesian community and its large Jewish population (Acts 19:8-9). Jesus made a point of identifying their lack of "first" love which would indicate their lack of intensity and preoccupation with Him as they had when they first met Him as their Savior (v. 4). Remember that the Revelation was written as a circular epistle to be read by all seven churches of the Lycus Valley. The warning to the Ephesians was not only to their church members but to the other six and to us. Jesus tells this church how to recapture their first love experience: He told them to remember (μνημονευε, v. 5) from where they have fallen, to repent (μετανοησον, v. 5), "and do the first works" (και τα πρωτα εργα ποιησον, v. 5). Jesus wanted them to remember how passionately they had expressed their love for Him and the Kingdom in the past. He wanted them to return to their original passion for Him or else He would "remove your lampstand from its place" (κινησω την λυχνιαν σου εκ του τοπου αυτης, v. 5). Remember that the angel explained to John that the seven lampstands symbolized the seven churches of the Lycus Valley association of churches. Therefore, when Jesus told John that He would remove their "lampstand" from its place, Jesus meant that He would take away their position of influence and mentoring that they enjoyed over the six other Lycus Valley churches if they refused His command for them to repent.

But Jesus complimented them for rejecting the influence of the Nicolaitans whose doctrine of fornicating and eating idol meat was decried by Jesus here and in the next chapter. Some scholars take note that the fornication mentioned in chapter 3 was not just extramarital sexual indiscretion, but possibly ritual prostitution during Christian love feasts influenced by cult prostitutes of Diana/Artemis in the Ephesus temple when the prostitutes were converted to Christianity in that city.[40] Jesus was adamant that He would judge the church members who practice both of these activities which offend the consciences of those watching and those practicing these sins. Jesus closed His comments to the pastor of the Ephesians as He did do to the other six churches: He told this church and the six others that their congregants should heed what the Spirit was saying not just to their church but really to all believers (v. 7). Jesus also promised that the victorious ones who returned to their first love of Christ would eat from the "Tree of Life which is in the Paradise of God" (ξυλου της ζωης ο εστιν εν τω παραδεισω του θεου, v. 7). Obviously, this was a reference to the Tree of Life of the Garden of Eden which also appears in the New Jerusalem in Revelation 22:2. Just as the fruit of this Tree caused rejuvenation and eternal longevity in the Garden on earth and in the New Jerusalem, Jesus also promised that its partakers would enjoy heretofore unlimited benefits from heaven. Jesus was promising the Ephesians the wellspring of Holy Spirit power and presence if they repented and returned to the "first works" of passionate Christian experience.

---

[40] John Henry Blunt M.A., F.S.A., ed., *Dictionary of Sects, Heresies, Ecclesiastical Parties, and Schools of Religious Thought* (London: Rivington's, 1874), 371–73.

Revelation: The Fifth Gospel

I think the Tree of Life's fruit in the New Jerusalem is packed with the nutrients of the Holy Spirit that we only get a glimpse of from Adam and Eve's experience in the Eden account in Genesis and from John's comments in Revelation 22. From the latter account, we can surmise that the fruit of the Tree produced each month supplies some of the rejuvenating nutritional needs of New Jerusalem citizens and the leaves of the tree supply the medicinal needs for the wholeness of the nations: "and the leaves of the tree are for the healing of the nations" (και το φυλλα του ξυλου εις θεραπειαν των εθνων—Rev. 22:2). I think that Jesus is not only promising future benefit to the Ephesians when they correct their thoughts and actions with "first love" passion, but He also is promising present enhancement through the ministry of the Holy Spirit represented by the symbology of the Tree of Life.

In summary, the Ephesian church was one of the premier churches outside of Jerusalem and had a pedigree of the very best preachers, prophets and teachers in Paul, John, Timothy, and Apollos. But despite such wonderful mentoring and examples to follow, the Christians of Ephesus became technocrats of the Word and not lovers of God and their fellowman which was egregious to Jesus. He commended their work efforts, projects, and patient endurance in the face of an ever-increasing threat of being identified as a *religio illicita* since Christianity was no longer being considered by various Roman provinces as a sect of Judaism. Jesus commended their stance against the sin compromises advocated by the Nicolaitans and encouraged them to listen closely to the voice of the Holy Spirit and be overcomers allowed to eat from the Tree of Life. Jesus continued His letter to the churches about their future and their relationship to His Kingdom and the New Jerusalem by addressing the closest church to Ephesus in the Lycus Valley, Smyrna, about 35 miles north of Ephesus near the Aegean Sea.

Message to the Church at Smyrna: Suffering and Poor Church without Fault

Revelation 2:8-11

Smyrna's name was likely derived from "myrrh" which was a resin extracted from several different trees of the genus Commiphora growing around this town near the Aegean Sea. In ancient times the myrrh resin was used as a medicinal ointment, as a fragrance, as an incense in the Temple, and as an analgesic with wine. The early city of Smyrna (35 miles north of Ephesus) was sacked by Alyattes around 550 BC, but restored by one of Alexander the Great's generals, Lysimachus, around 300 BC. The city built two temples one for Zeus and one for Cybele and then later created the Roman goddess Roma and a cult in her name in order to curry favor with Rome and protection from the Empire to thwart the Pergamum King Eumenes. By John's time, Smyrna had a large population of Jews and several synagogues and boasted a population of nearly two hundred thousand.[41] The city was wealthy with a robust seaport and trade routes passing through the outskirts of the city. By the AD 23, the city had built a temple in honor of Emperor Tiberius and his wife Julia and also built a theater holding up to twenty thousand people.[42] It was one of the top three royal cities in Asia along with Ephesus and Pergamum.

Emperor worship became very prominent in the city by the writing of John's *Revelation* due to Caligula, Nero, and Emperor Domitian's influences. These three emperors believed that Roman citizens should not only pay taxes but should also worship them as gods through

The Ancient ruins of Agora of Smyrna in Izmir, Turkey

---

41 F. L. Cross and E. A. Livingstone, eds., "Smyrna," *The Oxford Dictionary of the Christian Church*. (Oxford, England: Oxford University Press, 2005).

42 David Treybig, "Smyrna," *Life, Hope, and Truth*, accessed May 3, 2021, https://lifehopeandtruth.com/prophecy/revelation/seven-churches-of-revelation/smyrna/.

required animal sacrifices, incense offerings, and verbal prayers offered for them in their cult temples. This of course was repugnant to the Christians of the Empire who did not worship idols nor sacrifice animals to their God and certainly not to any "gods." The Romans tolerated the Jews because of policies adopted by the Empire when Palestine became a vassal state of Rome after Titus conquered and subjugated them in 68 B.C.

Some historians have posited that Judaism was officially a *religio licita* from then until the demise of the Roman Empire five hundred years later. But more recent historical investigation has indicated that the Romans usually tolerated *all* ancestral religions of its subjugated citizens except when threats were perceived against Rome or its official pantheon of gods.[43] Christianity, initially thought by the Romans to be a sect of Judaism, eventually was regarded as a threat to the Empire after John's death at the beginning of the second century. The Jews of Smyrna and Philadelphia, after first allowing their Jewish Christian brothers and sisters shelter and use of their synagogues, became antagonistic toward the Christians and did not allow them to meet and carry on their religious activities within their places of worship as many had during Paul's day. As you may remember, Paul and his missionary teams would first go to the synagogues of the cities they visited which always welcomed him as a revered rabbi as well as god-fearing Greeks. Granted, in a few cities such as Pisidian Antioch (Acts 13:13-52), Iconium (Acts 14:1-7), and Thessalonica (Acts 17:1-9) after Paul challenged their thinking by presenting Jesus as Messiah, the synagogue leaders threw him out of their synagogues for his "blasphemy." God the Father was particularly concerned that the Jews of Smyrna and Philadelphia were not the magnanimous people that He wanted them to be toward His "grafted-in" Gentile believers and of course Jewish Christians who loved and followed His Son.

Jesus began His message to the Smyrna church by introducing Himself as "the One who is the first and the last who became dead but is now alive again" (ο πρωτος και ο εσχατος ος εγενετο νεκρος και εζησεν, v. 8). He mentioned His past death and resurrection history to bolster the faith and hope of those Christians about to die for their testimony which Jesus would shortly reveal to the Smyrnaeans. Jesus acknowledged their suffering (θλιψιν, v. 9) and their poverty (πτωχειαν, v. 9)–quite a compliment from the Champion of both who left the glorious riches, position, and

---

43   John J. O'Keefe, "*Religio licita*," *A Dictionary of Jewish-Christian Relations* (Cambridge, England: Cambridge University Press, 2005), 371.

power of His seat in heaven to become a poor carpenter from Nazareth and rabbi with a fishermen brigade from Capernaum! Jesus wanted the persecuted church in Smyrna to know that their sacrifices mattered, particularly in a city where the Christians were being discriminated against by Roman citizens suspicious of their rituals and reluctance to worship their beloved Emperors.

The Agora of Smyrna, built during the Hellenistic era at the base of Pagos Hill and rebuilt under Marcus Aurelius after they were destroyed by an earthquake in 178 AD.

Jesus' comment that they were "poor" indicated that the citizens of the city were excluding the Christ followers from the Smyrnaean trade guilds and doing business in the two storied bazaar/open air mall in the center of their city. This was one of the largest of its kind in the world. Jesus also wanted this church to be aware of the Jews who did not want to be associated with a people becoming ostracized by the Roman government. Jesus told the Smyrna Christians that their poverty really made them "rich" (πλουσιος, v. 9): I think He was referring to the abundance of spiritual truths, gifts and fruit that become cultivated in the "fields" of persecution (cf. Jn. 15:1–6) as well as the influence on seekers who watch the faithfulness of persecuted believers.

Next Jesus blamed the suffering and poverty of these Christians on the Smyrna Jews who were excluding and likely exposing them to Roman censorship and imprisonment for their unwavering stance against Emperor worship (Domitian at the time) and faithfulness to the God that the Jews should have been following but were not: "and the blasphemy from those saying they are Jews, but they are not, *but are from the Synagogue of Satan*" (αλλα συναγωγη του σατανα, v. 9). This is a very harsh indictment against God's chosen; almost unbelievable. Yet Jesus was clear that the attitude of exclusion of the oppressed is not the way He wanted the Jews to treat His young church. The synagogue of Satan reminds us of the modern Church Age of the Satanic temples of the twentieth and twenty-first centuries. Jesus next told His beloved Smyrnaean church that some in their midst would be challenged with prison time lasting ten days. He told them that, "The devil is about to

Revelation: The Fifth Gospel

Ancient Arches of Smyrna, LIEU SONG

throw some of you into prison" (μελλει βαλλειν ο διαβολος εξ υμων εις φυλακην, v. 10). I find it fascinating that God, who knows the future, actually allowed His people to know about their persecution before it happened. In fact, He even told them specifics of their hardship: "you will have suffering for ten days" (εξετε θλιψιν ημερων δεκα", v. 10) eventuating for some into death. The knowledge of future persecution might be overwhelming. But Jesus encouraged this persecuted congregation to be faithful to Him even if it meant death because He would give them the "prize/crown of life" (στεφανον της ζωης, v. 10). He assured them that their natural fears about the permanence of death was unfounded in the face of His resurrection and victory over death. He told them that overcoming to the very end would result in "the second death not hurting" (μη αδικηθη εκ του θανατου του δευτερου, v. 11), a reference to the unwavering power of Jesus' sacrifice in delivering His followers to God and to His Kingdom despite physical death.

As with Jesus' church in Philadelphia, as we will see, the church in Smyrna reflected the best of faithfulness, obedience, and endurance in the setting of what would become severe persecution. Indeed, Christ was preparing this faith community for a legacy of suffering. Jesus

Polycarp (69-155 AD), disciple of the Apostle John and pastor of Smyrna church

had no criticism of this group mentored by John as they faced such strenuous opposition. About fifty years later, while still experiencing persecution from Pliny, Lucius Quadratus, and other Roman officials, Polycarp (AD 69-155), a protégé of the Apostle John and at one-time a pastor of the Smyrna church, was burned at the stake for refusing to offer incense to the Roman Emperor. His last words before his death were, "I bless you, Father, for judging me worthy of this hour, so that in the company of the martyrs I may share the cup of Christ."[44]

Message to Church at Pergamum: The Church in Satan's Home

Revelation 2:12-17

Pergamum was likely the third largest city (125,000 people) and the third most important city of Asia and considered a royal city by the Romans. The city was located 16 miles inland from the Aegean Sea, 2 miles north of the Caicus River (modern Bakir Cay) in southern Mysia. Ancient Smyrna was about 57 miles north of modern-day Izmir and was built on a precipice about 1,165 feet above sea level, one thousand feet above the surrounding plain. The image of strength and permanence is obvious at first glance of the city's remains. The terraces that overlook the Caicus River valley led to the entry gate of the city. The two small tributaries of the Caicus that neared the city, the Selinus to the west, the Cetius to the east, were navigable by small vessels that transported goods in the ancient period from the sea inland. The city was also joined to a road climbing toward Thyatira and on into Sardis. Today, the modern Turkish town of Bergama (population forty-five thousand) surrounds the ancient precipice, and partially covers the ruins of Roman Pergamum.

---

[44] Fr. Paolo O. Pirlo, SHMI. "St. Polycarp." *My First Book of Saints* (Parañaque City, Philippines: Quality Catholic Publications, 1997), 58-59.

Revelation: The Fifth Gospel

Ancient Pergamum

Jesus wanted John to write to the pastor and church at Pergamum that He was fully aware of their proximity to Satan. But He began His thoughts to them by reminding them that He was the One who had "the double-edged sharp sword" (ρομφαιαν την διστομον την οξειαν, v. 12) and had the real authority over Satan and his threats to their community. He acknowledged their tenacity in holding on to Jesus' Name and their faith in Him as they resisted Satan's onslaught against them. Jesus told them that impressive to Him was that "you did not deny your faith in Me" (ουκ ηρνησω την πιστιν μου, v. 13) even during the darkest days of the Christian community when one of their fellow believers named Antipas, appointed pastor of the church at Pergamum by John, had been burned alive in a hot furnace by the Temple of Dionysus priests during Nero's latter reign sometime around 66–68 AD.[45] Jesus did not specifically identify Antipas' killers but placed the blame for his death on Satan (v. 13). As the third largest city of Asia behind Ephesus and Smyrna, Pergamum had several large temples to the Greek gods Athena and Dionysus (Greek male god of the harvest, wine, and fertility; was known as the god Bacchus by the Romans)[46] surrounding a very large altar. Jesus spoke of Satan's influence here and that Satan's throne/dwelling was in Pergamum (v. 13). The church had some members who were syncretists—they were attempting to follow Jesus and the purity of His message but were also following the error of Ballam who taught Balak to place the stumbling blocks of fornication and eating idol meat as a temptation to the Israelites (Numbers 22–24). Both practices were forbidden for Israel and for those following Jesus (cf. Rom. 14:14–23). As with the Nicolaitans in Ephesus, the Pergamum temple influences over new Christian converts caused havoc in Pergamum when some refused to give up the fornication and eating the idol meat which had been offered earlier in the day to Athena and to Dionysus (vv. 14–15). Jesus was quite upset with those of His disciples following the teachings of

---

45 "Hieromartyr Antipas, Bishop of Pergamum and Disciple of Saint John the Theologian," *Orthodox Church in America*, accessed May 11, 2021, https://www.oca.org/saints/lives/2013/04/11/101052-hieromartyr-antipas-bishop-of-pergamum-and-disciple-of-saint-joh.

46 Rosemarie Taylor-Perry, *The God Who Comes: Dionysian Mysteries Revisited* (New York: Algora Publishing, 2003).

Balaam and the Nicolaitans. He unequivocally expressed His displeasure to them and told them if repentance did not occur soon, He would come to them and "would make war with them from the sword from My mouth" (πολεμησω μετ αυτων εν τη ρομφαια του στοματος μου, v. 16). This would have been even more frightful to them had they been

Ruins of Ancient Pergamum CC By 4.0, Besbudak

aware of John's vision of the first Armageddon recorded in Revelation 19 when John described the slaughtering of the Beast's armies and his kings from Jesus' weaponized mouth-laser sword and the amount of blood that flowed from this slaughter as he describes in Revelation 14.

Jesus continued His message to the Pergamum church by promising those who listened to His words that He would reward those who repented and/or were victorious in their Christian walks. Jesus described the rewards using two familiar metaphors: hidden manna and a white pebble. The Jewish Christians who made up a large portion of the church understood the manna reward because their religious heritage included Moses and the children of Israel surviving during their forty years of wilderness wandering by the daily manna and quail that God supplied (Ex. 16). But Jesus told them "and I will give the hidden manna to him" (δωσω αυτω του μαννα του κεκρυμμενου, v. 17); Jesus would be blessing their lives with spiritual bread from His own body. His comments to the synagogue crowd in Capernaum that John recorded in John 6:35, 41, 48–51 indicate that Jesus truly is the bread of life and will sustain all believers committed to following Him with life and life with abundance. His bread was far better to "eat" than the food offered to idols. Jesus also offered to the Pergamum overcomers "a white pebble and a new name written on the pebble that no one knows except the one receiving it" (ψηφον λευκην και επι την ψηφον ονομα καινον γεγραμμενον ο ουδεις οιδεν ει μη ο λαμβανων, v. 17). Several Revelation scholars have suggested that the "white stone" (ψηφον λευκαν) signifies the following:

- A magical amulet (good luck object thought to give protection from evil or disease)
- A token of Roman hospitality
- A ticket as a martyr to the gladiatorial games
- A ticket to one of the many theaters in Pergamum
- A vote of acquittal in a court of law[47]

However, in the context of Jesus rewarding saintly behavior and obedience to His commands throughout a lifetime of suffering, opposition and temptation, I think it is clear that the "white pebble" is a personalized, monogrammed ticket at death to enter heaven and spend the rest of eternity with Christ.

Jesus wanted His observations, warnings, and promises to the Christians of Pergamum to also be heeded by Christians in the other churches of the Lycus Valley network and by Christians throughout the ages. In short, despite the disadvantages of the church at Pergamum including the recent murder of one of their pastors, the Satanic presence in their city, and the obstinance and sin of the Balaamites and Nicolaitans in their congregation, Jesus gave this church optimism and pointed out a path for realignment with the Truth. As with their sister church in Ephesus, Jesus told them that repentance from their errors would lead to rewards. As in the case of the Smyrnaeans who corrected their errors, those Christians in Pergamum would receive reward including the "hidden manna" and the "white pebble" but only to those who repented and who once again became faithful followers of Christ.

Message to the Church at Thyatira: Hold on to What You Have

Revelation 2:18-29

Thyatira was wealthy in ancient times, with its gentle rolling hills and fertile valleys about 40 miles east of Pergamum. Ramsey stated that the inland road through Thyatira was what made this city so important. Thyatira was a garrison city guarding

---

[47] Rick Renner, "Why did Jesus promise a white stone?" accessed from the internet on October 4, 2021, https://renner.org/article/why-did-jesus-promise-a-white-stone/.

the road and keeping it safe for traders repelling robbers wanting to pirate from the unsuspecting or ill-prepared. The Seleucids guarded the city and the road through it until the Pergamines took over, who wanted to keep the road navigable to enhance their trading fortunes. Finally, the Romans took over because this road was the main connection from Rome to the East. Ramsey notes that the condition of Thyatira was the "best measure of the power of Pergamum."[48] It was considered by some ancients to be a city of the province of Mysia, but to others a city of the province of Lydia.

The first Scriptural reference to Thyatira was Luke's account in Acts of Paul and his second missionary team meeting Lydia in Philippi. Luke stated, "Now a certain woman named Lydia, a dealer in purple cloth from the city of Thyatira" (και τις γυνη ονοματι Λυδια πορφυροπωλις πολεως Θυατειρων, Acts 16:14). Lydia became the first

Ruins of Thyatira

Christian convert in all of Europe as Luke discusses in Acts 16. The city that she was from, Thyatira, was noted for its brilliant red-purple dye and for the purple cloth produced from its dye guild industry.[49] In fact, the trade guilds that flourished not only included the dyers but also many others including wool workers, garment workers, linen workers, leather workers, bakers, potters, slave dealers, and bronze

---

48   William M. Ramsey, *The Letters to the Seven Churches of Asia and Their Place in the Plan of the Apocalypse* (London: Hodder & Stoughton, 1904), 324-35.
49   John Cumming, *Butler's Lives of the Saints* (Collegeville, MN: The Liturgical Press, 1998), 24.

smiths. Each guild was accompanied by its patron gods, and in many cases, included immoral practices in participation with the guild members, including sexual intercourse with established guild members or with guild prostitutes.[50] A faithful Christian may have found it difficult to live his/her faith, as well as practice his/her craft. Without compliance with these pagan practices, the Christian would have been shut out of the mainstream of his/her business commerce and would likely not be as successful as the pagans who would comply with the initiation rites or maintenance dues.

The Amphitheater at Thyatira

Jesus commended them for their spiritual activities and stated that their recent efforts were more complete than their earlier efforts for the Kingdom. The Lord specifically identifies what appears to be considerable spiritual maturity: their works, ministry, love, faith, and patient endurance (v. 19). In contrast to the church at Sardis (3:1), Jesus told the pastor that "your most recent works were more complete than your former works" (το εργα σου τα εσχατα πλειονα των πρωτων, v. 19); this compliment sounded as if the Thyatirans were maturing in what they were doing for Christ, including their specific ministries and roles in the Church. At first blush, the Thyatirans appeared to be model Christians. But Jesus had much to say about the dysfunction produced by Jezebel, the woman associated with the church claiming to be a prophetess. Jesus confronted the church concerning this woman and her unfettered access and influence on their church members. Jesus stated that the pastor and his staff of leaders allowed this woman to "teach and deceive My servants to fornicate and eat idol meat" (διδασκει και πλανα τους εμους δουλους πορνευσει και φαγειν ειδωλοθυτα, v. 20). Jesus expressed His displeasure with their failure to confront and eliminate her behavior from their congregation. Jesus told the pastor that He had been very patient giving her time to change her ways and had even prompted her to repent—likely through the Holy Spirit's work on her

---

50 E .J. Banks, "Thyatira," *International Standard Biblical Encyclopedia*, James Orr, gen. ed., (Chicago, IL: Howard-Severance Co., 1915, PD), accessed October 6, 2021, https://www.biblestudytools.com/encyclopedias/isbe/thyatira.html.

conscience and direct pastoral confrontation. Because of inscriptions on building fragments found in archeologic digs, it is evident that Thyatira had many guilds of trade organizations, similar to Pergamum. Jezebel could have been the president or one of the major organizers of these guilds or maybe was one of the wives of a guild official. From Jesus' comments about her activities, she was encouraging prospective guild members who were Christian to comply with pagan guild entry customs. According to John's narrative, this included eating idol meat (which had previously been offered to temple gods) and fornicating with guild prostitutes. So, He told His leaders that He would take matters into His own hands and "make her sick and those who fornicate with her causing great suffering" (βαλλω αυτην εις κλινην και τους μοιχευοντας μετ αυτης εις θλιψιν μεγαλη, v. 22). The Greek, "βαλλω αυτην εις κλινην," literally translates, "I will throw her onto a bed" of sickness. This metaphor indicates that the Holy Spirit will make her so sick she will become incapacitated for a time. But Jesus indicated that her followers will be punished even more harshly. Jesus continued His diatribe against Jezebel by telling her church that He would "kill her children with death" (τα τεκνα αυτης αποκτενω εν θανατω, v. 23)—quite a threat to the sinners of their church. I wonder whether Jesus was using hyperbole or if He really would physically kill her "disciples." Of course, Dr. Luke described the Holy Spirit inducing fatal heart attacks or strokes in Ananias and Sapphira for their lies in Acts 5. This couple's *single* treachery would seem to be far less of a violation of Kingdom mores and commands than the perpetrators of fornication and offending fellow Christians by eating idol meat here in Thyatira. Jesus told John and His reading audience that all churches receiving this circular letter and those reading Revelation would realize that He was "the One searching [men's] desires and hearts" (ο εραυνων νεφρους και καρδιας, v. 23). The Apostle Paul described this seeking phenomenon as an activity of the Holy Spirit whom the Father sends out on behalf of His Son as we see in 1 Corinthians 2:10-16. Jesus as the Judge of the Universe, and in particular, of His churches, has a specific task to purge destructive behavior out of His congregations. This may sound harsh; but when people like the Jezebel of Thyatira and her unrepentant "children" refuse God's grace and continue to pollute the atmosphere and culture of the church and tarnish the witness to pagans and seekers in Thyatira, then Jesus assured them that He would intervene with definitive discipline which may sadly require removal from this world:. "and I will give to you each according to your works" (και δωσω υμιν εκαστω κατα τα εργα υμων, v. 23).

Jesus did not want to dwell too long on the Jezebel and Satanic influence through her. Jesus turned to the majority of the church who had been faithful to the dogma

Revelation: The Fifth Gospel

of Christ and had rejected Jezebel's deceptive teaching. Jesus told them two important things: "hold on to what you have until I return" (ο εχετε κρατησατε αχρις ου αν ηξω, v. 25) and "the victorious one and the one guarding My works to the end (ο νικων και ο τηρων αχρι τελους τα εργα μου, v. 26), I will give him authority over the nations and he will rule them with a rod of iron and will crush them like pottery" (vv. 26-27). Jesus wanted the marginalized church members at Thyatira to understand that despite His terrible indictment against Jezebel and her cohort, the faithful would be honored by Jesus with authority over the pagan world if not in this world, certainly in the next. Jesus used a metaphor for this dominance of "crushing the clay pottery" (a reference to Ps. 2:9) referring to the ease at shattering clay pottery with an iron staff. Jesus was referring to His Conquering Messiah role at His return (Armageddon I) and possibly immediately before the devil is thrown into the lake of fire (Armageddon II). We will see these later in the narrative when His weaponized mouth-laser destroys the armies of the nations of the dragon/Beast (19:21) and when "fire came down out of heaven and utterly destroyed them" (20:9). The armies of heaven are made up of the saints, some of whom will be the obedient members of the Thyatiran church.

The Lord gave the Thyatirans hope that, despite the difficulties with Jezebel and the fallout from their brothers' and sisters' poor behavior with the trade guilds, He would honor and reward those who deserved recognition for their faithfulness to Jesus. He would allow them to dominate their pagan neighbors and privileged guild members just as the early morning Venus star dominates all the other stars of the Eastern horizon (v. 28). I am also somewhat surprised that Jesus avoided using Jezebel's real name maybe in hopes that she would come to her senses and not be embarrassed to genuinely repent from her errors of judgment and sin. Indeed, even in this narrative, we see that Jesus tried to woo her back to righteous living. Her situation is somewhat remindful of the young man Paul rebukes in 1 Corinthians 5 who had fornicated with his stepmother. After being excommunicated from the Corinthian church and delivered for a short time to Satan for discipline, he repented as we see from Paul's comments some six to nine months later in 2 Corinthians 2:5-11. I think it possible that the Holy Spirit targeted this woman Jezebel for not only the discipline mentioned, but for her reinstatement after her repentance. If she truly had the gift of prophecy and engaged in the role of prophet for that Christian community, I think it hard to imagine Jesus not wanting to rescue her from her indiscretions and restore her back to her body of believers. She was a valuable member of their assembly and obviously possessed ability to connect them to the harvest of pagan guild souls in their city. Of course, Queen Jezebel, her namesake, wife of King Ahab, opposed the Lord and Elijah throughout his ministry culminating with Elijah's confrontation with her 850 Baal priests (cf. 1 Kings 18) and her bloody death (cf. 2 Kings 9:30-37).

REVELATION 3

Messages to the Churches at Sardis, Philadelphia, and Laodicea

Sardis:

1 "And to the pastor of the church in Sardis write, The One holding the seven Spirits of God and the seven stars says these things: 'I know your works. You have a reputation of being alive yet you are really dead; [2] become alive and strengthen the rest of your works about to die because I have found them incomplete before My God. [3] Remember then what you received and heard. Hold on to it and repent. If you will not wake up, I am coming like a thief, and you will not know which hour I will come to you. [4] Now you have a few people in Sardis who have not soiled their clothes but who walk with Me in white robes because they are worthy. [5] The victorious one will be dressed in white clothes, and I will surely not wipe his name out of the Book of Life; indeed, I will confess his name before My Father and

before His angels. ⁶ The one with ears let him hear what the Spirit is saying to the churches.'"

Philadelphia:

⁷ "And to the pastor of the church in Philadelphia write, The Holy and True One says these things: 'The One with the key of David: what He opens no one can shut, and what He closes, no one can open. ⁸ I know your works. I have placed an open door before you that no one can shut. I know you that you have little energy, yet you have obeyed My word and you did not deny My name; ⁹ indeed, I will make those who say they are Jews but they are not but are liars from the Synagogue of Satan, I will make them come and bow down before your feet and they will know that I loved you. ¹⁰ Because you have obeyed my command of patient endurance, I will guard you from the time of testing about to come upon the whole earth to test those living on the earth. ¹¹ Behold I am coming soon; hold on to what you have so that no one will receive your crown. ¹² The victorious one I will make a pillar in the Temple of My God and he will never go out from it; and I will write the Name of My God on him and the name of the City of My God, the New Jerusalem coming down out of heaven from My God, and My new name. ¹³ The one with an ear, let him hear what the Spirit is saying to the churches.'"

Laodicea:

¹⁴ "And to the pastor of the church in Laodicea write, The Amen, the faithful and true Witness, and the Ruler of God's creation says these things: ¹⁵ 'I know your works that you are neither cold nor hot; I wish you were either cold or hot ¹⁶ but because you are lukewarm and neither hot nor cold I am about ready to vomit you out of My mouth. ¹⁷ Indeed you say, "I am rich, I have become wealthy and I need nothing." But you do not know that you are really the wretched one—pitiable, poor, blind, and naked. ¹⁸ I counsel you to buy gold refined by hot fire from Me that you might become rich, and white clothes that you might be clothed and that the shame of your nakedness may not be revealed, and eye salve to rub on your eyes that you might see. ¹⁹ Those whom

I rebuke and discipline I love. So be genuine and repent. ²⁰ Behold, I stand at the door and knock; if anyone would hear My voice and open the door, I will come into him and I will dine with him and he with Me. ²¹ The victorious one I will allow him to sit with Me on My throne just as I conquered and sat down with My Father on His throne. ²² The one with an ear, let him hear what the Spirit is saying to the churches.'"

Message to Church at Sardis: The Wealthy-Sleeping Church

Revelation 3:1-6

Approximately 30 miles east of Thyatira, Sardis was a Lydian city somewhat destroyed by an earthquake twenty years before John's letter. The city boasted a beautiful acropolis and necropolis as it looked over the Hermus Valley at the foot of Mount Tmolus. That mountain fed its streams into the Pactolus River which flowed through the city carrying with it "golden" sands from the mountain which were actually minute pellets of gold mixed with silver. King Croesus (560-546 BC) of the early Lydian Kingdom commissioned his metallurgists to separate the gold from the silver using magnets. Because of this process, the gold and silver of Sardis were the purist in the Roman Empire and were minted into coinage for the Empire making Sardis a very wealthy city. In fact, metallurgists consider the Sardis coinage the beginning of modern minting.[51] Sardis was also known for its production and dying of wool and other delicate garment materials. Sardis had the largest synagogue in Asia built by arguably the wealthiest

---

51   Andrew Ramage and Paul Craddock, *King Croesus' Gold: Excavations at Sardis and the History of Gold Refining*, Archaeological Exploration of Sardis, (Cambridge, MA: Harvard University Press, 2000).

Jewish community of that province. Excavation work from Nicholas Cahill from the University of Wisconsin at Madison indicated that the synagogue was in continuity with an impressive gymnasium-bath complex.[52] Christians lived in peace with their Jewish and Roman neighbors and likely were allowed to use the synagogue and thus be identified as Jews by the Empire officials. Persecution was never mentioned in John's Revelation message to Sardis. Sardis was never conquered in the daytime by invading armies but was twice captured during the night due to lack of vigilance. It was also flattened by a terrible earthquake in AD 17 but was rebuilt by Tiberius Caesar due to the importance of the city's coin minting business and because of its critical role in commerce. Tiberius exempted Sardis from Roman taxes for five years because of this damage and their inability to pay Rome its annual duties.[53]

Ruins of the Temple of Artemis at Sardis

Jesus began His message to the pastor and church at Sardis by depicting Himself as the One who held/possessed (εχων, v. 1) the Holy Spirit identified as "the seven spirits of God" (τα επτα πνευματα του θεου, v. 1). The Apostle John also identified the Holy Spirit as "the seven spirits" in Rev. 1:4, Rev. 4:5, and in Rev. 5:6. The Holy Spirit is ubiquitous and is present in all seven continents of the world; seven is also a perfect number—the Spirit is perfect as well. Maybe these are the main reasons why the Holy Spirit is described as being made up of seven spirits; or the Apostle John could have actually seen seven spirits undulating as One Holy Spirit as he saw Him in the chapters cited.

Jesus then tells the Sardinian church that He knew their works and also knew that they had developed a reputation for being a vibrant, effective body of believers. But

---

52 Nicholas D. Cahill, ed., *Love for Lydia. A Sardis Anniversary Volume Presented to Crawford H. Greenewalt, Jr.*, Archaeological Exploration of Sardis Reports. (Cambridge, MA: Harvard University Press, 2008).

53 Tacitus, *The Annals of Tacitus*, 2.47, Alfred John Church and William Jackson Brodribb, trans. (New York: Macmillan, 1906, PD), accessed May 30, 2023, http://classics.mit.edu/Tacitus/annals.2.ii.html.

Jesus could see right through their smug and proper Christianity. He confronted them and told them that they were really asleep and near spiritual death: "You have a reputation for being alive, yet you are dead" (ονομα εχεις οτι ζης και νεκρος ει, v. 1). The Greek word "νεκρος" (death) that Jesus used to describe the Sardinians brings with it the meaning of "corpse-like" and suggests the malodor of death. As He mentioned to the church at Thyatira, the Spirit of Christ had searched their spirits and souls and knew that their relationship with Him had died. We can only speculate that maybe this was because their focus was on the accoutrements of life since their city was so wealthy. Jesus implored them "to come alive" (γινου γρηγορων, v. 2) and strengthen their works because Jesus perceived them to be "incomplete" (ου πεπληρωμενα, v. 2). Jesus knew that the way back to their genuine life with potent and sincere works was to remember the teachings, preaching, and life lessons communicated to their Christian community through Jesus' leaders—the Apostle John, the Apostle Paul, Timothy, Apollos and others. But Jesus told them that remembering was only a first step to recovering effectiveness; they also needed to repent and "hold on to"/"obey" (τηρει, v. 3) what they had heard and received from their mentors. Spiritual posterity means nothing if *application* of Kingdom truths are ignored. Jesus wanted them to "wake up" (γρηγορησης, v. 3); if they remained asleep—as their past citizens had been when invading armies did so in the middle of the night—then they would miss His visitation to their body to judge them. He didn't let them know *what* His judgment to them would be but told them He would be coming to them like a "thief" (κλεπτης) breaking into their homes. Maybe by this, Jesus was suggesting to them that He would be taking something away from them—possibly their wealth.

Ancient Sardis

But all was not negative with the wealthiest of Christian churches in Asia. Jesus told them that some from among them were not soiling their clothing. Jesus told their pastor that they were walking before the Lord wearing white clothes. Later in Revelation 19:8, the Apostle identifies "white fine linen" as the "righteous acts of the saints" which Jesus tells the victorious church members in Sardis they will be wearing with Him at the end. He also told the victorious one that He will make sure "his name is not wiped out from the Book of Life" (μη εξαλειψω το ονομα αυτου εκ της βιβλου της ζωης, v. 5) and assured him that Jesus will make the victorious one's name known to His Father and to His angels. Their victory over spiritual inertia, compromise, and decadence (prevalent among them) would be greatly honored by Jesus. This church more than any of the other Lycus Valley churches has been identified by dispensationalists as representing the rise of American Christian Liberalism and the sleeping of the American Evangelical Church.

The rise of liberal thinking in the church world and theological circles dominated the late nineteenth and first half of the twentieth centuries, particularly in America. The Tubingen School in Germany and the influence of Kant, Rauschenbusch, and Bushnell created the liberal influence on denominational Christianity. The most vulnerable denominations were the most socially aware ones, including Presbyterians, Methodists, Episcopalians, and Congregationalists. As previously mentioned, Immanuel Kant (1724–1804) influenced the development of liberalism in Germany and in turn on the church in America by his insistence that the Bible represents man's consciousness and is not an historical or objective account of God's interaction with His world. He believed the Bible to be man's creation and should be evaluated as any other book should be with a scientific approach. He denied the veracity of miracles and rejected the deity of Christ. He posited that God and Christ are a figment of our imagination. Walter Rauschenbusch's (1861–1918) social gospel emphasized experience over the Scriptures and encouraged the Christian to concentrate on the humanity of Christ and ignore his deity. He felt that religion and the Bible are expressions of man's dependence on God and indicate that man is emotionally dependent on a higher being. The miracles and supernatural events of the Scriptures were explained away by the scientific influences of the "higher" and "lower" biblical criticisms. Original sin, Christ's atonement through the sacrifice of His holy life on the cross, and even the doctrine of salvation through faith alone were disdained and minimized by many theologians at this time. The Sunday school efforts of Horace Bushnell (1802–1876) caused the American education of children to take several steps backward concerning matters of faith. Bushnell, a Congregationalist minister, felt that the child should not have to experience conversion if he were exposed to Christianity from early childhood. He was opposed to divine justice and scoffed at the concept of Atonement for sin and original sin.

These three influenced the American Christian church more than they should have; many denominations by the mid-1950s began to lose their grip on the fundamentals of our faith due to some of this thinking, beginning the slow slide into spiritual ineffectiveness and lethargy. Maybe the wealth of these liberal denominations was another reason why this spiritual drift away from orthodoxy was not noticed and not corrected.

Message to Philadelphia: The Persecuted Church

Revelation 3:7-13

About 30 miles southeast of Sardis, the ancient city of Philadelphia guarded and commanded an important pass through the mountains between the Hermus and Meander valleys. It was the "keeper of the key" to the door, or the gateway into the eastern Asian highlands. The officials had the power to open and close this door as they willed. Through this portal passed the mail, trade, and commerce of the west to the regions of central and eastern Asia and Lydia. The city of Philadelphia was subject to frequent and severe earthquakes. No city of Asia Minor suffered more or as much. The historian Strabo, who lived between 64 BC and AD 21, said Philadelphia was "full of earthquakes." He may have been there in AD 17 the year of the great earthquake that destroyed the city of Sardis (as previously mentioned), and ten other cities in the area. Strabo mentioned that the city was exempted from Roman taxes for five years just like Sardis and the other cities devastated by the great quake.[54] In fact, the historian Pliny the Elder described this great megaquake

---

54   The Geography of Strabo, 12.8.18 and 13.4.10, H.L. Jones ed., (Cambridge, MA: Harvard University Press, 1924), accessed May 29, 2023, https://www.perseus.tufts.edu/hopper/text?doc=Strab.+13.4.10&fromdoc=Perseus%3Atext%3A1999.01.0198.

Revelation: The Fifth Gospel

as "the greatest earthquake in human memory."[55] Unfortunately, that was only one of a series of quakes which kept the citizens in a state of fearful expectancy. Ancient Philadelphia, like Sardis and the other Lycus Valley cities, had several temples dedicated to the gods and to the Roman Emperors.[56] The Philadelphia church, like Smyrna, had been expelled from the Jewish synagogue and community and therefore had no protection from Roman persecution. The Christian community rejected emperor worship so were political/religious targets by the Roman officials of the city. Jesus told the Apostle John to tell the pastor of the church at Philadelphia that He, "the Holy and True One says these things" (ταδε λεγει ο αγιος ο αληθινος, v.7) and therefore would fully support them. This congregation had been challenged by the threat of the Roman Empire and the expectation of its subjects worshipping the Emperor by various acts previously described. As in Pergamum and Thyatira, the Christians refused to worship any other except the one and only Almighty God of the Hebrews as revealed through His Son Jesus. Therefore, they knew Jesus as the Holy and True One who possessed "the key of David" (την κλειν Δανιδ, v. 7), as King David's offspring. The "key of David" occurs in the Scripture in only one other place—Isaiah 22:22. The prophet speaks of Eliakim, a descendent of David, receiving the "key of David" and then telling the people of Israel that what Eliakim opens, no one can shut and what he shuts no one can open. The "key of David" likely had special meaning to the Philadelphians since their city had the "key" to the gate opening the highway from the East to the West and vice versa. Jesus described Himself as the gate/door in His teaching to His disciples overheard by the religious elite in John 10:7–10. In Revelation, Jesus went on to expand upon the significance of the key of David and the power that this key gives the One possessing it. He told them that what He opened, no one could shut, and what He closed, no one could open. The Philadelphians could see that following Jesus gave them access to the Kingdom and its protection, blessings, and witnessing potential as He explained in the next verses.

Jesus told them that He could see that they "had little energy" (μικρον εχεις δυναμιν, v. 8), but that they "obeyed My word and did not deny My name" (ετηρησας μου τον λογον και ουκ ηρνησω το ονομα μου, v. 8). Because of this faithfulness, Jesus promised to turn the tide of rejection and suffering against them by making

---

55   Elizabeth Keitel, "Tacitus and the Disaster Narrative," in Christina S. Kraus, John Marincola and Christopher Pelling, ed., *Ancient Historiography and Its Contexts: Studies in Honour of A. J. Woodman.* (Oxford, England: Oxford University Press, 2010), 335.

56   "Philadelphia, Seven Churches of Revelation," *Bible Study*, accessed May 18, 2021, https://www.biblestudy.org/biblepic/churches-of-revelation-philadelphia.html.

those who opposed them "bow down at their feet" (προσκυνησουσιν ενωπιον των ποδων, v. 9). This would be quite extraordinary for the enemies of the church—specifically Jews resenting their Jewish Christian brothers and sisters who were reporting them to the Roman authorities—to repent of their activities and then come to the realization that their Yahweh really did love Christians. Jesus said it this way, "and I will make those who say they are Jews but are really liars from the synagogue of Satan bow down before your feet and *they will know that I loved you*" (γνωσιν οτι εγω ηγαπησα σε, v. 9).

Ruins of Ancient Philadelphia

Then Jesus promised them protection from the distress about to come over the whole earth. He told them not to worry about this because He would "guard you from the time of testing about to come upon the whole earth *to test those living on the earth*" (πειρασαι τους κατοικουντας επι της γης, v. 10). I wonder what the "time of suffering about to come" actually was? Some have suggested this may be a veiled reference to more Christian persecution from Emperor Trajan (AD 98–AD 117), the collapse of the Roman Empire, invading Mongol hoards, pestilence, or more natural disasters like earthquakes to which the area was prone.[57] One possibility of a global catastrophic event that Jesus was warning the Philadelphians and all subsequent Christians about was the eruption of the Krakatoa Volcano between Java and Sumatra on the Island of Rakata in Indonesia. This took place in AD 535 and caused the coldest year on record from the previous 1,500 years on earth. The event may have precipitated the Dark Ages causing a series of catastrophic events including global loss of sunlight, crop failures, famine, and pestilence for decades.[58] Jesus encouraged His reading audience to hold on to their faith and the

---

57   Heinrich A. W. Meyer, "Revelation 3:10," *Meyer's New Testament Commentary*, accessed May 19, 2021, https://biblehub.com/commentaries/meyer/revelation/3.htm.
58   "Catastrophe! Part 2: How the World Changed," *Secrets of the Dead*, directed by Gary Johnstone (2000; New York: A 3BM Television Production), accessed May 19, 2023, https://www.youtube.com/watch?v=t7Xi3M8xoCQ&list=PLeTVzyt4IP4tIIEANtCihtXrwDt6ZMTEt&index=21.

teaching they had received so that "no one could take away your crown" (μηδεις λαβη τον στεφανον σου, v. 11). He promised the victorious believer that He would make him a "pillar in the Temple of My God" (στυλον εν τω ναω του θεου μου, v. 12). This was particularly meaningful to the Philadelphians because they had experienced numerous earthquakes and damaged temple buildings from them. The idea of being a pillar in God's Temple protected from natural disasters, spiritual threats, or physical suffering and a critical "pillar" at that supporting the work of the Kingdom was appealing, particularly with the promise Jesus made with His next statement: "and he will never go out from it" (και εξω ου μη εξελθη, v. 12). This metaphor of fellowship with the Father by remaining in His presence (His Temple) was a beautifully encouraging glimpse of heaven. Not only this, but Jesus gave the Philadelphian conquerors three more features of His blessing and protection—He will write on them three names: His Father's name, the New Jerusalem's name, and His new name. Toward the end of the Apocalypse in Revelation 21, John received a spectacular view of the Holy City coming down out of heaven and being established on the earth. Here in verse 12, Jesus was making reference to the Philadelphians becoming permanent residents in New Jerusalem without fear of cataclysm such as earthquakes that regularly threatened their lives. John also stated in the last chapter of Revelation that His servants would not only see His face and worship Him but would have His name written on their foreheads (Rev. 22:3-4). I believe this is a metaphor for the closeness of the relationship that God will share with His children—quite comforting to the Philadelphian church which was experiencing alienation and persecution at the hand the Philadelphian Jews and Roman citizens. Jesus' "new name" may be reference to the "High Priest after the Order of Melchizedek" discussed by the writer of Hebrews in 5:6-10—a new name and role Jesus acquired after perfectly living, dying on, and resurrecting from the cross. This intimates that He models the role of priest for us and is making us into a kingdom of priests mentioned by John in Revelation 1:6 and 5:10.

The dispensationalists feel that the church at Philadelphia represents the underground church in Muslim and Chinese Communist countries. It is no secret that the Christians and missionaries in these areas of the world sacrifice safety and well-being as they evangelize the unevangelized people groups there. As in Philadelphia, Christians in China, Afghanistan, and Syria must make hard choices and sacrifices, often resulting in "little energy." However, none of the other churches except for Smyrna were enticed with greater rewards than were the victorious Christians in Philadelphia.

Message to Church at Laodicea: The Wealthy-Lukewarm Church

Revelation 3:14-21

Laodicea was a city almost 50 miles southeast of Philadelphia and 95 miles east of Ephesus in western Asia Minor (Turkey). It was a wealthy city with a renowned medical school. It exported fine woolen garments (black wool) and was famous for its eye salves. This city was totally destroyed by an earthquake in AD 60. But its residents refused Roman Empire help and money to rebuild the city. They reconstructed their city into an attractive one, even better than before.[59] The city had a large Jewish population, well over two thousand families which sent at least 20 lbs. of gold each year (around four hundred thousand dollars a year) to Jerusalem as their contribution to the Temple.[60] Laodicea did not have adequate potable water. Therefore, water from the hot springs 6 miles south was piped into the city via an aqueduct system. When it reached the city, the water was lukewarm. Water from the mountains north of Laodicea was cold but by the time it arrived in Laodicea by the aqueduct pipes, it was also lukewarm.[61] Christ rebukes the church in Laodicea as being neither hot nor cold, but lukewarm (like the water). The original site of Laodicea is now abandoned, but the ruins of a Roman aqueduct are still there. As with some of the other Lycus valley churches, Laodicean Jews were never threatened by the emperor; neither were the Christians of this community

---

59   Tacitus, *The Annals of Tacitus*, xiv.27, accessed May 29, 2023, http://classics.mit.edu/Tacitus/annals.8.xii.html.
60   Flavius Josephus, *The Works of Flavius Josephus*, xii.3.4, William Whiston, AM, trans. (Buffalo, NY: John E. Beardsley, 1895), accessed May 29, 2023, https://www.perseus.tufts.edu/hopper/text?doc=J.+AJ+12&fromdoc=Perseus%3Atext%3A1999.01.0146.
61   "Laodicea—The Lukewarm Church Is Neither Hot Nor Cold," *Never Thirsty*, accessed October 15, 2021, https://www.neverthirsty.org/bible-studies/evaluating-health-your-church/the-lukewarm-church-is-neither-hot-nor-cold/.

which may explain their lack of religious zeal. Jesus states that whom He loves He rebukes. Obviously, His harsh rebuke is backed up by His love for the Laodicean church. Unfortunately, Jesus had no positive comments about the church in this community.

Jesus began His message to the Laodicean church by reminding them that as the "amen" and the "faithful and true witness," He was "the ruler of God's creation" (η αρχη κτισεως του θεου, v. 14). The term "αμην" means "truly" or "so be it" and suggests that what Jesus says goes. Jesus was without sin and was fully trusted by Father God to deliver Kingdom truths to the world. His words reflected the heart of His Father which is why He refers to Himself as the "amen." He was fully justified in referring to Himself as faithful and true as a witness for God in contrast to the lack of witness for the King by the Laodicean's. Jesus described Himself as the ruler of the kings of the earth in Revelation 1:5 but here as the ruler or originator/creator (αρχη) of God's creation highlighting His dominance over the highly inflated Laodicean view of themselves and over the supercilious medical school opinions and their influence over the city.

Ruins of Ancient Laodicea

Jesus immediately launches into what was wrong with the Christians in Laodicea telling them that, just like their water, they were lukewarm (χλιαρος, v. 16)—neither hot (ζεστος, vv. 15-16) nor cold (ψυχρος, vv. 15-16). Jesus told them that their "lukewarmness" was not acceptable to Him, likely meaning that their commitment and resolve to follow Him and their motivation to evangelize and teach were lacking in intensity. He told them that He preferred they be uncommitted and turned off toward Him because He could at least get their attention through the Holy Spirit pricking their consciences to repent and turn around their lethargy and syncretism. Jesus intimated by His comments that they were not really living completely committed lives for Jesus but just enough to get by as Christians. He told them that He had enough of their behavior and was about "to vomit you out of My mouth" (σε εμεσαι εκ του στοματος μου, v. 16). The metaphor is stark. Jesus was expressing extreme frustration. Yet He told them how to rectify their behavior—

by first ceasing their self-talk of "I am rich, I have become wealthy, I have need of nothing" (v. 17). Jesus had seen this pompous, self-righteousness, and hypocrisy among the religious elite of Judaism during His ministry on earth. He objected to it then, and as expected, objected to it among the Laodiceans. Jesus told the Laodiceans that they were really the exact opposite of who they thought they were. He considered them to be "the wretched one, pitiable, poor, blind and naked" (ο ταλαιπωρος και ελεεινος και πτωχος και τυφλος και γυμνος, v. 17). Jesus wanted Laodicea to recognize that despite its financial prosperity, it was spiritually impoverished and in need of spiritual riches: gold (the Word), white clothes (good works), and eye salve (spiritual discernment).

Jesus began His advice to restore spiritual well-being by suggesting that they, "buy gold from Me refined in hot fire" (γορασαι παρ εμου χρυσιον πεπυρωμενον εκ πυρος, v. 18). In Scripture, "gold" has been a metaphor for the Word of God because, just as gold is a precious metal with many uses, so too the Word of God is alive and active in all aspects of life and is the key to successful Christian living (cf. Ps. 19:10; 119:72, 127). Jesus told them that if they "purchased gold" from Him they would truly be wealthy (v. 18), an interesting perspective and insightful for societies like the Laodicean's that were wealthy, self-sufficient, and self-absorbed.

Jesus' second suggestion to restore spiritual health for this lukewarm community was, "(buy) white clothes [from Me] in order to be clothed" (ιματια λευκα ινα περιβαλη, v. 18). Jesus was wanting them to perform works worthy of His call. We know this because John later described in Revelation 19:8 "white clothes" as the "righteous acts of the saints." Jesus was concerned about their spiritual nakedness marked by not executing the works necessary to build the Kingdom in their city. He said it this way, "so that the shame of your nakedness not be revealed" (μη φανερωθη η αισκυνη της γυμνοτητος σου, v. 18).

I think it interesting and revealing that Jesus regards our actions so seriously. So often as Christians, we consider the faith expressions of the heart and confessions of our mouths to be adequate for spiritual health. But James reminded us that faith by itself is not adequate to please the Father. Pleasing Him also comes from our faith-based actions/works (James 2:26). His agenda for every local church depends on timely execution of His plan which cannot occur with lethargic Christians unconcerned about witnessing for Christ, helping the poor and disadvantaged, and being neighborly to our acquaintances.

Jesus ended His treatment plan to reverse their lukewarm behavior by giving them His third suggestion—to acquire "eye ointment to rub on your eyes in order for you to see" (κολλουριον εγχρισαι του οφθαλμους σου ινα βλεπης, v. 18). The Lord Jesus wanted this church in Asia to exercise spiritual discernment and *see* that their recent past behavior had fallen short of Kingdom values. The medical school in Laodicea produced an eye ointment for various eye maladies. But Jesus introduced *His* eye ointment as effective in restoring spiritual sight. Jesus appealed to the Laodicean's by telling them that His "rebuke and discipline" (ελεγχω και παιδευω, v. 19) only comes to those He loves (φιλω, v. 19). Even though Jesus did not commend this church for any good behavior, He still loved them and longed for them to change. Jesus asked them to do what He requests of all His children when they do wrong—He told them to be "genuine and repent" (ζηλευε ουν και μετανοησον, v. 19).

Jesus' final appeal is a statement which has given much comfort to believers over the centuries and insight into Jesus' raison d'etre: "Behold, I stand at the door and knock; if anyone hears My voice and opens the door, *I will come into him, and I will dine with him and he with Me*" (εισελευσομαι προς αυτον και δειπνησω μετ αυτου και αυτος μετ εμου, v. 20). He wanted the Laodiceans to understand that He had been attempting for some time to reach out and connect with them. He assured them that if they responded to His voice of invitation, they would begin to experience the intimacy and fellowship that had been lost from their lives. Jesus promised the lethargic, lukewarm Christians in Laodicea that if they repented from their spiritual smugness and ineptitude, became intimate with His Spirit once again, and became overcomers in this life, He would allow them to "sit with Me on My throne, just as I conquered and *sat down with My Father on His throne*" (εκαθισα μετα του πατρος μου εν τω θρονω αυτου, v. 21). What a privilege Jesus extends to those who are successful at the Kingdom life. He told the Laodiceans that whoever conquered would sit with Him on His throne of authority, confirming what the Apostle John reported in Rev. 22:5—the inhabitants of New Jerusalem will have the Name of their Father on their foreheads and will live the overcomers life, and *will reign as kings forever and ever*.

Many theologians and Revelation scholars over the decades have associated the Laodicean wealth-based ministry approach with spiritual smugness modeled by the Modern American Evangelical denominations, including Baptists, Assemblies of God, Pentecostal Holiness, and others. Although these denominations have prided themselves on Kingdom living and outreaches to their respective communities,

Messages to the Churches at Sardis, Philadelphia, and Laodicea

their individual congregants have been noted to be spiritually smug by those from their own ranks and hiding behind the programs of their denominations. Not only these church groups but the Traditional non-Evangelical denominations have been accused of the same pompousness. The Laodicean problem was not unique for that era. Even today with the COVID-19 pandemic and post-epidemic policies, the Church has been marginalized by the fear of gathering and meaningful engagement. To appease consciences, churches have delivered online podcasts and YouTube services that looked good for the first four to six months of the pandemic but did not meet the needs of hurting and lost Americans. Barna reports that the average church during the first six months of the pandemic lost at least 35 percent of their members and around 50 percent of their millennial participants with little hope that their members will return.[62] Some Christians have decided that an upper respiratory virus should command more fear and respect than the God of the Universe and His Son who has conquered all viruses. I'm wondering if Jesus' words of warning to the Laodiceans would be apropos to the post-COVID American Church of today.

Church	City	Church Positives	Church Negatives	Rewards	Punishment
Ephesus	Chief Asian city; three trade routes through; Temple of Diana; two emperor worship temples	Industrious; persevering, discerning, rejected Nicolaitans	Lost first love; replaced relational with the technical	New Jerusalem residence; right to eat from tree of life	Remove church from its place
Smyrna	One of top 3 cities in Asia; open air market largest in world	Despite persecution were faithful; refused to worship Emperor; were poor but really rich	None	Crown of eternal life despite martyrdom	None

---

62 George Barna, "State of the Church," The Barna Group, 2020, accessed May 24, 2021, https://www.barna.com/research/new-sunday-morning-part-2/.

Revelation: The Fifth Gospel

Church	City	Church Positives	Church Negatives	Rewards	Punishment
Pergamum	One of top 3 cities in Asia; considered royal city by Romans, guilds, theaters	Resisted Satan despite persecution and death of Antipas, remained faithful	Some followed Balaam and Nicolaitans	Hidden manna; white stone with new name = entrance into heaven	Sword fight with Jesus
Thyatira	Wealthy guild town; extensive commerce;	Maturing; noted for love, faith, and works	Jezebel forced guild protocol: idol meat eaten and sex with guild prostitutes	Resist Jezebel and Jesus will allow them to dominate over the pagans (give the morning star)	Repay each according to deeds
Sardis	Destroyed by earthquake in AD 17; rebuilt by Romans; minted gold and silver coins for the Empire largest/ wealthiest Jewish community	Some not complacent and not tolerant; dressed in white	Walking dead	If they wake up Jesus will give white robes – Book of Life	Jesus will judge if they don't repent
Philadelphia	Keeper of pass, many earthquakes; one destroyed city in A.D. 17	Persecution like Smyrna; did not denounce Christ despite death; love for Jesus	None	Open door; Jesus would protect from worse tribulation on world; pillar in temple; three names	None
Laodicea	Medical school; eye salve, cold water from North; hot water from south flowed into city lukewarm	No positive	Lukewarm behavior; spiritual lethargy	Jesus still loved them; will allow to sit with Jesus if they overcome	Jesus will "spit" them out

REVELATION 4

The Throne Room

The Throne Room Scene with the Father, Holy Spirit, Seraphs, and Twenty-Four Elders

1 "After these things, I saw a door opened in heaven and the voice that I first heard speaking to me like a trumpet said, 'Come up here and I will show you what must happen after these things.' ² Immediately I was in the Spirit and behold, a throne in heaven and One sitting on the throne. ³ And the One sitting was similar in appearance to jasper and ruby stones; and an emerald like iris encircled the throne and ⁴ surrounding the throne were twenty-four thrones and twenty-four elders were sitting on the thrones dressed in white clothes with golden crowns on their heads. ⁵ And out of the throne came lightening, rumblings, and thunder. And before the throne were seven burning lamps of fire which are the seven spirits of God ⁶ and also before the throne was a sea of glass, like crystal. And in the middle of the throne and around it were four living beings with eyes covering in front and behind. ⁷ And the first living being was like a lion, and the second like a young ox, and the third having the face of a man, and the fourth was like a flying eagle. ⁸ And each of the four living beings had six wings covered with eyes outside and inside; and they never stop saying day and night, "Holy, holy,

> holy is the Lord God Almighty who was and is and is to come." ⁹ Now, when the living beings give glory, honor, and thanksgiving to the One sitting on the throne living forever and ever, ¹⁰ the twenty-four elders bow down before the One sitting on the throne and worship the one living forever and ever and cast their crowns before the throne and say, ¹¹ 'You are worthy our Lord God to receive glory, honor and power, because You created all things and by Your will they were created and have their being.'"

The Throne Room (cf. Isaiah 6:1–5, Ezek. 1:4–28, Daniel 7:9–14)

The Apostle John heard Jesus' voice telling John to come up into heaven through the open door. John's spirit via the Holy Spirit's action levitated through the door into heaven's throne room and described the scene. John's visit to heaven and Paul's near-death experience and subsequent visit to heaven as mentioned in 2 Corinthians 12 are not unusual for many in this country. In fact, some studies and research in the last few decades have indicated that as many as 50 percent of all those victims of near-death have experienced identifiable stages before death and eternity begin. Scientists are divided as to why humans experience near death experiences (NDEs) so often. They offer three different explanations:

1. Physiological
2. Psychological
3. Transcendental

Kenneth Ring, a neuroscientist, has proposed a five-stage continuum of experiences in the NDEs which includes:

1. Peace
2. Out of body feelings (body separation/hovering)
3. Entering darkness (seeing and entering the tunnel)

4. Seeing the light (travelling through the tunnel)
5. Entering the light (entering heaven)

He suggests that around 60 percent of humans with NDEs experience stage 1 but only about 10 percent experience stage 5.[63] Over 2,500 of these events have been researched and recorded from 1975 to 2005 and many have involved cardiac arrest, shock related to hypovolemia, electrocution, traumatic brain injury, stroke, near drowning, asphyxia, sepsis, and attempted suicide.[64] The latter sufferers or the unreligious have not necessarily experienced "unpleasant" NDEs. By calculation if only 10 percent (250) of those with verifiable NDEs actually enter heaven, then even fewer actually experience heaven. Three-and-a-half-year-old Colton Burpo from Nebraska experienced one of the most astounding of these heavenly visits including meeting Jesus, his great grandfather Pop, and his unborn sister. His father recorded Colton's two to three week visit as Colton related his experience over several years.[65] We learn much about Paradise but from a distance from the neurosurgeon Eben Alexander who became septic from a bacterial meningitis and comatose but was flown on the wings of a giant butterfly to destinations in the afterlife.[66] His experience was quite different from Colton's and others who were Christians at the time of their excursions to heaven. Reading Eben's story makes it quite clear that Eben was *not* a Christian at the time of his journey—he has no interaction with heaven's citizens but saw its brilliance from afar. These stories and more suggest that John's journey through heaven's open door was genuine and accurate and not some deluded apostle's imagination.

Obviously, John's presence in heaven does not alter the activities including focused worship of the Father on His throne by the Seraphim and elders, in the presence of the seven lamps of the Holy Spirit. Some well-meaning pre-tribulation theologians believe that John's entrance into heaven signifies Jesus' rapture of the Church. However, Jesus' description during the last days of His Passion Week of His followers experiencing great suffering during the End Times contradicts this perspective (Mt.

---

63 Kenneth Ring, *Life at death: A Scientific Investigation of the Near-Death Experience* (New York: Coward, McCann, & Geoghegan, 1980), 40.
64 Janice Miner Holden, EdD, Bruce Greyson, MD, and Debbie James, MSN, RN, eds., "The Field of Near-Death Studies: Past, Present and Future," *The Handbook of Near-Death Experiences: Thirty Years of Investigation* (Santa Barbara, CA: Praeger Publishers, 2009), 1–16.
65 Todd Burpo and Lynn Vincent, *Heaven is for Real: A Little Boy's Astounding Story of His Trip to Heaven and Back*, (Nashville, TN: Thomas Nelson, Inc., 2010).
66 Eben Alexander, *Proof of Heaven: A Neurosurgeon's Journey into the Afterlife* (New York: Simon & Schuster, 2012).

Revelation: The Fifth Gospel

24:22). If the Church avoids the distress and suffering of the Tribulation Period, then Jesus' discussion of the End Times with His five closest disciples on that Passion Week Monday evening on Mount Olivet would make no sense. The idea that John himself symbolically represented the Church being raptured into heaven violates the principle of "metaphor exposure and explanation" which the angel indicated to John at the end of chapter 1, vis-à-vis "'The mystery of the seven stars that you saw in My right hand and the seven golden lampstands: the seven stars are the messengers (pastors) of the seven churches and the seven lampstands are the seven churches.'" (Rev. 1:20). The angel indicated that metaphors and symbolic language are *explained* when God's Revelation narrative needs it. Throughout the Book of Revelation, symbolic language is *always* explained. However, John's application of his terms for future events are uniformly *not* explained because John was the recipient of the Apocalyptic vision and no one else was allowed by the Holy Spirit to modify John's words. Any who would try to add to them God would add the plagues discussed in this Book to their lives, and any who would detract or subtract from these words, God would eliminate their participation in the New Jerusalem (Rev. 22:18-19). Besides, the rapture of the Church is far more likely depicted in Revelation 7 when John is shown an innumerable heavenly crowd shouting out with palm branches in the hands, "Salvation belongs to/is by our God, the One sitting on the throne and through the Lamb" (Rev. 7:9-10).

The Apostle Paul's experience in heaven was likely precipitated by his near-death experience with the stoning mob in Lystra as Luke records in Acts 14:19-20. Paul described his entrance and experience in heaven as so exhilarating that Satan was allowed to place a "thorn of the flesh" in his life to keep Paul from becoming conceited (2 Cor. 12:2-8). Despite Paul's desperate request three times to God that the thorn be removed, God refused saying, "My grace is sufficient for you, for My power is made perfect/complete in weakness" (2 Cor. 12:9).

Jasper Stone

John heard the thunderous voice that spoke to him about writing down the message of the Apocalypse to the seven Lycus Valley churches back in chapter 1.

Presumably this voice from the open door in heaven (likely Jesus') invited John up into heaven so that he could see things happening in the future. Jesus told John, "Come up here and I will show you what must happen after these things" (αναβα ωδε και δειξω σοι α δει γενεσθαι μετα ταυτα, v. 1). As Revelation 4 continues, John immediately was transported by the Spirit through the door and first noticed the throne of the Father and the Father's image—really only His silhouette. But Daniel saw a clearer picture of the Father which he reported in Daniel 7. Daniel saw the Father taking His seat: "His clothing was as white as snow; the hair of His head was white like wool. His throne was flaming with fire, and its wheels were all ablaze. A river of fire was flowing, coming out from before him" (Dan. 7:9-10, NIV). Moses saw the backside of the Father as God passed by him after Moses asked to see Him (Ex. 33:21-23). But John was obviously watching the throne room from above because he saw the throne's four sides as he described it and the elders and twenty-four thrones surrounding God's throne. John observed radiant light both green/jasper (ιασπιδι, v. 3)—which is the main precious stone comprising the New Jerusalem described in Revelation 21:9-14—and red/ruby (σαρδιω, v. 3) emanating from the Father. John also saw the rainbow dominated by emerald (σμαραγδινω, v. 3), another shade of green, encircling the throne in dazzling light. It would seem from John's reporting that the Father *really* likes green as we see throughout the earth's surface with grass and tree leaves. The Apostle noticed "twenty-four elders" (εικοσι τεσσαρας πρεσβυτερους, v. 4) "wearing white clothes" (περιβεβλημενους εν ιματιοις λευκοις, v. 4) and "golden crowns on their heads" (τας κεφαλας αυτων στεφανους χρυσους, v. 4).

Many have speculated over the centuries as to the identity of the twenty-four elders. It is clear that these individuals are human and wear clothes that would indicate revered status. In Revelation, white raiment is associated with righteous acts of the saints (cf. Rev. 19:8) and golden crowns with royalty. Some

Natural Ruby Stones

have suggested the elders in John's vision are the twelve patriarchs and the twelve apostles, an interesting proposition particularly if the Apostle John was actually observing himself many centuries in the future.[67] Another suggestion is that these are martyrs or beings from other worlds in light of recent congressional testimony on UFO's and on Area 51 acquisitions.

Despite lightning, rumblings, and thunder exploding from the throne, John noticed the crystal calm "sea of glass" (θαλασσα υαλινη, v. 6) unaffected by these commotions and the "seven burning lamps of fire" (επτα λαμπαδες πυρος καιομεναι, v. 5) of the Holy Spirit before God's throne. The sea of glass appears to be a water supply for Jesus, humans in heaven, and likely the source of "the river of the water of life" described by John in the Holy City, New Jerusalem (cf. Rev. 22:1). I find it fascinating that the Holy Spirit represents Himself as seven burning lamps. Of course, seven is considered a perfect number. God is very mathematical. There are seven continents on the earth; maybe the seven spirits before the throne each have responsibility to minister to one continent apiece as previously noted. The "burning lamps" could suggest that the Holy Spirit's essence is boundless energy in the form of light and fire; the light to guide and the fire to judge the world and burn away impurities from the hearts of His children.

The Throne of Heaven, painting by Davin Arries

John then focused on the "four living beings" (τεσσαρα ζωα, v. 6) hovering over and around the throne. John noticed that these creatures were "full of eyes" (γεμοντα οφθαλμων, v. 6) on their fronts and on their backs. In contrast to Ezekiel's vision of the seraphim, each of which demonstrated four faces simultaneously (Ez. 1:10), John noticed that the first seraphim looked like a lion (λεοντι, v. 7), the second like a young ox (μοσχω, v. 7), the third had the face of a man (προσωπον ως ανθρωπου, v. 7), and the fourth looked like a flying eagle (αετω πετομενω, v. 7). I wonder if the seraphim can morph in appearance depending upon the situation and depending on their feelings at the time. If that's the case, then both Ezekiel and John's vision

---

67 "The twenty-four (24) elders in Revelation—Who are they?" *Compelling Truth*, Accessed May 27, 2021, https://www.compellingtruth.org/24-elders.html.

of the seraphim make sense. John also remarked that each of the seraphim had "six wings with eyes covering outside and inside" (πτερυγας εξ κυκλοθεν και εσωθεν γεμουσιν οφθαλμων, v. 8). Then John witnessed one of the most intense worship experiences that a human could witness—both the seraphim and the elders worshipping the Father with unbridled, intense, spontaneous worship. According to John, the seraphim repeat day and night the trisagion: "Holy, holy, holy is the Lord God Almighty, who was, and is, and is to come" (αγιος, αγιος, αγιος κυριος ο θεος ο παντοκρατωρ ο ην και ο ων και ο ερχομενος, v. 8).

The word, "seraphim," is derived from a Hebrew term for "burning ones/fiery serpents" likely due to each of the four seraphs' burning desire to love and worship Father God as we see here. They are also burning because they are receiving untold roentgens of radiation from God, being so close to Him. Each of these magnificent angel beings surrounding the throne probably could care less about angel rank. They have the most enviable position in the universe because they are the closest beings to Father God. As indicated later in this chapter, these "living beings" lead the worship activities in heaven. Worship seems to be the most important celestial activity because it sustains the lives of the spirit beings living there. God is light and His light energy energizes the dwellers of heaven particularly when they worship Him. The whole Church community in the New Jerusalem as is illustrated from Revelation 21 and 22 is also energized by worshipping the Father. So, it is almost unimaginable the amount of energy radiating from God's throne into the four seraphim engulfing the Father. As I have pointed out, John's vision of heaven's throne room included the description of each of the seraphs and what many theologians have interpreted their body habitus to represent:

- eyes covering their bodies
- three pair of wings
- four recognizable features

    - lion: authority
    - young ox (calf): perseverance
    - face of a man: intelligence
    - flying eagle: execution of God's commands [68]

---

68   Albert Barnes, "Revelation 4:7," *Notes on the Bible*, accessed May 10, 2023, http://biblehub.com/commentaries/barnes/revelation/4.htm.

Revelation: The Fifth Gospel

Several other ideas have been promulgated concerning the significance of these four kinds of animals. One writer suggests that the lion represents wild animals, the ox represents domesticated animals, of course the man represents humans, and the eagle represents birds. All of this signifies the breadth of seraphim service to the Godhead, including the prospect of even executing His will as it involves His creation.[69] Some theologians feel that the lion seraph represents Jesus depicted by Matthew as the lion of Judah, the ox represents Jesus as the servant of the world as depicted by Mark, the human represents Jesus as the Son of Man in Luke's Gospel and the flying eagle as the universal Son of God as John depicted Him in his Gospel.[70]

In Isaiah 6:2-6, the prophet saw the throne room like the Apostle John did. But Isaiah saw that the seraphim cover their eyes with their upper wings; they cover their feet with their lower wings; and they fly with their middle wings. The covering of the eyes may be due to their humility. But it also may be because their head eyes or more sensitive to the Father's light than the other eyes on their bodies. They may cover their feet out of respect for the Father.[71] But they also may cover their feet because they may be sensitive to the heat from the radiation coming from the throne. In Isaiah's vision, they cry out, "Holy, Holy, Holy is the Lord God Almighty, the whole earth is full of His glory" (Is. 6:2, NIV) which is almost exactly what John heard in the throne room at the end of time: "Holy, Holy, Holy is the Lord God Almighty, who was and is and is to come" (Rev. 4:8). The prophet Ezekiel refers to the seraphim as cherubs which may add confusion to the position and function of the cherub versus the seraph. I think Ezekiel described his vision with great accuracy. He likely saw the same "living beings" the Apostle John saw. But each of his seraphim had the four faces demonstrated by the single forms of each of the four seraphim in John's account. In Ezekiel's account, the seraphim were also transported across the throne room with "wheels" which moved them up, down, and laterally. John saw a single face for each seraph because it was likely necessary as deemed by the Holy Spirit for John to be able to identify each of the four for their roles in the future apocalypse.

---

69   **Alice Wood**, *Of Wings and Wheels: A Synthetic Study of the Biblical Cherubim* (New York: Walter de Gruyter, 2008),*137*.

70   Victorinus of Pettau, Chapter 4, *Commentary of the Apocalypse*, Ante-Nicene Fathers, vol. 7., Robert Ernest Wallis, trans., Alexander Roberts, James Donaldson, A. Cleveland Coxe, and Kevin Knight, ed. (Buffalo, NY: Christian Literature Publishing Co., 1886), accessed May 28, 2021, https://www.newadvent.org/fathers/0712.htm.

71   William Owen Carver, "Seraphim," *International Standard Biblical Encyclopedia*, James Orr, gen. ed., (Chicago, IL: Howard-Severance Co., 1915, PD), accessed May 10, 2023, accessed October 6, 2021, https://www.biblestudytools.com/encyclopedias/isbe/seraphim.html.

The Throne Room

Besides attending to the Father and leading heaven's worship in the place of Lucifer, we see another function of this order of angels—one involving the spiritual purification of the those executing Kingdom work. Isaiah was one of the greatest prophets of Old Testament times and quoted by Jesus more than any other prophet. Isaiah prophesied and helped direct the affairs of five kings of Judah (Uzziah, Jotham, Ahaz, Hezekiah, and Manasseh). He was largely considered the greatest of the Jewish prophets by the kings (with the exception of Manasseh) and the people he served. However, while receiving his first vision and call to the prophetic ministry, Isaiah became acutely aware of his spiritual decadence and unfitness to minister on behalf of Yahweh. As he received his vision of the throne room of God and observed Yahweh and the seraphim surrounding His throne, Isaiah cried out in anguish, "Woe to me! . . . I am ruined! For I am a man of unclean lips, and I live among a people of unclean lips, and my eyes have seen the King, the Lord Almighty" (Is. 6:5, NIV). Immediately one of the seraphim flew over to the future prophet and touched a hot coal from the altar onto Isaiah's lips. As the seraph ministered to Isaiah, he said, "See, this has touched your lips; your guilt is taken away and your sin atoned for" (Is. 6:7, NIV).

The seraph was acutely aware of the potential for Isaiah to renege on his calling as a prophet of God. The Lord prompted the seraph to remedy the situation by taking away Isaiah's feelings of inadequacy and sinfulness and purified him physically, mentally, and most importantly spiritually with the coal from the holy Altar of God placed on his lip. With this action, Isaiah felt up to the challenge of bringing God's word to a dysfunctional and downright evil generation of Israelites.

The seraphim execute more than leadership, worship, and purifying activities in heaven. They are also responsible for critical roles in the unfolding of End-Time events as the Apostle John records in Revelation. All four are instrumental in the execution of the first four seal judgments which begin the first three- and one-half years of the Tribulation period (i.e., The Time of Sorrows) as John records this in Revelation 6. They each yell out "Come!" in booming voices to the four horsemen of the Apocalypse which unleash each of the first four judgements for that time on earth including:

- white horseman: one world government establishing economic prosperity
- red horsemen: international mistrust and global conflict; suspension of international treaties

- ▸ black horseman: famine with inflation
- ▸ pale green horseman: global war resulting in death of one fourth of the earth's population

In Revelation 8:13, John saw a "flying eagle" yell out "Woe, woe, woe to those living on the earth because of the trumpet blasts about to be sounded by the other three angels." I think the flying eagle is really the fourth seraph described by John in Revelation 4:7 as the one who appears like a "flying eagle" who sets the stage for the next series of three "woe" trumpet judgments which are far more devastating to the earth's inhabitants than the previous four. We are not told which seraph, but John indicated in Revelation 15:7 that one of the seraphs gives the seven bowl (vial) judgments to seven angels as the last act before the bowl judgments against the earth occur. Because the seraphim are in such close proximity to Father God, they would be most likely to know the most intimate thoughts of God. Ezekiel noticed that the seraphim's wings touched one another (Ezek. 1:11) which might assist them in thinking and acting in unison, which John noticed as they worshipped together. They would be the most likely to reflect God's will outside of the Triune God and the most likely to understand His commands and execute His desires. In summary, seraphim appear to be the closest to the Lord of His angel beings and likely receive information necessary for the execution of critical apocalyptic events which the archangels and the angels do not initially receive. They not only lead the angel hosts in the worship activities of God (Rev 4, 5, 7, 14, 19), but they execute judgment activities necessary for the final seven years of the earth as we know it.

Then John observed an amazing sequence. He noticed after the seraphim's trisagion that the elders continued the adoration of the Father by bowing down before their sitting Father and "casting their crowns before the throne" (βαλουσιν τους στεφανους αυτων ενωπιον του θρονου, v. 10). Evidently the excitement of unabashed worship and adoration of the Almighty caused the elders to forget about orderly protocol and throw their golden crowns in the direction of the throne. Presumably the crowns would not be damaged and the throwers would retrieve their crowns before doing this again. I wonder how many times in a day they would do this. But it would seem from John's account that no matter how many times they worshipped the King in this fashion, they never tired doing so; each worship sequence was as fresh as the previous one, as if they had never worshipped the Father in this manner before. They also never tire of their response to the seraphim trisagion: "You are worthy our Lord God to receive glory, honor, and power, because You created all things, and *by Your will they were created and have their being*" (δια το θελημα σου ησαν και εκτισθησαν, v. 11). I think that the Apostle could see that this incessant worship from the seraphim and elders indicates that the Lord truly loves to be worshipped; if He has one weakness or need it is the desire to be loved; as Saint Augustine stated, "God thirsts that we might thirst for Him."[72]

---

[72] Saint Augustine Quotes, Catholic Link, accessed May 29, 2021, https://catholic-link.org/images/god-thirsts-that-we-may-thirst-for-him-st-augustine/.

REVELATION 5

The Scroll

Jesus as the Lamb taking seven seals scroll from Father's right hand

1 "Then I saw in the right hand of the One sitting on the throne a scroll with writing on the inside and outside having been sealed with seven seals. ² Then I saw a mighty angel announce in a loud voice, 'Who is worthy to open the scroll and break its seals?' ³ But no one in heaven, or on earth or under the earth was able to open the scroll or even look on it. ⁴ Then I cried and cried because no one was found worthy to open the scroll or even look on it. ⁵ But one of the elders said to me, 'Do not cry. Behold, the Lion of the tribe of Judah from the root of David, conquered and can open the scroll and its seven seals.'

⁶ "Then I saw the recently slaughtered Lamb standing in the middle of the throne surrounded by the four living beings and the elders having seven horns and seven eyes which are the seven Spirits of God sent to the whole world. ⁷ And He went to take the scroll from the right hand of the One sitting on the throne. ⁸ And when He took the scroll, the four living beings and the twenty-four elders fell down before the Lamb each having a harp and golden bowls filled with incense which are the prayers of God's people. ⁹ And they sang a new song

> saying, 'You are worthy to take the scroll and open its seals because you were slaughtered and by your blood you purchased for God those from every tribe, people, nation, and language. ¹⁰ And You made them into a kingdom of priests for our God and they will reign on the earth.'
>
> ¹¹ "Then I looked and heard the voice of many angels numbering myriads upon myriads and thousands upon thousands accompanied by the elders and the living beings surrounding the throne; ¹² and they cried out with a loud voice, 'Worthy is the slaughtered Lamb to receive glory, honor, power, praise, strength, wealth and wisdom.' ¹³ Then I heard all creatures in heaven, on the earth, under the earth, and in the sea say, 'Blessing, glory, honor, and power forever and ever to the One sitting on the throne and to the Lamb.' ¹⁴ Then the four living beings said 'Amen.' Then the elders fell down and worshipped.'"

John's vision of the throne room now gets even more interesting. The worship scene was spectacular, but the next scene gets very emotional for him. He noticed a book "in the right hand of the One sitting on the throne" (δεξιαν του καθυμενου επι του θρονου, v. 1). The right hand was always considered the most important hand and one that would mediate judgment in the Roman courts of law and when extended represented trust, a pledge, and sometimes power.[73] Obviously the Father's left hand is also important. But holding a book (βιβλιον, v. 1) in His right hand with "writing on the inside and outside and sealed with seven seals" (γεγραμμενον εσωθεν και οπισθεν κατεσφαγισμενον σφραγισιν επτα, v. 1) accentuated the importance of the book. Legal documents of John's day were sealed which could be indicating this was one of the most important books in the universe; in addition, the document contained the description and activation of the coming End-Time events as we see when Jesus opens the scroll seals in chapter 6. Barclay thinks the scroll is, "God's will, his final settlement of the affairs of the universe."[74] In the first century, people wrote on papyrus (παπυρος) made from papyrus plant pith and parchments

---

[73] Karl E. Georges, *Ausführliches lateinisch-deutsches Handwörterbuch*, Leipzig, Hahn'sche Verlags-buchhandlung Lateinisch-deutscher theil. 1879-80. 2 v.—Deutsch-lateinischer theil 1882 2 v (reprint Berlin 2007), s.v., "dexter," cf. *Lewis-Short* s v "dextera," cf. *LSJ* s.v., "δεξιά."

[74] David Guzik, "Revelation 5—The Lion, the Lamb, and the Scroll," *Enduring Word Bible Commentary*, accessed May 29, 2021, https://enduringword.com/bible-commentary/revelation-5/.

(μεμβρανος, 2 Tim. 4:13) or the finer vellum[75] which were specially prepared goat, sheep, or calf skins.[76] These were either connected and rolled together in scrolls or later in the first century were cut into rectangles and bound together in codex (book) form. An official Roman document was often sealed with at least seven seals which indicated to the recipient of the document that it was legitimate, authentic, and represented the authority of its originator. The sealing process consisted of a cord or strand which had knots associated with the sections of the rolled-up scroll. The seals were usually dried wax or clay with the originator's imprimatur overlying the wax/clay and were placed over the knots of the string. These seals could only be opened by the designated recipient. In John's day, books as we know them existed but were rare and only associated with the larger libraries and Rome. John may never have seen a book or "codex" as they were called in the first century.[77] Of course, the Lord could use anything He wanted for John's vision. Throughout Revelation, the angel, through whom the Father sent the Apocalypse to John, utilized familiar *sitz im leben* (the environmental features of his first century world) wherever and whenever possible. I think the *scroll* was the most likely "book" of this scene; John would better understand what was transpiring in the events mediated by the writing in the scroll rather than in a book over the next few chapters.

Then a mighty angel (αγγελον ισχυρον, v. 2), likely one of the archangels Gabriel (the announcing angel) or Michael (the warring angel), cried out in a loud voice, "Who is worthy to open the book and break its seals" (τις αξιος ανοιξαι το βιβλιον και λυσαι τας σφραγιδος αυτου, v. 2)? The angel's question triggered a *massive* search effort throughout the universe to find that person who had the authority, purity, and the legal position to take the book, open its seals, read its pages, and presumably speak its words into action.

---

75 According to David Bianco who produced the vellum for both the cover art and for the Lycus Valley church paintings of this commentary, the process of transforming the lamb skin into parchment or vellum involves soaking the hide in a hydrated lime bath, then rinsing and stretching the hide like a drum on a "herse"; then the treated hide is scraped, dried over days, and then it is scraped a second time for parchment production but if vellum is desired then it is scraped a third time to remove all residual epidermis; the parchment or vellum is sanded multiple times with increasing finer abrasive surfaces; then it is removed from the herse frame; finally, it is cut to the size desired by the artist or production designer.

76 *Conservation of Leather and Related Materials*, Marion Kite and Roy Thomson, ed. (London: Taylor & Francis Group, 2007).

77 "A Scroll, Sealed with Seven Seals, Revelation 5:1," *Understanding the Book of Revelation/Hello Bible*, accessed May 29, 2021, https://hello-bible.com/index.php/bible-study/item/70-31-a-scroll-sealed-with-seven-seals-revelation-5-1#:~:text=According%20to%20the%20Roman%20law%2C%20wills%20and%20testaments,on%20the%20document%20were%20allowed%20to%20open%20it.

Revelation: The Fifth Gospel

I find it very interesting that the search involved looking for a worthy person "under the earth" (υποκατω της γης, v. 3). Maybe by this time in the future, the earth's surface will be more difficult to live on due to global warming, earthquakes, famines, and pandemics that Jesus mentioned in His Mt. Olivet sermon, and which would occur with increasing frequency as the End Times come near. I can easily imagine that the elite of the world will not only seek other planets on which to live, but also subterranean spaces in which to survive and escape the dangers of the earth's surface. These subterranean habitats are suggested by John's vision in Revelation 12 when the "woman" flees the dragon to the wilderness and the wilderness helps her escape from the pursuing serpent/dragon by opening its mouth and swallowing its water torrent (Rev. 12:13-16). This could indicate a subterranean channel.

John doesn't tell us how long the search lasted; but he reports that "no one was found worthy . . . to open the book or even look upon it" (ουδεις εδυνατο . . . ανοιξαι το βιβλιον ουτε βλεπειν ουτο, v. 4). Based on John's response of uncontrolled grief and anguish marked by his "weeping much" (εκλαιον πολυ, v. 4), John evidently was watching the entire search process with great interest and much hope. Not finding this person was devastating to him. Maybe the Lord wanted John to feel the gravity of the moment and how important Christ's work on Calvary was to the future of the End-Time events that John certainly knew would be revealed during his Revelation experience. At the very least, John's emotional response indicates how lost we all would be had Jesus not conquered death through His sacrifice, fulfilled all requirements for a perfect life, and then sat down with His Father on His throne (Rev. 3:21; Heb. 10:12-14).

I wonder why John didn't think about asking Jesus to open the book whom he had met in His conquering Messiah form in Revelation 1. But obviously he was overwhelmed with the frustration of not finding anyone to take and open the book. One of the elders took pity on John; maybe the elder was John himself in the future. This elder approached and told him not to worry about the unsuccessful search party. It appears that even the elders were not worthy enough to take and open the special book. But they were wise and knew who could. The elder told John not to cry anymore because the Lion of the tribe of Judah, from the root of David, has conquered and "He [is able to] open(s) the book and its seven seals." (ανοιξαι το βιβλιον και επτα σφραγιδας, v. 5)

I'm sure immediate relief and great hope came over John, particularly when he saw Jesus standing around the throne of the Father. The elder told him that Jesus as the Lion Conqueror was the only qualified person to open the seals of the book. But Jesus as the Suffering Messiah *actually* was the One who performed the honors as we see in the next few verses. The elders and four living beings continued their activity of worshipping the Godhead when Jesus, suddenly appearing "as the Lamb recently slain" (ως εσφαγμενον, v. 6), approached the Father sitting on the throne and took the sealed book from the Father's hand. John interjected that Jesus appeared as "a lamb" (αρνιον, v. 6) with "seven horns" (κερατα επτα, v. 6) and with "seven eyes" (οφθαλμους επτα, v. 6). John doesn't explain the significance of the seven horns, but the seven eyes he said represents "the seven spirits of God sent to the whole world" (v. 6). Usually horns in Revelation mean authority, even kingship. Of course, the Father released the Holy Spirit into the world as Jesus successfully completed His mission on earth and returned to His Father's side. When Jesus took the scroll, the four living beings and the twenty-four elders prostrated themselves before the Lamb as they each clutched a harp and "golden bowls full of incense" (και φιαλας χρουσας γεμουσας θυμιαματων, v. 8) which John explains are "the prayers of the saints (God's people)" (αι προσευχαι των αγιων, v. 8). It is interesting that both groups of worshippers (the elders and seraphim) were also involved with transporting and releasing the incense of believers' prayers to the Father, as we see more clearly a few chapters ahead in Revelation 8.

Then John reported what the worshippers now say about the Lamb. In one worshipful statement, the elders and the seraphim proclaim that Jesus is worthy to take the scroll and open it seals because He perfectly executed His mission from the Godhead by submitting to the cruelest of deaths. By shedding His blood, He redeemed those from every tribe, people, nation, and language, and transformed them into a kingdom of priests ministering before God. John stated that the worshippers began to sing a new song like this, "You are worthy to take the scroll and open its seals because You were slaughtered (εσφαγης, v. 9) and by Your blood You redeemed to God those from every tribe, people, nation, and language; and You made them into a *kingdom of priests to our God and they will reign on the earth.*" (τω θεω ημων βασιλειαν και ιερεις και βασιλευσευσιν επι της γης, v. 10). John saw the Lamb bearing the marks of recent sacrifice which accentuates the reality of it to the Father and the active reliance of believers on Jesus' death and resurrection. F. F. Bruce states, "The crucial event of all time is the sacrifice of Calvary; that was the decisive victory which has ensured the final triumph of God's cause and God's people over all the forces opposed to them."

Jesus took the scroll because He was worthy by giving up His life as payment for each sinner's sins past, present, and future. The Book of Romans and Paul's development of systematic theology and the doctrine of soteriology (salvation) are included here in the worship sung by the seraphs and elders with harps and incense filled bowls (of the prayers of the saints). In this one phrase, "purchased for God" (ηγορασας τω θεω, v. 9), the seraphim and elders sum up what Paul discusses at length in Romans 1-8: namely the *grace* of, the *redemption* by (buy back/repurchase), the *justification* before (legal pardon), and *reconciliation* between (overt conciliatory behavior to restore relationship) God with believers. Soteriology (the doctrine of salvation; see Romans 3:22-25) can be understood by knowing the meanings of these four key words upon which this most important of Christian doctrines is based:

- Grace: unmerited favor

  - Common: God's blessing on all humans
  - Free: no works necessary to receive
  - Irresistible: Calvinistic concept that if God pursues a person he/she cannot resist
  - Prevenient: God's initial grace before conversion mediated by the pursuit of the Holy Spirit of that person

- Redemption ("repurchase"; "buy back"): merciful act reconciling sinful man to the perfect Father through Christ's perfect atoning sacrifice

  - Propitiation (payment): required for penalty of our sins; Jesus' perfect sacrifice: Jesus' perfect life was given as our sacrifice (Eph. 5:2, Heb. 9:23, Rom. 3:25, Heb. 9:22)
  - Substitutionary: Jesus took our place on the cross (II Cor. 5:21)
  - Ransom paid to release Christ followers from sin and death bondages (Mt. 20: 28, Mark 10:45)

- Justification: God the Father declares a sinner "righteous" because of Jesus' sacrifice.

    - Legal act of pardon
    - Enacted through the Attorney Jesus Christ's representation for us before the Father
    - All receive justification who exercise faith in Jesus and His sacrifice and who:

- Repent: turning away from life of sin
- Confess: verbal request for Jesus' forgiveness and effects of His blood sacrifice be applied to our lives

    - Catholics/Eastern Orthodox

        - Initial: at baptism
        - Permanent: throughout a lifetime of righteous living

    - Protestants

        - At confession
        - Gift

- Reconciliation: conciliatory behavior to restore relationship

    - Because of Christ's perfect sacrifice for the sinner, he/she experiences atonement allowing for normalization of estranged relationship between God and His subject
    - This marks the end of hostilities between the two parties
    - The establishment of peace between humanity and God that results from the expiation of sin and the appeasement of God's wrath. [78]

---

[78] John Calvin, *Institutes of the Christian Religion*, (II.16.2), Henry Beveridge, trans. (Grand Rapids, MI: Christian Classics Ethereal Library, pd).

Revelation: The Fifth Gospel

The Apostle continued the events of the worship scene following the Lamb taking the scroll from His Father's hand by telling His reading audience that myriads of angels, elders, and seraphim proclaim that the slaughtered Lamb is worthy to receive "glory, honor, power, praise, strength, wealth and wisdom" (v. 12). All seven of these attributes genuinely characterize and describe the Conquering Messiah. No other being in the universe, save the Godhead, could claim any one of these attributes let alone all seven. Right after this acclamation, all beings from heaven, earth, under the earth, and on the sea also proclaim almost the same thing but also include the Father in their words of praise. They say, "Blessing, glory, honor, power, forever and ever *to the One sitting on the throne and to the Lamb*" (τω καθημενω επι τω θρονω και τω αρνιω, v. 13). The worship of the Godhead concludes with the seraphim saying, "Amen!" and the elders prostrating themselves and worshipping without restraint before the throne (v. 14). It seems that whenever a significant event occurs in the Apocalypse, the four living creatures and usually the twenty-four elders begin a worship sequence (cf. 4:9–10; 5:9–14; 7:11–12; 11:16–18; 19:4). This worship sequence is no exception: the seal events are about to unfold.

REVELATION 6

The First through the Sixth Seal Judgments

Introduction

Revelation chapter 6 cannot be understood unless we gain an understanding of Christian eschatology as developed through those passages in Scripture treating the subject. The main passages concerning the End Times are Daniel 9 and Matthew 24, Mark 13, and Luke 21. Daniel 9 discusses the seventy weeks of years of the End Times with sixty-nine weeks being fulfilled in the 483 years from the announcement to rebuild the city of Jerusalem (456 BC) to Jesus' death there in AD 27 or AD 28. The passages in Daniel 9 and in Matthew 24, Mark 13, and Luke 21 discuss the last "week" or seven years of the Tribulation Period also mentioned in Revelation 6–16. Jesus discussed the years leading up to this Tribulation Period recorded in Matthew 24 and divided this time generally into four events: birth pains, persecution, false prophets, and people group evangelization.

    a.   **Birth pains:** Jesus told His disciples that many "earth events" will occur before He comes including wars (fifty-three major wars in twentieth century alone, far more than in nineteenth century), famines (sixty major famines in twentieth century alone with seventy-five million deaths, far more than in nineteenth century) and earthquakes (310 major earthquakes in twentieth century alone of 6.0 or greater magnitude, far more than in nineteenth century).

Revelation: The Fifth Gospel

    b. **Persecution increase:** Jesus was clear to His disciples that persecution is always a part of the Christian life but will increase when His coming nears; each year between 100,000 and 175,000 Christians are executed for their faith in largely Muslim, Buddhist, or communist nations; in other words, one Christian dies every five minutes for his/her faith. The persecution of Christians will continue to increase, particularly as the western hemisphere becomes less tolerant of Christ and His followers.

    c. **False prophets:** Christ was clear to His disciples that some will claim to be Christians but will lead many away from Himself as His coming draws near. Of course, many pseudo ministers of the gospel have attempted to deceive the vulnerable and unsuspecting. Recently, this has included such false prophets as David Koresh, Jim Jones, Laurie Cabot, Dali Lama, Reverend Moon, Sylvia Browne and others. Many more will arise to deceive before the Rapture.

    d. **The gospel preached to all people groups:** Some estimate that 3.36 billion people (of a total world population of over eight billion people) are unreached for Christ and nearly seven thousand people groups of ten thousand or more individuals are not yet reached for Christ. [79] Jesus told His disciples He would not return until all these events occur.

The specifics of the last days comprising the Tribulation Period are not mentioned here in Jesus' discourse to His disciples. But He *does* mention that had these days not been cut short, even the elect would not have survived (Mt. 24:22) which gives me the perspective that Christians *will be* persecuted in the coming Tribulation Period. The latter is a seven-year period divided into two three and a half year periods: "the time of sorrows" and "the great tribulation period"; the latter period is marked by the beginning of the "abomination of desolation" (Mt. 24:15; Dan. 9:27) which Jesus mentioned to His disciples in passing during the Mt. Olivet discourse.

    a. **The time of sorrows:** this three-and-a-half-year period marks the beginning of the seven seal judgments on the earth of Revelation 6–7 and the seven trumpet judgments of Revelation 8, 9, and 11.

    b. **The great tribulation period:** this three-and-a-half-year period marks the beginning of the rise of the Beast and the "abomination of desolation"

---

[79] Joshua Project, A Ministry of Frontier Ventures, accessed May 12, 2023, https://joshuaproject.net.

after his assassination of Revelation 13-14. The abomination begins when the Beast (i.e., the Antichrist) sponsors the rebuilding of Temple in Jerusalem and then forces his image to be worshipped in the Temple as described by Daniel in his vision while in Babylon (Dan. 9:25-27). The prophet Daniel enumerates what he refers to as "seventy sevens" (Dan. 9:24) and explains to some degree what this means:

"Seventy 'sevens' are decreed for your people and your holy city to finish transgression, to put an end to sin, to atone for wickedness, to bring in everlasting righteousness, to seal up vision and prophecy and to anoint the Most Holy Place. Know and understand this: From the time the word goes out to restore and rebuild Jerusalem until the Anointed One, the ruler, comes, there will be seven 'sevens,' and sixty-two 'sevens.' It will be rebuilt with streets and a trench, but in times of trouble. After the sixty-two 'sevens,' the Anointed One will be put to death and will have nothing. The people of the ruler who will come will destroy the city and the sanctuary. The end will come like a flood: War will continue until the end, and desolations have been decreed. He will confirm a covenant with many for one 'seven.' In the middle of the 'seven' he will put an end to sacrifice and offering. And at the temple he will set up an abomination that causes desolation, until the end that (which) is decreed is poured out on him." (Dan. 9:24-27, NIV)

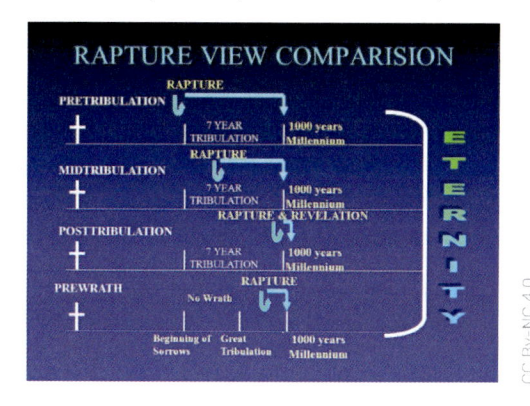

Comparison of Christian Rapture and Tribulation Views

Christians are divided when it comes to understanding when the Rapture occurs in relationship to the Tribulation Period. There are five major views and all with support from Scripture. Most evangelical Christians are either pre-tribulationists or mid-tribulationists. Here is a discussion of the five Rapture positions:

▸ *Revelation 4: Pre-tribulationists* believe that all Christians then alive will be taken bodily up to Heaven (the Rapture—2 Thess. 4:16-17) before the Tribulation begins (Lk. 21:36, 2 Thess. 5:8-10, Rev. 3:10, 4:1). Those who become Christians after the Rapture will live through (or perish during) the Tribulation. After the Tribulation, Christ will return.

- *Revelation 7 (Seventh Seal): Mid-tribulationists* believe that the Rapture will occur halfway through the Tribulation after the breaking of the sixth seal but before the seventh seal is broken and before the trumpet judgments occur (Dan. 7:23-25, Mt. 24:24-31, Rev. 7:7-14). In other words, they believe the Rapture occurs and is reported by John in Revelation 7, right after the sealing of the "Jewish Billy Grahams." The seven-year period is divided into two halves—the "beginning of sorrows," the first half, and the "great tribulation" period which takes place during the second half and begins when the "Beast"/Antichrist sets up his image in the rebuilt Temple in Jerusalem (Rev. 13:14-15) as previously mentioned.

- *Revelation 11 (Seventh Trumpet): Mid-tribulationists* believe the rapture will occur during the tribulation, halfway through or after, but before the seven bowls of the wrath of God. Specifically, at the sound of the Seventh Trumpet (Rev. 11:15, 1 Cor. 15:52).

- *Revelation 15 (Pre-wrath): Mid-tribulationists* believe the Rapture will occur during the tribulation, halfway through or after, after the Seventh Trumpet is blown but before the seven vials (bowls) of the wrath of God are poured out (Rev. 15).

- *Post-tribulationists* believe that Christians will not be taken up into Heaven but will be received or gathered by Christ into the Kingdom of God on earth at the end of the Tribulation. "Immediately after the tribulation . . . then the sign of the Son of Man (Jesus) will appear..and they will gather his elect" (Matthew 24:29-31, see also Mark 13:24-27; Luke 21:25-27). The idea of a post-tribulation coming can also be seen in 2 Peter 3:10-13, where Christ's return is equated with the "heavens on fire will be destroyed and the elements being burned will melt." and "the earth also and the works that are therein shall be burned."

- Millennialism or Millenarianism is a belief, based on Revelation 20:1-6, that Christ will establish a kingdom on earth for one thousand years. Interpretations of the Millennium's temporal relationship with Christ's second coming differ considerably among various branches of Christianity:

    - *Premillennialists* believe that the return of Christ (the second coming of Christ) occurs *before* the millennial kingdom (premillennialism). For premillennialists, the return of Christ is a cataclysmic event

The First through the Sixth Seal Judgments

initiated by God to bring a very sharp break from the wicked reality of the world by inaugurating the millennial kingdom.

- *Postmillennialists* believe Christ's return will happen *after* the millennial kingdom (postmillennialism). For postmillennialists, the return of Christ (His second coming) happens after Christians in the millennial kingdom responsibly establish cultural and political foundations to receive Him.
- There is a third view called *amillennialism*. It has a symbolic interpretation of the millennium kingdom, saying that it is simply the duration of the imperfect Church on earth between Christ's first coming and his return, and that the real kingdom of God is in heaven beyond the Millennium.

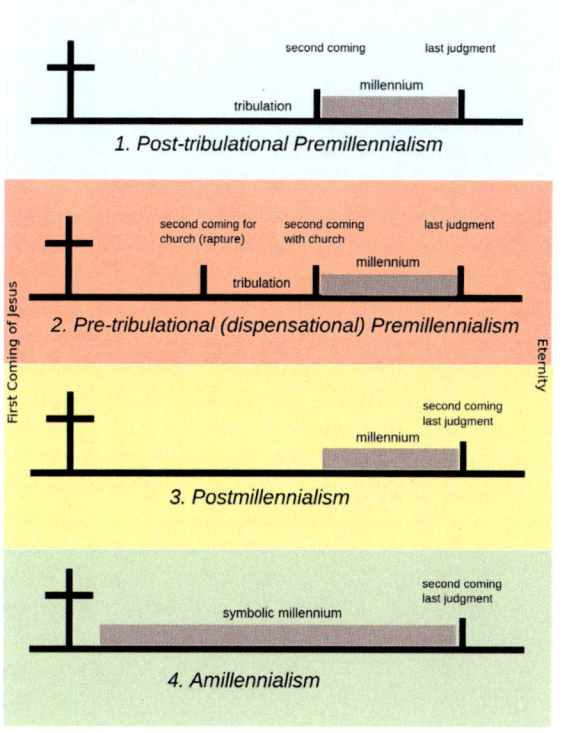

Comparison of Christian millennial teachings

Comparison of Christian Millennial Teachings

The First through the Sixth Seal Judgments

[1] "Then when I saw the Lamb open the first of the seven seals, I heard one of the four living beings shout in a voice like thunder, 'Come!' [2] And behold, I saw a white horse and the one sitting on it holding a bow and he was given a crown and he went out as a conqueror bent on conquering. [3] And when He opened the second seal, I heard the second living being say, 'Come!' [4] And another horse came out, a fiery red one. And its rider was given a large sword and he also was given the task of taking peace from the earth and they will slaughter one another. [5] Then when He opened the third seal, I heard the third living being say, 'Come!' And behold, I saw a black horse and its rider held a balance scale in his hand. [6] And then I heard a voice from the middle of the four living beings say, 'A quart of wheat for a denarius (a day's wages) and three quarts of barley for a denarius (a day's wages) and do not harm the olive oil and the wine.' [7] When he opened the fourth seal, I heard the voice of the fourth living being say, 'Come' [8] And behold, I saw a pale green horse. And its rider was named 'Death' and following close behind him was 'Hades'; and they were given authority over one quarter of the earth to kill by the sword, by famine, by plague and by the wild beasts of the earth.

[9] "Then when He opened the fifth seal, I saw the souls of those slaughtered for their testimony and the Word of God underneath the altar. [10] And they cried out with a loud voice, 'How long Sovereign Lord, holy and true, until You judge the inhabitants of the earth and avenge our blood?' [11] Then each was given a long, white robe and they were told to wait a little longer until the full number of their brothers and fellow servants were killed as they had been. [12] Then when He opened the sixth seal, I saw a great earthquake and the sun became black like a hairy sackcloth, and the whole moon became like blood, [13] and the stars of the sky fell to the earth like unripe (late) figs fall from a fig tree when a violent wind shakes it. [14] Then the heaven was moved away like a scroll is rolled up. Then every mountain and island were removed from their places. [15] Then the kings of the earth and princes and the generals and the rich and the powerful and the freedmen and the slaves hid themselves in the caves and among the rocks of the mountains. [16] And they cried out to the rocks and the mountains, 'Fall on us and hide us from the face of the One sitting on the throne and from the wrath of the Lamb; [17] because the great day of their wrath has come and who can stand?'"

The First Seal Judgment

Jesus opened the first of the seven seals of the scroll and the events of the aforementioned "Time of Sorrows" began. John noticed that the four living beings helped launch each of the events of the first four seals by commanding the horses and their horsemen to be released from their holding areas. Jesus opened the first seal and one of the seraphim boomed "with a voice like thunder, 'Come!'" (ως φωνη βροντης, ερχου, v. 1). We don't know which creature announced which horseman, but it would be intriguing to guess: I think the first announced by the young ox, a calf would be prone to lumbering, peaceful, non-aggressive; the second by the lion, a fierce fighter and aggressive; the third by the human, thinking required due to inflation; and the fourth by the eagle, able to see all of the destruction of human life with a bird's-eye view. But John's order of seraphim identified in chapter 4—lion, ox, human, eagle—may be the same order of seraphim announcements here in chapter 6.

Then, a white horse came out with its rider holding a bow. The horseman was given a crown and understandably went out to conquer those he was sent to. John stated it this way, "and he was given a crown and went out as a conqueror bent on conquering" (και εδοθη αυτου στεφανος και εξηλθεν νικων και ινα νικηση, v. 2).

To the Roman audience, the image of a horseman with white horse and bow suggested the feared Parthians who had recently defeated some Roman legions and were the only soldiers in the Empire who could effectively shoot from their horses with bow and arrow. The Parthians lived from 250 BC to AD 250 in present day Iran and Iraq and were known to make

Parthian Horseman

up the Arsacid Empire. They were highly respected and had notably defeated the Romans at the Battle of Carrhae in 53 BC when Parthian General Surena and his ten thousand horsemen fought against the Roman General Crassus and his forty-five thousand troops killing twenty thousand and capturing ten thousand.[80] But *this* conqueror in John's vision was riding on a white horse. He not only had a bow presumably representing his ability to inflict pain or to enforce his will but also wore a crown indicating that he was a world leader. Because the horse was white, the presumption and suggestion from some Revelation scholars is that this man successfully brings and enforces world peace. The horseman could signify the ruler from Rome (the Antichrist) or a precursor world leader trying to unite the nations to insulate from international financial catastrophes and unrest before he comes to power (Daniel 8:25).[81] However, this horseman may represent the desire for large governments, particularly those with nuclear capabilities, to expand influence over smaller countries in the pre-tribulation period causing the best political environment for the Antichrist (Rev. 13) to rise to power.

But the peaceful domination of the world to unite it was not enough to stave off the animosity that nations and peoples have against one another. I believe the white horseman and his leadership for the world is ultimately rejected because of what transpires during the next three years. But it is a compelling thought that a brilliant world leader offers mankind a solution for political and economic chaos. This "global solution" would *seem* to be executed by the "white horseman" who is allowed by the Father to align the world under him but ultimately against Christ and the Kingdom of God. I wonder if this person, the Antichrist or not, is a gifted banker maybe the president of the World Bank or the IMF (International Monetary Fund). Today, the World Bank, with 189 member countries and with headquarters in Washington, DC, has a stated mission of relieving world poverty by loaning the poorest world nations money for economic development. It also funds poorer governments' food programs and has committed to finance development of green energy projects in underdeveloped countries to mitigate global warming.[82] The IMF has 190 member countries also with headquarters in Washington, DC, and has a stated mission of promoting international trade, monetary cooperation, economic growth, and

---

80   Cassius Dio Cocceianus, *Dio's Roman History: Book 40*, 22.2, accessed May 30, 2023, https://www.gutenberg.org/cache/epub/11607/pg11607.html.

81   "Rev. 6:2: Who is the rider on the white horse? Christ or the antichrist?" *Evidence Unseen*, accessed November 5, 2021, https://www.evidenceunseen.com/bible-difficulties-2/nt-difficulties/jude/rev-62-who-is-the-rider-on-the-white-horse-christ-or-the-antichrist/.

82   "New Report Examines Risks of 4 Degree Hotter World by End of Century" (Press release). The World Bank November 18, 2012, accessed 12 October 2013, https://www.worldbank.org/en/news/press-release/2012/11/18/new-report-examines-risks-of-degree-hotter-world-by-end-of-century.

providing funds for member countries experiencing financial challenges.[83] Both organizations demonstrate global influence; but if led by a charismatic economist, his influence could usher the world into enraptured obeisance.

The Second Seal Judgment

But when the Lamb opens the second seal, all this world peace and cooperation goes away in the face of threats/rumors of war and global antagonism. We can only guess as to the particulars of the development of WWIII, which I think actually takes place *after* Jesus opens the fourth seal. But we are given a hint about this when John reported that when Jesus opened the second seal and after one of the seraphim called for the second horseman, a "fiery red" (πυρρος, v. 4) horse came out with its rider receiving both a "large sword" (μαχαιρα μεγαλη, v. 4) and the mission to "take peace from the earth" (λαβειν την ειρηνην εκ της γης, v. 4). Indeed, John stated that this horseman caused massive distrust between governments and disregard for human life by using the next phrase, and "they *will* slaughter one another" (αλληλους σφαξουσιν, v. 4). John wrote the Greek word for "slaughter," σφαξουσιν, in the future tense which could very well indicate that the actual global slaughter occurs, as I mentioned previously, when Jesus opens the fourth seal. But the red horseman sets the table for global conflagration by causing presumption of ulterior, self-serving motives between heads of state and mistrust of governmental efforts at international diplomacy. Previous world trade unions such as the European Union and NAFTA/USMCA (the United States-Mexico-Canada Agreement) during this second seal period would likely fall apart.[84] The world becomes a frightening place to live in which would cause those of the Church and those seeking Jesus and His peace and truth to become more committed to Him and Kingdom citizenship—not unlike the feeling American citizens have about the United States and our rivals China and Russia. I think God allows the seven seal judgments to play out as John reported them in order to strengthen the resolve and commitment of Christians and to turn hundreds of millions of unbelievers to

---

83   Arturo Escobar, "Power and Visibility: Development and the Invention and Management of the Third World," *Cultural Anthropology* 3 (4) November 1988: 428–443.

84   Eugene Beaulieu and Dylan Klemen, "You Say USMCA or T-MEC and I Say CUSMA: The New NAFTA—Let's Call the Whole Thing On." *The School of Public Policy Publications*, 17:7, April 2020, University of Calgary, accessed May 30, 2023, https://www.policyschool.ca/wp-content/uploads/2020/04/final2_NAFTA-Trade-Beaulieu-Klemen.pdf.

Christ. The Antichrist doesn't really declare himself or reveal himself as such until later when he is called the "Beast" for the first time several years later (Rev. 11:7). Until he thrusts himself onto the *political* world scene, the Church, still on earth as God's witnessing force, continues to effectively reveal to the world the Answer to its problems.

The Third Seal Judgment

This worldwide turmoil heightens to a fever pitch when pervasive inflation comes to the world economy. When Jesus opened the third seal, the third seraphim called out for the third horseman and a black horse appeared with its rider holding a "balance scale" (ζυγον, v. 5) in his hand. John was describing the loss of buying power and the erosion of international currencies. Indeed, a voice from among the four living beings describes the economic situation: *"A quart of wheat for a denarius [day's wages] and three quarts of barley for a denarius [day's wages], and do not damage the olive oil and the wine"* (χοινιξ σιτου δηναριου και τριες χοινικες κριθων δηναριου, v. 6). In the first century, business owners paid their hired workers a silver coin called a denarius for a day's wage. One denarius could purchase ten donkeys which by the first century had been upgraded to sixteen donkeys.[85] Thus the word "denarius" had the root word *"deni"* from the Latin word for "containing ten."[86] If a day's wage only purchases a quart of wheat and three quarts of barley, then currency is devalued as in inflationary times. As economists say, inflation occurs when too much money chases too few goods. Inflation occurs with a general rise in the costs of goods because of loss of real value in a country's money unit.[87] With international trade interrupted, the developed and underdeveloped countries experience shortages of heavy equipment, goods, agricultural supplies, food, metals and other raw materials, and technological systems to name just a few. This economic milieu produces international turmoil and such shortages of materials and supplies, that countries begin to look beyond their borders for the resources they lack. The inflation of the third seal is not unlike what we are experiencing here in recent pandemic America and throughout the world with supply chain

---

[85] Kenneth W. Harl, *Coinage in the Roman Economy, 300 B.C. to A.D. 700* (Baltimore, MD: John Hopkins University Press, 1996), 94-95.

[86] David. L. Vagi, *Coinage and History of the Roman Empire, c. 82 B.C.-A.D. 480*, vol. 2, (New York: Routledge, 2015).

[87] Paul H. Walgenbach, Norman E. Dittrich, and Ernest I. Hanson, *Financial Accounting*, (New York: Harcourt Brace Javonovich, Inc., 1973), 429.

interruptions, lack of workers to produce and transport goods, and the economic hardships resulting from this reactive global inflation. As previously mentioned, the lack of peace and trust between governments allow for the "rumors of wars" and skirmishes that Christ discussed on Mount Olivet with His disciples indicating that these would occur near the beginning of the End Times (Mt. 24:6). As is indicated by the third seal period, international economic hardship pushes the whole world to the brink of WW III.

The Fourth Seal Judgment

Jesus opened the fourth seal and literally Hell breaks out all over the earth after the fourth living being calls out the fourth horseman riding on a "pale green horse" (ιππος χλωρος, v. 8). Pale green is considered the color of a corpse, appropriate for what happens during this seal. John saw that the rider of the horse was "Death" (θανατος, v. 8) and that "Hades followed along after him" (αδης ηκολουθει, v. 8). I think it telling that Death is accompanied by Hades which suggests that most of those dying will not only die but will be escorted to Hades (Greek term for Sheol)—the holding place of the souls of unbelievers. John discussed what takes place after seeing Death and Hades riding together: "And they were given authority to kill one quarter of the earth *by the sword, by famine, by pestilence, and by the wild beasts of the earth*" (εν ρομφαια και εν λιμω και εν θανατω και υπο των θηριων της γης, v. 8). According to population experts, the world presently has about 8 billion people. By the year 2050, population experts predict nearly 9.7 billion people, which should reach a peak of around 10.4 billion people during the 2080s. The population is expected to remain at that level until the end of the twenty-first century.[88] John stated that the fourth horseman of doom kills one quarter of the population which would be over two billion people dying if the fourth seal judgment occurred today. The death toll from the fourth seal release of Death and Hades would be staggering considering that the costliest war to date, WW II, produced nearly eighty million deaths.

The sequence of catastrophic events in verse 8 causing the loss of life deserves attention. John mentioned "the sword" first which would make sense when nations

---

88   "World population to reach 8 billion this year, as growth rate slows," *UN News*, July 11, 2022, accessed May 30, 2023, https://news.un.org/en/story/2022/07/1122272.

Revelation: The Fifth Gospel

make war against each other. Of course, the modern implements of war would not include swords, but automatic weapons, missiles, tanks, as well as the nuclear arsenal of at least eighteen countries (see the above chart). The number of deaths from the First and Second World Wars was massive. During WWI, twenty-five million humans died.[89] During the most deadly war, WWII as previously mentioned, eighty million humans died, including many people living in the two Japanese cities, Hiroshima (140,000 people died) and Nagasaki (74,000 people died) when the United States dropped two atomic bombs in August 1945.[90] John actually saw a vision of these modern weapons when he described the events of the fifth and sixth trumpets (Rev. 9). Even though hundreds of millions would not survive the world war described in verse 8, more will likely die due to the famine, pestilence/plagues, and "wild beasts" as direct fallout from the war. Agricultural devastation with loss of crops and destruction of the topsoil occurred after both world wars for nearly a decade in the countries where the wars took place. Germany lost nearly 70 percent of their agricultural production immediately after the Second World War and did not recover until many years after.[91] Famines will occur as the result of the devastation to the biome from the nuclear fallout of the "sword" of the fourth seal. Already the annual death rate from famine across the world is around nine to ten million people. But as can be ascertained by recent compilation of famine data since 1860, the decades of the 1920s (WWI) and the 1940s (WWII) were marked by much higher famine rates. After the largest and most costly war known to humans during the fourth seal period of presumably months to a year, famine (λιμω, v. 8) becomes rampant across the globe and, with it, dead humans—too many to properly bury or cremate.

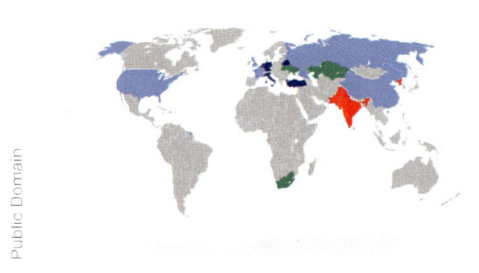

Depiction of Nations with Nuclear Capabilities

Public Domain

---

89 Jay Robert Nash, *Darkest Hours: A Narrative Encyclopedia of Worldwide Disasters from Ancient Times to the Present* (Rowman & Littlefield, 1976).
90 Seren Morris, How many people died in Hiroshima and Nagasaki? *Newsweek*, 8/3/2020, accessed May 30, 2023, https://www.newsweek.com/how-many-people-died-hiroshima-nagasaki-japan-second-world-war-1522276.
91 Wirtschaft und Statistik October 1956, Journal published by Statistisches Bundesamt Deutschland.

Famine victims worldwide since the 1860s

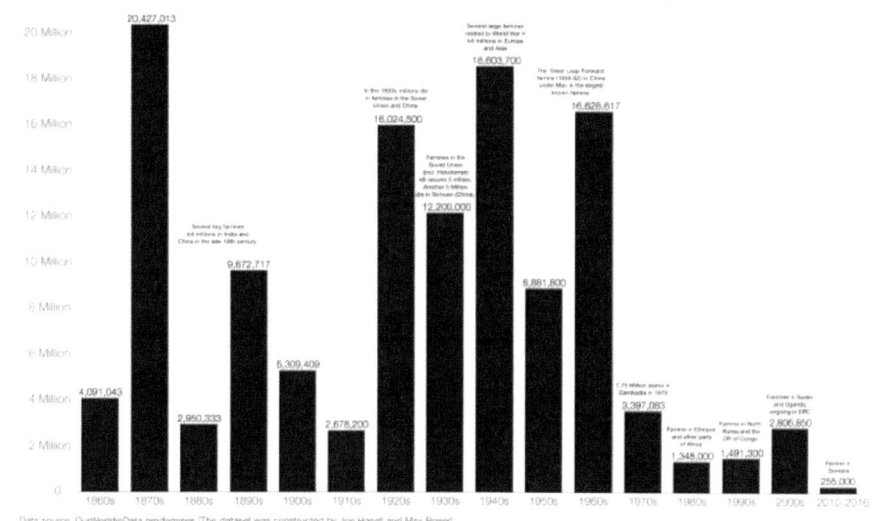

Remember that a single adult's gastrointestinal tract (GI tract) contains at least thirty trillion bacteria.[92] If dead bodies are not properly disposed of as in a post-war period, plagues (θανατω, v. 8) of bacteria occur because of bacteria from the dead infiltrating ground water sources and soil contamination, resulting in rampant disease and further death. This is the third of the four tools by which Death and Hades slaughters one quarter of the earth. The fourth remains a mystery: "the wild beasts of the earth" (των θηριων της γης, v. 8).

Two viable possibilities exist for identity of "the wild beasts of the earth." Some theologians and Revelation experts think that this passage could literally indicate that because of the devastation of war, famine, pestilence, and the resulting paucity of humans in large areas of the earth, that the normal check on the numbers of "wild beasts" from hunters becomes absent. This allows for the carnivorous animals

---

92   Andrew Holmes and Carly Rosewarne, "Gut Bacteria: the inside story," Australian Academy of Science, April 4, 2016, accessed June 7, 2021, https://www.science.org.au/curious/people-medicine/gut-bacteria.

to proliferate, threaten civilization, and kill humans.[93] The Lord told the Israelites before they occupied the Levant on their journey out of Egypt that He would not eradicate the Canaanites from Palestine immediately upon their entry because then there would not be enough humans to hunt and limit the "wild beasts" roaming the land (Ex. 23:29). The Lord punished the Northern Kingdom of Israel when they began to worship foreign gods, Asherah poles and practiced infant sacrifice. He sent lions among them to devastate them and make them turn back to the Lord (2 Kings 17:25).

But I have another thought about what or who the "wild beasts of the earth" could be. The Greek word, "θεριων" (beast), can also mean "wicked person" or "dangerous person" (cf. Titus 1:12). As we have seen, the massive loss of life with destruction of reliable food sources during the fourth seal period could cause the proliferation of "proteinaceous infectious particle" (AKA prion) diseases. These are fatal neurodegenerative illnesses caused by collapsed, misfolded proteins that when ingested cause the same collapse of the cells they infect. This protein particle causes mad cow disease, causes chronic wasting disease in deer, and has been linked to scrapie in sheep. Some of the more common prion-like diseases already infecting some Americans include fatal familial insomnia, kuru, and amyotrophic lateral sclerosis (i.e., ALS, Lou Gehrig's disease). Prions may play a part in producing the amyloid proteins of Alzheimer's disease and of Parkinson's disease.[94] I can easily speculate that "wild beasts" may actually be prion infected humans whose brains are so infected that they become unrecognizable and threats to their fellow humans. It is well known that brain tumors can alter the personalities of cancer victims. Prion disease does the same in primates and humans. That's why I believe the "wild beasts" of verse 8 could be the "walking dead" of the fourth seal.

In summary, the four seal judgments triggered by the "Lion of Judah" are the following:

- ▸ First seal judgment: flimsy financial stability and forced political cooperation
- ▸ Second seal judgment: loss of world peace, distrust of international diplomacy, and increasing international discord

---

93   Richard T. Ritenbaugh, "What the Bible Says about Wild Beasts," *Bibletools*; accessed November 6, 2021, https://www.bibletools.org/index.cfm/fuseaction/Topical.show/RTD/cgg/ID/3395/Wild Beasts-.htm.
94   Susan Lundquist, "What is a Prion?" *Scientific American*. October 21,1999, accessed June 8, 2021, https://www.scientificamerican.com/article/what-is-a-prion-specifica/.

- Third seal judgment: destruction of international business treaties and commerce with resulting supply chain difficulties causing shortages of goods, technology, materials, food, and agricultural supplies resulting in worldwide inflation
- Fourth seal judgment: World War III with massive loss of life due to combat, famine, pestilence, and "wild beasts of the earth"

The Fifth Seal Judgment

John continued describing the seal judgments of chapter 6 by noticing a striking scene taking place underneath the altar near the throne of God. Jesus has just opened the fifth seal. John had seen or heard about the deaths of his fellow apostles and disciples. Nearing one hundred years old, he had outlived every one of his friends from Galilee. He had witnessed terrible Christian deaths in Jerusalem and imprisonment at the hand of Saul (Paul) of Tarsus. He also saw the gruesome treatment of Christians on the Palace grounds and in the Circus Maximus and Roman Amphitheater under Nero and Domitian during his sojourns to Rome earlier in his life. So it was particularly emotional for him to see the souls of his martyred comrades and others underneath the altar. The offerings of the people in Old Testament times were placed by the priests under the altar. So it was appropriate for the Holy Spirit to escort the souls of those martyred for Christ to the altar floor after giving up their lives on earth in His service. In a sense, they, with Jesus, are the first fruit offerings of believers from the Kingdom of God on earth to the Father. What is even more compelling about this scene is that these slaughtered beings are dialoguing with their God. In fact, we can see by their very pointed and poignant question that they likely were allowed to see the events of the previous seal judgments and the continued and devastating slaughter of their fellow Christians: "How long, Sovereign Lord, holy and true, until You *judge the inhabitants of the earth and avenge our blood*" (κρινεις και εκδικεις το αιμα ημων εκ των κατοικουντων επι της γης;, v. 10)? They had seen enough. They had enough. Their patience had run out. So, they were appealing to God's sense of justice and fair play, of mercy and love for His people. But in their minds and souls, the past, present, and near future held too much sadness, anguish, and terror for their fellow brothers and sisters in Christ. So, they appropriately asked God, who they stated was holy and lived by Truth, to intervene and reverse the frightful slaughter of Christians.

God responded as He so often does with a tacit, "No, not yet!" John then noticed that a detail of angels served each martyred soul under the altar by giving him/her a long white robe (στολη λευκη, v. 11). In the first century, the "στολη λευκη" were worn by those who held high office or high social status. Here, Jesus honors His brothers and sisters by authorizing their apparel for the wedding feast of the Lamb. In the near future, as discussed in Revelation 19:8, those invited to the wedding feast of the Lamb are given fine, white "linen"/clothes—not unlike the description of our martyrs here in Revelation 6. In Revelation 7:9, the same "long white robes" (στολας λευκας) are worn by the raptured Church. But God is not done appeasing the martyrs for Christ under the altar. He actually tells them His divine reasoning for the delay of their vengeance. He reveals to them that they must wait a little longer until the "full number of their brothers and fellow servants have been killed just as they had been" (πληρωθωσιν και οι συνδουλοι αυτων και οι αδελφοι αυτων οι μελλοντες αποκτεννεσθαι ως και αυτοι, v. 11).

Maybe God allowed continued suffering as a reinforcement to the brethren since it is essential to the success of the Kingdom and its believers. Another reason for God's reticence to stop the martyrdom of His children is the evangelization of people groups is still not complete by this time in Revelation 6, and Christian persecutions and deaths are great witnesses to pagans who see what believers endure for Christ. As patristic father Tertullian once wrote, "The blood of the martyrs is the seed of the church."[95] Another reason to continue their ultimate sacrifices is God needed more martyrs to take their positions of authority over the earth during Christ's millennial reign in chapter 20. In chapter 6, the Lord may not have enough martyrs to take their thrones of rule over the earth during the millennium reign. This may very well be why He was delaying His intervention.

The Sixth Seal Judgment

The seal judgments continue with the focus now on the stratosphere around the earth and on the earth itself. The sixth seal triggers cataclysmic changes to the earth not seen with the previous seal judgments. I think severity of the seal events *increases* from the first seal to the sixth seal. When Jesus opens the sixth seal, the

---

[95]   Tertullian, *Apologeticus*, 50, 13, *Ante-Nicene Fathers* Vol. III, Sydney Thelwall, trans., accessed May 30, 2023, https://www.tertullian.org/fathers2/ANF-03/anf03-05.htm#P478_246152.

first scene that John noticed is the tremendous earthquake that causes the sun to become "black like hairy sackcloth, the whole moon became like blood, and *the stars fell from the sky to the earth like unripe figs fall from a fig tree when a violent wind shakes it*" (και οι αστερες του ουρανου επεσεν εις την γην ως συκη βαλλει τους ολυνθους αυτης υπο ανεμου μεγαλου σειομενη, v. 13). The earth itself takes a big hit from the judgment God unleashes on it from a mega-earthquake, likely larger than has ever occurred on the earth in the past. Some Revelation experts believe that the earthquake John sees and describes in Revelation 16:18 is the same one that he sees when Jesus opens the sixth seal. These scholars think that the seal judgments are repeated by the seven vial judgments and that John is watching the same judgments repeated two or three times. But a close look at all the seal, trumpet, and vial judgements demonstrates multiple differences between them. John does not witness a circular, repetitive cycling of judgments but a linear, progressive intensity of judgments. In other words, the megaquake John sees here in Revelation 6 has great effects on the earth and atmosphere but not as severe as the one he sees later for the seventh vial judgment in Revelation 16. The sixth seal quake not only causes the mountains and islands in its wake to "be removed from their places" (εκ των τοπων αυτων εκινηθησαν, v. 14), but it causes significant changes in the earth's atmosphere.

The largest earthquake in modern times occurred on May 22, 1960, in southern Chile near a town called Valdivia with a magnitude of 9.5. This quake killed nearly six thousand people in Valdivia and its surroundings but, possibly more significantly, created a powerful tsunami that travelled at speeds of over 200 mph across the Pacific Ocean to Hawaii, Philippines, and Japan and killed hundreds in these countries a day later. The sea level rose some thirty feet and obscured many islands by ten feet.[96] John mentioned that "the sun became black and the whole moon became like blood" (ο ηλιος εγενετο μελας και η σεληνη ολη εγενετο ως αιμα, v. 12) likely because the volcanos triggered by the megaquake caused such a large amount of atmospheric ash that those in the area could not see the sun's light.[97] The effects of the ash during the sunsets and sunrises caused the moon's light to look red. John also noted that the stars in the sky "fell to the ground *like unripe figs fall to the ground when a violent wind shakes it*" (ως συκη βαλλει τους ολυνθους αυτης υπο ανεμου μεγαλου σειομενη, v. 13).

---

[96] "World's Largest Recorded Earthquake," Geology.com, accessed June 13, 2021, https://geology.com/records/largest-earthquake/.
[97] "Volcanoes and Earthquakes," U. S. Geological Survey, accessed June 13, 2021, https://pubs.usgs.gov/gip/earthq1/volcano.html.

Revelation: The Fifth Gospel

At present, there are approximately three thousand four hundred active satellites, three thousand inactive satellites, and twelve thousand pieces of catalogued space junk orbiting the earth in three major orbits. The high orbit for most weather, telecommunications, and solar satellites is around 22,300 miles above the earth. The medium orbit for the GPS and for Sirius radio network is around 12,500 miles above the earth. The low orbit for scientific and some weather satellites including the International Space Station is from 250 to 400 miles above the earth. Control centers on earth alter satellites orbits' inclination, height, and eccentricity by activating the satellite thrusters on the satellites so that they avoid collisions in orbit with the active and inactive satellites and the twelve thousand pieces of debris.[98] I think that John was describing catastrophic collisions between the satellites and others in free fall toward the earth because their remote control centers on earth are destroyed by the mega quake he observed in verse 12. These satellite collisions cause quite an impressive fireworks show that John described as stars falling to the earth (v. 13). John also witnessed another megaquake even larger than this one, as previously mentioned, in Revelation 16 when he observes "millstone" sized hail each weighing about one hundred pounds striking the earth after the megaquake occurs. I think the same thing in Revelation 6 happens in Revelation 16—the satellites orbiting the earth becoming disoriented by the loss of their command centers being destroyed by the megaquake, and then the satellites free fall onto the earth like "giant hail" (cf. Rev. 16:21). John also reported that the mountains and islands in the vicinity of the megaquake are "moved from their places" (εκ των τοπων αυτων εκινηθησαν, v. 14) referring to the effects of the continental tectonic plate shifts which flatten mountains. The energy of the earthquake also produces tsunami tidal waves which devastate the lower lying land masses such as islands and peninsulas, totally obliterating them. I think John describes this same language of change to creation as we see in post-quake events affecting the atmosphere. He stated that the "sky was moved away as a scroll is rolled up" (ο ουρανος απεχωρισθη ως βιβλιον ελισσομενον, v. 14). Again, I think the release of so much energy from the tectonic plate shift producing the quake releases volcanoes on the earthquake fault lines with a tremendous discharge of energy into the sky—not unlike a nuclear-bomb explosion. This produces the *shock wave* and then the *fallout* of radioisotopes produced by collision of atmospheric hydrogen and oxygen molecules—what John describes as "the sky was moved away."

---

[98] "Catalog of Earth Satellite Orbits," NASA, , accessed 13, 2021, https://earthobservatory.nasa.gov/features/OrbitsCatalog.

To end the chapter, John discussed the insight that the unbelievers of the world have during these seal judgments, particularly after the devastation of the sixth seal. I find it fascinating that their comments are very accurate and knowledgeable even to the point of being prophetic. It can be easily surmised that the Church is still present in the world to point out that all of these events including the megaquake have occurred because of earth's citizens' refusal to listen to God and His Son. They have rejected the Word and because of their penchant for sin; destruction of God's creation; and love of power, position, and money; they are being punished. John reported that the leaders ("kings") of the world and their subjects including their administrators (princes), generals, the rich and the powerful, and the slaves and the free were so fearful that they decided to go to underground shelters (caves, σπηλαια, v. 15) to flee. They made a striking admission about the etiology of the world's troubles by calling out to the rocks and mountains, "fall upon us and hide us from the face of the One sitting on the throne and from the wrath of the Lamb" (πεσετε εφ ημας και κρυψατε υμας απο προσωπου του καθημενου επι του θρονου και απο της οργης του αρνιου, v. 16).

All of these comments reflect a tremendous sensitivity to God's direction of the events of the seal judgments likely coming from their relationships with believers. The idea promoted by pre-tribulationists that the Church is raptured out of the earth in Rev. 4:1-2 is preposterous, particularly in light of the passage here in Revelation 6 and the very specific and insightful comments from pagans about the sixth seal judgment. How could unbelievers at this time know that the sixth seal came from "the One sitting on the throne and from the wrath of the Lamb" (Rev. 6:16) if not informed about this by the Church? I think that the Bible and the access of the public to the Book of Revelation and the other apocalyptic Scriptures during the last seven years of the Time of Sorrows and Great Tribulation Period is severely limited as is indicated by a lack of knowledge of the events of the twenty-one judgments that befall the earth (via the seal, trumpet, and vial judgments). But here at the end of Revelation 6, due to the witness of the disciples of Christ, the pagans of the world realize that God and His Son are the authors and perpetrators of the havoc they are experiencing. One would think that with this insight these folks would turn from their wicked ways and embrace the Lamb and His Father. Also interesting is their comment directed to "the rocks and the mountains" (τοις ορεσιν και ταις πετραις, v. 16) as if these inanimate objects could listen and respond to their request to be hidden from God. By this time in the world's history, this and other passages in Revelation (vis-à-vis Rev. 9:20) indicate a naivete and primitive animism (e.g. calling out to rocks and mountains) practiced by people who should have known better than to trust in anything or anybody other than the God of the universe and of the earth.

REVELATION 7

Sealing & Commissioning of the Christian Jewish Evangelists

The Rapture

[1] "After this, I saw four angels having taken a stand at the four corners of the earth to control the four winds of the earth so that the wind would not blow on the land, the sea, nor any of the trees. [2] Then I saw another angel coming up out of the East holding the seal of the living God and he shouted with a loud voice to the four angels given the task of harming the land and the sea saying, [3] 'Do not harm the land, the sea, nor any of the trees until we have sealed the servants of God on their foreheads.' [4] And I heard the number sealed, 144,000 sealed from every tribe of the nation of Israel: [5] twelve thousand sealed from the tribe of Judah, twelve thousand from the tribe of Reuben, twelve thousand from the tribe of Gad, [6] twelve thousand

from the tribe of Asher, twelve thousand from the tribe of Naphtali, twelve thousand from the tribe of Manasseh, ⁷ twelve thousand from the tribe of Simeon, twelve thousand from the tribe of Levi, twelve thousand from the tribe of Issachar, ⁸ twelve thousand from the tribe of Zebulon, twelve thousand from the tribe of Joseph, twelve thousand sealed from the tribe of Benjamin.

⁹ "After this, behold, I saw a multitude that no one could count standing before the throne and before the Lamb from every tribe, people, nation, and language having been dressed in long white robes with palm branches in their hands. ¹⁰ And they cried out with a loud voice saying, 'Salvation is through our God, the One sitting on the throne, and through the Lamb.' ¹¹ And all of the angels accompanied by the elders and the four living beings stood around the throne and they fell down on their faces before the throne and they worshipped God ¹² saying, 'Amen. All the glory, honor, power, praise, strength, thanksgiving and wisdom to our God forever and ever. Amen.'

¹³ "Then one of the elders asked me, 'These clothed in the long white robes, who are they and from where did they come?' ¹⁴ And I replied to him, 'You know, my Lord.' Then he replied, 'These are those who have come out of the Great Affliction and have washed their long robes and have made them white in the blood of the Lamb. ¹⁵ Therefore, they are before the throne of God and they worship Him in His Temple day and night; and the One sitting on the throne will come to dwell/tabernacle with them. ¹⁶ No longer will they hunger or thirst; the sun will no longer beat down on them and scorch them. ¹⁷ The Lamb in the center of the throne will shepherd them and He will lead them to springs of living waters and God will wipe every tear from out of their eyes.'"

John continued his vision of the End-Time-seal period by noticing that the four angels given the task of "harming the earth and the sea" (αδικησαι την γην και την θαλασσαν, v. 2) through their manipulation of the four winds from the four corners of the earth are actually discontinuing their actions and standing. They likely were instrumental in some of the destruction noted in the second through the sixth seal judgments (except the fifth seal). They may have allowed the volcano plumes to be transported through the wind currents they controlled across the globe to obscure the sunlight and contribute to the "blackness of the sun" and the blood red color of the moon during the sixth-seal period. These winds would have also contributed to the nuclear winter which likely resulted from the volcanic ash being transported around the globe. Some have suggested that "the four winds" may not refer literally to the wind but to the earth and the four angels' dominance over it.[99] However, if "wind currents" are taken literally, they are responsible for the successful pollination of much of earth's biomass and in the future may be a major worldwide source of power; thus, no wind blowing for a significant time could significantly impact the agricultural and energy supply of the world. But these angels are responsible for *sending* devastating winds throughout the earth, which is likely the meaning of the passage. Sustained F3, F4, and F5 tornadoes and hurricanes could wreak havoc on the earth. As previously suggested, if these angels already were responsible for some of the destruction of the sea (plankton), land (topsoil), and trees (oxygen), the consequences of their actions would be catastrophic. John then informed his reading audience *the reason* why these four angels were "holding back/controlling the four winds of the earth" (κρατουντας τους τεσσαρας ανεμους της γης, v. 1).

Illustration from the Ottheinrich Bible from an unknown artist of Angels Holding the Four Winds and the Sealing of the 144,000

An angel with God's seal—probably signet ring seal representing God's authority or maybe even an image of the seal of God on a flag or banner—rose up from the east and told the four "wind" angels not to harm the earth until the 144,000 chosen and anointed Jews following Jesus were sealed for the Kingdom and their roles solidified in the late Time of Sorrows period. The angel said it this way, "Do not harm the land, the sea, nor any tree *until we have sealed the servants of God on their*

---

99   "Four Winds of Revelation Bring On the Time of Trouble," Revelation of Jesus, accessed June 17, 2021, https://revelationofjesus.net/en/important-questions/four-winds-of-revelation-bring-on-the-time-of-trouble/.

Revelation: The Fifth Gospel

foreheads" (αχρι σφραγισωμεν τους δουλος του θεου ημων επι των μετωπων αυτων, v. 3). Speaking in the first-person plural, the angel from the East was taking responsibility for the sealing. This raises a very interesting possibility—that the Holy Spirit developed these young evangelists, who John describes as "without blame" (cf. Rev. 14:5), with help from this and likely other angels. The writer of the Book of Hebrews mentions that angels truly are "ministering spirits sent out to serve on behalf of those inheriting salvation" (Heb. 1:14). I'm sure God uses His angel corps to assist in developing His children in their faiths. Certainly, angels help in the execution of the saints' ministries while on the earth. Certainly, these of the most gifted evangelists the world has ever seen will face the greatest opposition ever faced by Christians requiring angel assistance and protection. Ultimately, each of these completed Jews will be martyred for their uncompromising stand for Christ and their undeniable witness for Christ during the three and a half years of the Time of Sorrows (cf. 14:1-5).

Therefore, arguably, the main reason for stopping the wind destruction was to allow the Jewish Christians uninterrupted time to be solidified in their faith and calling. Because the believers of Christ's Church are to be shortly raptured (Rev. 7:9), these Jewish evangelists would need some mentoring without upheaval and persecution in order to later contend with pagan retaliation for the Lamb's judgment experienced right after the sixth seal was broken. Another reason to exclude destructive wind currents may be to minimize complications during the Rapture; if the Rapture occurs during windy moments, much destruction could occur with those being raptured and those left behind such as in the cases of airline pilots and public transportation drivers being raptured while performing their jobs.

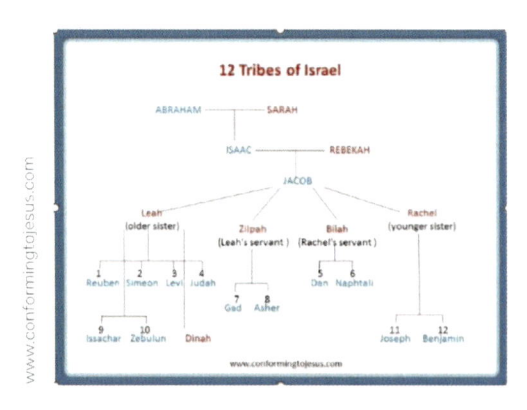

Another explanation for no earth wind during this time of sealing of the Christian Jewish Evangelists might be because God wants the pagans to not confuse earth wind with the "wind of the Holy Spirit," vis-à-vis the baptism of the Holy Spirit as experienced by the apostles in Acts 2. The "sealing" of these Christian Jews may not be necessarily a private matter. Maybe some of the pagans of the world, who just indicated in Revelation 6:16-17 that they understood that the seal judgments came from God and the Lamb. If they could see the "wind of God" during this special time and not confuse this spiritual wind with earthly wind, they might be attracted to Jesus and the Kingdom. The Apostle next described the Jewish Christian contingent and the importance of their sealing for the work of Christ's Kingdom on earth. He heard the number of Jews sealed for Christ: 144,000. The number is significant because it is a derivative of twelve, a perfect number.

John began his description of the Jews for Christ by mentioning the tribe of Judah first. Likely Judah was honored as the first patriarch in this "list" because, even though he was the fourth born of Jacob and Leah, King David and Jesus came from the lineage of Judah. Judah was protective of Joseph and the plans that God had for him by suggesting to his brothers bent on killing Joseph that he be sold to the Midianite slave traders (Gen. 37:26-28). I think Judah's sensitivity to the plans of the Lord endeared him and his descendants to God and gave them a place of preeminence not matched by any of the other eleven tribes of Israel.

John mentioned Reuben Jewish Christians next because Reuben was the eldest son of Jacob and showed strength of character and sensitivity to the mores and call God had for his little brother Joseph by sticking up for him and directing Joseph's brothers to place him in the pit instead of killing Joseph as they wanted to do (Gen. 37:21-22).

Gad Jewish Christians are the third mentioned in the list of tribes of Israel because Gad, as Jacob's seventh son, was the closest to Reuben and settled with his oldest brother on the East bank of the Jordan River. He and his descendants were known for their persistence in battle and their ability to finish off their enemies.

Map of the Twelve Tribes of Israel

Revelation: The Fifth Gospel

Asher Jewish Christians were mentioned next. Asher, as Jacob's eighth son, and his children were known for their generativity and ability to build consensus and unity among their brothers and fellow Jews.

Naphtali Jewish Christians were the fifth mentioned. Naphtali was Jacob's sixth son. He and his descendants were noted to possess great energy for the Lord, they knew how to live with God's favor, and they were expert at blessing and encouraging others.

Manasseh Jewish Christians were next in the list. Manasseh— the oldest of two sons of Joseph, the eleventh son of Jacob—was obviously positively influenced by his father Joseph and understood the value of perseverance and faith. Yet Jacob gave his younger brother Ephraim the blessing of the first born at Jacob's death thinking that Ephraim would be more worthy than his older brother. Actually, Manasseh's descendants were more faithful to the teachings of the Torah and commands of Yahweh than Ephraim's descendants and resisted the tendency Ephraimites exhibited in committing idolatry.

Simeon Jewish Christians were next. Simeon, the second son of Jacob, came from a tribe judged for its treachery against Shechem and were consequently scattered throughout Judah as Jacob prophesied in Genesis 49:5-7. However, later in their history, this tribe began to understand the consequences of anger unchecked. This knowledge and mastery of their emotions will propel these Jewish Christians to great success in delivering the gospel to the pagans of the End-Time world making them disciples of our Christ.

Levi Jewish Christians also came from a tribe (Levi was the third son of Jacob) which matched the vindictive anger of the Simeonites and assisted them in killing the helpless Shechemites. But they were the progenitors of the Aaronites who became the priests of Yahweh. They were not allowed any inheritance of land in Palestine because their "portion was the Lord" (Num. 18:19-21). They were honored however for their valiant stand with Moses against the three thousand Jews who worshipped the golden calf (Ex. 32:26-32). This zeal for the Lord will be obvious with the Christian Levites who give up their lives for Christ as we see in Revelation 14.

Issachar Jewish Christian were the descendants of Issachar, the ninth son of Jacob. The tribe of Issachar was known for the aggressive proselytization of non-Jewish neighbors and were possibly the best of the twelve tribes at teaching the

Sealing & Commissioning of the Christian Jewish Evangelists

THE TWELVE TRIBES OF ISRAEL – GENESIS 49

Tribes	Mother	Jacob's Blessing Genesis 49	Moses' Blessing Deuteronomy 33	Total - Numbers 1	Total - Numbers 26	Position round tabernacle	Judges	Well known figures	Historical events
REUBEN	Leah	Thou art my firstborn, my might, and the beginning of my strength. Unstable as water, thou shalt not excel	Let Reuben live, and not die; and let not his men be few	46,500	43,730	South		Dathan and Abiram took part in the rebellion of Korah (Num 16)	Chose to dwell on the east bank of Jordan (Num 32.1-5); failed to answer the call of Deborah (Judg 3.15-16)
SIMEON	Leah	I will divide them in Jacob, and scatter them in Israel		59,300	22,200	South		Zimri slain by Phinehas due to his brazen immorality at Shittim (Num 25.10-15)	
LEVI	Leah		Let thy Thummim and thy Urim be with thy holy one, whom thou didst prove at Massah					Moses Aaron Samuel	Levi stood with Moses in the matter of the golden calf (Ex 32.26); the tribe that provided the priestly family and the others to be servants in the Tabernacle and the Temple
JUDAH	Leah	The sceptre shall not depart from Judah, nor a lawgiver from between his feet, until Shiloh come	Hear, Lord, the voice of Judah, and bring him unto his people; let his hands be sufficient for him; and be thou an help to him from his enemies	74,600	76,500	East	Othniel	Boaz David	The tribe from which David and the Kings of Israel came
ZEBULUN	Leah	He shall be for an haven of ships	Rejoice, Zebulun, in thy going out; and Issachar, in thy tents	57,400	60,500	East			Many of them came to Jerusalem for Hezekiah's passover (2 Chr 30.11)
ISSACHAR	Leah	A strong ass couching down between two burdens		54,400	64,300	East	Tola		
DAN	Bilhah	An adder in the path that biteth the horse heels	Dan is a lion's whelp; he shall leap from Bashan	62,700	64,400	North	Samson		They set up idol worship (Judg 18.30-31) and became a centre of idolatry; Jeroboam's idolatrous calves were set up in Bethel and Dan (1 Kings 12.28-30)
GAD	Zilpah	A troop shall overcome him; but he shall overcome at the last	Blessed be he that enlargeth Gad; he dwelleth as a lion	45,650	40,500	South			Settled on the east bank of the Jordan with the Reubenites (Num 32.1-5)
ASHER	Zilpah	His bread shall be fat, and he shall yield royal dainties	Let Asher be blessed with children; let him be acceptable to his brethren	41,500	53,400	North			Many of them came to Jerusalem for Hezekiah's passover (2 Chr 30.11)
NAPHTALI	Bilhah	A hind let loose; he giveth goodly words	O Naphtali, satisfied with favour, and full with the blessing of the Lord: possess thou the west and the south	53,400	45,400	North			
JOSEPH - EPHRAIM JOSEPH - MANASSEH	Rachel	Joseph is a fruitful bow ... whose branches run over the wall	Blessed of the Lord of his land ... His glory is like the firstling of his bullock, and his horns are like the horns of unicorns	40,500 32,200	32,500 52,700	West West	Abdon Gideon	Jeroboam	Many slain by the Gileadites under Jephthah (Judg 12.5-6); became the leading tribe of the northern kingdom of Israel (1 Kings 12.19-20)
BENJAMIN	Rachel	Benjamin shall ravin as a wolf: in the morning he shall devour the prey, and at night he shall divide the spoil	The beloved of the Lord shall dwell in safety by him; and the Lord shall cover him all the day long, and he shall dwell between his shoulders	35,400	45,600	West	Ehud	Saul Jonathan	Many of them came to Jerusalem for Hezekiah's passover (2 Chr 30.11); remained with Judah as the southern kingdom of Judah after Jeroboam's revolt (2 Chr 11.1)

believersmagazine.com *Facts on Tribes*

Revelation: The Fifth Gospel

Torah and Midrash. They devoted so much of their energies to the religious world that they needed the members of the tribe of Zebulon to support them financially and agriculturally. I believe that the world will be blessed during this End-Time period of the "Time of Sorrows" through the tribe of Issachar which was noted for its fierce loyalty to Judaism. During many campaigns while possessing Canaan under Joshua's command, the Issacharites gave up their lives without hesitation.

Zebulon Jewish Christians came from their descendants of the sixth son of Jacob who were known for their love for their brothers and sisters from the neighboring tribe of Issachar whom they supported with agricultural and fishing industries. They protected King David when he was still being pursued by Saul and his forces. Because of their close relationship with the tribe of Issachar, the best teachers of the Torah, the descendants of Zebulon were known for their faithfulness to Yahweh and His Word—quite a heritage for these Jewish Christians who cherished the Word of God.

Joseph Jewish Christians were mentioned next in this list. Most lists of the tribes of Israel do not mention Joseph, the eleventh son of Jacob, because he was so financially blessed and had vast land holdings in Egypt. Nonetheless, despite his son Manasseh already listed, God honors Joseph with posterity throughout the ages including a central role in the evangelization of the pagan world during the End Times. Joseph was noted to be resourceful, persistent, loving, and very spiritually intelligent—qualities his descendants will be sure to demonstrate when the Church vacates the earth during the Rapture.

Benjamin Jewish Christians, descendants of Benjamin, the twelfth son of Jacob, were known to be pugnacious, left-handed fighters during the conquest of Canaan. But because one member of their tribe raped a concubine belonging to a member of the tribe of Levi, all of Israel fought against them almost wiping out the tribe of Benjamin. Six hundred men were allowed to survive. Benjamin descendants learned from this and other incidents to be aggressive people in order to survive hardship, good qualities for the End-Times trumpet judgments about to come on the earth.

The tribe of Dan is curiously not mentioned in this End-Times army; no real explanation exists as to why the tribe is not included. The Old Testament listings of the patriarchs usually do not include Joseph because his two sons Ephraim and Manasseh substitute for him and for Levi. Levi's inheritance is always stated to be the Lord (see Num. 18:20; Deut. 10:9; 18:1; et. al). One clue for Ephraim and Dan not being a part of the 144,000 may be because of their tendency for idolatry. They are indicted by the prophets because of several episodes of idolatry before the Assyrian and Babylonian campaigns (Gen. 49:17; Deut. 29:18-21; Judges 18:30; 1 Kings 12:29; and Amos 8:14). Maybe this is God's judgment for their earlier unfaithfulness? Some scholars think that Ezekiel 48 states that the Lord allows the original sons of Joseph to be named at each of the entrances of the New Jerusalem. But the passage in Ezekiel likely does not refer to the New Jerusalem, but to Jerusalem being rebuilt after the Babylonian captivity. The Israel Central Bureau of Statistics has kept record of the tribal origins of each Israeli Jew which makes the enumeration and listing of twelve thousand Jews from each tribe believable in the near or far future, whenever this sealing and commissioning of the 144,000 takes place.[100] Of course, the best written record of the twelve thousand from each of these twelve tribes comes from the Book of Life, introduced to John's reading audience at the most critical time in human history—the Great White Throne Judgment (Rev. 20:12).

Some Revelation experts feel that the 144,000 actually represent the Church because John does not initially see them, but only hears about their number (v. 4). However, in Rev. 14:1-5 John not only saw the 144,000 Jews but described them as being virgins without reproach who were offered as first fruits to the Father and Jesus. It would seem contradictory that the Spirit would represent the Church as specifically being from each Jewish tribe when, a few verses later in chapter 7, He revealed to John that the saints come from every people group on the earth.

The "sealing" of the Jews probably refers to their conversion and reception of the Spirit as Paul discusses in Ephesians 1:13; 4:25-30. The sealing of our lives by the Spirit enables us and these Jews to serve the Lord without fear and boldly proclaim the gospel throughout the world as it experiences the worst hardship since the beginning of time. Later in Revelation 12-14, the Beast and the Dragon pursue the Jewish Christians because they hold to their testimony of Jesus and adhere to His commandments without wavering despite the persecution and suffering (Rev. 12:17). In Revelation 14:1-5, they are identified as virgins who never had sexual relations with women, followed Jesus wherever He desired to go to expand the Kingdom, and spoke no lie throughout their lives. These three characteristics caused John to remark that they were "blameless" (Rev. 14:5). I think it simply amazing that these Christian Jews forsake all distractions for the sake of their Lord

---

[100] "The Roles of the Central Bureau of Statistics (CBS) and Methods of Operation," The State of Israel, accessed May 15, 2023, https://web.archive.org/web/20101121103949/http:/cbs.gov.il/engprfl.htm.

and the Kingdom. Of course, they are familiar with the Book of Revelation and know that they will all die martyrs' deaths.

After identifying the 144,000 Jewish-Christian evangelists, John's attention switched to a massive crowd "that no one could number" (ον αριθμησαι αυτον ουδεις εδυνατο, v. 9). He identified these individuals as those who "have come out of the Great Tribulation" (οι ερχομενοι εκ της θλιψεως της μεγαλης, v. 14) and have come from every people group on earth (v. 9). These are probably not the same Christians who were martyred in Rev. 6:9-12, because the ones identified here have not necessarily died martyrs' deaths but have suffered and been persecuted. John stated that they appear in white robes with palm branches in their hands and are speaking/shouting words of praise to God. They shout that "salvation belongs to our God, the one sitting on the throne, and to the Lamb" (η σωτηρια τω θεω ημων τω καθημενω επι τω θρονω και τω αρνιω, v. 10). They all have experienced the thrill of personal salvation from God the Father through His Son and express their joy with a deafening shout. I wonder if they all speak the same language as with other important events in heaven—a sort of language of heaven as in the tongues of the Spirit since they are from a multitude of languages. I also wonder, as have some scholars, if Jesus is actually presenting this massive crowd of Christians through the ages to His Father. This is why many feel this scene marks the moments right after the Rapture. If the innumerable Christian throng worshiping the Godhead was not enough, John then described the next scene involving the seraphim, all the angels, and elders taking their stand around the throne; then they "fell down on their faces before the throne" (επεσεν ενωπιον του θρονου επι τα προσωπα αυτων, v. 11). This is unabashed worship from holy beings. They all fall down and then in unison as if all are directed to speak the same words of adoration they shout, "Amen; glory, honor, power, praise, strength, thanksgiving, and wisdom to our God forever and ever, amen" (αμην, η ευλογια και η δοξα και η σοφια και η ευχαριστια και η τιμη και η δυναμις και η ισχυς τω θεω ημων εις τους αιωνας των αιωνων αμην, v. 12). The seven adjectives the crowd uses to worship the Father are the most descriptive of His nature in all of Scripture; interestingly, the Greek word translated "wealth" (πλουτον, Rev. 5:12), used as an adjective back in chapter 5 when the redeemed crowd was worshipping the resurrected slaughtered Lamb, was *not* used in the worship of God during this worship sequence. Instead, the Greek word for "thanksgiving" (ευχαριστια) was used. Maybe the Holy Spirit used this term because the Raptured Christians had just been safely delivered to heaven and the heavenly beings had the responsibility of their protection were breathing a sigh of relief mixed with thankfulness.

Then one of the elders asked John who all those in long white robes were and where did they come from. I wonder if John in the future was the elder (assuming the identity of the twenty-four elders were the patriarchs and the apostles) that came to the earth-bound John and asked him this question. John *wisely* answered the question by telling the elder, "My Lord, you know" (κυριε μου, συ οιδας, v. 14). The elder proceeded to answer his own question by telling John that these had come out of "great suffering" (θλιψεως της μεγαλης, v. 14). In my opinion, the Great Tribulation's three and a half years does not begin until *after* all the seal judgments have occurred, and not until the "abomination of desolation" takes place in the newly built Temple in Jerusalem catalogued in Daniel and in Revelation 13. Therefore, the elder's comment that these white robed saints "came out of" (ερχομενοι, v. 14) this great suffering period refers to the Time of Sorrows inferred by Daniel (Dan. 9:24–27) and mentioned by Jesus in His Olivet Discourse (Mt. 24:21). Did John's vision jump to the period after Revelation 13 or was he truly seeing just those Christians persecuted during the Time of Sorrow and before. Was he just using a descriptor for the Time of Sorrow and not referring to the actual Great Tribulation period? The myriad of believers from every "tribe, people, nation, and language" probably represents the raptured Christians *after* the sixth seal who had experienced the devastating effects of seals one through four; this would support the mid-tribulation perspective for the Rapture. The elder told John that these Christians had washed their long robes in the blood of the Lamb and made them white (ελευκαναν, v. 14) by that process. Of course, "washed" (επλυναν, v. 14) refers to the cleansing and sanctification that Jesus appropriated by His sinless life and work on the cross that each believer experiences living the life of faith in Jesus (Rev. 1:5; Heb. 9:14).

The elder also elaborated on these blood-washed Christians and their activities after their arrival in heaven. He told John that "as a consequence" (δια τουτο, v. 15) they stand in a privileged place: before the throne of God. He also told John that the redeemed get to worship the Father "day and night" (ημερας και νυκτος, v. 15) in His Temple. They can sustain this intensity of activity because God sitting on His throne will "tabernacle" (σκηνωσει, v. 15) with them. Later in his vision of the End Times, John saw the New Jerusalem and the unrelenting worship of the saints for Him and the Lamb sustained by their proximity to Him and His light which continually energizes them. In these later passages in Revelation, God's tabernacle activities with the saints allow them to see His face. They also become so at one with Him that His name is on their foreheads (Rev. 21:23; 22:3–5). Any of those of us on earth who have intimate worship experiences with God understand the refreshing and sense of well-being with time in His presence. The elder tells John that these Christians will no longer experience the hardships of the seal judgments and the suffering all Christians experience on earth including hunger, thirst, and "any scorching heat from the sun" (ο ηλιος ουδε παν καυμα, v. 16).

When I first started my dermatology practice, I would diagnose patients with first time melanomas about once every six months. Now, at times, I make a melanoma diagnosis once or twice each week. Dermatologists across the United States have experienced the same increase in skin cancers among their patients somewhat due to the ozone layer of the lower stratosphere breaking down secondary to greenhouse gases and hydrocarbons increasing-although of late, ozone depletion has been somewhat reversed.[101] The loss of ozone and resulting ozone depletion above our cities allows for less filtering of damaging ultraviolet A and B waves. But too much light energy will produce the "scorching" of the earth and the burning of our epidermis as the elder described for John here and as John sees for himself in the fourth bowl judgment of Revelation 16:8-9.

The saints also can count on a very close relationship with Jesus, the Lamb. He gently "shepherds them and leads them to springs of living water" (ποιμανει αυτους και οδηγησει αυτους επι ζωης πηγας υδατων, v. 17). I think the "river of the water of life sparkling like crystal" (Rev. 22:1) in the "middle of the great street" (Rev. 22:1) in New Jerusalem is not just a delicious water source but a metaphor for the Holy Spirit. I think Jesus facilitates the saints' connection to the life sustaining activities of the Holy Spirit in heaven and in heaven on earth called the New Jerusalem. The elder ended his comments concerning the future of these once suffering saints: "God will wipe away every tear from out of their eyes" (εξαλειψει ο θεος παν δακρυον εκ των οφθαλμων αυτων, v. 17). This comment about the exquisite comfort the Father delivers to the often but not-now-suffering saints also occurs later in Revelation 21:4 when John described the saints living in the newly deployed New Jerusalem and being comforted by the Father from the trauma of Armageddon I (Rev. 19) and II (Rev. 20). The thought that God would be aware of *every* tear from the eyes of the saints is mind-blowing. But that He would actually take the personal responsibility of wiping each tear from their eyes is inconceivable. But because this sentence occurs twice in the Book of Revelation, John's vision emphasizes that we serve a God dedicated to knowing not just each hair on our heads but each moment of fear, sadness, joy, anger, and any other emotion triggering tears from the eyes of the saints.

---

101 John Bowden "Ozone hole shrinks to lowest size since 1982, unrelated to climate change: NASA". The Hill (2019-10-21).

REVELATION 8

Wormwood

1 "And when He opened the seventh seal and there was silence in heaven for about a half an hour. [2] Then I saw seven angels standing before God; and they were given seven trumpets. [3] And another angel came and stood before the altar holding a golden censer; and he was given much incense which are the prayers of all God's people (the holy ones) to offer on the golden altar before the throne. [4] And the smoke of the incense which are the prayers of God's people went up before God by the angel's hand. [5] Then the angel took the censer and filled it with fire from the altar and hurled it to the earth. Then came lightening, rumblings, thunders, and an earthquake.

[6] "Then the seven angels holding the seven trumpets prepared to blow them. [7] Then the first angel blew his trumpet and fire and hail mixed with blood were hurled to the earth and burned up one third of the land, one third of the trees, and all of the green grass. [8] Then the second angel blew his trumpet and something like a big, burning, fiery mountain was hurled into the sea and one third of the sea became like blood [9] and one third of the sea creatures, the living ones, died and one third of the ships were totally annihilated. [10] Then the third angel blew his trumpet and a mega-star, burning like a torch, fell from the sky and it fell on one third of the rivers and fountains of water; [11] the

Revelation: The Fifth Gospel

> name of the star is 'Wormwood' and one third of the water became bitter and many humans died because the waters became bitter. ¹² Then the fourth angel blew his trumpet and one third of the sun was struck, one third of the moon was struck, and one third of the stars were struck; and one third of them did not shine and one third of the day was dark as well as the night. ¹³ Then I looked and heard an eagle flying in midheaven and he shouted with a loud voice saying, 'Woe, woe, woe to those living on the earth because of the other trumpet blasts about to be sounded by the three angels.'"

The Seventh Seal

The half hour of silence at the breaking of the seventh seal probably indicates the beginning of a series of events more extraordinary than the previous six-seal events. The heavenly "pregnant pause" could also mean that its inhabitants listen to the saints' prayers sent out during the fifth seal and the prayers about to be mentioned in the first few verses of Revelation 8. Silence, particularly in heaven, accentuates or magnifies the importance of events happening immediately thereafter. The events in chapter 8 begin the more serious trumpet judgments meant to create the environment of fear for the Lord and respect for His ways and ultimately to assist these Jewish Christians in their evangelization of the world. As we see in Revelation 14, their efforts result in the greatest harvest for Christ since the Church Age began.

Comet hitting Earth

After the pause in heaven, John noticed seven angels taking a stand before God; he also observes that "seven trumpets are given to them" (εδοθησαν αυτοις επτα σαλπιγγες, v. 1). Angels appear before the throne for specific and important tasks (vis-à-vis Rev. 7:11, 19:4). Some scholars feel that according to Jewish literature seven archangels exist. These seven trumpet angels may be archangels. When Jesus breaks the seventh seal, this ushers in the seven trumpet judgments

(Rev. 8–11) which lead to the severe seven bowl (vial) judgments which John reported in Revelation 16. As with the trumpet judgments, John reported that seven angels also facilitate their activities by pouring out their vials onto the earth. Some have suggested that these seven *trumpet* judgment angels are the same seven angels that mediate the seven *bowl/vial* judgments. But a close look at the text indicates that one of the seven *vial* judgment angels, *not* one of the seven *trumpet* judgment angels, showed John the New Jerusalem and took him on a tour of that marvelous city beginning in Revelation 21:9–10. So, I think God uses two different sets of seven angels each for the execution of each judgment given to mankind and the earth.

During this time, they blow the seven trumpets for specific judgments against the earth; this begins what some prominent Revelation scholars, most notably Marvin Rosenthal, think is the beginning of "The Day of the Lord" which initiates God's specific wrath against the heathen and the Antichrist with the seven trumpets and the seven vials.

John saw another very important angel also taking a stand but this one stood before the golden altar. He noticed that this angel is "holding a golden censer" (εχων λιβανωτον χρυσουν, v. 3). This angel is also likely the same angel that the Apostle observed tending the fires on the golden altar later in the Apocalypse (Rev. 14:18). This golden altar angel has the responsibility to release the seven trumpet angels to perform their judgments on the earth. But John digressed with an explanation of what is *in* the angel's golden censer.

On earth, the priests would prepare the incense offerings from very specific ingredients, as many as eleven,[102] such as myrrh, storax gum/balsam, *shehelet* from a seashell from the Red Sea, ferulah herb, frankincense, and salt and then burn these ingredients in their censers while performing the duties of high priest before the Lord, particularly on the Day of Atonement. The aroma would waft up before Yahweh as a pleasing odor. But in this scene, the smoke of the incense wafted up to the Father from the angel's hand reminding Him of His children's suffering and request to end their pain soon. This angel in Revelation 8 does what the high priests would do on the golden altar before God. Instead of aromatic incense oils, his incense offerings were "the prayers of all God's people" (ταις προσευχαις των

---

[102] ʰImmanuel Benzinger and Judah David Eisenstein, "Incense," *Jewish Encyclopedia*, accessed June 23, 2021, https://www.jewishencyclopedia.com/articles/8099-incense.

αγιων παντων, v. 3). The prayers of the saints are likely to include the prayers of the martyrs of Revelation 6; God finally judges those who martyred the saints with the impending destruction of the earth. The angel combines their prayers with the fire from the altar as a symbol of judgment and a fitting representation of the great comet "Wormwood" which hits the earth and unleashes the events of the ensuing first four trumpets. The prayer sacrifice to the Father mediated through the actions of the altar angel precedes the events of the trumpet judgments. Throughout Revelation, altar activities are often paired with and precede seal judgments (Rev. 5:8-14), trumpet judgments (Rev. 8:3-6) and vial/bowl judgments (Rev. 15:1-7) which heighten the importance and centrality of worship and prayer activities in heaven and their impact on the history of the earth. Jesus' words to His disciples on earth align with this thought when He told His disciples: "What you bind on earth will be bound in heaven, and what you loose on earth, will be loosed in heaven" (Mt. 16:19). He also told His disciples, "If you have the faith like the seed of a mustard plant, you can say to this mountain be removed from here to there and it will move" (Mt. 17:20). These altar activities accentuate the importance of Jesus' role now and in the future as our great High Priest and our role on the earth since we also are a kingdom of priests.

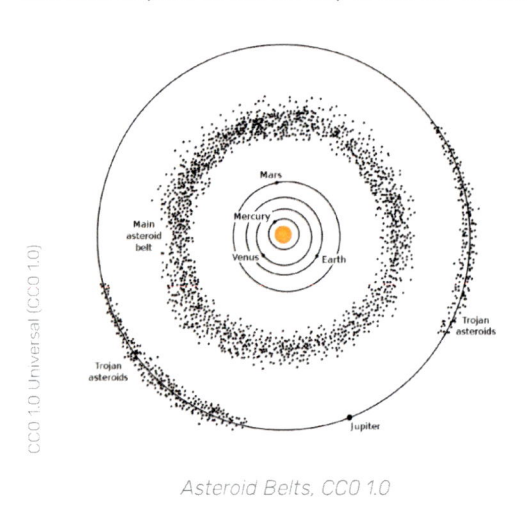

Asteroid Belts, CC0 1.0

The First Trumpet Judgment

John then observed that the seven angels with their trumpets got ready to blow them. The first angel blew his trumpet and immediately "hail and fire mixed with blood was thrown onto the earth" (χαλαζα και πυρ μεμιγμενα εν αιματι και εβληθη εις την γην, v. 7) The text does not indicate who or what actually threw the hot mixture to the earth—maybe the first trumpet angel actually performed the launch of the burning mixture toward the earth. I think the key to the origin of the burning up of a third of the earth's land and trees as well as all the green grass was the "star" that the third trumpet angel released onto the earth. Some Revelation experts have posited that the star called "Wormwood" was likely a comet or asteroid which, by the time the first angel blew his trumpet, was passing its tail at and through the earth. Asteroids don't usually have tails because their volatile gases are burned off from their tails as they pass close to the sun. But comets *do* have tails because they spend most of their time in the outer Solar System at quite a distance from the sun allowing their tails to persist. I don't think the comet's tail striking the earth could explain the scorching of the earth as John described. As far as we know, the only comet's tail in modern history striking the earth was Halley's Comet, which passes by the earth on its elliptical orbit around the sun every seventy-five years or so. Its tail of nearly 24 million miles barely grazed the earth's atmosphere for about six hours on May 19, 1910, causing *no damage* to the earth but some reports of red bands of light in the sky.[103] Most comets have three tails, a *gas tail* (i.e., ion tail/ type I tail) which points directly away from the sun, a *dust tail* (type II tail) which points away from the sun but is curved, and an *anti-tail* leading the front of the comet. These tails average about 100 million miles long. The nuclei of most known comets (about 4,600 comets have been identified[104]) are from 300 feet to 25 miles wide and are composed of ice, rock, dust, ammonia, carbon dioxide, volatile and noxious methane, and carbon monoxide.[105] When the comet approaches the sun on average at about 25 miles per second (range of 5 to 40 miles per second)[106], the sun's radiation causes weaker areas of the surface of the comet to release volatile gases, dust, and ice chunks which feed into the gas and dust tails of the comet. Comet gas tails in most instances are inconsequential to the earth. But the dust trails of the larger comets are sometimes composed of massive ice chunks rather than the more usual sand or pebble sizes. In fact, when many meteors are dragged along in the comet's type II tails, spectacular meteor storms can be observed on the earth, if the comet's tail passes through the earth's orbital path. The most common and observable annual meteor showers/storms are the Perseids meteor showers,

---

103 Ian Ridpath, "Through the Comet's tail," *A Comet Called Halley* (Cambridge, England: Cambridge University Press, 1985), accessed 15 May 2023, revised extracts, http://www.ianridpath.com/halley/halley12.html.
104 Minor Planet Center, International Astronomical Union; accessed June 27, 2021, https://minorplanetcenter.net.
105 J. Mayo Greenberg, "Making a comet nucleus," *Astronomy & Astrophysics,* September 24, 2997, 375-380, accessed June 28, 2021, https://articles.adsabs.harvard.edu//full/1998A%26A...330..375G/0000375.000.html.
106 "How fast is a comet moving when it crosses earth's orbit?" from Astronomy Stack Exchange, accessed May 15, 2023, https://astronomy.stackexchange.com/questions/6384/how-fast-is-a-comet-moving-when-it-crosses-earths-orbit.

Revelation: The Fifth Gospel

derived from the Comet 109P/Swift-Tuttle, which peak yearly in mid-August[107] and the Leonid meteor showers, derived from Comet 55P/Tempel-Tuttle, which peaks yearly in mid-November.[108] Sometimes these showers can produce as many as several thousand meteors per hour. I think that based on John's observation that the earth impact of the mixture of hail, fire, and blood caused so much "scorching" of the land, trees, and grass, that the earth will experience the worst meteor storm that ever struck the earth. Whether or not the scorching meteor storm comes from the dust tail of the mega-star Wormwood remains to be seen. However, this could be possible since dust tails of comets can be hundreds of millions of miles long and many hours and days away from the comet nucleus itself. One of these volatile gases discovered at the surface of the comet called 67P/Churyumov-Gerasimenko is methyl isocyanate (CH_3NCO), a potent chemical used as a pesticide but very toxic to humans.[109] This same comet also has traces of iron oxide (FeO) in its nucleus which is a red mineral also found on Mars.[110]

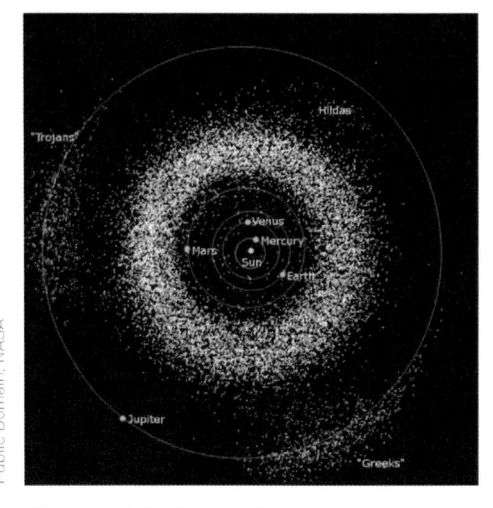

The inner Solar System, from the Sun to Jupiter, with Asteroid Belts

---

107 "Perseid Meteor Shower 2023," Farmer's Almanac (Dublin, NH: Yankee Publishing, Inc., 2023), accessed May 16, 2023, https://www.almanac.com/content/perseid-meteor-shower.

108 "Leonid Meteor Shower: A Reliable November Event," Farmer's Almanac (Dublin, NH: Yankee Publishing, Inc., 2023), accessed May 16, 2023, https://www.almanac.com/extra/leonids-meteor-shower; "Meteor Showers 2023: Where, when and how to see them," Space.com, accessed May 15, 2023, https://www.space.com/39469-best-meteor-showers.html#section-november-taurids.

109 "Science on the Surface of a Comet," European Space Agency, July 30, 2015, accessed May 15, 2023, https://www.esa.int/Science_Exploration/Space_Science/Rosetta/Science_on_the_surface_of_a_comet.

110 Martin Rubin, Kathrin Altwegg, Hans Balsiger, et al. "Elemental and molecular abundances in comet 67P/Churyumov-Gerasimenko"; Monthly Notices of the Royal Astronomical Society, Oxford University Press: 489 (1), 594-607, July 24, 2019, accessed May 15, 2023, https://core.ac.uk/download/pdf/237313106.pdf.

The Second Trumpet Judgment

When the second angel blew his trumpet a "big burning fiery mountain" (ορος μεγα πυρι καιομενον, v. 8) fell from the sky onto the sea. One third of the sea became blood and one third of the living sea creatures died. I wonder if a portion or large chunk from the nucleus of the comet Wormwood broke off as it neared the earth due to the shearing effects of earth's gravitational pull producing a miniature impact. The impact from this comparably smaller meteor would be much less when compared to the impact of the comet Wormwood as we see with the third trumpet. John stated that this "mountain"/meteorite strikes the ocean and causes the water to become red due to its iron oxide crystals and because of its methyl isocyanate, a third of the sea life perishes. Its impact, including the mega-tsunami(s) it inevitably produces, destroys a third of the ships. By definition, meteors are less than three feet in diameter. But asteroids are classified as greater than three feet in diameter and up to 600 miles wide (Ceres is the largest asteroid so far identified). Asteroids were formed between the Sun and Jupiter and, because of these warmer temperatures, are not composed of ice and don't usually have dust tails as do comets but are composed of minerals, rock, and carbon.[111] The second trumpet judgment creates so much havoc to the earth's maritime activities and destruction to the ocean water and fish, that a small meteor can hardly be imagined to be what John observed.

I think John saw an asteroid or comet of considerable size strike the earth's Atlantic Ocean. The destruction that John records here in Revelation 8:8-9 is not unlike the destruction that an asteroid caused in Siberia in 1908 in wiping out a forest near Tunguska River of 830 square miles. The asteroid was nearly 300 feet wide. It exploded when it entered the earth's atmosphere and did not directly strike the earth.[112] Since the population centers are greater in the Northern Hemisphere and therefore because there are more sinners in North America, Europe, Russia, and China than elsewhere, I can imagine the Lord directing the impact of a comet tail's meteor shower (first trumpet judgment) on to Northern Hemisphere land. I believe

---

[111] "What is the difference between an asteroid and a comet?" Infrared Processing and Analysis Center. *Cool Cosmos*, Infrared Processing and Analysis Center, California Institute of Technology, accessed June 29, 2021, https://coolcosmos.ipac.caltech.edu/ask/181-What-is-the-difference-between-an-asteroid-and-a-comet-.

[112] Paolo Farinella, L. Foschini, Christiane Froeschlé, R. Gonczi, T. J. Jopek, G. Longo, and Patrick Michel, "Probable asteroidal origin of the Tunguska Cosmic Body," *Astronomy & Astrophysics.* 377 (3), July 17, 2001: 1081–1097, accessed May 30, 2023, https://www-th.bo.infn.it/tunguska/aah2886.pdf.

that an asteroid from one of the millions of asteroids in one of the major asteroid belts, or a large meteor breaking off of a comet (I favor the latter: second trumpet judgment) could strike the ocean.

Meteors are usually pebble size or smaller and have minimal impact when they collide with the earth's crust. When most meteors enter the earth's atmosphere, they produce dazzling streaks of light but because of the friction between the stratosphere and their great speeds, they are destroyed before striking the earth. Those meteors that actually make it to the earth's surface are called "meteorites." But most meteorites striking the earth create minimal damage because they are so small when they strike, as previously mentioned. But the Apostle observes a mountain-like meteor or asteroid from the second trumpet judgment causing considerable damage to the ocean and shipping. If this meteor/asteroid strikes land, then it will produce more damage to the earth. The ocean, I think, would act as a buffer to many of the effects of the meteorite/asteroid impact including negating the plume effect and nuclear winter described by John from the mega-star hitting the earth in the third and fourth trumpet judgments. But as indicated from the text, the second trumpet judgment was bad enough: destroying one third of sea life wreaks havoc on the world's food supply. Today 15 percent of the world's protein needs come from our oceans' fish. The loss of a third of the world's ships devastates the timely delivery of goods and supplies to the world's economy, not unlike the supply chain disruptions due to the shipping debacle in our country and throughout the world during the COVID pandemic. Shipping in today's world is critical for international trade: the world depends on ships to deliver 90 percent of its goods and supplies.[113] You can imagine the havoc produced by a loss of not only tankers and ocean barges but also the loss of tourist ships from the tsunamis that form after the impact of the maritime meteor.

The Third Trumpet Judgment

The third angel blew his trumpet and the "mega-star" (αστηρ μεγας, v. 10) that John identified as "Wormwood" (Αψινθος, v. 11, Greek word for "bitter"; the Hebrew word for wormwood, וְלַעֲנָה, is used as a curse seven times in the Old Testament—Deut. 29:17;

---

113   Interesting Ocean Facts, Save the Sea" *SavetheSea.com*, accessed June 28, 2021, https://www.savethesea.org/STS%20ocean_facts.htm.

Prov. 5:4; Jer. 9:14; 25:15; Lam. 3:15, 19; and Amos 5:7) strikes the land's rivers and springs of water. "Wormwood" is described by John as a star but would technically be either a comet or an asteroid *forming* from a comet. Comets possess tails as we see from the first trumpet judgment; asteroids and comets are both classified as near-Earth objects. Asteroids are made of rock, metal, and carbon and comets mainly ice, rock, and dust. As previously mentioned, astrophysicists think asteroids are created in the warmer inner solar system this side of Jupiter from fragments breaking off of comets as the comets near their perihelion elliptical paths around the sun. They also think that planets early on in their creation, particularly Jupiter, could have released the ingredients producing asteroids after being hit by asteroids and comets.[114] When asteroids collide, smaller rocky bodies called meteoroids often result. Meteoroids are also formed when a comet passes near the sun and the solar heat releases dust particles from the comet's icy dust tail or more often from the nucleus of the comet itself. As the comet's black surface warms up from the solar radiation pelting it, the comet nucleus extrudes meteoroids as it circles the sun and is flung back into the solar system. When a meteoroid or asteroid/comet enters the Earth's atmosphere, it ignites, creating a visible streak of light called a meteor as previously described. If the meteor or asteroid/comet doesn't vaporize completely and crashes into the Earth, it's called a meteorite. If the asteroid or comet was of sufficient size, it likely would not vaporize and would successfully strike the earth with the severe consequences as John foresees with the third trumpet judgment.

Wormwood would more likely strike land of the Northern Hemisphere because it possesses more land mass than the Southern Hemisphere and would also be where most Christians would have been persecuted. Therefore, as previously indicated, I think God would be more likely to judge the Beast and his minions by dropping Wormwood on the land mass of the Northern Hemisphere. John reported that Wormwood's impact caused one third of the fresh water of the earth to become undrinkable. At present, according to World Health Organization, about two billion people have unpotable water contaminated by feces to drink.[115] The water from the impact of the asteroid/comet and the radioactive isotopes, sulfur dioxide, and methyl isocyanate released at the target site will directly kill many people, but possibly even more humans die from the methyl isocyanate infiltrating the water table.

---

114   William F. Bottke, Jr., Daniel D. Durda, David Nesvorny, Robert Jedicke, Alessandro Morbidelli, David Vokrouhlicky, and Hal Levison, "The fossilized size distribution of the main asteroid belt," *Icarus*. 175 (1): 111, March 14, 2005, access May 30, 2023, https://astro.troja.mff.cuni.cz/davok/papers/fossil05.pdf.

115   "Drinking-Water: Key Facts," World Health Organization, March 21, 2022, accessed May 30, 2023, https://www.who.int/news-room/fact-sheets/detail/drinking-water.

Revelation: The Fifth Gospel

Four Largest Asteroids, CC By A 4.0, NASA

One of the world's most brilliant astrophysicists, the late Stephen Hawking, warned that the most likely cause of earth destruction from our Solar System would be from an asteroid striking the earth. He wrote, "The biggest threat to the future of the planet is an asteroid collision."[116] NASA astrophysicists have estimated that there may be millions of asteroids in the main asteroid belt between Jupiter and Mars. There are at least two hundred asteroids identified with diameters greater than one hundred kilometers and those with diameters greater than one kilometer number from 700,000 to 1.7 million.[117] The four largest asteroids Ceres (587 miles), Vesta (326 miles), Pallas (318 miles), and Hygiea (217 to 300 miles)[118] make up 50 percent of the total asteroid mass—about 4 percent of the mass of the moon. I have stated my bias concerning the third trumpet judgment: I think it is a comet hitting the earth instead of an asteroid. Comets have tails and asteroids do not. The comet's tail spins off a meteor shower onto the earth for the first trumpet judgement. But Hawking would beg to differ; and he may be right. If Wormwood "burning like a torch" (καιομενος ως λαμπας, v. 10) is a meteor from an asteroid and not from a comet, the impact effects would be the same as if it was a comet or its meteor.

The Fourth Trumpet

John described the effects of the fourth angel blowing his trumpet as an impact plume in his first century words: "one third of the sun was struck, one third of the moon, and one third of the stars" (επληγη το τριτον του ηλιου, και το τριτον

---

[116] Stephen Hawking, *Brief Answers to the Big Questions*, (New York: Bantam Books, 2018), 149–159.
[117] "New study reveals twice as many asteroids as previously believed," European Space Agency, April 4, 2002, accessed May 16, 2023, https://sci.esa.int/web/iso/-/29762-new-study-reveals-twice-as-many-asteroids-as-previously-believed, based on Edward Tedesco, Leo Metcalfe, "The Infrared Observatory Deep Asteroid Search, *Astronomical Journal*, April 2002.
[118] "Largest Asteroids: List of the largest asteroids," SolarStory.net, 2016, accessed May 16, 2023, https://solarstory.net/asteroids/largest-asteroids.

της σεληνης και το τριτον των αστερων, v. 12). The light from the sun, moon, and stars are blotted out because of the resulting debris and radioactive plume created by the impact of the comet (or asteroid) Wormwood striking the earth's surface. The impact of a sufficiently large comet or asteroid could cause food chains to collapse both on land and at sea by producing dust and particulate aerosols and thus inhibiting photosynthesis. This series of catastrophic events is what astrophysicists call an *extinction level event*. Impacts on sulfur-rich rocks could emit sulfur oxides precipitating poisonous acid rain, contributing further to the collapse of food chains. Such impacts could also cause mega-tsunamis and/or global forest fires.[119]

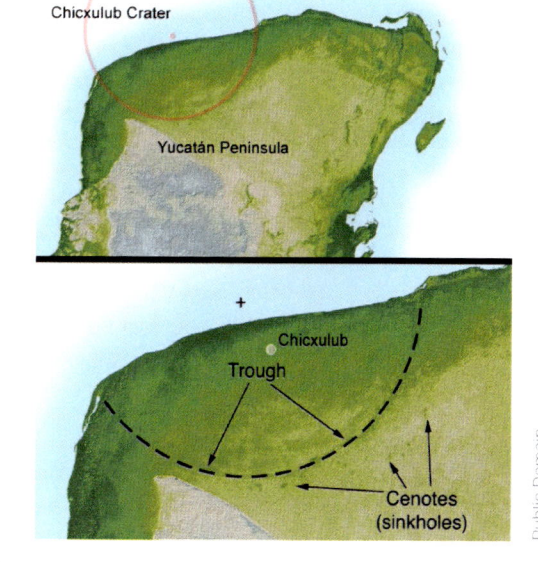

The Yucatan Peninsula was hit by an asteroid 65 million years ago

Most paleontologists now agree that an asteroid *did* hit the Earth at the Yucatan Peninsula near what today are the towns of Chicxulub Puerto and Chicxulub Pueblo. A Glasgow geology team estimates the Chicxulub asteroid struck the earth about 66 million years ago from the northeast at from 8 to 12 miles per second creating an impact hole 60 miles wide and 20 miles deep. The impact released tremendous energy, about 1.3–58 yottajoules, equivalent to over 500 billion H-bombs (one hydrogen bomb killed 140,000 Hiroshima residents and flattened 5 square miles of the city[120]) or about 100 million megatons of TNT.[121] The Chicxulub impact

---

[119] Donald K. Yeomans, "Why Study Asteroids?" Jet Propulsion Laboratory/California Institute of Technology, April 1998, https://ssd.jpl.nasa.gov/?why_asteroids (accessed July 2, 2021).
[120] Seren Morris, "How many people died in Hiroshima and Nagasaki?" *Newsweek*, August 3, 2020, accessed June 30, 2021, https://www.newsweek.com/how-many-people-died-hiroshima-nagasaki-japan-second-world-war-1522276.
[121] Hector Javier Durand-Manterola, Guadalupe Cordero-Tercero, "Assessments of the energy, mass and size of the Chicxulub Impactor," Correll University, March 19, 2014, accessed May 16, 2023, https://arxiv.org/abs/1403.6391.

Revelation: The Fifth Gospel

produced winds of over 600 mph and a tsunami reaching the southern United States coastline with waves over 300 feet high. The impact also produced a mega-earthquake of around 12 on the Richter scale which spawned many aftershocks and volcanos hundreds of miles away.[122] The asteroid impact also caused an ejection plume of dust, sulfur aerosols, and carbon that eventually covered the earth causing an exaggerated greenhouse effect, acid rain, and decreased sunlight and photosynthesis for up to ten years. The greenhouse effect also lowered the global temperature to approximately 40 degrees causing a dearth of food and an inhospitable environment for 75 percent of the non-avian dinosaurs. Some think that the effects from Wormwood could be as devastating—particularly if the fourth trumpet judgment causes this same blanketing of the impact plume over the surface of the earth. The impact plume would obscure the sun, the moon and the stars "so that one third of them became dark and a third of the day would not shine as well as the night" (ινα σκοτισθη το τριτον αυτων και η ημερα μη φανη το τριτον αυτης και η νυξ ομοιως, v. 12).

The flying eagle of verse 13 announces that the next three trumpet blasts, known as the three woe judgements, would be more extensive and devastating to the earth and its citizens than the previous four trumpet judgments. The "flying eagle" could very well be the fourth seraphim identified as a flying eagle in Revelation 4:7. Remember that all four seraphim have a role in announcing critical events of the Apocalypse, including each announcing the four horsemen of the Revelation 6.

---

122 "Chicxulub Impact Event: Regional Effects," *Lunar and Planetary Institute*, accessed June 30, 2021, https://www.lpi.usra.edu/science/kring/Chicxulub/regional-effects/.

REVELATION 9

The Fifth and Sixth Trumpet Judgments

1 "Then the fifth angel sounded his trumpet and I saw a star having fallen from heaven to the earth and he was given the key to the deep pit of the Abyss. ² And he opened the deep pit (shaft) of the Abyss and smoke went up from the deep pit like smoke from a giant furnace. Then the sun was darkened as well as the sky from the smoke of the deep pit. ³ Then locusts came out of the smoke onto the land and they were given authority just like scorpions of the earth have authority. ⁴ And they were told not to harm the earth's grass nor any plant nor any tree except the people who did not have the seal of God on their foreheads. ⁵ They were not allowed to kill them but could torment them for five months. Their torment was like the torture of a scorpion when it stings a man. ⁶ In those days men will seek death, but will by no means find it; they will long to die, but death flees from them.

⁷ "Now the locusts looked like horses prepared for battle, they wore something like golden crowns on their heads and their faces resembled human faces ⁸ and they had hair like women's hair and teeth like lions' teeth ⁹ and they wore breastplates made of iron and

the sound of their wings was like the sound of many horse-drawn chariots rushing into battle. [10] Their tails had stingers like scorpions and in their tails they were given authority to torment men for five months. [11] And they had as king over them the angel of the Abyss who in Hebrew is called 'Abaddon' and in Greek 'Apollyon', which means 'Destroyer.' [12] This is the first woe; two woes come shortly thereafter.

[13] "Then the sixth angel sounded his trumpet and I heard one voice from the four horns of the golden altar the one before God [14] speaking to the sixth angel with the trumpet, 'Release the four angels bound at the Great River Euphrates'; [5] These four angels have been kept ready for this very hour, day, month, and year so that upon their release they might kill one third of mankind. [16] The number of the soldiers of the army was twice ten thousand times ten thousand; I heard their number. [17] Then I saw the horses of the vision and their riders with fiery red, deep blue, and yellow sulfur breastplates. The heads of the horses were like the heads of lions; and fire, smoke, and sulfur went out of their mouths; by these three plagues, [18] one third of mankind was killed, by the fire, smoke and sulfur going out of their mouths. [19] And the power of the horses was in their mouths but also in their tails; indeed, their tails were like snakes having heads with which to harm. [20] The rest of the people not killed by these plagues still did not repent from the works of their hands; they kept worshipping demons and idols of gold, silver, bronze, stone and wood which do not see, hear, nor walk. [21] In addition, they did not repent from their murders, from their sorcery, from their fornication, nor from their thefts."

The Fifth Trumpet Judgment: Hybrid Locusts

The First Woe

The flying eagle (possibly the fourth seraphim of Rev. 4:7) announced to the world and to the Apostle that three woes were about to occur. John then saw the fifth angel blow his trumpet and a series of events were triggered starting with "a star having fallen from heaven to the earth" (αστερα εκ του ουρανου πεπτωκοτα εις την γην, v. 1). An angel who fell out of heaven to the earth (likely a bad angel and not the good angel who binds Satan and locks him in the Abyss in Rev. 20:1-2) is given the assignment to release stinging locusts onto earth to physically sting and torment non-Christians. Is the falling star really the asteroid/comet "Wormwood" releasing the thick smoke from the Abyss because of the tremendous impact when it struck the earth? Could the impact plume from Wormwood's striking the earth of chapter 8 really actually be the smoke from the Abyss? I think the star is a very bright object moving very fast from heaven to earth that John couldn't quite see. This "star" is possibly the angel of the Abyss identified later in this chapter as Abaddon/Apollyon who receives the key to open the Abyss and begin the judgment on those pagans of the earth who do not have the seal of God on their foreheads. (v. 4) I think it unlikely that the "star" is an inanimate object like an asteroid because John is clear that the bright "star" (αστερα, v. 1) falling is the same agent opening the pit's entrance with a key. This seems to be the same "deep pit of the abyss" (φρεαρ της αβυσσου, v. 2) that John sees the mighty angel of Revelation 20:1-2 throw Satan into and imprisoning him in for a thousand years. For now, the pit may be occupied by "locusts"—possibly locked up in the abyss. Or maybe Wormwood's impact caused so much release of radioactive isotopes from fusion and fission atoms produced that the locusts in the area morphed into "stinging machines" quite different from the grasshopper grazers they usually are.

But the fifth angel blows his trumpet which triggers the opening of the door of the abyss releasing the thick smoke from it which obscures the sun and the atmosphere around it. John saw the release of the smoke this way, *"And he opened the deep pit of the abyss, and smoke went up from the deep pit like smoke from a great furnace, and the sun was darkened as well as the sky around it from the smoke from the deep pit"* (και ηνοιξεν το φρεαρ της αβυσσου και ανεβη καπνος εκ του φρεατος ως καπνος καμινου μεγαλης και εσκοτωθη ο ηλιος και ο αηρ εκ του καπνου του φρεατος, v. 2). Immediately, John saw the locusts which come out of the smoke and not necessarily from out of the abyss. He stated, *"Then locusts came out of the smoke onto the land and they were given authority like the scorpions of the earth have authority"* (και εκ του καπνου εξηλθον ακπιδες εις την γην και εδοθη αυταις εξουσια ως εχουσιν εξουσιαν οι σκορπιοι της γης, v. 3). According to the text, the scorpion-like locusts come from the smoke and spread throughout the world. It appears that the smoke from the Abyss alters the appearance and the behavior of these locusts who take orders from the angel of the Abyss, identified later in this chapter (v. 11). As previously suggested, the locusts may have been morphologically altered by the radioactivity of their environment.

Could John's locusts really be viruses or *unmanned computer directed assault devices* or maybe even sophisticated killer drone aircraft? Could these locusts be hybrid locusts allowed to proliferate during the ensuing five months because their normal competitors and food chain rivals would be decreased from the radioactive fallout of the fourth trumpet? Wormwood would have decreased the sun exposure for several months secondary to global darkening and lack of photosynthesis upsetting normal food chain balance; this would allow the locusts to dominate the earth for the five months because they would have no viable predators. Some have suggested that the locusts are actually released from the impact of the comet on the earth's surface from the "shaft of the Abyss." Whoever and whatever these "locusts" are, they have the ability to listen to and execute as the angel of the Abyss directs them. John stated that the locusts are directed not to harm the earth's grass, plants, or any of its trees, quite the opposite of what normal locusts particularly in large numbers would do (v. 4). But the locusts are allowed to harm those without God's forehead seal (v. 4). In other words, these scorpion-like locusts are tasked with stinging any human who are not sealed by the Holy Spirit, as He sealed the Israeli Christians for Jesus in Revelation 7. These Jewish Christians are protected from these "locpions" (locust/scorpion hybrids) during the five months of their mischief. The sting of these locusts is like the sting of the scorpion "when it stings a human" (οταν παιση ανθρωπον, v. 5). On average each year, about a million people are stung by scorpions from stingers in their tails. Very few deaths occur from these stings—about one person every two and a half years in the United States.[123] The sting of these locusts appears to cause severe pain maybe from neuraminidase, leukotrienes, prostanoids or other pain mediators causing those who receive the inoculations to want to die. But John is clear that the pagans who receive the stings will not die even if they try to escape their pain by suicide.

The Apostle states, "In those days men will seek death, but they will never find it; they will long to die, but death flees from them" (και εν ταις ημεραις εκειναις ζητησουσιν οι ανθρωποι τον θανατον και ου μη ευρησουσιν αυτον και επιθυμησουσιν αποθανειν και φευγει ο θανατος απ αυτων, v. 6). I find it fascinating that worldwide suicides appear to be nonexistent during this time. The national suicide rate is around 10:100,000; the worldwide rate is around 16:100,000, with over eight

---

123   "10 Deadliest Animals in the US," *World Atlas*, accessed December 4, 2021, @https://www.worldatlas.com/articles/10-deadliest-animals-in-the-us.html#:~:text=Scorpions%20are%20small%20but%20potentially%20deadly.%20Being%20killed,around.%20Healthy%20adults%20usually%20survive%20a%20scorpion%20sting.

hundred thousand global suicides each year, with one suicide every 40 seconds somewhere in the world.[124] But just imagine that no one dies from suicide at least among those stung by the "locpions" during this five-month period to allow for God's fifth trumpet judgment to have maximum effect and to allow opportunity for the Christian Jews to evangelize these troubled souls.

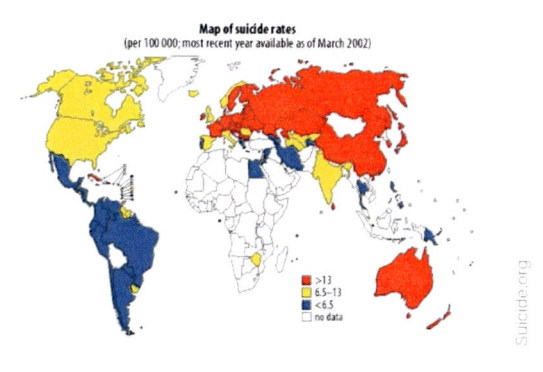

Map of Suicide Rates

John describes the locusts as "looking like horses prepared for battle" (ομοια ιπποις ητοιμασμενοις εις πολεμον, v. 7). There was no question in John's mind about the intent of these weaponized Abyss derived organisms. John continued his description of the locusts as wearing "something like golden crowns on their heads" (επι τας κεφαλας αυτων ως στεφανοι ομοιοι χρυσω, v. 7). I wonder if these "golden crowns" are really something like radio transmitters or receptors which allow them to receive directions from their leader who we later find out is the "angel of the Abyss." The crowns could be symbolic for their authority over men who do not have the seal of God in their lives. But I think John's description is too detailed to just be symbolic. I believe he is giving the best description for these demonic organisms using the language of his day to describe what he sees, as he does throughout the Apocalypse. He continued with a portrayal of their faces as resembling human faces, and "hair like women's hair, their teeth were like lions" (τριχας ως τριχας γυναικων και οι οδοντες αυτων ως λεοντων ησαν, v. 8). To some degree, several species of locusts resemble human faces with hair (τριχας, antennae) and teeth (οδοντες, incisor like teeth on their mandibles[125]) as John describes. John also mentions that these supernatural predators also wear "breastplates of iron" (θωακας

---

124   Saloni Dattani, Lucas Rodés-Guirao, Hannah Ritchie, Max Roser and Esteban Ortiz-Ospina, "Suicide," Our World in Data, 2023, accessed November 22, 2021, https://ourworldindata.org/suicide.
125   Pranav Baskar, "Locusts Are A Plague Of Biblical Scope in 2020. Why? And . . . What Are They Exactly?", NPR, June 14, 2020, accessed July 4, 2021, https://www.npr.org/sections/goatsandsoda/2020/06/14/876002404/locusts-are-a-plague-of-biblical-scope-in-2020-why-and-what-are-they-exactly#:~:text=When%20locusts%2.

σιδηρους, v. 9) which could be his impression of what the locust thorax looked like. Most likely, the angel, through whom Jesus was communicating His Apocalypse to John (Rev. 1:1), told him that their thoraces were covered with iron (σιδηρους) which would somewhat protect these predators for their five-month mission to torment humans. John was impressed with the sound of their wings and stated that they sounded like "many horse-drawn chariots rushing into battle" (αρματων ιππων πολλων τρεχοντων εις πολεμον, v. 9).

Close up photograph of a Grasshopper

Locusts are actually various species of short-haired grasshoppers which possess swarming behavior. Recent research has identified that swarming behavior is a response to overcrowding. Increased tactile stimulation of their hind legs causes an increase in levels of serotonin. This causes the locusts to change color, eat more, and breed much more easily—phenomena called *phenotypic plasticity* by botanists.[126] The transformation of the locusts to the swarming variety is induced by several hind leg contacts per minute over a four-hour period. It is estimated that the largest swarms have covered hundreds of square miles and consisted of many billions of locusts.[127] The swarming locusts have insatiable appetites. They eat the equivalent of their own weight each day, and, flying at night with the wind, may cover some 500 kilometers/300 miles. The largest known swarm covered 1,036

Full Body of a Grasshopper

---

126 Michael Antsey, Stephen Rogers, S. Ott, Malcolm Burrows, S. J. Simpson, 30 January 2009, *Science* 323 (5914): 627-630, "Serotonin Mediates Behavioral Gregarization Underlying Swarm Formation in Desert Locusts," accessed May 16, 2023, https://www.semanticscholar.org/paper/Serotonin-Mediates-Behavioral-Gregarization-Swarm-Anstey-Rogers/2eb8e5b4d5793003cd56b1952dd9897a31ded14c.

127 P. A. Stevenson, "The key to Pandora's box," *Science* 323 (5914): 594-595 January 30, 2009, accessed May 16, 2023, https://www.science.org/doi/10.1126/science.1169280.

square kilometers (400 square miles), comprising approximately forty billion insects.

In summary, John remarked that these creatures are commanded and ruled by Satan's underworld cherub angel named Abaddon/Apollyon who likely is the angel John described as "having fallen out of heaven to the earth" (εκ του ουρανου πεπτωκοτα εις την γην, v. 1). I think John indicated that the angel Abaddon was the angel given the key because John described the angel as *already* "having fallen" (πεπτωκοτα) by using the perfect tense of the verb πιπτω (to fall). John explained and described the fallen state of Satan and his angels in Revelation 12:4, 9. All of John's descriptions about *God's* angels leaving heaven to do His bidding never "fall" from heaven but leave or go out of heaven (cf. Rev. 10:1, Rev. 18:1). As the leader of the demons of the Abyss, this angel, identified by Moses as the death angel who killed the Egyptian firstborn in the tenth plague immediately before the Exodus of Israel from Egypt (Ex. 12:23), was given permission to open the door of the Abyss and release the locusts under his control (v. 1). He did so with the key he was given as we see in the first two verses. God gives Abaddon specific directives concerning what the weaponized locusts should do—attack and torment but not kill unbelievers for five months and not harm those sealed on their foreheads—obviously referring to the Jewish Christians—the 144,000 evangelistic "Billy Grahams" from the twelve tribes of Israel who take the place of the raptured Church from Revelation 7, as previously described. Also, very unlike the swarms of locusts in our present world, these supernatural locusts *do not* eat plants, trees, and crops in John's Apocalypse because they are directed not to do so (v. 4). Instead, they are presumably well controlled by their "king" Abaddon which is why I feel that the locusts may really be demonic spirits with locust/scorpion like bodies or demons infecting (possessing) hybrid locust bodies.

The intelligence of the hybrid locusts is truly impressive as we see from John's description of what they do, particularly when it concerns their torment of humans. John stated that the locusts are directed to sting humans for five months causing so much intense pain that they "long to die" (επιθυμησουσιν αποθανειν, v. 6) and

Christian and Apollyon

"seek death" (ζητησουσιν . . . θανατον, v. 6) but "death flees from them" and "they will not find it" (v. 6). I find it interesting that Abaddon/Apollyon is torturing the very pagans who assist the Antichrist against the forces of heaven, particularly at the Battle of Armageddon. John ends this section by stating that this fifth trumpet judgment is the first woe and two other woes will come shortly after (v. 12; cf. Rev. 9:13, 11:15).

The Sixth Trumpet Judgment: Nuclear Warfare

The Second Woe

An attack helicopter fires rockets

The Apostle reported that the sixth angel blew his trumpet triggering the following: John heard a solitary voice come from the golden altar's four horns. The voice commanded the sixth angel to "release the four angels bound at the great River Euphrates" (λυσον τους τεσσαρας αγγελους τους δεδεμενους επι τω ποταμω τω μεγαλω Ευφρατη, v. 14). Again, I think that these four angels are fallen ones who have been bound at the Euphrates River which will be the staging area for the fourth world war. I think that even the End-Time-judgment events are orchestrated by God the Father as we see in the previous verses with Abaddon executing God's desire for the five months of torment on those who reject His Will and His ways. These four Euphrates angels, likely fallen spirit colleagues or students of Abaddon, were kept ready for this very hour, day, month, and year (v. 15). John stated that they are responsible for the killing of a third of the world's population. Remember that one quarter of the world died from the fourth seal judgment leaving about six billion people still on earth, based on the current world population of 8.033 billion people (cf. Rev. 6:8-WWIII). But at this time, one third of the world dying would be about two billion deaths. After speculating about the tremendous loss of life, John saw the agent of this terrible loss of life—a standing army of two hundred million troops and stated, "The number of the soldiers of the army was twice ten thousand times ten thousand" (ο αριθμος των στρατευματων του ιππικου δισμυριαδες μυριαδων, v. 16). In the first century there were two hundred million people on the earth and China had around fifty-seven million of that total.[128] In John's day, a discussion of two hundred million soldiers was preposterous—and John knew this, which is why he reiterated to his reading audience that "I heard their number" (ηκουσα τον αριθμον αυτων, v. 16). Interestingly, in 2015 China has boasted about its active army of "2.3 hundred million troops serving on the ground, in the air and in the increasingly robust force China is deploying on the high seas."[129] John gives his reading audience further description of this massive army. He stated that the army consisted of horses with riders on them dressed in fiery red, azure blue, and sulfur yellow (v. 17). These have been the colors of the Chinese Liberation Air Force division for at least a decade or more.[130] John described how the army will wreak havoc on mankind by the "horses" attacking with the three plagues of fire, sulfur, and smoke "coming out of their mouths" (εκ των στοματων, v. 17). This may be his way of expressing the horrendous nuclear warfare mediated through aircraft such as attack helicopters or through ground vehicles like nuclear upfitted tanks: horses with heads of lions and tails like snakes (vv. 17–19). Remember, John was describing in terms of first century language what he sees many centuries in advance.

Soldiers of the Chinese People's Liberation Army

---

128 Dina Spector and Eric Goldschein, "15 crazy facts about life in the first century", *Insider*, November 11, 2011, accessed July 5, 2021, https://www.businessinsider.com/what-life-was-like-in-the-first-century-2011-11.

129 Julie Makinen, "China's Military: How Strong is the People's Liberation Army?" The Los Angeles Times, September 2, 2015, accessed July 8, 2021, https://www.latimes.com/world/asia/la-fg-china-military-pla-q-and-a-20150902-story.html.

130 "Type 07 [Military Uniforms] (Chinese: 零七 式军服,07式军服)," accessed July 9, 2021, https://en.wikipedia.org/wiki/Type_07#cite_note-8.

Revelation: The Fifth Gospel

As to the origins of this terrible nuclear holocaust, John offered a few clues. Remember WW III took place as the result of Jesus opening the fourth seal and releasing the pale green horseman (Death) with Hades (Rev. 6:8). But the nuclear slaughter evident here in chapter 9 is directed by a voice authorizing the sixth angel to release the four bound fallen angels imprisoned at the Euphrates River. I wonder if two of these angels direct the East army and if two direct the West army triggering the nuclear global holocaust. John reported that one third of mankind was slaughtered during this war possibly starting at the Euphrates River. I can imagine that those angels caused the opposing army generals to resort to all-out nuclear warfare resulting in frightful loss of life throughout the world. This same army several years later will march on a dried-up Euphrates riverbed in Revelation 16:12. According to this account, they march into the Valley of Megiddo in Revelation 16:12 where, in Revelation 19:11-21, Christ and His armies from heaven annihilate this large army and the nations' armies which join it. As previously mentioned, the costliest war in human history so far was WWII with a loss of nearly eighty million lives, about 3.5 percent of the world's population (2.3 billion in 1940). This conflict in Revelation 9 results in catastrophic loss of life thirty times greater than WWII. I wonder if the four angels of Rev. 9 utilize suspicion and doubt between world leaders who have experienced a short time of world peace under the economic genius of the Revelation 6 white horseman (the Antichrist)? WWI was triggered by French resentment over Germany's annexation of Alsace Lorraine in 1871 and the assassination of the Archduke Ferdinand and his wife Sophie of Austria-Hungary in July 1914 by a Serbian nationalist. WWII was caused by similar suspicion and resentment of the German people who had been punished by the Versailles Treaty of 1918 after WWI. The German public became dissatisfied with the prohibition of unification with Austria and the loss of three of their territories as consequence of their role in WWI (Danzig, Eupen-Malmedy, and Upper Silesia). Based on the previous two world wars, these four angels of Revelation 9 would not have to work very hard to foment revenge and a bellicose spirit between nations of the East and the West, particularly in light of the political suspicion the West has and will have in the future concerning the Chinese Communist Party, the Khomeini's of Iran, the dictators of Russia and their Marxist ideologies evident even today.

The last few verses of Revelation 9 paint a disturbing picture of opposition to God and His Will, as we see from John's description of the reticence of the pagan citizens of the world to repent. John found it incredulous that despite the seal judgments and the six trumpet judgments experienced by mankind at this point in the End Times and the global loss of life because of them, despite the insight they have received from the Church that these judgments are occurring because of God's anger with their rejection of His Word and Son and their refusal to follow accepted mores of their consciences (Rev. 6:16–17), they *continue* "worshipping demons and idols of gold, silver, bronze, stone, and wood" (προσκυνησουσιν τα δαιμονια και τα ειδωλα τα χρυσα και τα αργυρα και τα χαλκα και τα λιθινα και τα ξυλινα, v. 20).

Demons are alive and active today. The Apostle John reported the fall of Lucifer and his angels in Revelation 12. He saw a vision of Satan as a seven-headed and ten-horned dragon sweeping one third of his angels from heaven down to the earth (12:4). The devil was once in charge of the worship of God before this war took place and, as one of three archangels, was in charge of one third of the angels in heaven (See Isa. 14:12–15 and Ezek. 28:11–19). Because he sinned by coveting God's place, those angels under his charge also sinned by subjecting their wills to his and not to God's. The demons await their final judgment and banishment to the Abyss/Hell. But in the meantime, they are worshipped by humans not only in the Church of Satan, but in other branches of the occult, new thought mysticism, shamanism, and even progressive socialism. It is insightful and revealing that John linked demon worship with idol worship (v. 20). I find it shocking that a world of the future End Times with all of its technologic and informational advances would embrace what seems obviously spurious to Christians. Their preoccupation and dedication to idols (which at times can be indwelt by demonic spirits) is at the least a waste of time and at the most dangerous activity resulting in loss of eternal life. John told us that, despite the obvious, these idols "cannot see, nor hear, nor walk" (ουτε βλεπειν δυνανται ουτε ακουειν ουτε περιπατειν, v. 20). Also astounding is that mankind does not feel compelled to embrace the One and Only God responsible for the past three years of hell on earth. These Apocalyptic humans also produce the fruit of their defiance of God; not only do they not repent from their sorceries, but they also refuse to stop their murdering, their fornicating, and their stealing (v. 21).

In 2020, in the United States, the murder rate was 7.8 homicides for every one hundred thousand people with nearly 21,570 murder victims; 16,608 deaths per year come from firearm use (6 for every one hundred thousand people).[131] These figures have been steadily rising. We are living in a progressively violent culture not

---

131 John Gramlich, "What we know about the increase in U.S. murders in 2020," Pew Research Center, accessed May 17, 2023, https://www.pewresearch.org/short-reads/2021/10/27/what-we-know-about-the-increase-in-u-s-murders-in-2020/.

helped by the recent trend to defund police in larger cities and from the pressures brought to bear against society by Satan and his demons, heightened by the economic downturns during the COVID-19 pandemic.

The adultery rate also is climbing in America but with divorces actually decreasing. In 2019, the rate of divorce was 7.6 per one thousand marriages. In 2009, the divorce rate was 9.7 per one thousand marriages.[132] But the adultery rate has risen over the years with 15 to 20 percent of couples cheating in 2019, usually after twenty to thirty years of marriage. The majority of these marriage cheaters are between fifty and sixty years of age.[133] Men cheat more often than women, the percent growing wider in older age groups. But women are cheating more on their spouses due to greater work force involvement and because of pervasive Internet dating platforms.[134]

Stealing comes in many forms. But grand larceny is likely the most prevalent and causes the largest economic losses in the United States because vehicles are some of the most costly items purchased. The rate of motor vehicles stolen in 2022 was over one million—an economic loss of over 8.6 billion dollars.[135]

I believe Satan will target these four types of sin and facilitate humans in sinning in these ways during the End Times because each are particularly egregious violations against God (sorcery and idolatry), humans (murder and stealing), and marriages (fornication).

---

[132] Linda Anderson and Zachary Scherer, "US Marriage and Divorce Rates Declined in Last 10 Years," United States Census Bureau,; accessed July 11, 2021, https://www.census.gov/library/stories/2020/12/united-states-marriage-and-divorce-rates-declined-last-10-years.html.

[133] Gabrielle Applebury, "Infidelity Statistics on Men, Women, and Relationships," *Love to Know*, May 6, 2020, accessed July 11, 2021, https://www.lovetoknow.com/life/relationships/rates-divorce-adultery-infidelity.

[134] "Who Cheats in America? Institute for Family Studies, accessed May 17, 2023, https://ifstudies.org/blog/who-cheats-more-the-demographics-of-cheating-in-america.

[135] "Vehicle Thefts Nationwide Surpass One Million For the First Time Since 2008," Insurance Information Institute, March 8, 2023, accessed May 17, 2023, https://www.nicb.org/news/news-releases/vehicle-thefts-nationwide-surpass-one-million-first-time-2008.

REVELATION 10

John and the Mighty Angel

1 "Then I saw another mighty angel coming down out of heaven clothed in a cloud with a rainbow on his head and his face like the sun and his feet like pillars of fire; [2] and he held an open little scroll in his hand and he placed his right foot on the sea and his left on the land. [3] Then he shouted with a loud voice like the roar of a lion; and when he yelled the voices of the seven thunders spoke. [4] And when the seven thunders spoke, I was about to write, but I heard a voice from heaven say, 'Seal what the seven thunders spoke and do not write them down.' [5] Then the angel who I saw standing on the sea and on the land raised his right hand toward heaven [6] and then he made an oath by the One living forever and ever, who created the heaven and the things in it, and the earth and the things on it, as well as the sea and the things in it saying, 'there will now be no more delay; [7] for in the days when the seventh angel is about to blow his trumpet, the mystery of God will be fulfilled as He announced to His servants, the prophets.'

[8] "Then I heard the voice from heaven again speaking to me saying, 'Go and take the scroll, the one opened in the hand of the angel, the

Revelation: The Fifth Gospel

> one standing on the sea and on the land.' ⁹ So I went to the angel and asked him to give me the little scroll. And he said to me, 'Take and eat it up; it will make your stomach sour, but in your mouth, it will be as sweet as honey.' ¹⁰ Then I took the little scroll from the angel's hand and ate it up; sure enough, in my mouth it was as sweet as honey but as I was digesting it, my stomach became sour. ¹¹ Then they said to me, 'You must again prophecy to peoples, nations, languages and to many kings.'"

John continued his fast-moving Apocalypse by slowing his story down to describe a very touching scene between an unidentified "mighty angel" (αγγελον ισχυρον, v. 1) and John himself. John saw this very large angel "clothed in a cloud" (περιβεβλημενον νεφελην, v. 1). Clouds are found usually several thousands of feet above the earth; but this angel was so large that his "clothing" included a cloud surrounding his body. This was an astonishing scene to John. I doubt that even in his earlier experiences of the Apocalypse did he see an angel quite this size except perhaps when John used the same phrase "mighty angel" in Revelation 5:2 to describe the heavenly being who asked if anyone in the universe was worthy to open the scroll God the Father held in His right hand and break its seals. The angel of Rev. 5 was not the same angel of his vision and experience in Revelation 10 because he described *this* angel as "another" (αλλος, v. 1) mighty angel. I wonder if the announcing angel Gabriel was the "mighty angel" that John saw here with "rainbow on his head" and "face like the sun and feet like pillars of fire" (v. 1).

Angel of Revelation 10, painted by William Blake in 1805

I find it interesting that this angel presented himself with a "rainbow on his head" (η ιρις επι της κεφαλης αυτου, v. 1). To Jews and even Jewish Christians, the rainbow was a sign of God's promise to mankind-that He would never again destroy the world as He had done during the Flood. John had seen tremendous destruction and the death of billions during the seal and trumpet judgments. But maybe to John, seeing the angel with a rainbow was comforting and indicated to him that God still remembered His promise to Noah that He would never totally destroy humans as He had with the Flood (Gen. 9:8–16). But the angel had a very imposing appearance: "his face was like the sun and his feet like pillars of fire" (το προσωπον αυτου ως ο ηλιος και οι ποδες αυτου ως στυλοι πυρος, v. 1) The radiation from standing in the presence of the Father likely caused this angel's face and feet to emit light rays just as if his face *was* the sun and his feet *were* on fire. Remember the appearance of Jesus in Revelation 1:15–16. His face also shown like the sun at noon and His feet appeared as if they had been in a white-hot furnace. We also have the description of Moses as he came down from Mt. Sinai with the Ten Commandments after being with God the Father for forty days. The people saw his face shining like the sun which caused great concern on their part. Moses allayed their fears by covering his face (Ex. 34:29–35).

The angel is so large that John observed him placing his "right foot on the sea and his left on the land" (τον ποδα αυτου τον δεξιον επι της θαλασσης τον δε ευωνυμον επι της γης, v. 2). I think the angel is an archangel because of his size. Scriptures indicate that there *may* be a hierarchy of angels with archangels being the tallest, then seraphim (30 to 50 feet), then angels (9 to 12 feet), and finally cherubim (7 to 9 feet). From eyewitness accounts and from the Apostle John's experience with this and the other large angel (5:2), archangels may be from 50 to 100 feet tall. A few comments may be in order concerning angels and what we know about them.

The study of angels, called "angelology," reveals multiple different angel traditions from most religions. Jews and Christians believe that angels are spirit beings created by God to live for eternity, to execute His will for the world and humans, and to promote kingdom activities particularly when involving humans (cf. Heb. 1:14). The Scriptures mention angels over 270 times. Orthodox Jews believe that there are ten archangels named Michael, Gabriel, Raphael, Metatron, Raziel, Tzaphkiel, Tzadkiel, Khamael, Haniel, and Sandalphon. But most Christians feel that God created just three archangels each with control over one third of angels below their rank. This would explain why Lucifer took one third of the angels with him when he was thrown out of heaven after his sin of pride and covetousness as mentioned in Revelation 12:4, Ezekiel 28, and Isaiah 14. Scholars think the Archangel Michael, in charge of God's heavenly army, controls the critical events of the End Times whenever God's army is needed. He is usually called on to intervene and frustrate Satan's plans and seems to be God's choice for hand-to-hand combat with Satan (vis-à-vis 12:7; 20:1–2).

St. John the Evangelist with Angel on Patmos

The Archangel Gabriel has evidently been given the task of announcing God's plans to humans: he announced John's birth to Zacharias and Elizabeth (Lk. 1:11-20); he announced Jesus' birth to Mary (Luke 1:28-37). As previously mentioned, I think Gabriel may have been the archangel interacting with the Apostle John in Revelation 10. The gentleness and care that he demonstrated to John is very touching: consider allowing John to take the book from his left hand so as not to expose his ninety-five-year-old body to the sea where Gabriel had the right side of his body; and the obvious bending down to let John take the book from his hand; and the warning that eating the book would cause his stomach to sour and give him a stomach ache.

In Revelation 10:2, John told his reading audience that the mighty angel held an "open little scroll/book in his hand" (εν τη χειρι αυτου βιβλαριδιον ηνεωγμενον, v. 2). Likely this scroll held the developments of the next three and a half years—the period of time referred to as the "Great Tribulation Period." John then sees the angel placing his right foot on the sea and his left foot on the land signifying dominance and coming judgment (v. 2). I think the angel put his right foot on the sea so that he could "officially" swear with his unoccupied right hand about the coming judgment of the world unleashed by the seventh angel which he soon mentions—the right hand has always been considered the proper hand for the execution of oaths. If he held the little book with his right hand, then his left hand would have been the one available for the oath giving; it turned out that John took the little book from the angel's left hand because the angel's left leg was standing on the land; a nonagenarian would have had difficulty retrieving the little book from the angel's right hand had it been held over the ocean as previously indicated.

John then saw the angel yell at the top of his voice "like the roar of a lion" (ωσπερ λεων μυκαται, v. 3) which caused "the voices of the seven thunders to speak" (ελαλησαν αι επτα βρονται τας εαυτων φωνας, v. 3). The "seven thunders" could very well be the Holy Spirit since He is referred to in the earlier chapters of Revelation as the Being represented by the number seven. The Holy Spirit is identified as the "seven spirits before His throne" (Rev. 1:4), "seven burning lamps" before the throne of the Father (Rev. 4:5), and the seven eyes and seven horns on the Lamb (Rev. 5:6). Because of John's history and experience with the Holy Spirit from the days of the outpouring on Pentecost to the shaking of the Upper Room where the young Church was praying after their tussle and persecution from the Sanhedrin (Acts 5) to the numerous miracles of the Spirit through Peter, Paul, and others, John understood the importance of the Holy Spirit. So, when John heard "the seven voices," i.e., the Holy Spirit, say something, he naturally began to write down what he was hearing. John had such a brilliant mind and great memory even into his nineties, the angel showing him this Apocalypse had to remind him to write down what he thought he could just commit to memory (cf. Rev. 21:5). But in *this* instance, hearing the Holy Spirit speak critical information about the End Times, John immediately started writing down what he heard. But "a voice from heaven" (φωνην εκ του ουρανου, v. 4) spoke to John telling him to "seal up what the seven thunders spoke" (σφραγισον α ελαλησαν αι επτα βρονται, v. 4) and "do not write them down" (μη αυτα γραψης, v. 4). John complied and obviously the record of the statements or words spoken by the Holy Spirit did not become a permanent part of the Apocalypse. Maybe the information shared with John was not apropos to Christendom or maybe more likely the Holy Spirit's words, had Satan heard them, would have given the devil an advantage against God's saints during Armageddon I or II or the timing of the events of the last judgments. This was likely information that if Satan knew about, God's campaign against Satan's forces might become compromised; this was secret information that was critical for the forces of life but detrimental to them/us if Satan learned about the contents of the message from the seven thunders. Of course, Satan knows Revelation by heart so that he can offer stiff resistance to the forces of light and be a formidable opponent throughout

Revelation: The Fifth Gospel

the Tribulation Period. I can assure my reading audience that I will ask Jesus what was spoken during this part of the Apocalypse. Maybe He will tell me, but likely He will not until the events of Revelation have entirely taken place.

This angel roared like a lion because he had some judgment to execute beginning with making an oath before his God. He dramatically "raised his right hand toward heaven" (ηρεν την χειρα αυτου την δεξιαν εις τον ουρανον, v.5). Swearing is forbidden by Jesus (Mt. 5:34–37) and by His half-brother in James 5:12. But the angel was holy and had God's authorization to proclaim the inevitable end to time as we know it. Then John told us that the Father who created everything in the universe including in heaven, on the earth, and in the sea will allow "no more delay"/"time shall be no longer"-χρονος ουκετι εσται, v. 6). The archangel indicates that God had been patient; He has been restraining His penchant for judging unrighteousness as well as avenging His martyred saints' request that He stop the murder of His saints (Rev. 6:10–11). God would rather delay His plans for His kingdom on earth (New Jerusalem) to save more pagan souls during the Tribulation as Peter indicates in 2 Peter 3:9, 15. But the angel swears by the Father that time has run out and the seventh angel will blow the last trumpet soon (Rev. 11) triggering the fulfillment of the "mystery of God" (μυστηριον του Θεου, v. 7) as God spoke through "His servants the prophets" (εαυτου δουλους τους προφητας, v. 7). I think the mystery refers to the execution of the End-Time prophecies and the reestablishment of God's kingdom on earth as revealed to Daniel, Ezekiel, Isaiah, Jeremiah, Hosea, and others.

Then the voice that John had heard from heaven directing him not to write down the words of the seven thunders spoke again to him telling him to go and take the opened book from the hand of the angel, "the one standing on the sea and the land" (του εστωτος επι της θαλασσης και επι της γης, v.8). John was likely dreading to have to retrieve the opened little book from the mighty angel who roared like a lion and in holy fervor had sworn an oath with God's authorization. But remember—and certainly John remembered—that even the archangels and seraphim had not been worthy enough to open and read the sealed scroll from the Father's hand in Revelation 5. Maybe because of that, along with the encouragement from the "voice from heaven," John cautiously took the initiative and walked up to the mighty angel and asked for the opened little book. Maybe to John's surprise, the angel acquiesced and then told him, "Take and eat; for it will make your stomach sour but, in your mouth, it will be as sweet as honey" (αλλ εν τω στοματι σου εσται γλυκυ ως μελι, v. 9). This, of course, occurred after John took the scroll and ate it and may indicate that the words of the scroll are enlightening (sweet) but tough to deliver (sour or bitter) as prophecy against the nations as the angel commands him to do. The Lord told Ezekiel in Ezekiel 2:8-9 to eat the word offered to him as he prophesied to the Israelites. The word of the Lord is often associated with sweetness and honey as we see from Psalms 19:10; 119:103; and Proverbs 24:13-14. John's task of continuing to record the unfolding of the Revelation to Christendom and to the pagan world about to experience the most severe judgments that the world has ever seen from the Father, makes his job very difficult and in many ways repulsive as we see by his description of the scroll causing his stomach to become "sour." Another reason for the scroll causing stomach upset for John is the suffering and death of the two beloved Jerusalem prophets at the hand of the Beast about to be introduced in the next episode of John's Apocalypse.

Chapter 10 ends with presumably the voice from heaven telling him that he must prophesy again to "peoples, nations, languages and to many kings" (λαοις και εθνεσιν και γλωσσαις και βασιλευσιν πολλοις, v. 11). John's life's work was not over; through the words of this last verse of Chapter 10, John realized that the events about to take place in the Apocalypse triggered by the seventh angel's trumpet blast (Rev. 11:15) culminates in the final events of the Great Tribulation Period including the execution of the seven vial judgments.

REVELATION 11

Two Jerusalem Prophets

1 "Then a measuring rod like a stick was given to me and I was told, 'Rise up and measure the Temple of God, the altar, and those worshipping in it; ² but exclude the outer court and do not measure it because it has been given to the Gentiles and they will trample the holy city for forty-two months. ³ Then I will give my two witnesses and they will prophecy for 1,260 days clothed in sackcloth.' ⁴ These are the two olive trees and two lampstands, the ones standing before the Lord of the earth. ⁵⁶ And if someone wants to harm them, then fire goes from out of their mouth and annihilates their enemies; this is how anyone must die who wants to harm them. ⁶ And they will be given the power to shut the sky so that rain will not be sent during the days of their prophecy; they also have the authority over the waters to turn them into blood and can strike a blow to the earth with every plague whenever they desire.

⁷ "Now when their testimony is complete, the Beast will rise up from the Abyss and will make war against them, will conquer them and will kill them ⁸ and their dead bodies will lie in the main street of the great city figuratively called Sodom and Egypt where also their Lord was crucified. ⁹ For three and a half days some from every tribe, people, nation, and language will gawk over their dead bodies, and will not allow their dead bodies to be placed in a tomb. ¹⁰ Those living on the

earth will rejoice over them and are made glad and will send each other gifts because these two prophets tormented those living on the earth. [11] But after three and a half days, the breath of life from God entered them and they rise to their feet and great fear fell on those watching them; [12] then they heard a loud voice from heaven say to them, 'Come up here!' Then they rose into heaven in a cloud and their enemies watched them. [13] At this very hour, a great earthquake occurred and one tenth of the city was destroyed and seven thousand people were killed by the earthquake; and the rest became terrified and then they gave honor to the God of heaven. [14] This is the second woe, behold, the third will come shortly.

[15] "Then the seventh angel sounded his trumpet and there were loud voices in heaven saying, 'The kingdom of this world has become the kingdom of our Lord and of His Christ and He will reign forever and ever.' [16] Then the twenty-four elders sitting on their thrones before God fell down on their faces and they worshipped God [17] saying, 'We thank You Lord God Almighty, the One who was and is, because You received Your great power and You reigned. [18] Now the nations became incensed; but Your wrath has come. The time has come to judge the dead and to reward your servants the prophets and the saints and all those fearing Your Name, the small ones and the big ones, and for destroying those who destroy the earth.' [19] Then the Temple of God in heaven was opened and the Ark of the Covenant was seen in His Temple. Then came lightening, rumblings, thunder, an earthquake and large hail."

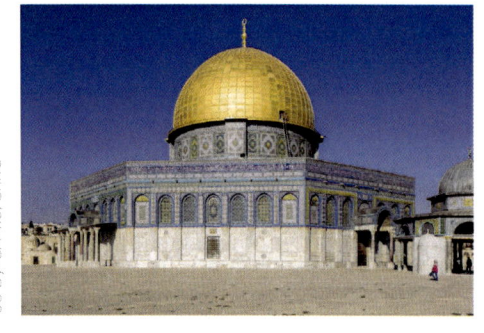

Dome of the Rock

I think the Antichrist brokers a peace between Israel and the Palestinians/the Muslims which allows the Islamic shrine, Dome of the Rock, (present today) to coexist with the rebuilt Temple. After the second Temple (Herod's) was destroyed by General Titus in AD 70, the Temple Mount was unoccupied until in AD 692

Two Jerusalem Prophets

when the first Islamic shrine was built over the Foundation Stone upon which Abraham offered up Isaac to Yahweh and where Muslim's believe Muhammed ascended into heaven assisted by the angel Gabriel.[136] However, the dome collapsed in AD 1015 and was rebuilt in AD 1023.[137] The Dome of the Rock is considered the third most holy site in the Muslim world behind the Kaaba in Mecca, the most holy site, and the Prophet's Mosque in Medina, the second most holy site.[138]

The Temple Movement in Israel has gained much momentum at present with the development of the Red Heifer program: transferring Red Angus cattle embryos from America to Israel and impregnating kosher heifers. This program is in its infancy with the first red heifer born in Israel in 2018. Before then, one had not been born in Israel for nearly two thousand years.[139] The red heifer program should result in many more kosher red heifers to facilitate the Yom Kippur sacrifices and others required by the Sacerdotal code from Moses (Numbers 19:1-10). The Temple Movement has also been developing the priestly skills of the Kohanim (priests) from the tribe of Levi-Aaron in the sacrifice of animals and in performance of the prayers and other rituals (such as the production of

Red Heifer

Larval Eggs

---

136   Amikam Elad, *Medieval Jerusalem and Islamic Worship: Holy Places, Ceremonies, Pilgrimage,* Islamic History and Civilization, Vol. 8, 1999, 2nd ed., 40–50.
137   Gulru Necipoglu, "The Dome of the Rock as Palimpsest: 'Abd al-Malik's Grand Narrative and Sultan Suleyman's Glosses," in *Muqarnas: An Annual on the Visual Culture of the Islamic World,* XXV. 17–90.
138   Chandler Stark, "The Holiest Sites in Islam," *Grunge,* accessed May 19, 2023, https://www.grunge.com/1089749/the-holiest-sites-in-islam/.
139   "Update on the Building of the Third Temple," *The Jewish Voice,* accessed July 17, 2021, https://www.jewishvoice.org/read/article/update-building-third-temple.

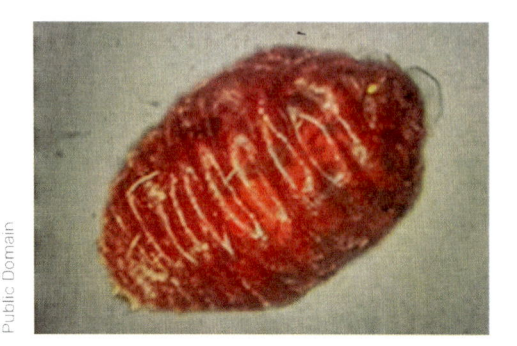

Crimson Worm

the sacred mikveh water for priestly ceremonial washings) for the successful resumption of Temple activity. Another recent development is the discovery that biblical crimson can be recreated with the use of the larval eggs of the crimson worm called *"tola'at shani."*[140] The deep red-bluish dye is made into a kosher dye for priestly garments, for the Holy of Holy's curtain, and for other priestly items. Researchers have found that pulverizing cochineal berries produces Biblical scarlet. The female crimson worm called Coccus ilicis (Heb. תּוֹלַעַת שָׁנִי, *tola'at shani*) attaches to the twigs and leaves of the palm-oak and lays its eggs (i.e., cochineal berries) from where they can be harvested to produce the kosher dye.[141]

The Israeli Temple Movement has already spent twenty-seven million dollars as of 2020[142] and expects to spend billions more for the actual rebuilding of the Temple. When Solomon built his Temple in the tenth century BC (recorded in 1 Kings 5-9), he used over eight million pounds of gold and over seventy-five million pounds of silver which calculates using gold and silver prices of today at over 194 billion dollars' worth of gold and about twenty-three billion dollars of silver. The over 150,000 laborers building the Temple and the other Temple materials including the bronze, cedar wood, iron, ivory and precious metals would push the price tag for Solomon's Temple at well over five-hundred billion dollars in today's money values.[143] Because rebuilding the Jerusalem Temple would be such a politically charged event, I believe that *only* the Antichrist will be able to appease the Muslim world and satisfy the Jewish leaders enough to allow for the reconstruction of the third Temple. However, I would expect the Dome of the Rock to coexist on the twenty or so acres of the Temple Mount with the newly rebuilt Temple for the Jews.

---

140 "Update on the Building of the Third Temple," *The Jewish Voice;* accessed July 17, 2021.
141 "Crimson," *Cyclopedia of Biblical, Theological, and Ecclesiastical Literature*, Bible Portal, John McClintock and James Strong, eds., accessed December 30, 2021, https://bibleportal.com/encyclopedia/cyclopedia-of-biblical-theological-and-ecclesiastical-literature/crimson.
142 "Final Preparations to Rebuild the Temple in Jerusalem," accessed July 17, 2021, https://www.bibleguidance.co.za/Engarticles/Temple-rebuild.htm.
143 Pita Kang and Red Johnson, "How much did Solomon's Temple cost?" *The Exodus Myth: A research resource for people on the quest for truth*, accessed December 30, 2021, https://exodusmyth.com/2017/07/29/how-much-did-solomons-temple-cost-pita-kang/.

I would have liked to see John's reaction when he saw the rebuilt Temple in this vision of the future after hearing about its total destruction by the Romans in AD 70. The Apostle made it clear that the Temple in Jerusalem is indeed standing before him because of the task he was given in his vision: "Rise up and measure the *Temple*

Foundation Stone of Dome of the Rock

of God, its altar, and those worshipping in it" (εγειρεκαι μετρησον τον ναον του θεου και το θυσιαστηριον και τους προσκυνουντας εν αυτω, v. 1). The process of measuring requires that John use a "measuring rod like a stick" (καλαμος ομοιος ραβδω, v. 1) which was given to him for this task of evaluation. Maybe the instrument was similar to the laser light measuring rod the angel gave him to calculate the dimensions of the New Jerusalem in Rev. 21:15–17. John is asked to measure two inanimate objects—the Temple and the altar. He would have been familiar with the quality of construction of the previous second Temple expanded and improved by Herod the Great. He likely would also have seen the altar for the sacrifice of the red heifer and other animals on the three great feast days when he would travel to Jerusalem with his family and relatives including with the young Jesus. Remember he was a first cousin to Jesus because his mother Salome was the sister to Mary. But the idea of "measuring" people is interesting. How could John measure people with a ruler? Maybe John's task is to simply count the number of worshippers in the Temple. Or maybe he was to evaluate their worthiness to worship there, particularly in juxtaposition to his divine directive to "exclude the outer court *and do not measure it because it has been given to the Gentiles*" (και μη αυτην μετρησης οτι εδοθη τοις εθνεσιν, v. 2). Gentiles were never allowed in the Temple by Jewish law except in the Court of the Gentiles outside the Court of Women. All Jews and Roman citizens living in Jerusalem during the days of the Temple understood that to go past the barriers erected separating the Court of Gentiles from the Temple proper would mean death as is confirmed by Josephus[144] and by the archeologic

---

144   Lawrence Schiffman, "Descriptions of the Jerusalem Temple in Josephus and the Temple Scroll," accessed July 18, 2021, http://orion.mscc.huji.ac.il/symposiums/4th/papers/Schiffman99.html; "Court of the Gentiles," *Bible History*, accessed May 20, 2023, https://bible-history.com/jerusalem/court-of-the-gentiles.

find in 1871 in Jerusalem of one of the Temple signs which warned Gentiles on pain of death not to pass the barrier. The archeologic find stated: "No foreigner is to go beyond the balustrade and the plaza of the Temple zone. Whoever is caught doing so will have himself to blame for his death which will follow."[145]

In verse 2, the "Gentiles" (εθνεσιν, v. 2) are represented by the Antichrist and his minions who, after allowing the Jews to rebuild their Temple which was destroyed in AD 70 by General Titus of the Roman Empire, defile it. We know from Revelation 13, from Jesus' words during His Olivet Discourse (Mt. 24:15), and from the prophet Daniel (Dan. 9:27; 11:31; 12:11) that the Antichrist will ceremonially defile the Temple by allowing the "second beast" (Rev. 13:11–15), also referred to as the "false prophet" (Rev. 19:20; 20:10), to set up an image of the Beast as an idol to be worshipped within the Temple. John was given a peek at the future Temple in Jerusalem by the command to him not to measure its outer court because pagans are allowed on its premises. In addition, John was told that the pagans will "trample the Holy City for forty-two months" (την πολιν την αγιαν πατησουσιν μηνας τεσσερακοντα δυο, v. 2) This refers to the Beast and his forces who oppose everything and anyone who align with God. The Beast opposes the two prophets of God who take up residence in Jerusalem as we see in a few verses. I'm sure God balances the bullying of the Beast with the brilliance and power of the two prophets. In fact, John stated that God gives these two prophets to the people of Jerusalem and to the world who "will prophesy clothed in sackcloth for 1,260 days" (προφητευσουσιν ημερας χιλιας διακοσιας εξηκοντα, v.3). Their prophecies and miracles are a formidable force in the world as John states in verse 10. They are opposed by the Antichrist and by the many he sends to try to kill the two prophets. But God calls these two servants His "two olive trees and two lampstands" (δυο ελαιαι και αι δυο λυχνιαι, v. 4). These images depict life/peace (olive tree of Zech. 4:3) and light (lampstands of Zech. 4:11). They are both dear and valuable to God.

Their identities may never be known. Some Revelation scholars have suggested that Elijah (who never died) and Moses (Mt. 17:1–3) appeared or that Elijah and Enoch who was an eyewitness to the angel-human race (Nephilim) and who could warn the world effectively of the demonic deceptions could be the two prophets

---

145   A. vander Nat, "Temple Warning Inscription," *Early Accounts of the Temple of Jerusalem*, accessed July 18, 2021, https://avande1.sites.luc.edu/jerusalem/sources/temple-warning.htm.

of Revelation 11.[146] However, I find it difficult to believe that God would allow any of his saints of the past to return to receive the "honor" of being persecuted and ultimately assassinated and left to rot in the streets of Jerusalem for three and a half days. I think that these two witnesses are powerful Jewish Christian prophets possibly from the original 144,000 of Revelation 7 who are sent to Jerusalem to protect it from destruction and defilement by the Antichrist and his henchmen. They live as "mouthpieces" for God and speak His Word despite the world's rejection and opposition in this time of sorrows. I think their three-and-a-half-year ministry begins shortly after they are commissioned (Rev. 7) following the sixth seal earthquake judgment on the earth and ends with their assassination sometime before their fellow Jewish Christians are slaughtered by the Beast in Revelation 14.

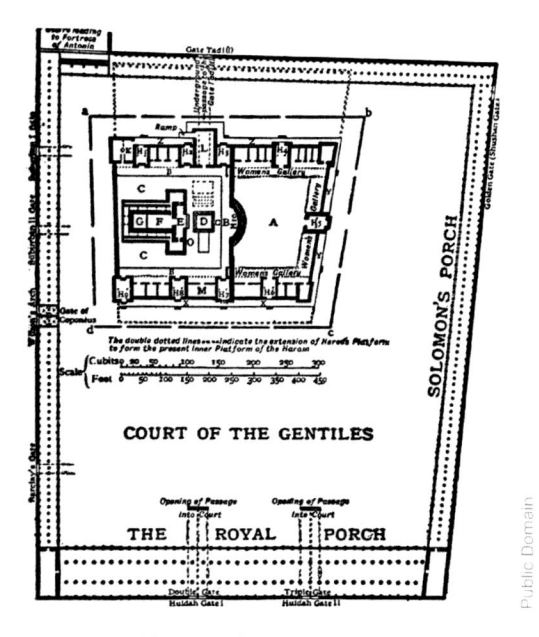

Diagram of Herod's Temple

Remember, prophets have the ability to speak God's thoughts for future events (foretelling) and His thoughts concerning past and present events (forth telling). The prophet is an integral part of the Kingdom of God and is critical in promoting Kingdom truths and revealing God's plans for future Kingdom building. These two prophets are God's mouthpieces who singularly dedicate their lives to proclaiming God's love and judgment on the world to whom they are sent. They are often persecuted and ostracized by pagans and sadly even ignorant Christians who don't understand the movement of the Holy Spirit and the passion of God for holiness and obedience. Prophets in John's day and in ours often lived and live solitary lives.

---

146   John MacArthur, "Who Are the Two Witnesses in Revelation 11," *The MacArthur New Testament Commentary*, quoted on Grace to You, accessed January 8, 2022, https://www.gty.org/library/bibleqnas-library/QA0087/who-are-the-two-witnesses-in-revelation-11.

Revelation: The Fifth Gospel

The Massacre of the Two Witnesses by the Beast, painted by Folio about 1255-1260.

The most dependable prophets are usually grounded under the authority of local church pastors even though their prophecies may have national or international relevance. The Apostle Paul revered God's prophets and honored the office of the prophet as depicted in his suggestion to the Corinthians that they all should strive to prophecy (2 Corinthians 14). Here in John's Revelation the prophet is also venerated in Revelation 10:7 and 11:18.

These two prophets represent God in the heart of the Middle Eastern world. Based on Revelation 19:10 ("the testimony of Jesus is the spirit of prophecy"), the gospel of Jesus is at the heart of all prophecy. Therefore, these two prophets represent the very heart and thoughts of the Lord. John described the constant danger that they face in this way: "If anyone wants to harm them, then fire comes out of their mouth and annihilates their enemies" (ει τις αυτους θελει αδικησαι πυρ εκπορευεται εκ του στοματος αυτων και κατεσθιει τους εχθρους, v. 5). Before their assassination, God felt that His message to the world through them was so important that He gave them the authority and power to protect themselves from the threats and attempts against their lives for the entire 1,260 days of their ministry. I wonder how many attempts to kill them occurred over this time. The world received many punishments for their actions against these two Jerusalem prophets including: drought for three and a half years (rain would not be sent for the days of their prophecy, v. 6), lethal "fire from their mouth," unpotable ground water (water changed to blood, v. 6), and other assorted plagues and environmental hardships not individually enumerated. John described that the two prophets were dressed in "sackcloth" which meant that they were mourning and likely *always* fasting. Their message to the pagan world was likely sorrowful, accusatory, and confrontational as can be ascertained by their clothes but also because of the reaction their audience gave them. You can also be sure that they will speak to their fellows Jews about Messiah Jesus and will always be willing to lead Jews, Muslims, and other pagans to faith in Christ Jesus during their ministry days in and around Jerusalem.

John told his reading audience that after the 1,260 days of their prophetic ministry was completed, God allowed the Antichrist/Beast to rise up from the Abyss and "make war against them, and will conquer them, and kill them" (ποιησει μετ αυτων πολεμον και νικησει αυτους και αποκτενει αυτους, v. 7). John continued by recounting details of the hate that the pagans of Jerusalem and the rest of the world have for these prophets by describing how the Beast and his security forces dishonored their bodies. The prophets' relatives and loved ones were not allowed to bury their sons who were assassinated on one of the main streets of Jerusalem. The Beast ordered that a squadron of soldiers, who likely were responsible for their deaths, be placed around the two prophets to prevent proper burial. (v. 8) They allowed passer-byes to gawk at their corpses which had rigor mortis after a day; they even "sent gifts to one another" (δωρα πεμφουσιν αλληλοις, v. 10) because they had been tormented so much by these two prophets (v. 10). But God had other ideas about His fearless martyrs. They are resurrected after three and a half days with the world watching through the news media, cell phones, twitter, etc. I believe that the Antichrist gave the orders not to bury the two prophets because he knew what Revelation states about these two rising into heaven, and he wanted to dare and maybe even prevent that from happening by refusing the normal formaldehyde perseverant during burial preparation, allowing their bodies to decay. We are not told what measures he used to ensure that their resurrection did not occur except for the refusal of a proper burial for them.

One clue that the Antichrist tried to prevent their resurrection was the utter fear and "terrified" reaction when the two prophets were raised from the dead as John reported in Revelation 11:11, 13. By these reactions, their enemies were very confident that the Beast's "resurrection prevention measures" were foolproof and ironclad. But God's will was to frustrate the Beast and circumvent his and his pagan minions' ideas about who was in charge of these prophets and whose power was preeminent. The Holy Spirit breathed life into their dead bodies depicted by John as, "the breath of life from God entered into them and they stood on their feet" (πνευμα ζωης εκ του θεου εισηλθεν εν αυτοις και εστησαν επι τους ποδας αυτων, v. 11). Then John reported that a voice called for them out of heaven. A cloud then encircled them as they rose into heaven, likely with the help of cherubim in full view of the shocked world (v. 12). John made it clear that "indeed their enemies watched them" (και εθεωρησαν αυτους οι εχθροι αυτων, v. 12) which could only mean that the Beast, his assistants, and security officers were watching their ascent very intently. Maybe they were relieved and hopeful that the prophets' influence over the world and the frustrations in dealing with their miracles had finally come to an end and

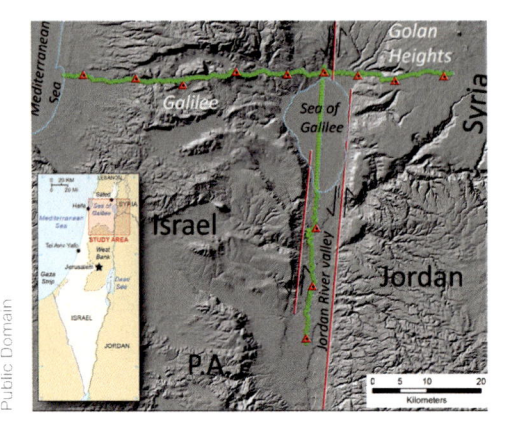

Dead Sea Fault Line

that their political, economic, and religious systems would now be unopposed. Whatever their hopes, these were dashed because within the next hour a massive earthquake shook downtown Jerusalem killing seven thousand people and destroying one tenth of the city (v. 13). John remarked that the rest of Jerusalem citizens were terrified with these signs from heaven and even gave honor to the God of heaven—at least for a short period of time after the earthquake.

Seismologists have studied the Great Rift Valley which is a 10-meter-wide separation between the African and the Eurasia Tectonic Plates running 3,000 miles from Syria through Jerusalem (as the Dead Sea Fault) down to Mozambique, Africa. This Great Rift has caused earthquakes in Jerusalem every eighty years or so. One was even mentioned by Zechariah when King Uzziah reigned which was estimated to be from 7.8 to 8.2 on the Richter scale (Zechariah 14:5). This fault line, which passes through Jerusalem near the Temple Mount area, rivals the San Andreas Fault.[147] Certainly the Great Rift-Dead Sea fault line will be activated by an angel or the Holy Spirit to wreak havoc on the Beast and his forces for murdering arguably the two greatest prophets of modern times. The Apostle John remarked that these events capped by the tremendous quake and loss of life in the Holy City are the second woe. He warned of the third woe occurring soon thereafter.

---

[147]   Amotz Agnon, "Earthquakes in Jerusalem: Geological Insights From the Bible," *Israel Today*, February 8, 2023, accessed June 9, 2023, https://www.israeltoday.co.il/read/earthquakes-in-jerusalem-whens-the-next-big-one/.

The Seventh Trumpet Judgment

John continued the post-earthquake vision by switching the setting of the Apocalypse from the city of Jerusalem to heaven. John observed the seventh angel blowing his trumpet. Remember the mighty angel of chapter 10 stated that in the days when the seventh angel blew his trumpet the mystery of God would be fulfilled (Rev. 10:7). The "mystery of God" likely refers to the events which John described at the end of chapter 11. John stated that he heard voices in heaven which proclaim the Lord's dominance on the earth: "The kingdom of this world has become the kingdom of our Lord and of His Christ and He will reign forever and ever" (εγενετο η βασιλεια του κοσμου του κυριου ημων και του Χριστου αυτου και βασιλευσει εις τους αιωνας των αιωνων, v. 15). The elders who seem to know about all of the major events before they take place express their understanding about what is about to happen. John reported their words as the following: "We thank you Lord God Almighty, the One who was and is, because You received Your great power and began to reign" (ευχαριστουμεν σοι κυριε ο θεος ο παντοκρατωρ ο ων και ο ην οτι ειληφας την δυναμιν σου την μεγαλην και εβασιλευσας, v. 17). They continue their perceptive worship of the Father and insight about His future actions by stating, "Indeed, the nations have become incensed" (και τα εθνη ωργισθησαν, v. 17). John observed that the elders have noticed at this time near the end of the Time of Sorrows that the pagan nations have lost their patience and have become furious with God. Remember, just as recently as a few verses and maybe a few hours to days previously, the Beast, his personal forces, and his allies from Europe and the Asian nations had "honored the God of heaven" (εδωκαν δοξαν τω θεω του ουρανου, v. 13) when they saw and heard about the resurrection of the two assassinated Jerusalem prophets and the great Jerusalem earthquake (v. 13). But the last three years were quite eventful—featuring the execution of the seal and trumpet judgments resulting in seven twelfths of the world's population's deaths (one quarter in Rev. 6:8, plus one-third in Rev.9:15). John indicated that although the seal and trumpet judgments were meant to punish godlessness, they were also meant to attract pagans to the God of heaven and His Son. The world was at times impressed with the events of the judgments (vis-à-vis their fear of the Lamb and the Father in Rev. 6:15–17), but ultimately rejected and became very antagonistic toward the Conquering Messiah. Here in Revelation 11, we see their disregard for God and His purposes for the earth and oppose Him by killing His prophets and other saints as we see in Revelation 13 and beyond.

Revelation: The Fifth Gospel

But John told his reading audience that the elders tell Father God that it is now time to do what He was reluctant to do when the martyred saints under the altar ask Him to take revenge on the pagans who killed them and their fellow believers in the future (Rev. 6:10-11). The twenty-four elders implore an angry God, "it is now time for You to judge the dead and to reward Your servants the prophets and the saints and those who fear your Name both great and small and *to destroy those who destroy the earth*" (διαφθειραι τους διαφθειροντας την γην, v. 18). Several other Scriptures intimate that God judges those who abuse the earth (e.g., Jer. 12:10-13, Ps. 73). But here, John reported the most direct relationship between God's judgment and those who destroy His creation. It is very clear that the world is on a collision course with the Godhead. Not only is it evident that the Beast has organized the nations into a loosely federated alliance that will become much more closely aligned by Revelation 13, but that the pagan inhabitants of the earth have been abusing it. John heard the elders state that God will destroy them for destroying His earth.

Even in this day, the world has become a very polluted place—its oceans are filled with plastics, chemicals, sewage, oil, fertilizers, and thermal/fossil fuel waste causing eutrophication (resulting in decreased ocean oxygen) and acidification (resulting in increased carbonic acid in the oceans resulting in fewer coral colonies/ coral reefs and shellfish). The amount of plastic polluting the ocean is staggering— eight million tons of plastic thrown into our oceans annually. By the year 2025, this will triple to nearly twenty-five million tons per year. By 2025, plastic pollution in our oceans will outweigh ocean fish by three times.[148]

Then the Temple in heaven opened and the Ark of the Covenant is revealed (v. 19). John's Revelation is the only place in the New Testament where the Temple in heaven and its Ark are actually seen. The Ark on earth, the Tabernacle Ark constructed by Moses after seeing the real Ark in heaven, contained manna, the Ten Commandments, and Aaron's rod (Heb. 9:4). I believe that these objects signify Jesus, the Father, and the Holy Spirit, respectively. I can only speculate about what may be in the Ark of Heaven. It may be that the same objects in Moses' Ark are in the heavenly Ark. However, nothing, or perhaps other objects may be in the heavenly Ark. The important point is that the Lord opens heaven and shows His Ark,

---

[148] Diptarka Ghosh, "The Causes and Effects of Ocean Pollution," *World Atlas*, accessed July 24, 2021, https://www.worldatlas.com/articles/what-causes-ocean-pollution.html#:~:text=%20Causes%20of%20ocean%20Pollution%20%201%20Dumping.

demonstrating His covenant commitment to His people. Though the time of the End is near, the open Temple shows that the Lord still desires new converts, even after the death of His two dearest prophets and His fierce anger over their deaths. These men are probably the finest examples of prophet the world has ever seen. They both demonstrated patience, love, and the other fruit of the Spirit despite their constant abuse by the culture of the world and the oppression of the Antichrist. Indeed, they defended themselves during their 1,260 day witness period but only because their testimony was necessary to touch Jerusalem Jews and Muslims and to expand God's kingdom there. They were desperate to promote God's word and demonstrate His love because they understood that their time and the world's time was short.

John closed out his remarks in Chapter 11 by mentioning severe weather events in verse 19, "then came lightening, voices, thunders, an earthquake, and large hail" (και εγενοντα αστραπαι και φωναι και βρονται και σεισμος και χαλαζα μεγαλη, v.19). Bad weather in Revelation always precedes or succeeds God's judgment (Rev. 6:12–17, 8:1–5). The New Jerusalem days of Revelation are fast approaching in heaven's time as indicated by the acceleration of John's commentary throughout the next few chapters; earth time, as we know it, is drawing to a close. John next reviewed the previous Age of the Patriarchs with its connection to Mary and the Messiah. He also reviewed the fall of Lucifer and his angels as well as a future war in heaven between Satan and his fallen angels and the forces of the Conquering Messiah and His angels. The development and future of the Church including its Jewish and Gentile roots are discussed in this seminal twelfth chapter of Revelation.

REVELATION 12

Satan's Fall and Expulsion from Heaven

The Survival of the Church

1 "Then a great sign appeared in heaven: a woman clothed with the sun and the moon underneath her feet and a crown of twelve stars on her head. *2* And being pregnant, tormented with her pregnancy, and about to deliver, she cried out with birth pains. *3* And another sign appeared in heaven: behold, a big fiery red dragon with seven heads and ten horns and seven crowns on his heads. *4* His tail dragged one third of the stars from heaven and flung them to the earth; then the dragon stood before the woman about to deliver so that he could devour when she gave birth. *5* Then the woman gave birth to a Son, a male child, who was about to rule all of the nations with a rod of iron, but her child was snatched up to God and to His throne; *6* then the woman fled into the wilderness to a place prepared for her by God that they might take care of her for 1,260 days. *7* Then war broke out in heaven; Michael and his angels fought against the dragon; and the dragon and his angels fought back. *8* But he was not strong enough; and their place in heaven was no more. *9* The great dragon was thrown out; that ancient serpent also known

> as the devil and Satan, who deceived the whole world, was thrown onto the earth and his angels were also thrown out with him.
>
> [10] "Then I heard a loud voice from heaven saying, 'Now has come the salvation, the power and the kingdom of our God and the authority of His Christ; indeed, the accuser of our brothers has been thrown out, the one accusing them before our God, day and night. [11] And they overcame him by the blood of the Lamb and by the word of their testimony; and they did not love their lives above death. [12] Therefore, rejoice heavens and those living in them but woe to the earth and the sea because the devil has come down to you, having great fury and knowing he has little time.' [13] When the dragon realized that he was thrown onto the earth, he pursued the woman who gave birth to the male child. [14] But she was given two wings of the great eagle so she could fly away to her wilderness place where she was taken care of for a time, times, and half a time [three and a half years] out of reach of the serpent. [15] But the serpent spewed water like a river out of its mouth to overtake the woman and sweep her away in its torrent. [16] But earth helped the woman by opening its mouth and swallowing the river that the dragon spewed from its mouth. [17] Then the dragon became furious with the woman and left her to make war against the rest of her offspring, those obeying God's commands and holding on to the testimony of Jesus. [18] Then the dragon stood on the seashore."

Revelation 12 is probably the most difficult of all the chapters of Revelation to understand and interpret. Some sections are symbolic, some sections have literal meaning, and some may have elements of both. In Chapter 10, a voice told John to prophecy against the world because of the treachery against His Church, His Temple, and His Holy City (Jerusalem). The remaining chapters (12 through 19), particularly with the execution of the vial judgments (16), illustrate the bitterness of John's task.

John told his reading audience that he next sees a great "sign" (σημειον, v.1) in heaven. He saw, "a woman clothed in the sun with the moon under her feet and a crown with twelve stars on her head" (γυνη περιβεβλημενη τον ηλιον και η σεληνη υποκατω των ποδων αυτης και επι της κεφαλης αυτης στεφανος αστερων δωδεκα, v.1). John was very intentional in using the term "sign" in describing the woman because, although his vision involved a woman, he knew that she represented *people* and/or *concepts*. John was always very specific when he described actual events or when he described symbols. He told his reading audience the meaning of symbols when it was necessary. But here, John indicated that the "woman" and the "dragon" (δρακων, v.3) are metaphors for concepts and for individuals. The "woman" represents the plan of God as expressed through the nation of Israel, Mary, and the Church. She is clothed with the sun illustrating the light of the Gospel which she will share with the world. She has twelve stars in her crown representing the twelve tribes of Israel. She has the

Woman of the Apocalypse

moon under her feet, possibly representing the dominance over Islam. The moon has been a symbol found on early Islamic coins by AD 695.[149] The Seljuk Turks introduced the crescent moon into Islam in the twelfth century as a symbol of their nation which was continued by the Ottoman Turks who conquered them. The Egyptians, Pakistanis, and other Islamic states adopted the moon symbol on their flags by the early twentieth century.[150] The moon may also represent the dominance of God's plan even over nature. John noticed that "[the woman] being pregnant, about to deliver and tormented with her pregnancy cried out with birth pains" (και εν γαστρι εχουσα και κραζει ωδινουσα και βασανιζομενη τεκειν, v. 2). This brings to mind Mary as she delivered Jesus and the Satanic opposition through Herod

---

[149] Richard Ettinghausen, "Hilal," Encyclopaedia of Islam, 2nd ed., Vol. 3, B. Lewis, V. L. Ménage, Ch. Pellat, and J. Schacht, ed. (Leiden, Netherlands: E. J. Brill, 1986), 381–385, accessed May 19, 2023, https://archive.org/details/ei2-complete/Encyclopaedia_of_Islam_vol_3_H-Iram/page/n1/mode/2up, in Patricia Baker, "What is the origin of the crescent moon symbol seen throughout Islamic cultures?" Notes and Queries, accessed July 25, 2021, The Guardian, https://www.theguardian.com/notesandqueries/query/0,5753,-1411,00.html.

[150] William G. Crampton, "What is the origin of the crescent moon symbol seen throughout Islamic cultures?" Notes and Queries, *The Guardian,* accessed July 25, 2021, https://www.theguardian.com/notesandqueries/query/0,5753,-1411,00.html.

and his henchmen during His first two years (Mt. 2:12–18). The pregnant woman may also represent God's plan of salvation (*Hielsgeschichte*) including the ministry, death, burial, and resurrection of our Lord Jesus and the "birthing" of the Church at Pentecost as well as His preservation of the remnant of Israel.

The big, fiery red dragon (δρακων μεγας πυρρος, v. 3) with seven heads, seven crowns on his heads and ten horns is the second sign that John mentions in his chapter 12 vision. The dragon represents Satan—his work of treachery and subterfuge to undermine God's plan is symbolized by the seven-headed and ten-horned red dragon symbolizing the previous seven dominant kingdoms: Egypt, Assyria, Babylon, Media, Persia, Greece, and Rome with ten presiding kings (horns) during the reign of these kingdoms. Immediately John noted that "his tail dragged one third of the stars from heaven and flung them to the earth" (και η ουρα αυτου συρει το τριτον των αστερων του ουρανου και εβαλεν αυτους εις την γην, v. 4) referring to the fall of Lucifer mentioned by Isaiah and Ezekiel.

We assume that God made Lucifer with a free will. Moses reported in Genesis 1:27 that God chose to make man in His image which would include instilling free will within him and then allowing him to exercise his will without divine control. We assume that God's angels also have free will and the ability to exercise this divine privilege whenever and wherever they choose to do so. Despite all the promise of Lucifer as one of three archangels and his role as God's angel worship leader, despite his proximity to God and the richness of his home, and despite his superior intellect and insight into all things spiritual, he began to move away from the Lord as he became self-absorbed and enamored with himself. I think it simply amazing that the all-knowing God created His most loved angelic being with the potential to sin. The Lord even knew that Lucifer would be the source of all things evil in the universe even before He created him. Yet He allowed Lucifer to exist and loved him with a perfect love before Lucifer's sin.

In Ezekiel 28:11–19, Ezekiel prophecies about the King of Tyre, who embodied the history of the archangel Lucifer in a microcosm. The prophet told us that the King of Tyre/Lucifer was:

> *the seal of perfection, full of wisdom and perfect in beauty. You were in Eden, the Garden of God; every precious stone adorned you: carnelian, chrysolite and emerald, topaz, onyx, and jasper, lapis lazuli, turquoise, and beryl . . . you were anointed as a guardian cherub, for so I ordained you. You were on the holy mount of God (Ezekiel 28:12–14, NIV).*

The King of Tyre could not have really been all these things. But God's number one archangel demonstrated all of these attributes and then some. I think it very interesting that God allowed Lucifer (i.e., "light bearer" and "morning star") to be closest to Him and most like Him despite knowing that Lucifer would one day sin and turn away from His unconditional love for him. He even allowed Lucifer to help Him organize and develop the Garden of Eden before He placed Adam there—maybe even helping God plant the Tree of Life and the Tree of the Knowledge of Good and Evil. As we see in Revelation 21, the nine precious stones which are the foundations of the city walls and which Lucifer wore could have been used to refract light waves as we see with our present-day lasers. Maybe Lucifer helped the Lord in the Garden of Eden by receiving God's light energy through these stones to refract them as in a portable mini-laser of sorts to construct, cut, and create the most perfect Garden for their future human guests.

But then our omniscient God allowed Lucifer to experience sin as we see from the passage in Isaiah 14. Lucifer began to regard himself not only as the top angel in beauty and function but as God's equal. Maybe we can't blame him for becoming somewhat narcissistic because he was responsible for arguably the most important job in the universe—the choir director of all the angel worship. So, the most beautiful being in God's creation began to notice how good he looked. Lucifer eventually developed frank pride in his worth which led to coveting God's position in the universe. His self-talk reflects these dangerous self-conscious musings according to the prophecy that Isaiah made about the king of Babylon in Isaiah 14:12–14:

> "You said in your heart, '*I* will ascend to the heavens; *I* will raise my throne above the stars of God; *I* will sit enthroned on the mount of assembly . . . *I* will ascend above the tops of the clouds; *I* will make myself like the Most High'" (NIV, emphasis added).

Clearly these thoughts reflect Lucifer's willingness to leave the comfort and security of his place/abode in heaven, his position in relationship to his brother archangels and other angels, his prestige and worth in the kingdom, and ultimately his relationship to the Triune God. Billy Graham in his classic book, "Angels," states that Lucifer's **five "I's"** of this passage in Isaiah constituted a rebellious state: "He exulted at the thought of being the center of power throughout the universe—he wanted to be the Caesar, the Napoleon, the Hitler of the entire universe."[151] God chose not to intervene as He watched His most promising creation slide down the slippery slope of self-indulgence, pride, and eventually outright rebellion against His God. God chose to allow Lucifer to rebel against Him and even take the angels committed to him from their creation in his rebellion described in Revelation 12:4, "Its [the dragon's] tail dragged a third of the stars of heaven and hurled them onto the earth."

So when Satan sinned by coveting God's power and authority, he was thrown out of his position in heaven. One third of the angels who aligned themselves with him were also thrown out of heaven onto the earth permanently—the so called First Heaven War. The Apostle made no mention of the struggle between Lucifer and God during this first expulsion from his position in heaven. After Satan took his angels with him to the earth, John stated that Satan, as the dragon in his vision, then "stood before the woman about to give birth so that he could devour when she delivered" (εστηκεν ενωπιον της γυναικος της μελλουσης τεκειν ινα οταν τεκη το τεκνον αυτης καταφαγη, v. 4). He and his fallen angels centered their efforts on the earth in attempts at frustrating God's plan including Satan's desire to identify and kill the baby Jesus as the Apostle John indicates in verse 4. But the birth of the newborn King took Satan off guard. He likely expected the Messiah to be born in Herod's Palace. It appears that Herod the Great's wives and their children had Satan's attention as their lives were marked by imprisonment and death at the hand of their husband/father who trusted no one and lived a paranoid life. He put to death his three sons Alexander (7 BC), Aristobulus IV (7 BC), and Antipater II (4 BC). In jealousy, he executed his second wife Mariamne I (29 BC). As soon as the devil figured out that the Messiah was born in Bethlehem as he learned from overhearing the conversation between Herod and the wise men from the East, he prompted Herod to send out the Temple guard which slaughtered all the boys in the Bethlehem area who were two years of age and younger (Mt. 2:16–18) as previously mentioned.

Satan continued his harassment of Jesus throughout His lifetime. We have no record of how the devil may have tempted or frustrated the Christ as a boy. But during Jesus' ministry—immediately after His baptism starting with His forty days of fasting in the wilderness and continuing on throughout His three and a half years

---

151   Billy Graham, *Angels: God's Secret Angels*, (Nashville, TN: Thomas Nelson, 1995), 61.

of ministry including His death, burial, and resurrection—it was apparent that Jesus was more than Satan's match even in His human form.

The apostle continued the saga of the dragon by mentioning that the woman successfully delivered the Christ child and that "He was about to rule all of the nations with a rod of iron; but her Child was snatched away/up to God and to His throne" (ος μελλει ποιμαινειν παντα το εθνα εν ραβδω σιδηρα και ηρπασθη το τεκνον αυτης προς τον θεον και προς τον θρονον αυτου, v. 5). The Greek word for "snatched away/up" (αρπαζω) is also used by the Apostle Paul in his first letter to the Thessalonians concerning the Rapture of believers to meet Jesus in the clouds and then forever be with Him (1 Thess. 4:17). The snatching up of the child, in this context, would refer to Jesus' ascension after His resurrection and to the Rapture revealed by Paul to the Thessalonians. But despite losing the opportunity to defeat Jesus and His Church with His ascension and their future Rapture, the dragon continues to thwart the Kingdom of God and the Conquering Messiah's work in the hearts' of humans by nurturing the development of the Occult, the Church of Satan, the media, the Internet, and through Satanic oppression and possession of various individuals.

As is apparent in Revelation 12, after Satan was censored and his angels expelled from God's presence, his main role was "the accuser of the brothers" continually before God, day and night. Jesus, as part of the Triune God, created Lucifer and knows Satan better than any person in the universe. He stated in John 10:10 that the thief (Satan) "comes to steal and kill and destroy." From the account in Revelation 12 and from other passages in Scripture, it is apparent that Satan fulfills at least three roles:

1. Satan acts as a prosecuting attorney against the Church and its members before the Court of Heaven and its Judge.
2. Satan also uses his considerable intelligence and leadership skills to thwart God's plan on earth by *stealing* the Church's possessions and members, by *killing* human beings (mind, soul, and spirit), and by *destroying* Kingdom thoughts, hopes, dreams, and the earth's beauty and resources mediated through his direction of his fallen angels.
3. Satan also directs, to some degree, his church called the Church of Satan. As the Church of Satan does not publicly release membership information, it is not known how many members belong to this church. However

according to an interview with the Church of Satan, "interest in the Church of Satan and Satanism is growing all the time if our mailboxes, answering and fax machines, and email is any indication."

After the ascension of Christ and His departure from the earth, John stated that the woman "fled to the desert to a place prepared for her by God so that they could take care of her for 1,260 days" (εφυγεν εις την ερημον οπου εχει τοπον ητοιμασμενον απο του Θεου ινα εκει τρεφωσιν αυτην ημερας χιλιας διακοσιας εξηκοντα, v. 6). From the context of the previous verses and the departure of the Messiah "child," the woman, now representing Christendom, also removes herself from the dragon threat. She flees to the wilderness/desert seemingly to a place described later in the chapter as not accessible by the "serpent" (v. 14). In fact, verse 14 expands on the manner in which she flees—by using "the two wings of the great eagle" (αι δυο πτερυγες του αετου του μεγαλου, v. 14). I'm wondering if the "great eagle" might be a reference to the United States and our only stated role in Revelation. If the woman represents the surviving Church during the tough years of the seal and trumpet judgments after the Rapture of the Church in Revelation 7, then the work of the 144,000 Jews for Christ was successful in re-evangelizing America or whoever else assists the "woman" in her efforts to flee. "Fleeing" also raises the question of why? If the woman represents the Jews for Christ and their fellow converts, why would they fear death? In fact, the Revelation 12 narrative states that those Christians living on the earth after the dragon has been permanently thrown out "did not love their lives above death" (ουκ ηγαπησαν την ψυχην αυτων αχρι θανατου, v. 11). More than likely, the choice to flee was meant to frustrate the plans of the devil. The devil wanted to kill the woman as we can see from his actions in trying to drown the woman in verse 15. Dead Christians can't evangelize a desperate but receptive world. However, despite fleeing to a safe place, maybe with the help of America's Air Force, these Christian leaders can utilize the Internet and other platforms of communications effectively spreading the Good News throughout the world. Maybe the United States gives sanction to these brave, Messianic Jews because of our long history of supporting Israel. The Apostle told us that the woman stays in her sanctuary for 1,260 days, exactly the same period of time that the two prophets of Revelation 11 execute their ministry. It would not be surprising if the two "super" prophets in Jerusalem communicate strategy, exchange encouragement, and cover the sequestered wilderness team with prayer and vice versa throughout their forty-two months of ministry time. The wilderness Church likely die martyrs' deaths just as their two brothers of Revelation 11 experience. I think we see a glimpse of their martyrdom in Revelation 14.

Eventually, probably during the early part of the Great Tribulation Period or slightly before it begins during the latter months of the Time of Sorrows, Michael and his angels launch an attack on Satan and overcome him. I wonder what an angel war looks like. Certainly, no nuclear warfare. But likely much action and likely hand-to-hand combat. There might even be thought or word sparring. However, no matter how angels fight, Satan is not strong enough to contend with Michael. John reported this in verse 7: "War broke out in heaven; Michael and his angels fought against the dragon; and the dragon and his angels fought back, but he was not strong enough" (εγενετο πολεμος εν τω ουρανω ο Μιχαηλ και οι αγγελοι αυτου του πολεμησαι μετα του δρακοντος και ο δρακων επολεμησεν και οι αγγελοι αυτου, και ουκ ισκυσεν…vv. 7-8). This is the Second Heaven War and results in Satan's *permanent* expulsion from heaven as reported by John who had seen the tremendous power Jesus used during His earth ministry when exorcising demons from unfortunate souls. John's apocalyptic narrative continues: "the great dragon was thrown out, the ancient serpent, the one called the devil and Satan, the one who deceives the whole world, *he was thrown onto the earth, and his angels were thrown out with him*" (εβληθη εις την γην και οι αγγελοι αυτου μετ αυτου εβληθησαν, v. 9). We know that this time Satan was permanently expelled from heaven and forever denied access to God because his plaintiff role as the accuser of the brethren before God was permanently suspended as we see in the next verse: "Now has come the salvation, and the power, and the kingdom of our God and the authority of His Christ because *the accuser of the brethren has been thrown out, the one accusing them day and night before our God*" (εβληθη ο κατηγωρ των αδελφων ημων ο κατηγορων αυτους ενωπιον του θεου ημων ημερας και νυκτος, v. 10). Satan now spends all his time on earth, no longer able to bring accusation of sin and shortcoming before Father God. Because the Accuser can bring no more accusation, Jesus' time is now better spent at finishing the New Jerusalem and organizing and training His heavenly army to engage Satan in Armageddon I and II, which comes in Revelation 19 and 20, respectively. The earth is warned of Satan's heightened efforts to derail God's plan. John mentioned that the devil takes stock of no longer having access to heaven and God's presence. Because of his expulsion, the devil understands that "his time is short" (ολιγον καιρον εχει, v. 12) causing him to immediately attack the woman and "her offspring" (του σπερματος αυτης, v. 17) with "great fury" (θυμον μεγαν, v. 12). Despite Satan's fury, the elect conquer him with two elements of the Kingdom that can never be overcome by the devil or his minions: "the blood of the Lamb and the word of their testimony" (το αιμα του αρνιου και δια τον λογον της μαρτυριας αυτων, v. 11). Jesus' death on the cross marked by the shedding of His sinless blood fulfilled all requirements

Revelation: The Fifth Gospel

for a Perfect Sacrifice once and for all for all accommodating but sinful humans (cf. Hebrews 10:8-10). The devil therefore has no more claim on those "bought with a price" (1 Cor. 6:20) and who think, speak, and act out the Word in their lives. The angel through whom God is giving the Apocalypse likely explains to John the thinking of the devil as he is repelled by the faith and obedience of even those who are martyred for their faith—all of the 144,000 of Revelation 7 and 14. John told his reading audience that when the devil realized that as a result of his expulsion from heaven he no longer had access to his estranged Father God, he decided to "pursue the woman who had given birth to the male child" (εδιωξεν τυν γυναικα ητις ετεκεν τον αρσενα, v. 13).

At this point in the history of the Church, "the woman" would be the Christian survivors of the terrible trumpet judgments including the 144,000 completed Jews who are "following Jesus wherever He goes" (ουτοι οι ακουλουθουντες τω αρνιω οπου αν υπαγη, Rev. 14:4). As previously mentioned, the ancient serpent's pursuit of these super-evangelists during their ministry and other believers ultimately forces them into a wilderness sanctuary site possibly in western United States such as Area 51 for 1,260 days (vv. 6, 14). The mention of the woman using two wings of the great eagle "to fly" (πετομαι, v. 14) to the sanctuary site suggests a massive airlift. As previously suggested, I would not be surprised if the United States Air Force was responsible for "Operation Israelis for Jesus"! John indicated that the woman flies to her desert place where she stays "away from the face of the serpent" (απο προσωπου του οφεως, v. 14). The serpent does not give up his relentless search for the underground church. In fact, John's narrative indicates that the serpent eventually *knows* where the woman fled because it knows where to direct "the water like a river to sweep her away" (v. 15).

John next saw a vision of a torrent of water like a river being spewed out of the serpent's mouth "in order to carry away the woman in its torrent" (ινα αυτην ποταμοφορητον ποιηση, v. 15). Maybe the water coming out of the serpent's mouth is John's first century understanding and vocabulary describing a nuclear cloud or plume detonating in the area of their wilderness hideout. It is possible that the torrent really *is* water since John described what he wanted his reading audience to take literally and specifically explained what is symbolic in his Apocalypse. Here in two successive verses, John mentioned the "river" (ποταμον, vv. 15-16) coming from the serpent/dragon's mouth and being "swallowed" (κατεπειν, v. 16) by the earth. I favor the perspective that the river is a considerable flood possibly released from a nearby dam like the Hoover Dam or a large dam like it which threatens "the woman" where she is hiding. The earth then opens its mouth to help the woman by "swallowing the river spewed from the dragon's mouth" (κατεπιεν τον ποταμον ον εβαλεν ο δρακων εκ του στοματος αυτου, v. 16). Maybe the United States opens one of its many underground water reservoirs. This action would dissipate the threat by containing the water. Maybe Revelation experts were consulted about the role the United States will take with End-Time events, and with this knowledge, thwart what the devil may try to do in Area 51 against its valuable "asset."

Area 51 in Nevada

The western United States have struggled with generations of drought. Most of the major cities there have developed large underground reservoirs to collect the rain that falls in large amount during only a few weeks out of each year. The underground reservoirs reduce the large amount of water evaporation which occurs in open, above ground reservoirs.[152] One or a few of these underground *empty* reservoirs around the sanctuary site would certainly offer a solution in protecting the valuable Kingdom guests attempting to stay alive for Christ from a significant flood threat. John states that despite the peril to their lives from the "water like a river" (v. 15), the underground saints survive—for now.

John made it clear that the dragon is incensed at being outfoxed by the earth and those aiding its quarry. The dragon left the woman to make "war against the rest of her offspring" (πολεμον μετα των λοιπων του σπερματος αυτης, v. 17). He also made it clear that her offspring are truly committed believers undeterred by Satan's threats and undiscouraged by all their brothers and sisters martyred for Christ. John stated that the offspring of the woman include those "who obey God's commands and who hold onto the testimony of Jesus" (τηρουντων τας εντολας του θεου και εχοντων την μαρτυριαν Ιησου, v. 17). I find it amazing that the two

---

[152] "UST [Underground Storage Tanks] Finder," Environmental Protection Agency, accessed June 9, 2023, https://www.epa.gov/ust/ust-finder; https://epa.maps.arcgis.com/apps/webappviewer/index.html?id=b03763d3f2754461adf86f121345d7bc.

most important believer qualities to the Godhead—obedience and faithfulness—are also the two easiest attributes for believers to inculcate into their lives—even easy for the children who follow Christ to demonstrate in their lives.

In summary, we see that the woman (representing the Church) with the help of two wings of the great eagle (United States Air Force planes; Area 51 in Nevada?) flees to a desert environment to avoid persecution from the dragon. Curiously, the earth opens its mouth to absorb the river which the dragon sends after the woman to engulf her. Could the "earth opening its mouth" indicate a massive underground water reservoir system surrounding extensive underground bunkering where the saints are protected to avoid previous and future nuclear warfare? For reasons that we will see later in the Apocalypse, God protects the woman for 1,260 days against the unholy trinity of Satan, the Antichrist, and the prophet who eventually beheads/annihilates "her" (the 144,000 Jewish Christian evangelists) by Revelation 14.

REVELATION 13

Rise of the Antichrist Beast

The Rise of the False Prophet

The Abomination of Desolation

1 "Then I saw a beast rise up out of the sea with seven heads and ten horns and blasphemous names on its heads and ten crowns on its horns. [2] And the beast I saw was like a leopard with feet like a bear's and with a mouth like a lion's. And the dragon gave his power, throne and great authority to the beast. [3] But one of the beast's heads was like slaughtered to death; but he was healed of his fatal wound and the whole earth was amazed at the beast and followed after him. [4] Indeed, they worshipped the dragon because he gave his power to the beast and they worshipped the beast saying, 'Who is like the beast and who has the power to make war against him?' [5] The beast was given a mouth speaking proud things and blasphemies and he was given authority for forty-two months. [6] He opened his mouth speaking blasphemies against God, against His Name, against His throne, and against those living in heaven. [7] He

> was given (authority) to make war against the saints and to conquer them; he was also given authority over every tribe, people, nation, and language. ⁸ And all those living on the earth worshipped the beast whose names are not written in the Book of Life of the Lamb, who was slaughtered from the creation of the world. ⁹ The one with an ear, pay attention. ¹⁰ If anyone is to go into captivity, into captivity he will go, and if anyone is to be killed by the sword, by the sword he will be killed. This situation calls for patient endurance and faith on behalf of the saints.
>
> ¹¹ "Then I saw another beast coming up out of the earth and he had two horns like a lamb but he spoke like a dragon. ¹² And he performed on behalf of the authority of the first beast, and he forced the world and its inhabitants to worship the first beast who was healed of his fatal wound. ¹³ Then he (the false prophet) performed great signs; indeed he even caused fire to fall from the sky to the earth before the people. ¹⁴ And he deceived those living on the earth by the signs given to him to perform before the beast. And he told those living on the earth to make an image of the beast who had the wound of the sword yet lived. ¹⁵ Further, he was given authority to give breath to the image of the beast so that the image of the beast could speak. And he also was given the power to kill those who refused to worship the image. ¹⁶ Then he made all (people), including the small ones and the big ones, the rich and the poor, and the freedmen and the slaves to receive a mark on their right hand or on their foreheads, ¹⁷ so that they could not buy or sell except the one with the mark, which is the name of the beast or the number of its name; ¹⁸ this requires wisdom. If anyone has insight, let him calculate the number of the beast, which is the number of a man; that number is 666."

The Church has been raptured (Rev. 7) and the Antichrist has been influencing the world scene indirectly since Revelation 6:1-2 as the white horseman. The 144,000 Jewish Christians sealed with a special anointing by the Holy Spirit (Rev. 7:4-8) have been assisting the two Jerusalem Jewish Christian prophets with evangelism and judgment against the world and its culture and have been bringing many millions to decisions for Christ. However, Satan begins to relentlessly attack these Jewish Christian evangelists, recently converted Jews, representing true Israel, and the pagans who have become Christians since Revelation 7. But God has engineered an airlift, possibly through the United States, providing refuge in the "desert" for the "woman" of Revelation 12 as the two prophets carry on their ministry in Jerusalem during the Time of Sorrows of the Tribulation period (1,260 days). The Apostle told us that the dragon stood on the seashore in the previous chapter because he was anticipating the appearance of the Beast from somewhere in the sea. Satan, as the dragon, ushers in the outwardly defiant and ferocious Beast from the sea as John described him. Remember earlier in Revelation 11, the Beast was exposed as a terrible threat to the Kingdom by ordering the assassination of the two Jerusalem prophets. Before the events of Revelation 11, the world considered the white horseman to be just the right person to bring economic prosperity to the world creating optimism and international peace. Indeed, this Beast even brokered a peace of sorts between Israel and the Palestinians and the Muslim world allowing for the building of the third Temple in Jerusalem as we see in chapter 11. However, the seal and trumpet judgments began to erode his international popularity; but not among his peers in the international banking and political world. He continued to create liaisons and build trust and confidence among his peers. Eventually he became their leader—maybe in an organization such as the EEC (European Economic Community).

John began his comments concerning the emerging Beast in the following manner: "Then I saw a Beast rising up out of the sea having seven heads with blasphemous names on them and ten horns with ten crowns on his horns" (v. 1). Maybe the Antichrist comes from the islands off the coast of Italy like Sardinia or Corsica. Or he may come from one of the countries bordering the oceans such as Italy, Portugal, or Greece, or maybe comes from an underwater community which our world has not yet developed. Indeed, the dragon was watching on the seashore as the Beast was "rising up" (αωαβαινον, v. 1) from the sea. He has seven heads which could symbolize Rome (city on seven hills). As previously mentioned in Revelation 12, the seven heads of the Beast who is Satan's understudy could represent the same empires: Egypt, Assyria, Babylon, Media, Persia, Greece, and Rome. This Beast also has ten horns which could represent ten presiding kings (horns) comprising a federation of nations set up by the Beast. These "horns" give allegiance to the Beast particularly after his apparent assassination. These heads of state are signified by the ten *diadem* crowns worn on their heads. John uses the Greek word διαδηματα (diadem crowns, v. 1) to illustrate that this type of crown is only worn by the supreme leader of each state/nation. The Beast's heads have "blasphemous names" written on them indicating his intentions to thwart the purposes and plans of the Kingdom of God. The Apostle described that his body is that of a leopard (Greece?), his feet is like a bear's feet (Medes-Persia?), and his mouth like a lion's mouth (Babylon?). Maybe these animals indicate the type of Beast the world will begin to see. The leopard is known for its stealthy, strategic behavior. The bear's feet may indicate strength and stability in the face of opposition. The lion's mouth is known to be very dangerous and lethal to its victims. The connection between the dragon and the Beast is confirmed by John's next statement: "And the dragon gave his power, his throne, and his great authority to him [the beast]" (και εδωκεν αυτω ο δρακων την δυναμιν αυτου και τον θρονον αυτου και εξουσιαν μεγαλην, v. 2).

The Antichrist probably unifies the world through political and economic hard times from his appearance in Revelation 6 to the end of the first half of the Tribulation period. He has considerable influence granted him by Satan as we see from 13:2. But that influence becomes markedly more because of what John describes next. I suspect that he will be an influential member or the president of the European Union and, as just mentioned, will already have brokered peace between Jews and Arabs when he is unexpectedly assassinated. I suspect that after his work in facilitating the rebuilding of the Temple in Jerusalem, an assassin is sent from one of the radical Muslim fringe jihadist groups or the assassin is a Jewish nationalist working largely on his own. John describes that fateful day this way: "But one of its heads was like slaughtered to death; but his fatal wound was healed" (και μιαν εκ των κεφαλων αυτου ως εσφαγμενην εις θανατον και η πληγη του θανατου αυτου εθεραπευθη, v. 3). In my opinion, the Antichrist becomes the "son" of Satan, the Beast, by the beginning of the second half of the Tribulation period (known as the Great Tribulation Period) when he assassinates the two Jewish Billy Graham Jerusalem prophets in *Revelation* 11. But, "what goes around comes around." The Beast is assassinated in the first portion of verse 3. However, it appears that Satan intervenes and miraculously heals him. It is very clear that in the future world of the Apocalypse, the news media, global Internet, and satellite systems for communication are at optimum effectiveness. When the Antichrist is assassinated, the world immediately hears about it and may even see it (e.g., President John F. Kennedy, November 22, 1963). The text indicates the world is amazed by what transpires. John explained: "but his fatal wound was healed and the whole world was amazed and they followed after the beast" (και η πληγη του θανατου αυτου εθεραπευθη και εθαυμασθη ολη η γη οπισω του θηριου, v. 3). The world was shocked by the Beast's assassination but amazed by his resuscitation. Gunshot wounds to the head are nearly uniformly fatal with victims dying 95 percent of the time.[153] John later in the chapter stated that the Beast experienced "the wound of the sword" (πληγην της μαχαιρης, v. 14) which can also be fatal but not as frequently fatal as cerebral gunshots. Of course, guns were not present in John's world because they did not appear until the fourteenth century.[154] But John may have actually meant a sword or long dagger for the would-be murder weapon used to try to kill the Beast based on John's tendency to describe exactly what he sees when his vision is not symbolic. He reported the attempted murder with very specific detail which makes me think that the beast's assassin used a sharp object and not a projectile. However, the attempt on his life was made and executed, and the world was "amazed" at his miraculous recovery and survival. It would be very likely that the wound of the sword was healed by the dragon/Satan himself since the dragon has so much invested in his understudy. John stated that the world's citizens "followed after the Beast" (οπισω του θεριου, v. 3) as a result of his miraculous recovery. John then explained some of the specific dynamics of the relationship that the dragon had with his apprentice, the Beast/Antichrist and the relationship the Beast had with his subjects.

As previously mentioned, the Beast received all of his supernatural leadership qualities from Satan: he was noted to have the power, the position (throne of the dragon), and the "great authority" of the dragon. He also had tremendous military power as we see from the John's observation that the public commented, "who has the power to make war against him?" (τις δυναται πολεμησαι μετ αυτου?, v. 4). No other *current* position of authority could be like John's description of the Beast except the leader of the present European Economic Community or the President of the United States. The Beast has ten horns and ten crowns which could possibly be symbolizing ten countries with ten rulers/presidents of those countries under his authority. The European Economic Community, now known as the European Union, presently has twenty-eight members, six original charter members, and seven original free trade members. But as *Megiddo*, one of the best movies produced about the End Times and rise of the Antichrist,[155] depicts, the Beast divides the world into ten sections with ten rulers over those sections of the world.

---

153 Vaishnavi Patil, "Gunshot to the Head: Does It Always Mean Instant Death?," Science ABC, Jan. 14, 2021, accessed August 4, 2021, https://www.scienceabc.com/humans/gunshot-to-the-head-does-this-mean-instant-death.html.

154 "Gun Timeline," *History Detectives*, PBS, accessed August 4, 2021, https://www.pbs.org/opb/historydetectives/technique/gun-timeline/#:~:text=Historical%20timeline.

155 *Megiddo: The Omega Code 2*, directed by Brian Medwin Trenchard-Smith (2002; Hollywood, CA: Gener8Xion Entertainment, 2002), DVD.

European Union

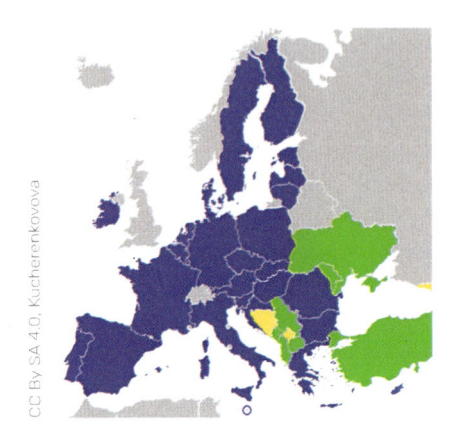

The European Union

To become a member of the European Union, an interested country must meet the Copenhagen criteria[156] developed in a meeting of the European Council in Copenhagen in 1993.[157] These criteria demand a stable democracy that respects human rights and the rule of law, a functioning market economy, and the acceptance of the obligations of membership—including European Union law. The European Council gives a periodic review of each European Union member country. No member state has ever left the Union except for Great Britain recently (2020)[158] and Greenland (an autonomous province of Denmark) which left the European Community in 1985.[159] The Lisbon Treaty now contains a clause providing for a member to leave the European Union.[160] Presently the "euro" is the currency for the European Union which generates around $16.89 trillion dollars (US dollars) in 2021,[161] slightly less than the United States income of 23.54 trillion dollars in 2021.[162]

---

[156] "European Neighourhood Policy and Enlargement Negotiations, European Commission, accessed May 23, 2023, https://neighbourhood-enlargement.ec.europa.eu/enlargement-policy/conditions-membership_en.

[157] Matthew J. Gabel, "European Union," Encyclopaedia *Britannica*, accessed May 23, 2023, https://www.britannica.com/topic/European-Union.

[158] "Brexit: UK Leaves the European Union" BBC News, 1 February 2020, accessed May 23, 2023, https://www.bbc.com/news/uk-politics-51333314.

[159] Henry Bodkin, "Greenland showed how to leave Europe as far back as 1984," *The Telegraph*, 24 June 2016, https://www.telegraph.co.uk/news/2016/06/24/greenland-showed-how-to-leave-europe-as-far-back-as-1984/ (accessed May 23, 2023).

[160] Michael Ray, "Lisbon Treaty," *Encyclopaedia Britannica*, November 24, 2022, accessed May 23, 2023, https://www.britannica.com/event/Lisbon-Treaty.

[161] "European Union GNP 1972-2023," *Macrotrends*, accessed May 23, 2023, https://www.macrotrends.net/countries/EUU/european-union/gnp-gross-national-product.

[162] "U.S. GNP 1962-2023," *Macrotrends*, accessed May 23, 2023, https://www.macrotrends.net/countries/USA/united-states/gnp-gross-national-product.

The Beast had a winsome personality to pagans but an aversive one to Christians and to the Godhead. John described the Beast's relationship with God and His allies: "And he was given a mouth to speak blasphemies and proud things . . . *he opened his mouth in blasphemy against God, blaspheming His Name, the Temple, and those living in heaven*" (ηνοιξεν το στομα αυτου εις βλασφημιας προς τον θεον βλασφημησαι το ονομα αυτου και την σκηνην αυτου τους εν τω ουρανω σκηνουντας, vv. 5–6). By this time in his political life, the Beast does everything to ingratiate himself to the leaders who support him and to the people across the globe who long for an answer to the world's economic and social problems. His intellect is superior to most who have come before him. The nations are quick to follow his programs for success and stability at the cost of freedom and independence. The Apostle John made it clear in this portion of the text that the Beast has preeminent international influence and power for forty-two months; the apostle stated, "And he was given a mouth to blaspheme and to speak proud things, and he was given authority for forty-two months" (και εδοθα αυτου στομα λαλουν μεγαλα και βλασφημιας και εδοθα αυτου εξουσια ποιησαι μηνας τεσσαρακοντα δυο, v. 5). John made it clear that now the assassinated official, likely involved in international political affairs before the attempt on his life, after his healing will be an extension of Satan for the next three and a half years. This period of time corresponds to the worst of the Tribulation referred to by theologians as the Great Tribulation Period.

From this point in the narrative, the Beast wages a political and economic war against the surviving Church. Eventually he begins to physically persecute and "conquer them" (νικησαι αυτους, v. 7). I would assume that "conquering" not only means imprisoning Christians, but also killing them as John stated in verse 15. The world begins to "worship" (προσκυνεω, vv. 4, 8) the Beast for all he does for them and against their enemies of the Church of Jesus Christ. John was clear to state that these are those "whose names are not written in the Lamb's Book of Life" (ου ου γεγραπται το ονομα αυτου εν τω βιβλιω της ζωης του αρνιου, v. 8). John Calvin would be pleased with these words depicting predestination which he thought was one of the major thrusts of God's covenant relationship with each believer, but which also explained the impossibility of some unbelieving souls from ever entering the Kingdom. By this time in the Great Tribulation Period, those predestined for Hell will dominate the activities of nations as they all follow the Beast and his magnetism. At this point in his apocalyptic narrative, John emphasized the inevitability of trauma and death to the redeemed: "If someone is to be taken into captivity, into captivity he will go; and if someone is to be killed by the sword, by the sword he will be killed" (ει τις εις αιχμαλωσιαν εις αιχμαλωσιαν υπαγει ει τις εν μακαιρη αποκτανθηναι αυτον εν μακαιρη αποκτανθηναι, v. 10). John's statement here leaves the reader with no doubt that persecution of believers will not bring with it intervention from God to reverse their fortunes, which is why John here interjects the phrase, "This situation requires patient endurance and faith on behalf of the saints" (ωδε εστιν η υπομονη και η πιστις των αγιων, v. 10).

John continued his report of this critical time by discussing the rise of the false prophet. Remember that Satan began his life around the Godhead—Father, Son, and Holy Spirit. It is understandable for him to want to mimic this formidable Trinity with one of his own. John stated, "And I saw another beast rise up out of the land, and it had two horns like a lamb but he spoke like a dragon" (και ειδον αλλο θηριον αναβαινον εκ της γης και ειχεν κερατα δυο ομοια αρνιω και ελαλει ως δρακων, v. 11). The second beast that John described does not look at all imposing like the first Beast with seven heads and ten horns. In fact, he appeared to be a gentle lamb with two horns. But John was quick to add that his voice was like a dragon—like Satan's. In other words, he was definitely from the same ilk as the Antichrist Beast but with a "golden tongue" who could persuade pagans to do about anything. The second beast, also identified as the "false prophet" (ψευδοπροφητης, Revelation 19:20; 20:10), was quick to solidify his appeal and persuasiveness with the world's pagans by performing unbelievably flashy miracles. John even mentioned that the false prophet "caused fire to fall from the sky to the earth before the people" (πυρ ποιη εκ του ουρανου καταβαινειν εις την γην ενωπιον των ανθρωπων, v. 13). John explains that the second beast's miracles caused mental assent and eventually deception of the whole world (v. 14). All this was necessary to motivate them to follow his command "to build the image of the beast" (ποιησαι εικονα τω θηριω, v. 14). The false prophet's tactic of using the miraculous to establish an *emotional* connection with the people *before* establishing mental rapport was the opposite of how Jesus treated His disciples. Jesus did not perform His first miracle at Cana until preaching and teaching His followers for nearly a year. He wanted to make sure that they assented mentally to His presentation of the Kingdom of God and accepted Kingdom values *before* solidifying their faith and trust in His being and character with miracles. He understood that miracles without teaching and the experience of encounters with Him often create relationships which are shallow, short-term and emotionally based. These are often unsustainable connections between the divine and the human. It appears that the false prophet is only interested in promoting outward allegiance and acquiescence to execute his plan to alienate the world from God and to institute worship of his boss the Antichrist in the newly constructed Temple.

A series of miracles beginning with the Beast brokering peace between Jews and Muslims, which paves the way for the construction of the Third Temple on the Temple Mount in Jerusalem, the miraculous recovery of the Antichrist from a head shot with "the wound of the sword" (την πληγην της μακαιρης, v. 1), and numerous miracles by the false prophet prepares the world for the false prophet's suggestion that they honor the first Beast with an idol commemorating his recovery and greatness. But the false prophet knew that it would be difficult to require worship of the Beast without first having somewhere for the whole world to worship him. As previously discussed, the second Temple was destroyed by General Titus and the Roman forces in AD 70. The Mosque of Omar built in AD 1023 and refurbished in AD 1193 has occupied the Temple Mount ever since.[163] But due to extraordinary efforts on behalf of the Beast and his prophet, the Muslims in charge of the Mosque agree to share the Temple Mount area and allow the Jews to rebuild their Temple, making it possible to fulfill prophecies from Daniel (Dan. 8:13, 9:27, 11:31, 12:11) and from Jesus (Mk. 13:14; Mt. 24:15) as regarding an idol built and placed inside the Temple.

The Prophet curried so much respect and favor with the Jews that they evidently allowed him to create an idol of the Beast with the help of robotic and artificial intelligence engineers. The Apostle John reported that "he told those living on the earth to make an idol of the Beast who had the wound of the sword yet survived" (λεγων τοις κατοικουντας επι της γης ποιησαι εικονα τω θηριω ος εχει την πληγην της μαχαιρης και εξησεν, v. 14). In this passage of Revelation 13, John did not reveal *where* the image of the Beast is placed. But we can surmise from Jesus' words recorded in the Gospels and from the passages in Daniel that the Beast commanded his image to be placed in the Third Temple, likely in the most important place on the planet for the Jews— the Holy of Holies. The Jews recently impressed with the Antichrist's skill and magnanimity, see his true motives and disregard for their religion. Despite their objections, the false prophet places the idol in the Holy of Holies in the newly built Jerusalem Temple and, to their horror, require all people to worship it. The idol likely is a robot-like humanoid with artificial intelligence (AI) able to speak to the worshippers of the Beast and his false prophet (v. 15). Maybe the superior intelligence and tracking methods contained in the idol's optic system can not only track mental assent in the confines of the Temple but could also track

---

163   Jerome Murphy-O'Connor, *"Two Mosques," The Holy Land: An Oxford Archaeological Guide from Earliest Times to 1700*. Oxford Archaeological Guides. (Oxford, England: Oxford University Press, 2008), 62-63.

response remotely through Internet computer connections throughout the world. Somehow, those refusing to worship the idol will be identified and killed by orders of the prophet: *"And he was given authority to give breath to the image of the beast so that the image of the beast could speak* and also was given the authority to kill those who refused to worship the image" (και εδοθη αυτου δουναι πνευμα τη εικονι του θηριου ινα και λαληση η εικων του θηριου, v. 15). This passage would have seemed fantastical to all generations reading John's account of this "abomination of desolation" in the Jerusalem Temple. But twenty-first century humans can readily see how John's description of the idol could exhibit the newer AI and mind reading capabilities being developed in today's computers. Computer engineers and designers are raising the possibility of "recursive self-improvement" (the ability of the AI to reprogram itself to exponentially improve performance)[164] and brain-computer interface capabilities (interfacing human neurons with AI technology from Elon Musk's company Neuralink and others).[165] The physicist Stephen Hawking warned about artificial intelligence stating,

> *The development of full artificial intelligence could spell the end of the human race. Once humans develop artificial intelligence, it will take off on its own and redesign itself at an ever-increasing rate. Humans, who are limited by slow biological evolution, couldn't compete and would be superseded.*[166]

Hawking was concerned about the concept of "technological singularity" which is artificial intelligence's ability to improve itself without human interference also described as "recursive self-improvement," as I have just mentioned.[167] Maybe by this time in the Apocalyptic future, the computers within robot-like devices possess superhuman intelligence with the ability to manage humans even in the realm of obeisance/worship and also in the management of economic activity as indicated in Revelation 18.

---

164   Stephen M. Omohundro, "The Nature of Self-Improving Artificial Intelligence: What Are the Potential Benefits and Implications?". October 27, 2007, presented and distributed at the 2007 Singularity Summit, San Francisco, CA, accessed May 23, 2023, https://medium.com/@emergingtechnology/the-nature-of-self-improving-artificial-intelligence-2a4b69bdd160.

165   Elon Musk, Neuralink, "An integrated brain-machine interface platform with thousands of channels," bioRxiv, Cold Spring Harbor Laboratory, accessed July 18, 2019, https://www.biorxiv.org/content/10.1101/703801v2.

166   Rory Cellan-Jones, "Stephen Hawking warns artificial intelligence could end mankind," *BBC News*, 2 December 2014, accessed October 30, 2015, https://www.bbc.com/news/technology-30290540.

167   Stuart J. Russell and Peter Norvig, *Artificial Intelligence: A Modern Approach*, 2nd ed. (Hoboken, NJ: Prentice Hall, 2003), 963.

With his great miracle working power, the prophet convinces the world to follow the Beast's economic program including requiring all to receive a computer chip on their foreheads or right dorsal hands with the number of his financial empire in the chip: 666. The chip technology is now widely used throughout the world as RFID (radio frequency identification) microchip implants in pets, Alzheimer's patients, livestock, and in cars.[168] I believe that verses 16–17 refer to the supranational currency (to some degree already developed in the European Union, i.e., the euro or throughout the world with bitcoin) that the Antichrist brilliantly forces onto the world as a foolproof way to avoid thefts that even John reported takes place during these times in Revelation 9:21. Eventually, this chip credit card implantation method allows for worldwide control of commerce and an exclusion of all those wary of the Beast who refuse to receive it underneath their skin: "Then the beast made all those living on the earth both great and small, rich and poor, free and slave receive a mark on their right hand or forehead *so that they could not buy or sell without having the mark which is the name of the beast or the number of its name*" (ινα μη τις δυνηται αγορασαι η πωλησαι ει μη ο εχων το χαραγμα το ονομα του θηριου η τον αριθμον του ονοματος αυτου, vv. 16–17). This "command economy" of the Beast (more fully discussed by the Apostle John in chapter 18) has already to some degree been introduced by the Chinese Communist Party through Mao Tse Tung in the early 1950s and is practiced by Iran, Belarus, and Cuba.[169] In 2020, China became even more controlling of its economy by instituting a Social Credit System within their national banking system for their citizens which is a national credit rating program based on gathered personal banking, employment, salary, and medical data. This system rates each individual's compliance with Chinese Communist Party (CCP) laws and standards and has generated a national blacklist of thirteen million people and a whitelist as well.[170] In case the reading audience of this Revelation passage believes that our generation of consumers will never see this, we have only to consider what is being discussed in our own country. American airline companies, major sports teams, and large businesses required

---

168 Angell, I., Kietzmann, J., "RFID and the end of cash?," *Communications of the ACM*. December 2006, 49 (12): 90–96, accessed May 23, 2023 https://web.archive.org/web/20140224155226/http:/beedie.sfu.ca/files/Research/Journal_Articles/Journal_Articles_misc/RFID_and_the_end_of_Cash.pdf.

169 Kimberly Amadeo, "What is a Command Economy," *The Balance*, August 7, 2022, , accessed from the internet on February 19, 2022, accessed May 23, 2023, https://www.thebalance.com/command-economy-characteristics-pros-cons-and-examples-3305585#:~:text=Here%20are%20examples%20of%20the%20most%20well-known%20countries,having%20suffered%20starvation%20during%20World%20War%20I.%20.

170 Louise Matsakis, "How the West Got China's Social Credit System Wrong," *Wired*, 29 July 2019, accessed May 23, 2023, https://www.wired.com/story/china-social-credit-score-system/.

their employees to receive COVID-19 vaccinations and documentation of these before continuing employment. Our federal government has mandated that all federal employees get COVID vaccinations and boosters and that these records be kept in a national data bank. However, the Supreme Court[171] and Texas Supreme Court[172] have suspended for now the implementation of this mandate due to too much OSHA control over personal liberties.

Many scholars and theologians have speculated about the "name of the beast and the number of his name" (v. 17). Some have suggested that the Beast will have a name which has letters which add up to 666 (gematria).[173] Some suggest that because 666 corresponds to the numerical values of the Greek translation of "Nero Caesar" that the beast must come from an Italian lineage with royal history.[174] Others suggest that 666 refers to an antichrist-like figure because 6 is the epitome of an imperfect number; others feel that 666 probably refers to the number of years, months, or days of the reign of the kingdom or family responsible for bringing the Antichrist into the world. The French seer Nostradamus (1503–1566) predicted floods in Europe and a twenty-seven year war before the Antichrist rises to power.[175]

Command Economy

- ✓ Government generates economic plan
- ✓ Government allocates resources of state according to this plan
- ✓ Government creates regulation and policies concerning the execution of this plan
- ✓ Government decides how the products of the economy are disseminated to the citizens and who does or who does not receive these products
- ✓ Government makes all economic decisions and
- ✓ Government prevents free market economy forces from "interfering" with the economic plan

Author

---

171 Dave Jamieson, "Supreme Court Blocks Biden's Vaccine or Test Rule For Large Employers," *New York Times*, Jan. 13, 2022, accessed May 23, 2023, https://www.nytimes.com/2022/01/13/us/politics/supreme-court-biden-vaccine-mandate.html.

172 Dave Jamieson, "Biden's COVID Vaccine Mandate For Federal Workers Blocked Temporarily in Court," *HUFFPOST*, January 21, 2022, accessed May 23, 2023, https://www.huffpost.com/entry/bidens-covid-vaccine-mandate-for-federal-workers-blocked-temporarily-in-court_n_61eb23b8e4b0b7eb1cd5052c.

173 Michal Hunt, "The Gematria of the Number of the Beast—666," Agape Bible Study, 2002, accessed May 23, 2023, https://www.agapebiblestudy.com/charts/Gemetria%20and%20the%20Number%20of%20the%20Beast%20666.htm.

174 Craig Koester, *Revelation: A New Translation with Introduction and Commentary*, The Anchor Yale Bible Commentaries (New Haven, CT: Yale University Press, 2014), 598.

175 Peter Lemesurier, *The Unknown Nostradamus: The Essential Biography for His 500th Birthday* (Winchester, Hampshire, UK: John Hunt Publishing, Ltd., 2003), xii–xviii.

But I doubt the validity of this "prophecy" for a number of reasons including his own rejection of the title "prophet."

Whoever the Antichrist is, John's description of his personality reveals that he was very verbal and likely highly critical and verbally abusive of Christians and the Kingdom but highly persuasive to his circle of leaders and their subjects. He will have a winsome personality which influences his ally, the false prophet also with a persuasive nature, who helps the Beast broker peace between Jews and Muslims. All of these End-Time developments including the rebuilding of the Third Temple in Jerusalem, the assassination and recovery of the Beast, and the institution of beast worship (the abomination of desolation) will occur with little or no insight or awareness from the pagan population. I think the global satellite communication systems, news media, Internet services, and computer search engines have little if any connection to the biblical and apocalyptic literature when these events transpire due to the censuring of anything related to Jesus and His Kingdom for decades. If God's Word was to be available to the people of the Beast's circles and the pagans of the time, much would be done to attempt to *avoid* the events John described in this chapter including the assassination of the Beast. As the Revelation unfolds, John continued the discussion of the worldwide influence of the Beast. He described "the unholy trinity's" three areas of worldwide influence in *Revelation* 17–19 as religious Babylon, economic Babylon, and political Babylon. The following is a summary of the Beast's influences in these three realms:

- *Religious Babylon* (Rev. 17) centers on the worldwide religious worship of the Beast starting with his idol in Jerusalem and propagated through "the harlot" described by John in *Revelation* 17 which some scholars identify as the Catholic Church centered in Rome and will be under direct control of the *prophet.*

- *Economic Babylon* (Rev. 18) centers on the *Beast's genius* as demonstrated in his leading of the EEC/EU to economic viability as the white horseman of Revelation 6. The Beast also leads the world back to some semblance of economic health with his institution of world currency marked by the global computer chip technology and bitcoin or something like it as mentioned in Revelation 13:16–18. But the worldwide economy is devastated by the catastrophic event described in Revelation 18—likely the cataclysmic megaquake of Revelation 16:18-21 inducing a nuclear power plant disaster or possibly even a nuclear attack on the capital city of economic Babylon.

- *Political Babylon* (Rev. 19) centers on the comment from John in verses 4-7 that the world follows the Beast because they realize that they cannot wage successful wars against the Beast and his allies. They therefore join his political machine by allowing him to organize and finance their armies as we see in Revelation 19. Of course, behind the Beast's power and authority is the Dragon, Satan himself, who the pagans unabashedly worship due to Satan's healing of the Beast whose life was threatened by the fatal wound discussed in verses 3-4.

REVELATION 14

Jewish Christian Martyrs

Last Great Christian Harvest

Second Judgment Seat of Christ

¹ "And I looked and behold the Lamb standing on Mt. Zion and with Him the 144,000 with His Name and the Father's Name written on their foreheads. ² Then I heard a voice from heaven like the sound of many waters, like the sound of loud thunder, the sound I heard was similar to the sound of harpists playing their harps. ³ And they sang a new song before the throne and before the four living beings and before the elders; and no one could learn the song except the 144,000, the ones redeemed from the earth. ⁴ These are those undefiled by women, because they are virgins, and these are those who follow the Lamb wherever He goes, these are purchased from mankind and are the first fruits to God and to His Christ. ⁵ They are blameless because no lie is found in their mouths.

⁶ "Then I saw another angel flying in mid-heaven with the eternal Gospel to proclaim to those residing on the earth, indeed to every

tribe, people, nation, and language. ⁷ And he shouted with a loud voice, 'Worship God and give Him glory because the hour of His judgment has come; indeed, worship Him who created the heaven, the earth, the sea, and the fountains of water.' ⁸ And then I saw another angel, the second one following saying, 'Fallen, fallen is Babylon the Great who made all the nations drink the maddening wine of her fornication.' ⁹ And then a third angel followed them and cried out, 'If anyone worships the beast or his image and receives the mark on his forehead or his hand, ¹⁰ then he himself will drink from the wine of the fury of God poured undiluted into the cup of His anger and he will be tormented with fire and brimstone before the holy angels and before the Lamb. ¹¹ And the smoke of his torment will rise forever and ever. And to those who worship the beast and his image and receive the mark of his name, he will not sleep day or night forever and ever.' ¹² This situation requires patient endurance on behalf of the saints who hold on to God's commands and have faith in Jesus. ¹³ Then I heard a voice from heaven say, 'Write, "Blessed are the dead, those who have died in the Lord from this day forward."' Then the Spirit said, 'Yes, because they will have rest from their labor and their works will follow them.'

¹⁴ "Then behold, I saw a white cloud and One like the Son of Man sitting on it with a golden crown on His head and a sharp sickle in His hand. ¹⁵ Then I saw another angel go out of the Temple calling out to the One sitting on the cloud, 'Swing your sickle and reap because the time to reap has come since the earth's harvest became ripe.' ¹⁶ Then the One sitting on the cloud swung His sickle on the earth and the earth was harvested. ¹⁷ Then another angel went out of the Temple in heaven with a sharp sickle. ¹⁸ And another angel with authority over the fire from the Altar shouted to the angel with the sharp sickle saying, 'Swing your sharp sickle and pick the grapes from the earth's grapevine because they have become ripe.' ¹⁹ So the angel swung his sickle on the earth and plucked the earth's grapevine and threw it into the great winepress of God's fury. ²⁰ And the winepress was trampled outside the city and the blood came out of the winepress as far as the horses' bridles 1,600 [180 miles] stadia away."

Jewish Christian Martyrs

The Apostle John continued his narrative by switching his attention from the Antichrist and his activities in Jerusalem and around the earth to heaven. John saw "Mt. Zion" (το ορος Σιων, v. 1) where the 144,000 sealed and delivered Jewish Christian evangelists from every tribe of Israel (Rev. 7:3-8) were standing. In contradistinction to the seal/mark of the Beast on the foreheads of all those following the Beast (Rev. 13:16-17), John knew that these are the Israeli Christians for Jesus he described to his reading audience because Father God's name and the Lamb's name were "written on their foreheads" (γεγραμμενον επι των μετωπων αυτων, v. 1).

Mount Zion is the center of the activities of heaven and identified by many of the prophets as the seat of the throne of God, the Father (e.g., Ps. 9:11; Is. 8:18; Joel 3:21). Earth's Mt. Zion is Mt. Moriah on which Abraham sacrificed Isaac, where the Jebusites lived, and where present-day Mosque of Omar is standing. David conquered the Jebusites and built his city of Jerusalem there. Mt. Zion in Revelation 14 refers to the heavenly Mt. Zion because the 144,000 Jewish Christian Evangelists by this time have been martyred by the Beast as we see in verse 3 ("redeemed from the earth") and verse 4 ("purchased from mankind, the first fruits to God and to the Lamb"). By Revelation 14, the Antichrist martyrs the 144,000 completed Jews who now stand victorious before the throne of God in heaven. John then noticed a peculiar sound that he relates reminds him of "the noise of a cataract/waterfall/many waters" (φωνην υδατων πολλων, v. 2) and the "sound of great thunder" (φωνην βροντης μεγαλης, v. 2). He expanded his description of the heavenly sound by stating that the noise reminds him of "harpists playing on their harps" (κιθαρωδων κιθαριζοντων εν ταις κιθαραις αυτων, v. 2). The noise is a victory song unheard of before and impossible for other redeemed Christians to learn because these 144,000 martyred Christians experienced extreme, extraordinary suffering from the Antichrist (v. 3). John stated that these unusually dedicated Christians from the twelve tribes of Israel were sexual virgins because they were preoccupied with pleasing Him and very sensitive to the leading of His Holy Spirit: *"These are those undefiled by women, because they are virgins*, and these are those who follow the Lamb wherever He goes, these are purchased from mankind and are the first fruits to God and to His Christ" (ουτοι εισιν οι μετα γυναικων ουκ εμολυνθησαν παρθενοι γαρ εισιν, v. 4). Some have suggested that their dedication gauged by their sexual purity was more symbolic than practical. But as previously indicated, the Apostle always tells his reading audience when he writes symbolically, which is not indicated here. John also stated that these Christians were particularly worthy to be a "first fruit offering to God and to the

Lamb" (απαρχη τω θεω και τω αρνιω, v. 4). Nothing was more important in their lives than seeking the face of God and following Jesus wherever and whenever He led them. John also indicated that not only were their actions above reproach, but that their words were blameless: "no lie was found in their mouth because *they were blameless*" (αμωμοι εισιν, v. 5).

It is easy to see the tremendous spiritual impact of these Charismatic, Spirit-led believers whose main desire was to introduce pagans to Jesus and turn their fellow Jews to Christ. They were so effective at evangelism that they were singularly hated by the devil and his minions of fallen angels. As discussed in chapter 12 through the symbolism of "the woman," these 144,000 were an integral part of the Church and are pursued by the Beast *after* the Rapture (Rev. 12:13). As expressed earlier, I think the United States Air Force performs an airlift to whisk away a large number of these Jewish Christians from the Antichrist's grasp to allow them to continue their tremendously successful evangelization of the world now more dominated by the Beast than ever before (Rev.12:14). Maybe in an underground bunkering system (Area 51 in Nevada?), they facilitated through the Internet or other media avenues the greatest harvest of souls for Christ the world has ever seen as John described in verses 15–16. The Beast and his religious lieutenant, the false prophet, eventually decided to end these evangelists' lives. I believe they were beheaded by contract assassins from the Muslim world and likely murdered by hitmen from religious Babylon who could be from the Catholic Church or from the organized "official" world-wide church of the Antichrist which I will explain later (cf. Rev. 17:6).

Because the Church had already been raptured (Rev. 7:9–10) and the completed Jewish evangelists murdered and beheaded, John indicated that the final effort at evangelizing the world will be executed by one of God's angels. He stated that an angel from heaven announces to the world that God's irreversible judgment is imminent, and His gospel will be proclaimed to all those who have survived the seal and trumpet judgments. John told his reading audience, "Then I saw another angel flying in midheaven *holding the eternal Gospel to proclaim to those living on the earth*, to every tribe, people, nation, and language" (εχοντα ευαγγελιον αιωνιον ευαγγελισαι επι τους καθημενους επι της γης, v. 6). God is sending a very talented and persuasive angel to proclaim the gospel to the almost doomed pagans of the earth. I wonder if this angel is Gabriel, known for his verbal abilities. These lost souls still have time to acknowledge the God of creation and honor Him by joining Jesus. John related that the angel proclaimed this to the world on the basis that creation including the heaven, the earth, the seas, and the springs of water are

God's handiwork (v. 7). I would think that because of the present-day introduction of the public to UFO's and non-earth beings, the pagan public at this time in earth's future history would not be intimidated by an angel from God speaking to them about Jesus.[176]

The next angel, identified as the second one, announces the destruction of Babylon described in great detail in chapters 17–18. Even at this late time, God sends the first angel with the task of evangelizing the pagan world one last time before He authorizes and releases the last seven vial/bowl judgments to strike the earth. As the Apostle Peter indicated in 2 Peter 3:9, the Father does not want anyone to die condemned to Hell. Therefore, He ensures that thousands and maybe even millions of pagans come to Christ even during the Great Tribulation period—yet before the beginning of the most frightful time the earth has experienced as described by John in chapter 16. But in chapter 14, John stated that a second angel announces the eventual destruction of Babylon who: "made all the nations drink from the maddening wine of her fornications" (εκ του οινου του θυμου της πορνειας αυτης πεποτικον παντα τα εθνη, v. 8). God is paying Babylon back for the deception and the treachery of misleading nations and peoples away from His ways and His Word. I think it significant that John used the inebriation metaphor for the influence that "Babylon" has on the world and its citizens. When a person imbibes too much alcohol, the hydroxy moiety from the alcohol molecule displaces the oxygen molecule carried by the red blood cell into the brain. When numerous hydroxy radicals displace oxygen in red blood cells, the brain receives far less oxygen than what is necessary for normal thinking, feeling, speaking, and walking. These altered activities create the drunkenness and the "maddening" (craziness) of the alcoholic or heavy drinker. John clearly stated that Babylon forced the world to "drink the maddening wine of its fornications." As previously discussed, the Beast and his false prophet institute an international monetary system forcing most humans to get a chip under their skin on their right hand or forehead in order to buy and sell needed goods and commodities (Rev. 13:16–17). This and other political and religious requirements cause a loss of individualism and personal freedoms and rights resulting in a strict form of political dictatorship and economic imperialism.

John described three Babylons in chapters 17–19. *Religious* Babylon is likely centered in Rome as described in Revelation 17 and may involve the Catholic Church

---

[176] David Grusch, Commander David Fravor, Ryan Graves, "House holds hearing on UFO's: government transparency"; CBS News, July 26, 2023.

as previously mentioned. *Economic* Babylon probably is the worldwide economic center and may be present day commerce capitals located near bodies of water such as New York, Los Angeles, Tokyo, London, or Rome. The location is likely close to one of the oceans because of the description of the sailors on ships witnessing the smoke rising from the destroyed city of the epicenter of world commerce (Rev. 18:18-19). *Political* Babylon may be near Israel such as Bagdad or Rome; but it becomes the dominant world power and the center of worldwide government during the last three and a half years of the Tribulation Period. Note that each person of the "unholy trinity" controls his sphere of expertise: the false prophet controls Religious Babylon as we saw in chapter 13:14-15; the Beast controls Economic Babylon as we see in Rev. 6:2, 13:16-17; and the dragon/the Devil controls Political Babylon as we will see in the events preceding Armageddon I (Rev. 19) and in the events preceding Armageddon II (Rev. 20).

I think it striking that the third angel warns any *individual* who "worships the beast and his image and receives his mark on his forehead or on his hand" (προσκυνει το θηριον και την εικονα αυτου και λαμβανει χαραγμα επι του μετωπου αυτου η επι την χειρα αυτου, v. 9) will be punished with "fire and sulfur" (πυρι και θειω, v. 10), an obvious reference to the lake of fire (Rev. 19:20; 20:9; 21:8). The third angel makes it very clear that at this time repentance is not an option and that reversal of the ultimate judgment against the perpetrators of the dragon's will and purpose will never take place.

The last angel of chapter 14 warns that those who have aligned themselves with the Antichrist by allowing his mark to be put on their forehead or hand will experience the lake of fire in hell. But John also heard an encouraging voice from heaven remind him to write down the following: "Blessed are the dead ones, the ones having died in the Lord from now on" (μακαριοι οι νεκροι οι εν κυριω αποθνησκοντες απ αρτι, v. 13). This emphasizes the great risk believers carry with their faith during this time of dominance of the Beast and the collateral damage to believers who die with pagans because of the vile judgments about to be unleashed on the earth. Even the Holt Spirit interrupts the narrative at this point: "Yes, says the Spirit, that they might rest from their labor, *and that their works might follow them*" (το γαρ εργα αυτων ακολουθει μετ αυτων, v. 13). Despite all the hardships, what appears to be little effect from righteous living, suffering, and the very real prospect of death, the followers of Jesus will find rest and peace in heaven. The Holy Spirit also intimates by His words in this passage that believers' lives will not go unnoticed even by the pagans who often carefully watch these peculiar people.

John then stated that he saw a white cloud presumably above the earth and that a person who looks "like the Son of Man" (ομοιον υιον ανθρωπου, v. 14) wearing a golden crown on His head is sitting on the cloud poised to swing His "sharp sickle" (δρεπανον οξυ, v. 14). John saw an angel going out of the Temple who presumably shouts to Jesus to go ahead and harvest the earth with His sickle because "the earth's harvest is ripe" (εξηρανθη ο θερισμος της γης, v. 15). It appears that the efforts of the Jewish Christian evangelists recently slaughtered for their faith and the efforts of the angel with the task of evangelizing the earth produced a harvest worthy of Jesus' efforts at harvesting believers.

I'm wondering what actually is meant by Jesus "harvesting the earth." It could be that Jesus escorts these believers' souls-spirits into the Kingdom of God exactly as He does with all believers on the earth when they repent and give their lives to Him. But it could also mean that He escorts them through death into the Kingdom. Interestingly, Jesus harvests the last believers on earth and, as we see in the next few verses, separates them from the followers of the Beast ushering them into paradise. Remember that the first Judgment Seat of Christ takes place after the Rapture (2 Corinthians 5:10) for the believers who have died and those alive at the Rapture as John reported in Revelation 7, likely *before* the Seventh Seal is broken in Revelation 8. Though not stated here, a second great judgment of believers before Christ (i.e., the Second Judgment Seat of Christ) would have to occur to validate their entry into heaven.

The next angel actually judges the rest of the world whose names are not in the Book of Life by gathering them to battle against Jesus and His forces at the Battle of Armageddon discussed in greater detail in chapter 19. John closed out Revelation 14 by giving his reading audience a quick glimpse into the utter destruction of Satan's forces at this final conflict before Christ's millennial reign on earth. He stated that another angel with a sharp sickle is commanded by the angel of Revelation 8—who has authority over the altar of Heaven's fire—to swing his sickle on the earth to harvest the earth's grapes because they are also ripe. These grapes are not the sweet grapes that the Son of Man harvested but are sour ones doomed to destruction (v. 19). This angel harvests not only the sour grapes but the grapevines on which they lie signifying that not only is the fruit of their lives worthy of destruction but also their very beings. The apostle stated: "So the angel swung his sickle on the earth and *plucked the earth's grapevine and flung it into the great winepress of the wrath of God*" (ετρυγησεν την αμπελον της γης και εβαλεν εις την ληνον του θυμου του θεου τον μεγαν, v. 19). The angel doesn't pluck each grape

Valley of Megiddo

from the grapevine as Jesus did for His harvesting, but surprisingly gathers not only the clusters of grapes but the entire grapevine from the earth as well. The angel didn't bother to pick each grape because he knew that all the grapes on this specific grapevine of the earth (pagans) were rotten and not worth saving. Furthermore, the angel hurls the bad grapes and the grapevine upon which they grow into the great winepress of God's anger. The symbology is stark. John stated that the "winepress is trampled outside of the city" (επατηθη η ληνος εξωθεν της πολεως, v. 20). He reported that the amount of devastation to the "grapevine" results in the "trampling" of the Beast's forces and their blood flowing out of the winepress as high as a horse's bridle (5 feet high) filling the Valley of Megiddo/Jezreel (180 miles). Because of the "trampling," I think that John indicated unequivocally that the grapes and grapevine refer to the Beast and his armed forces who fatefully surround the holy city Jerusalem as "the Rider of the white horse" annihilates them with His mouth laser. According to Revelation 19:14–21, His forces destroy the armies of the east as the Beast and his false prophet are thrown into the Lake of Fire. John gives a more detailed discussion of this annihilation in Revelation 19 as previously indicated. But in our winepress scene in *this* passage, the angel revealing the Revelation to John shows him the ghastly loss of blood pouring out of the winepress and filling the Megiddo Valley in central Israel. Each adult has between five and a half and six liters of blood. The Valley of Megiddo/Jezreel is 150 to 180 miles long. In order to fill the Valley with blood as indicated by this passage, anywhere from thirty thousand or as few as four thousand people have to die depending on the amount of blood that drains out from each person. If less than half the blood of each dead person drains out, then thirty thousand have to die; or if all the blood drains out of the soldiers' bodies, then only four thousand die.[177] But according to John in Revelation 19:21, the largest army ever assembled is decimated by the weaponized laser sword projecting out of Jesus' mouth. According to Ezekiel 39:12, birds of prey gorge themselves on

---

177   Gordon Hudson, "How many people will die at the Battle of Armageddon?" *Ecalpemos*, accessed 20, 2021, https://gordonhudson.blogspot.com/2006/09/how-many-people-will-die-at-battle-of.html.

the flesh of these soldiers for seven months. Based on the Armageddon I passage from Revelation 19:15-21, far more than thirty thousand die from encounter with Christ making the blood amount spilled from the battle entirely plausible.

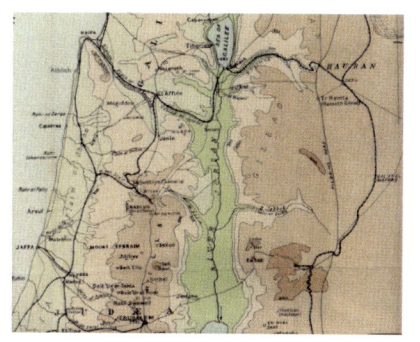

Map of the Valley of Megiddo

REVELATION 15

Seven Angels with the Seven Last Plagues

Temple of Heaven Opened

Smoke of God's Power and Glory Filled the Temple

No one Enters the Temple until Completion of Last Bowl Judgments

1 "Then I saw another sign in heaven, great and marvelous: seven angels with seven last plagues because after these, God's wrath is completed. ² Then I saw the sea of glass mixed with blood and those standing beside the sea victorious over the beast and over his image and over the number of its name holding harps of God ³ and they sang the song of Moses, the servant of God and the song of the Lamb saying, 'Your works are great and

> marvelous Lord God Almighty, and Your ways are true and just, King of the nations; ⁴ who would not fear You, Lord, or glorify Your Name? Because You alone are holy. Because of this, all the nations will be there and bow down and worship before You, because Your righteous acts have been revealed.'
>
> ⁵ "After these things, I saw the Temple of the Tent Testimony opened in heaven ⁶ and seven angels with seven plagues going out of the Temple dressed in pure white clothes with golden sashes around their chests. ⁷ Then one of the four living beings gave the seven angels seven golden bowls filled with the wrath of God, the One living forever and ever. ⁸ And the smoke of the glory and power of God filled the Temple. And no one could enter the Temple until the seven plagues from the seven angels came to an end."

The Apostle John next focused on heaven and what he calls a "great and marvelous" (μεγα και θαυμαστον, v. 1) "sign" (σημειον, v. 1). The Jews considered a "sign" to be a significant event or even a miracle. John saw a significant event occurring in heaven, as significant as the other sign he identified in Revelation 12 with the woman described in heaven who was pregnant and then delivered a Son. But here he saw God's terrible plan for the earth about to unfold involving seven judgment angels who bring specific judgments against the people of the earth which he describes in the next chapter. John revealed to his reading audience that these seven angels have "the last seven plagues" (πληγας επτα τας εσχατος, v. 1). John stated that this third series of judgments are the *last* ones for the earth and its people because by the end of these plagues, God's thirst for justice and appetite for punishment are satisfied. John also utilized the Greek word for last (εσχατος) which makes his narrative very clearly linear and not circular as some theologians have indicated. Some Revelation experts feel that the seven seal, seven trumpet and seven vial/bowl judgments should really be considered the same judgments but presented slightly differently by the Apostle. To me this perspective makes no sense because these twenty-one judgments all are very different and appear to take place sequentially, particularly in the light of John's use of language like "εσχατος" to describe the last seven (Rev. 15:1; 21:9). God purposely and very deliberately increases the stress and intensity of the seal and trumpet judgments so that the pagans resisting His will and purpose for mankind would repent and embrace His new and eternal life.

But as we have seen in the previous chapters, the dragon and his understudies, the Beast and the false prophet, do their best to frustrate the Lord. Finally, as we see in the next six chapters, the Lord has had enough of this opposition, and by chapter 15 He sends one of His seraphim to authorize the seven angels to release their bowl judgments onto the earth.

Before the release, John received a vision of people standing by the glassy sea presumably the one he saw in Revelation 4 when he first had a vision of the throne room of God. But instead of a calm sea, John saw a very disturbed sea "mixed with fire" (μεμιγμενην πυρι, v. 2)—likely indicating great turmoil from the Beast's persecution of the saints who he described as standing beside the sea. These were obviously martyrs who John told us had triumphed over the Beast, his image, and "over the number of his name" (εκ του αριθμου του ονοματους αυτου, v. 2). The "number of his name" refers to the international economic system based on the chip technology (RFID) or something like it and its connection to the Beast without which no one can subsist (cf. pp.191-193). Just as the 144,000 were able to sing an unknowable song of praise to the Father, so too John related that these martyrs near the fire-tinged sea sang a very specific song of Moses and a song from the Lamb Himself. Moses sang a song to the Lord with exuberant thankfulness when the Lord delivered the Israelites from Pharaoh and his chariots through the Red Sea as recorded in Exodus 15. The "song of the Lamb" (ωδην του αρνιου, v. 3) could possibly be one of the praising Psalms of David or even one of the Suffering Servant Songs of Isaiah. But it could also be an extemporaneous song that Jesus sang to the Father and Spirit as He rejoined them in heaven after His Passion, death, burial, and resurrection. I think some of the elements of both songs are found in verses 3-4 as the lakeside martyrs sing, accompanied with harps of God:

> Great and marvelous our Your works, Lord God Almighty, and true and righteous are Your ways, King of the nations. Who would not fear You, Lord? Or glorify Your Name? For You alone are holy; therefore, all the nations will be there and will bow down and worship before You, *because Your righteous acts have been revealed* (οτι τα δικαιωματα σου εφανερωθησαν, v. 4).

Even though their lives were prematurely ended likely by beheading or gunshots to their heads, these followers of Christ unabashedly, enthusiastically praised Father God and predicted that even the enemies of God and of His Christ would be bending their knees and acknowledging that Jesus Christ is Lord as the Apostle Paul stated they would in Philippians 2:10–11.

John's vision of heaven changes after he sees the lakeside martyrs singing for Jesus. He stated that the Temple in heaven is open. He also remarked that the Temple represents the Tent of the Covenant/Tabernacle: "After these things, I saw the Tabernacle of the tent of testimony open in heaven" (και μετα ταυτα ειδον και ηνοιγη ο ναος της σκηνης του μαρτυριου εν τω ουρανω, v. 5). God the Father wanted His Temple to be open at this moment because in a matter of moments the Temple will become inaccessible to all in the Universe due to His fierce wrath. He also wanted the saints and even the pagans of the earth if they could see the Temple to know that His Covenant through the Ages beginning with Abraham, Isaac, Jacob, David, and finally through Jesus was still in effect. Despite the tremendous Divine onslaught about to hit the earth in the form of seven vile plagues, God was still faithful to His Word and to His children.

After seeing the Temple open for business, John noticed seven angels with their plagues coming out of the Temple as if they had just been given final instructions for harming the earth. He noticed that they were "clothed in pure white robes and had golden sashes girded around their chests" (ενδεδυμενοι λινον καθαρον λαμπρον και περιεζωσμενοι περι τα στηθη ζωνας χρυσας, v. 6). Their garments bring to mind what Jesus was wearing when He reintroduced Himself to John in Revelation 1:13. The outfit of the seven angels signified the role of a judge highlighting the grim task each of the angels were assigned to execute on the earth. But as the angels came out of the Temple with their plagues, one of the four seraphim met them and gave them "seven golden bowls filled with the wrath of God" (επτα φιαλας χρυσας γεμουσας του θυμου του θεου, v. 7). It was as if the seven plagues that the seven angels carried were not terrible enough on their own and had to be synergized and potentiated with more punishment for mankind. God sent one of His living beings out to give each a golden bowl filled with His anger to accentuate each of their plagues. This, in fact, pleased the Father so much that He followed the exchange of golden bowls to His angels by filling the Temple with "the smoke of the glory and power of God" (καπνου εκ της δοξης του θεου και εκ της δυναμεως αυτου, v. 8).

Immediately, John realized that the smoke was so thick that no one could enter the Temple until "the seven plagues of the seven angels came to an end" (αχρι τελεσθωσιν αι επτα πληγαι των επτα αγγελων, v. 8). He understood that no manner of pleading or supplication could change God's mind concerning the delivery of the worst of God's judgments to the earth. The earth was doomed to judgments meant to punish the pagans of the earth who had been unmerciful to His Church and to the 144,000 Israeli Christians for Jesus.

REVELATION 16

The Seven Bowl Judgments

1 "Then a loud voice came out of the Temple speaking to the seven angels, 'Depart and pour out the seven bowls of God's wrath onto the earth.' ² Then the first departed and poured out his bowl onto the land, and a terrible, sick making sore broke out on the people, the ones with the mark of the beast and those worshipping his image. ³ Then the second poured out his bowl onto the sea and it became like the blood of the dead and every living sea creature died. ⁴ And the third poured out his bowl onto the rivers and fountains of water and they became like blood. ⁵ Then the angel over the waters cried out, 'You are the righteous One, the One who was, the Holy One because You judged these, ⁶ since they killed the prophets and the saints, You gave them blood to drink because they are deserving. ⁷ Then I heard the altar say, 'Yes, Lord God Almighty; Your judgments are true and righteous.' ⁸ Then the fourth poured out his bowl onto the sun. And he was given authority to scorch the people with fire; ⁹ and the people were scorched with searing heat; and they blasphemed the Name of God, the One in charge of the plagues. But they did not repent nor give God the glory. ¹⁰ Then the fifth poured out his bowl onto the throne of the beast and his kingdom became dark and they

Revelation: The Fifth Gospel

> bit their tongues because of the pain ⁱⁱ and they cursed the God of heaven because of their pain and because of their sores but did not repent from their works. ¹² Then the sixth poured out his bowl onto the Great River Euphrates and it dried up to prepare the way for the kings of the East. ¹³ And I saw three unclean spirits like frogs going out of the mouth of the dragon, and out of the mouth of the beast and out of the mouth of the false prophet. ¹⁴ These are demonic spirits performing signs. And they went out to the kings of the whole world to gather them to battle on the Great Day of God Almighty. ¹⁵ 'Behold, I am coming like a thief; blessed is the one watching and holding on to his clothes lest he walk around naked and his shame be seen.' ¹⁶ And they gathered them together to a place called Armageddon in the Hebrew. ¹⁷ Then the seventh [angel] poured out is bowl onto the air and a loud voice from the throne went out of the Temple saying, 'It is finished.' ¹⁸ Then came lightening, rumblings, thunders and a mega quake occurred; such a one has not occurred like this since man has been on the earth, the earthquake was so tremendous. ¹⁹ Then the great city split into three parts and the cities of the nations collapsed. Then God remembered Babylon the Great and gave her the cup of the wine of the fury of His anger. ²⁰ Then every island disappeared quickly and mountains were not found. ²¹ Then great hail each a talent weight fell from the sky onto the people, and they cursed God because of the plague of hail, the plague was so severe."

First Bowl Judgment

It must be noted that the timing of the seven plagues is in quick succession. The recipients of these plagues really had no time to recover from each plague. The plagues were additive and crushing to the world's wealth, food supply, and emotional health. John continued his frightful narrative of the worst judgments ever experienced by the earth: "Then I heard a

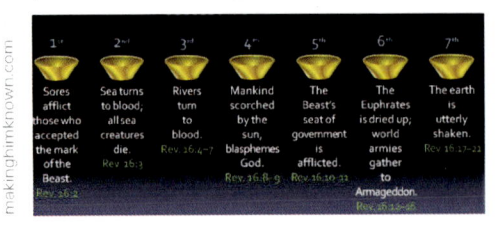

The seven bowls of judgement.

loud voice from the Temple speak to the seven angels saying, ' *Depart and pour out the seven bowls of the wrath of God onto the earth*" (υπαγετε και εκχεετε τας επτα φιαλας του θυμου του θεου εις την γην, v. 1). Remember that the seraph had just given the seven angels seven bowls—each full of the wrath of God. When the seven angels mixed their plagues with the God's wrath in the golden bowls given to them, their plagues were synergized with as much ferocity as possible to mete out God's maximum punishment on the Beast and his followers. The first angel poured out his bowl onto the land; the narrative states: "*a terrible, sick-making sore break out onto the people* who had the mark of the Beast and who worshipped his image" (εγενετο ελκος κακον και πονηρον επι τους ανθρωπους, v. 2). The Greek term for "sore" (ελκος) is singular in John's passage possibly meaning that the sore could arise from what each person in the Beast's kingdom possesses—a subdermal computer chip identification tag. The Greek word for "sick-making" (πονηρον) indicates that the ulcer each Beast follower gets causes *more* than a local reaction to his/her skin.

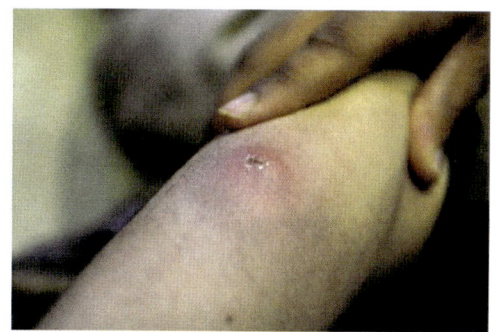

abscess of arm

It likely causes a systemic illness not unlike bacteremia or even septicemia, both caused by bacteria in the blood. The pathophysiology of the first angel's bowl punishment involves the skin—the largest organ of the body and the easiest to access. The angel's punishment could cause the intradermal or the subcutaneous tissue-(second or third layer of the skin) placed-computer chip to elicit a foreign body response activating the immune system which could trigger development of inflammatory abscesses. These abscesses compromise the barrier function of the skin and then become infected by super bacteria unresponsive to antibiotics or other measures. The skin is innervated by many nerves which could be activated by the inflammation around the chips and the bacteria collecting around them causing tremendous pain. No wonder the worshippers of the Beast who have received his chip become very sick.

Revelation: The Fifth Gospel

Second Bowl Judgment

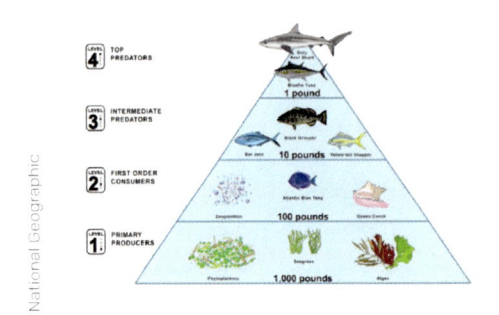

Ocean Food Chain (National Geographic)

Next, John wrote to his reading audience that the second angel pours out his bowl onto the world's oceans: "Then the second poured out his bowl on *the sea, and it became like the blood of the dead and every living sea creature died*" (την θαλασσαν και εγενετο αιμα ως νεκρου και πασα ψυχη ζωης απεθανεν τα εν τη θαλασση, v. 3). The second angel's bowl causes the oceans throughout the earth to become toxic killing all sea life. John stated that the sea became like "blood of the dead" which could mean that the ocean became toxic due to actual blood or something made the water look like blood such as the ferric oxide (cf. Rev. 8:8–9). Another thought is that this second angel's judgment bowl caused the toxic chemicals already in and moving into our oceans to finally cause our saltwater bodies to reach toxic levels. The amount of toxic waste materials entering the waters of our country is over two hundred million pounds per year.[178] This is disastrous for the earth because even plankton loss alone would mean loss of the greatest source of food on the earth's surface. But even if John's use of the singular form of "sea" (θαλασσα) means only the Mediterranean Sea, the loss of sea life in this large body of water would be disastrous for the entire Mediterranean Basin. If the "sea" means all oceans of the earth, then catastrophic effects would occur to all forms of life as we know it including devastating effects on human life which depends on the oceans for at least 10 percent of its protein needs.[179] Food chain disruption would likely produce famine and disease. Without sea life including the most critical

---

[178] Sean Breslin, "206 Million Pounds of Toxic Chemicals Dumped Into U.S. Waterways in One Year, Study Finds." The Weather Channel, September 29, 2014, accessed August 26, 2021, https://weather.com/science/environment/news/206-million-pounds-chemicals-water-study-20140923.

[179] Ocean, Importance of the Ocean; The Columbia Electronic Encyclopedia, 6th ed. (New York: Columbia University Press, 2023), accessed August 25, 2021, https://www.infoplease.com/encyclopedia/earth/geology-oceanography/info/ocean/importance-of-the-ocean.

autotrophs of the world, (phytoplankton like diatoms and dinoflagellates), the birds and many mammalian species would quickly decline, including bears, seals, penguins, birds, amphibians, and eventually humans.

Red Ocean

Third Bowl Judgment

The toxicity of the seawater was bad enough. But John reported that the third angel pours out his judgment bowl on the rivers and the underground water sources. Land water becomes undrinkable due to this bowl judgment; ocean water pollution would be devastating enough to world inhabitants, but land water pollution would be the death of most inhabitants over time since this is the most precious of human nutrients. It is well known that humans cannot survive longer than three days without water.[180] Dehydration would result within days of this plague and vulnerability to water borne diseases would eventually occur if humans lived long enough (e.g., typhoid, dysentery, protozoan diseases). John reported the third bowl judgment like this: "Then the third poured out his bowl onto the rivers and springs of water and they became blood" (και ο τριτος εξεχεεν την φιαλην αυτου εις τους ποταμους και τας πηγας των υδατων και εγενετο αιμα, v. 4). One can only imagine the difficulty for people living in the world at this time. Indeed, we get some insight into what they face with the water becoming unpotable by John's comments concerning the angel in charge of the land water: "Then I heard the angel in charge of the water say, 'You are righteous, the One who was, the holy One because You judged these since they killed the saints and the prophets and *You gave them blood to drink since they are deserving of it*" (αιμα αυτοις δεδωκας πιειν αξιοι εισιν, v. 6).

---

180 Jan Johnson, "How Long Can You Live Without Water?" *Medical News Today*, May 14, 2019, accessed August 29, 2021, https://www.medicalnewstoday.com/articles/325174.

It is possible that ocean water pollution could have extended to the land water since all ocean winds and water eventually get to land in the hydrosphere of the world; however, I believe that the third angel's bowl caused specific pollution to the land water including subterranean water sources in relatively quick succession to the second bowl judgment creating a water crisis that the world has never seen to that point. The fourth bowl judgment accentuates the global dehydration of the second and third bowl judgments.

The Fourth Bowl Judgment

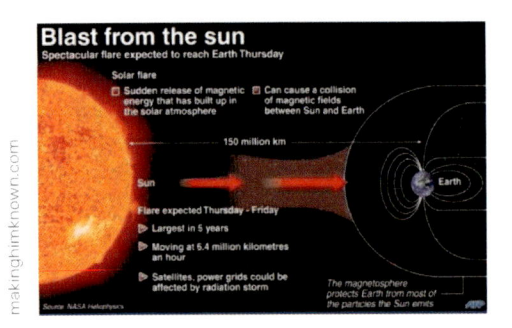

NASA representation of a sun flare

John described a frightful situation with the fourth angel's bowl judgment. But this one involves manipulation of the sun. "Then the fourth poured out his bowl onto the sun; and he was given authority to scorch the people with fire, *and the people were scorched with great searing heat*" (και εκαυματισθησαν οι ανθρωποι καυμα μεγα, v. 9). The sun occasionally creates offshoots of its dynamic atmosphere called solar flares and radiation storms. A portion of the sun's atmosphere on occasion ejects electromagnetic energy such as protons and plasma called coronal mass ejections. When these particles are ejected into the space immediately surrounding the corona of the sun, they hitch a ride onto solar winds and are transported within several hours to days to the earth causing satellite disturbances, threats to the electronics of space stations, and blackouts of the electrical grids on the earth. Our astrophysicists call these events *radiation storms*.[181]

---

181   R.A. Mewaldt; et al., "Space Weather Implications of the 20 January 2005 Solar Energetic Particle Event," paper given at an "American Geophysical Union" meeting, (April 2005), accessed August 27, 2021, https://www.researchgate.net/publication/234303812_Space_Weather_Implications_of_the_20_January_2005_Solar_Energetic_Particle_Event.

But here John was clear that the fourth bowl judgment actually is significant enough to cause severe sunburns and photodermatitis. He stated that they "were scorched with great searing heat" (v. 9). Second (into the dermis) and third (into the subcutaneous tissues) degree skin burns cause humans to lose more water which would accentuate the effects of loss of drinkable water and cause dehydration faster. John intimated that those on earth at this time experience the greatest amount of radiation ever released at one time by the sun onto the earth. Their sunburns are so pervasive that John reported that pagans throughout the world "blasphemed the name of God" (εβλασφημησαν το ονομα του θεου, v. 9). Furthermore, the impact of these four bowl judgments, instead of driving people to respect and honoring God and embracing the elements of the Kingdom including repentance from their evil thoughts and ways, they "did not repent nor did they give honor to Him" (ου μετενοησαν δουναι αυτου δοξαν, v. 9). As a dermatologist, I think John's narrative very interesting in that these solar radiation flares cause people significant cutaneous harm despite the development of very protective sunscreens and sunblocks. In the past few decades, pharmaceutical companies have developed SPF (solar protection factor) values at 110, considerably more than the protection we had thirty years ago. Even clothing has been manufactured with fibers possessing a 50 SPF value. Despite this technology, humans are hurt by this solar radiation released by the fourth angel likely indicating that the solar radiation storm happened quickly and without warning.

Fifth Bowl Judgment

Darkness falls over those who have the mark of the Beast who live in the capital city of Babylon. The fifth angel is very specific about pouring out the darkness over this leading economic city and no other city: "And the fifth angel poured out his bowl onto *the throne of the beast, and the kingdom of the beast became dark*"

Revelation: The Fifth Gospel

City in a blackout.
CC By 2.0, Eden, Janine and Jim

(τον θρονον του θηριου και εγενετο η βασιλεια αυτου εσκοτωμενη, v. 10). The effects on this city would certainly have a negative impact on others throughout the world. This occurs probably because of electrical brown and black outs causing paralysis of economy and accentuates dehydration and the treatment of their sores. Remember the previous judgment bowl causes solar flares/coronal mass ejections. Maybe this angel directed the massive amount of solar plasma and protons/electrons and X-rays at this city to cause electrical grid failure as occurred on March 13, 1989, when a geomagnetic storm blasted the earth causing a nine-hour power outage in Quebec.[182]

Electrical energy failures whether through solar flares or fossil fuel generator failures would be devastating to world economies including Babylon's. It is unclear where the "throne of the beast" actually is. But some Revelation scholars have suggested the Biblical Babylon located in present day Iraq near Bagdad or Basra could be the site.[183] Others suggest that Rome is a likely candidate, particularly in light of the angel's comment to John in Revelation 17:9 about the Beast with seven heads representing "seven hills"—an obvious reference to Rome.[184]

Water flow and pressure in the capital city would be one of the most critical resources compromised by the loss of power producing water shortages. Without electrical energy generated, water pressure would not be maintained, and water would then be unavailable; thus the "tongue gnawing" secondary to dehydration

---

[182] Eric J. Lerner, Eric J., "Space weather: Storms and hurricanes don't leave off where the atmosphere ends," *Discover*, August 1, 1995, accessed May 26, 2023, https://www.discovermagazine.com/the-sciences/space-weather.

[183] Kuudere-Kun, "Mystery Babylon, Jerusalem, and the Throne of the Beast," August 20, 2014, accessed August 28, 2021, https://midseventiethweekrapture.blogspot.com/2014/08/mystery-babylon-jerusalem-and-throne-of.html.

[184] John Gill, "Revelation 16:10," *Exposition of the Entire Bible*, accessed August 28, 2021, https://biblehub.com/commentaries/revelation/16-10.htm.

The Seven Bowl Judgments

and the pain the Apostle identified because of lack of wound healing for the abscesses of first bowl judgment: "and they bit their tongues because of the pain" (και εμασσωντα τας γλωσσας αυτων εκ του πονου, v. 10). John reiterated pagan resistance to "repentance from their deeds" (μετανοησαν εκ των εργων αυτων, v. 11) despite the pain of their sores (των πονων αυτων και εκ των ελκων, v. 11).

Euphrates River

Sixth Bowl Judgment

The sixth angel causes the Euphrates River to dry up secondary to the altered weather patterns of solar origin from the fourth and fifth bowls. But the sixth angel could cause the loss of Euphrates water by numerous other methods including natural disasters like earthquakes, which could redirect the headwaters of the river away from its natural riverbed, or by causing the Turkish authorities who control the Atatürk Dam (the third largest dam in the world completed in 1990) overlying

River Euphrates

the Euphrates to shut down all flow of water into the river.[185] The Euphrates is one of the largest and longest in the world; it is about 1,800 miles long and well over a mile wide in some areas. It has an average width of about 400 yards throughout its entire length.[186] Because of the construction of the Atatürk Dam, this judgment may be relatively easy to execute. John wrote that he watched the sixth angel pour out his bowl onto the Euphrates River, and the resulting judgment causes the riverbed to dry up allowing for the passage of the armies of the Kings of the East. The world begins now to implode with the Satan's unholy trinity marshaling the troops "from the Kings of the East" (των βασιλεων των απο ανατολης, v. 12) as they traveled down the dried-up Euphrates River.

Ataturk Dam

The Apostle stated that the sixth angel enacted war preparation activities by not only causing one of the greatest rivers to dry up but to set the stage for the costliest war that the world has ever seen. Because God had a date from the beginning of time to engage the military forces of the Beast/Antichrist, I surmise that the sixth angel authorized the release of demonic spirits to come out of the devil's mouth, the Beast's mouth, and out of the false prophet's mouth. These evil spirits performed signs through the representatives of the unholy trinity and, as John stated, these demonic spirits *"were sent out to the kings of the whole earth* to gather them for battle on the great day of God Almighty" (εκπορευεται επι τους βασιλεις της οικουμενης ολης, v.1 4). John made it clear that the kingdom of the Beast had considerable influence and the Beast, the false prophet and their envoys obviously utilized verbal persuasion and supernatural acts to influence the Beast's circle of ten nations (cf. Rev. 17:12-14) to join the Beast against Christ. Chief among the kings of the ten heads of state who join the Beast's political and army alliance are those nations from the East which would obviously include China and Russia, who have

---

185 S. Malla, M. Wieland, and R. Straubhaar, "Monitoring Atatürk dam," *International Water Power & Dam Construction*, October 17, 2006, accessed May 26, 2023, https://www.waterpowermagazine.com/features/featuremonitoring-ataturk-dam.

186 "Euphrates River," *Encyclopaedia Britannica*, https://www.britannica.com/place/Euphrates-River (accessed May 26, 2023).

already developed political and economic treaties.[187] I am sure these pagan leaders and the armies under their control understood that they were gathering to fight against the forces of God Almighty and those on earth who chose to fight with Him. I wonder if the United States will be fighting with the forces of heaven against the Beast and political Babylon or by this time might have been annihilated by several of the trumpet judgements, particularly the 6th trumpet judgment (cf. 9:16-20).

John closed out the sixth bowl judgment with a warning from Jesus Himself. The ten kings and their nations are flexing their political and military muscles which I would imagine generates a sense of false security and bravado. In light of this, it is appropriate that Jesus speaks a warning to the world at this time: "Behold, I am coming like a thief; blessed is the one watching and holding onto his clothes that he not walk naked and his shame be seen" (ιδου, ερχομαι ως κλεπτης μαρκαριος ο γρηγορων και τηρων τα ιματια αυτου ινα μη γυμνος περιπατη και βλεπωσιν την ασχημοσυνην αυτου, v. 15). I think Jesus' comments about nakedness are more for the Church *now* before these bowl judgments transpire. If these words happen to be delivered to the confederation of the ten nations of the Antichrist through the Internet, I imagine they would scoff at Jesus' warning that He will "come like a thief." But Jesus is likely being very honest with His enemies. He is likely also telling those leaders that capitulating to the selfish, bellicose, and shortsighted behavior of the Beast and his false prophet, causes them to become "naked." The nakedness that Jesus discusses here is not physical nakedness but spiritual bankruptcy which those from the Kingdom and even from the pagan world later will identify as shameful behavior. Despite the ten kings' confederacy and efforts in joining the Beast, they are doomed. Within months, Jesus and His heavenly forces will strike the Beast and his armies unexpectedly, with fury, and with surgical accuracy as John reported in Revelation 19:19-21.

As we can see, the unholy counterfeit trinity mobilizes the world's armies against Jesus at the Valley of Megiddo for the first Battle of Armageddon before Christ's millennial reign on earth. The entire conflict will likely be primarily nuclear holocaust between Jesus and His heavenly forces using Jesus' mouth-laser (Rev. 19:15) against the nuclear-toting forces of the Kings of the East (China and Russia) and their allies from the Islamic world (Put [Libya], Egypt, Iran, Iraq) as indicated by the prophets Daniel and Ezekiel.

---

187   Marc Champion, "Why Closer Ties Between Russia and China Have Democracies Worried" accessed from the internet on July 29, 2023, @https:// bloomberg.com/news/articles/2022-06-14/why-increasing-russia-china-ties-worry-democracies-quicktake#xj4y7vzkg

Revelation: The Fifth Gospel

Seventh Bowl Judgment

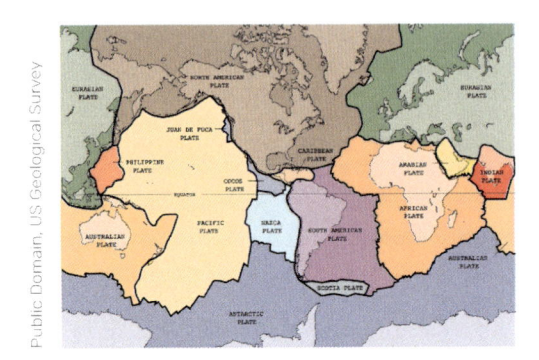

Map of the tectonic plates of the Earth

The seventh bowl judgment initiates the most destructive earthquake to ever strike the earth erasing mountain ranges, displacing islands and destroying large cities. There are eight tectonic plates across the surface of the earth which slide toward (convergent) and away (divergent) from each other and which comprise the lithosphere (crust and outer mantle of the earth). When tectonic plates collide or pull away from each other, they produce faults (breaks in the surface) and release large amounts of energy in the form of earthquakes, volcanos, mountain range building, and trench formations. There are three main types of tectonic plate shifts creating earthquakes (normal, reverse, strike-slip), but the worst are probably *reverse* tectonic plate movements which arise from converging tectonic plate shifts. Reverse fault shifts produce the megaquakes with magnitudes greater than 8.0; seismologists estimate that 90 percent of the energy released from worldwide earthquakes come from reverse plate shifts.[188] I think the megaquake occurs with epicenter near Rome, Bagdad, Basra, Kuwait City, Abu Dhabi, Dubai or any number of seaside cities with

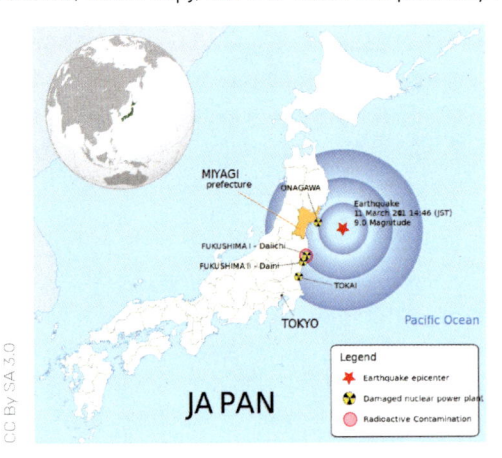

In 2011, a megaquake hit the northeast coast of Japan.

---

[188] Robert J. Stern, "Subduction Zones: Seismogenic Zone," *Reviews of Geophysics*, 40 (4), December 31, 2002, accessed May 26, 2021, https://agupubs.onlinelibrary.wiley.com/doi/10.1029/2001RG000108.

magnitude >9.0 and may involve the Eurasian tectonic plate. Those greater than 9.0 (only four recorded to date:1960, Chile; 1965, Prince William Sound; 2005, Indian Ocean/Indonesia; and 2011, Japanese East Coast) are devastating and, thankfully, rare.

In 2011, a 9.1 mega-earthquake with epicenter 45 miles from Japan in the Pacific Ocean struck Sendai, Japan, on March 11. Its residents had 8 to 10 minutes to run for cover. The megaquake lasted for 6 minutes and was followed by a tsunami with waves over 100 feet high traveling at 400 mph when it struck the Japanese coast. The destruction of the earthquake and the tsunami which travelled 6 miles inland into Japan from its Eastern shore was massive including nearly twenty thousand deaths, six thousand injured, and twenty-five hundred missing. Nearly a quarter of a million Japanese were still displaced from their homes four years after the disaster.[189] If these figures are not enough, the earthquake caused the Fukushima Daiichi nuclear disaster several days later due to the meltdowns of three nuclear reactors which eventually exploded, damaging an area of 12 miles radius around the nuclear plant. The immediate economic loss was estimated at over thirty billion dollars but the long-term loss at over two hundred billion dollars.[190] Japan's megaquake will pale in comparison to the seventh bowl's quake, the granddaddy of them all. This quake effectively clears the earth of its filth and readies it for God's final judgment Armageddon I/II and ultimately the New Jerusalem. This destruction includes the world's economic center Babylon which demise is more specifically catalogued in Revelation 18.

In 2011, a megaquake hit the northeast coast of Japan.

---

189   Kirk Spitzer, "250,000 Japanese still displaced 4 years after quake," *USA Today*, March 9, 2015, accessed May 26, 2023, https://www.usatoday.com/story/news/world/2015/03/09/japan-tsunami-radiation-fourth-anniversary-fukushima/24254887/.
190   Victoria Kim, "Japan damage could reach $235 billion, World Bank estimates," *Los Angeles Times*, March 21, 2011, accessed May 26, 2023, https://www.latimes.com/business/la-fgw-japan-quake-world-bank-20110322-story.html.

John began the narrative of the last of God's worst bowl judgments: "Then the seventh poured out his bowl on the air. Then a loud voice from the throne came out of the Temple saying, 'It is finished.' Then came lightening, rumblings, thunders and a great earthquake occurred; *such a one has not occurred since man has been on the earth, the quake was so great*" (οιος ουκ εγενετο αφ ου ανθρωπος εγενετο επι της γης τηλικουτος σεισμος ουτω μεγας, v. 18). I wonder if the loud voice from the throne was actually God the Father's voice declaring that the bowl judgments have about come to the end. It would make sense that John heard the *Father's* voice since God the Father has established the timing of the Apocalypse events according to Jesus' comments in Acts 1:7. The striking feature of this seventh bowl judgment is that this megaquake is the largest the earth has ever experienced in recorded history. John described the extent and severity of the quake by stating that Babylon "the great city was split into three parts; and the cities of the nations collapsed" (και εγενετο η πολις η μεγαλη εις τρια μερη και αι πολεις των εθνων επεσαν, v. 19). As previously mentioned, I think that the seventh angel triggered a massive tectonic plate *reverse* shift with release of billions of pounds of equivalent TNT energy, accounting for the massive destruction to the earth and its inhabitants. The destruction would be immediate from the actual megaquake damage but also would trigger tsunamis as a result (as was observed with the Japanese megaquake in 2011) and would spawn volcanos. John left no doubt in the reader's mind about God's wrath behind the devastation: "God remembered Babylon the Great and gave her the cup of the wine of the fury of His anger" (και βαβυλων η μεγαλη εμνησθη ενωπιον του θεου δουναι αυτη το ποτηριον του οινου του θυμου της οργης αυτου; v. 19). John intentionally stacked the description of God's anger with "wrath/fury" of His "anger"; his readers easily grasped that this bowl judgment is the worst ever seen on the earth. John intensified his description of the effects of the earthquake by mentioning that "every island quickly disappeared, and the mountains were not found" (και πασα νησος εφυγεν και ορη ουκ ευρεθησαν, v. 20).

The Apostle finished his account of the effects of the megaquake by describing the massive hailstones raining down from the sky onto the earth causing terrible danger, destruction, and death. John stated that each hailstone is about as heavy as a talent weight, about 90 to 100 pounds. He then ends the discussion of the seventh bowl judgment by stating that *"the people blasphemed God because of the plague of hail, the plague was so great"* (εβλασφημησαν οι ανθρωποι τον θεον εκ της πληγης της χαλαζης οτι μεγαλη εστιν η πληγη αυτης σφοδρα, v. 21). Geologists have discovered the earth's most active volcano ring in the Pacific Ocean is also associated with the most active earthquake ring where 80 percent of all earthquakes occur. This earthquake/volcano belt is called the circum-Pacific seismic belt. Often earthquakes here cause a shift in the ocean floor tectonic plates resulting in ocean trenches. Then magma swiftly ascends through the open ocean trenches in the plates to produce active volcanos.[191] When volcano eruptions are massive, as would be the case with the megaquake that John describes in Revelation 16, the eruption could easily spew rocks into the atmosphere for many miles causing the destructive "hailstones" that John described. However, another explanation for the 100-pound hailstones would be what I think John observed with the 6th seal judgment in Rev.6:12-17. As previously suggested, the tsunamis unleashed by the megaquake could incapacitate the command control centers on the surface of the earth for the 18,000 satellites circling the globe. This would result in thousands of large and heavy objects losing their orbit pathways, striking other satellites, and then hitting the earth after free-falling from their orbits to the earth. Many humans die as attested by people cursing God Who they know is behind the megaquake and its effects (v.21). Their knowledge of God and His connection to the recent bowl judgments against the earth and against their religious, economic, and political systems come from the unholy trinity. Remember that the false prophet is the mouthpiece for the Beast and for Satan as he masterfully generates propaganda against Jesus through his world religious system centered in Rome and in the rebuilt third Temple in Jerusalem. But his influence over the world's population becomes severely limited due to the effects of the 7th bowl judgment, which he could not prevent. The world is about to destroy this counterfeit world religion as we see in the next chapter.

---

[191] Joe Ford, "What is the relationship between earthquakes and volcanic activity?" *Answers to All*, March 12, 2021, accessed August 31, 2021, https://answerstoall.com/object/what-is-the-relationship-between-earthquakes-and-volcanic-activity/#What_is_the_relationship_between_earthquakes_and_volcanic_activity.

REVELATION 17

Destruction of Religious Babylon

1 "Then one of the seven angels with the seven bowls came and spoke with me saying, 'Come here and I will show you the judgment of the great prostitute sitting on many waters ² with whom the kings of the earth fornicated and the nations of the earth became drunk on the wine of her fornication.' ³ Then he carried me away by the Spirit into the wilderness and I saw a woman sitting on a scarlet beast full of blasphemous names having seven heads and ten horns. ⁴ Now the woman was dressed in purple and scarlet and adorned in gold, precious stones, and pearls and she held a golden cup in her hand full of what is detestable and unclean things of her fornication. ⁵ And a secret name was written on her forehead, 'Babylon the Great, the Mother of Fornicators and the detestable things of the earth.' ⁶ And then I noticed that the woman was drunk from the blood of the saints and from the blood of the martyrs for Jesus. And I was astonished when I saw her. ⁷ Then the angel asked me, 'Why were you astonished? I will tell you of the mystery of the woman and of the beast carrying her, the one with seven heads and ten horns. ⁸ The beast that you saw once was and now is not, he is about to ascend from the Abyss but will go to his destruction; and

Revelation: The Fifth Gospel

those living on the earth, whose names are not written in the Book of Life since the creation of the world, they will be amazed when they see the beast who was, and is not, but is to come.

⁹ "This requires a mind of wisdom. The seven heads are seven hills on which the woman sits and seven kings; ¹⁰ five have fallen, one still is, and one has yet to come. When he does come, he must remain for a short time. ¹¹ The beast who once was and now is not, is an eighth king who belongs to the seven and will go to his destruction. ¹² The ten horns that you saw are ten kings who have not yet received a kingdom but who for one hour will receive royal authority from the beast. ¹³ They have one purpose and will give their power and authority to the beast. ¹⁴ These will make war against the Lamb. But the Lamb will conquer them because He is Lord of lords and King of kings, and those with Him, the called, the chosen, and the faithful. ¹⁵ And he said to me, 'The waters that you saw where the prostitute sits are tribes, peoples, nations and languages; ¹⁶ and the ten horns that you saw and the beast hate the prostitute and will make her desolate, and naked, and they will eat her flesh and will burn her down with fire; ¹⁷ because God put it into their hearts to accomplish His purpose, indeed, His sole purpose—that they give their kingdoms to the beast until God's words are fulfilled. ¹⁸ The woman that you saw is the great city which rules over the kings of the earth."

Whore of Babylon illustration from Martin Luther's 1534 translation of the Bible.

The devastation from the seven plagues makes the world a difficult place to live in due to the damage from the seven bowl events to the water, atmosphere, and land. These judgments would most certainly cause dehydration and terrible sickness to the people of the earth and to the crown city of "Babylon" which was "split into three parts" (Rev. 16:19) yet survived the seventh bowl megaquake enough to continue to "rule the over the kings of the earth" (εχουσα βασιλειαν επι των βασιλεων της γης, v. 18) as indicated in the last verse of this chapter. The delusion to fight God overtakes the rulers and authorities of the world. All of these world judgments make it easy for the Beast and his false prophet to persuade the ten horns/rulers to fight against their archenemy and amass their armies against the armies of God at Armageddon. As previously described in the sixth bowl judgment, lying spirits from the unholy trinity (Satan, the Antichrist, and the prophet) infect the world leaders to convince them to fight against Jesus at the last great battle in the Valley of Megiddo (Rev. 16:16; 19:17-21). The political alliance with the ten rulers that solidifies from the influence of the Satanically driven Beast and his false prophet becomes apparent in Revelation 16:13-14. But here in Revelation 17, John showed his reading audience the beginning of the end of the religious system that had been orchestrated by the false prophet depicted by the Apostle John in Revelation 13. After establishing the Beast's international economic system based on RFID (chip technology), after instituting the false prophet's religious system by rebuilding the Jerusalem Temple and instituting the worship of the idol of the Beast, the dragon himself sent the "three lying frogs" (Rev. 16:13) to the kings of the earth to establish the political and military alliance to oppose and eventually fight against the Christ and the Kingdom of God. Throughout the next few verses of chapter 17, John described the rise and fall of the religious Babylon and its relationship with the economic (chapter 18) and the political (chapter 19) systems established by the Beast and his team.

The narrative begins with one of the seven bowl angels approaching John and telling him, "Come here, and I will show you the judgment of the great prostitute who sits on many waters with whom the kings of the earth fornicated and *those living on the earth became drunk on the wine of her fornication*" (εμεθυσθησαν οι κατοικουντος την γην εκ του οινου της πορνειας αυτης, v. 2). The phrase "wine of her fornication" also occurs in Revelation 14:8 and 18:3. This phrase underscores the loss of human judgment and right thinking when associating with the unholy trinity. John complied and approached the angel who immediately transports him through the Spirit to a wilderness location where he sees a striking/astonishing scene. He sees "a woman sitting on a scarlet beast full of blasphemous names with seven heads and ten horns" (γυναικα καθημενην επι θηριον κοκκινον γεμοντα ονοματα βλασφημιας εχων κεφαλας επτα και κερατα δεκα, v. 3).

This is the same Beast of Revelation 13; he heads the worldwide council of governments with ten presidents making up the core of the leadership who preside over ten major districts and who eventually give their power and authority to the Antichrist. The Antichrist is the leader of the eighth kingdom—the revived Roman Empire. The seven previous kingdoms were Egypt, Assyria, Babylonia, Media, Persia, Greece, and Rome. He is assassinated as John noted in Revelation 13:3. He then is revived by the power of Satan and becomes the unanimous choice of the worldwide Council to lead the new government (revived Roman Empire). Daniel 2 discusses four world governments from Daniel's time to the End Times as represented by the image of the statue (Babylon, 605-539 BC; Persia, 538-531 BC; Greece, 332-168 BC; Rome, 168 BC–AD 476); its two legs were the Eastern (Constantinople) and Western (Rome) branches of the Roman Empire and its ten toes represent the future kingdom of the Beast—the ten leading countries (possibly the European Union) and rulers at the end of this age discussed in Revelation 17. After his "resurrection," some scholars suggest that the revived Roman headquarters will shift from Rome to present day Iraq which may better explain "Babylon." However, verses 9 and 18 indicate that the likely location of "Babylon the Great" would not be Bagdad or Basra in Iraq, but Rome. I will discuss more about this later.

John continued his description of the woman sitting on the beast by discussing her attire, jewelry, and golden goblet: "And the woman was clothed in scarlet and purple; and she was adorned with gold, pearls, and precious stones; and *she had a golden goblet in her hand full of what is detestable and the unclean things of her fornication*" (εχουσα ποτηριον χρυσουν εν τη χειρι αυτης γεμον βδελυγματων και τα ακαθαρτα της πορνειας αυτης, v. 4). The woman that John described is dressed like a prostitute. He likely did not include some of the details that he could have included in describing her. She is wearing evocative and risqué clothing consistent with her intention of playing the harlot with the souls of the Beast's confederacy and the pagans following them. She even wears gaudy jewelry pieces including necklaces, bracelets, and earrings of gold, precious stones, and pearls. Of course, she holds a large golden goblet in her hand which John told us is full of the detestable and unclean elements of her fornication. I'm not sure how John knew what was inside the goblet, but maybe he was allowed to see its contents or could see some of its remnants on and around her mouth. He noticed two other very important features of her appearance. The first was the secret name written on her forehead: "Babylon the Great, the Mother of Fornicators and of the detestable things of the earth" (Βαβυλων η μεγαλη η ματηρ των πορνων και των βδελυγματων της γης, v. 5). John confirmed that the woman really does represent the great center of the Beast's activities by his comment in the last verse of this chapter that the woman is "the great city" (η πολις η μεγαλη, v. 18) previously mentioned which rules over the kings of the earth. The name she bears on her forehead is in sharp contrast to the name the 144,000 Jewish Christian evangelists bore on their foreheads (Rev. 14:1) and the name the saints will have on their foreheads when they enter the New Jerusalem (Rev. 22:4).

The second feature that John noticed is the fact the prostitute is actually "drunk on the blood of the saints and on blood of the martyrs for Jesus" (μεθυουσαν εκ του αιματος των αγιων και εκ του αιματος των μαρτυρων Ιησου, v. 6). John admitted that he was "astonished" (εθαυμασα, v. 6) when he saw the woman inebriated. Maybe John was shocked because she is involved with the killing of many Christians which he would not have suspected.

Vatican City

Whether or not the harlot is the Catholic Church remains to be seen. John was astonished by what he initially saw, maybe because he recognized the Roman Catholic Church as it had morphed into the *universal* Catholic Church. If the harlot represents the Catholic Church, his astonishment would be understandable. However, this conjecture would require much change in the culture of the Catholic Church that we now know which usually champions conservative Christian teaching and values and, as of this writing, seems to be capably led by the sincere and humble Pope Francis. Whoever "she" ends up being, "she" ultimately becomes the antithesis of the true Church of Jesus Christ because she is responsible for the martyrdom of many Christians (she is drunk with their blood in verse 6).

Another possibility for the prostitute of this chapter is the World Council of Churches, formed in 1948, which presently boasts about six hundred million people from 352 denominations including Presbyterians, Lutherans, Methodists, Moravians, Reformed, Eastern Orthodox, as well as some Pentecostal and

Baptist denominations, and many others, but excludes Roman Catholics.[192] This organization includes around 500,000 pastors, and 525,000 local congregations from more than 120 countries with its headquarters in Geneva, Switzerland. In order for the Catholic Church or the World Council of Churches to be responsible for the deaths of thousands of Christians, particularly those during the Tribulation Period, it would have to make an unholy alliance with the Beast and his world council of ten leaders. This may have occurred by the beginning of the Tribulation Period when the first seal was opened in Revelation 6 and the first horseman with his bow rides off to make conquering peace with the world, or more likely, this alliance between organized religion and the Beast could have occurred by the time the prophet sets up "beast" worship in Revelation 13. By the end of Revelation 17, the angel told John that the "woman that you saw is the great city, the one which rules over the kings of the earth." (v. 18). Therefore, the woman of John's vision not only attempts to control the religious environment of the world desperate to stem the dominance of the true God and Christ, but also is involved with the political and economic spheres of Babylon's influence.

The angel noticed John's surprise at seeing the inebriated, blood-drinking prostitute and asked John why he was astonished. The angel didn't wait for a response and offered to answer John's questions concerning the identities of the Beast and the woman riding it. The angel told John, "The beast you saw once was but now is not; he is about to ascend from the abyss and will go to his destruction; and those living on the earth are amazed, whose names are not in the Book of Life from the creation of the world, *at seeing the beast who was and is not and is to come*" (βλεποντων το θεριον οτι ην και ουκ εστιν και παρεσται, v. 8). Of course, the angel was confirming to John that this is the same Beast that John described arising from the sea in Rev.13:1-3 (the one "who was") who rose to prominence as the white horseman in Revelation 6 and created a stable economic environment for the world. He was assassinated (the one who "is not") and then his fatal wound was healed (the one who "is to come"). Then the angel continued his discussion of the Beast by describing the meaning of its seven heads. He revealed that the seven heads stand for seven "hills/mountains" (ορη, v. 9) and seven "kings" (βασιλεις, v. 9). The angel stated that the prostitute "sits" (καθηται, v. 9) on these seven mountains indicating

---

192   "What is the World Council of Churches?" World Council of Churches, accessed February 2, 2022, https://www.oikoumene.org/member-churches?search_api_fulltext=&location_filter_2=All&field_wcc_n_church_family_single=All&glossaryaz_title=S (Accessed May 27, 2023.

her existence at this location. The text suggests a "seven hill" city as the center of religious Babylon. Rome is the most likely candidate for this "honor" although to date there are eighteen cities built on seven hills in the United States including Seattle, San Francisco, and Cincinnati; thirty-eight cities in Europe; and eight cities in Asia/Middle East including Jerusalem, Tehran, and Mecca. The seven kings of the seven dominant empires as previously mentioned include the five who have already died at the time of the angel's words to John (Pharaoh Thutmose III from Egypt, Tiglath-Pileser from Assyria, Nebuchadnezzar from Babylon, Cyrus from Media-Persia, and Alexander the Great from Greece). Emperor Domitian of Rome who was alive at the time John received Apocalypse is the king "who is." The seventh king is the one who has "not yet come" and could be any of a number of rulers/dictators including, as some have thought, Hitler or even a dictator with a global influence prior to the rise of the Antichrist in Revelation 13. Indeed, the seventh king could be the Antichrist as the economic leader of the world at the World Bank represented by the white horseman of Revelation 6:2 during the first half of the Tribulation period as suggested earlier. Indeed, John made the comment that the seventh king will only have a short reign: "when he does come, he will only remain for a short time" (και οταν ελθη ολιγον αυτον δει μειναι, v. 10). In other words, the Antichrist of the Time of Sorrows becomes the Beast of the Great Tribulation Period after his assassination and resuscitation making him an eighth king of sorts mentioned in this narrative that "belongs to the seven" previous kings because he operates in their shared spirit of opposition to the God of the universe.

Next John discussed the Beast again and his relationship to the "ten horns": "The beast who was and now is not is an eighth (king) who belongs to the seven and will go to his destruction"- (και το θηριον ο ην και ουκ εστιν και αυτος ογδοος εστιν και εκ των επτα εστιν και εις απωλειαν υπαγει-v.11). John reiterated the role of the Antichrist during this very trying time on earth. The world has just experienced the outpouring of the seven bowl judgments with millions dying from the skin abscesses, the sea and water pollution and the resulting dehydration, the solar flares causing painful second and third degree burns, the electrical blackouts, the prospect of final battle, and the devastating earthquake with damage of the capital city and many other major cities on the earth. The Beast has a three-and-a-half-year rule on the earth ending in his army's annihilation and his subsequent casting into the lake of fire (cf. Rev. 19:20). But God allows the Beast to mentor and lead "ten horns." As John described, "The ten horns that you saw are ten kings who have not yet received a kingdom; *but they will receive royal authority for one hour through the beast*" (αλλα εξουσιαν ως βασιλεις μιαν ωραν λαμβανουσιν μετα του θηριου, v. 12). The "one hour" of time for the ten kings and their rule may translate to several months to several years of a "ten kings' confederacy." I think that time at the end is very accelerated because of so many events happening at once. It would make sense that the ten rulers are part of the European Union. However, at the time of the events recorded here by John, the confederacy of ten might be another group possibly associated with Muslim and Sino-Asian countries. One feature emphasized by John in chapter 17 is that these kings "have one purpose—to give their power and authority to the Beast" (μιαν γνωμην εχουσιν και την δυναμιν και εξουσιαν αυτων τω θηριω διδοασιν, v. 13). Because of the worldwide destruction, great hate has developed in the hearts of these leaders and their citizens against God. As He did with Pharaoh (Ex. 9:16; Rom. 9:17), I think the Lord will harden their hearts and will solidify their hate against Himself to ensure that they will be resolute in attempting to annihilate God. God does an excellent job at getting them ready to fight Him. *"And they will make war against the Lamb, but the Lamb will conquer them because He is Lord of lords and King of kings and those with Him—the called, the chosen, and the faithful"* (ουτοι μετα του αρνιου πολεμησουσιν και το αρνιον νικησει αυτους, v. 14). The angel gave John a glimpse into the near future ahead of the present narrative and allowed him to see the results of Armageddon. I find it comforting that those on earth and in heaven who follow the Lamb are considered partners with Jesus against His enemies. The angel identified these people as "the called, the chosen, and the faithful" (κλητοι και εκλεκτοι και πιστοι, v. 14). The contrast is striking. His saints, God's answer to the entrenched pagan support of the Beast and rage against the Lord, are just as dedicated and enmeshed with the Trinity as are the leaders and pagan followers of the Antichrist and the unholy trinity. The angel speaking to John also celebrated the Lion of Judah, the Conquering Messiah, and His complete victory with his words about the Beast and the confederacy of ten kings/nations being dominated by the King of kings and Lord of lords.

The angel completed the vision of the prostitute and the Beast by giving John insight into "the waters" which the prostitute was sitting on at the beginning of the chapter. He told John that "the waters that you saw where the prostitute sits are tribes, people, nations, and languages" (τα υδατο α ειδες ου η πορνη καθηται λαοι και οχλοι εισιν και εθνη και γλωσσαι, v. 15) again indicating the extent of her influence over the nations under the Beast's rule. I wonder if by this time the United States is under the Antichrist's rule. The indication from Revelation 12 is that the "two wings of the eagle" (possibly indicating the United States) rescued "the woman" representing the beleaguered followers/saints of Jesus Christ and protected her for 1,260 days (forty-two months) until the saints were martyred. But by the latter half of the Tribulation, during the Great Tribulation, America may have succumbed to the wiles of the enemy and joined in the fight against the Lord of lords and the King of kings.

Then the angel revealed the awful demise of the prostitute. He told John that the ten kings and the Beast end up hating the prostitute and, turning on her, destroy religious Babylon as well as burn down the facilities that house her administrative staff. Perhaps political and economic Babylon began to hate her because she couldn't appease God Almighty and prevent the devastating hit their world experienced at the hand of the seven angels with the seven bowl judgments. The angel told John, "Then the ten horns that you saw and beast *hate the prostitute and make her destitute and naked; and they eat her flesh and burn her down with fire*" (μισησουσιν την πορνην και ηρημωμενην ποιησουσιν αυτην και γυμνην και τας σαρκας αυτης φαγονται και αυτην κατακαυσουσιν εν πυρι, v. 16). In case there was any question concerning who the woman was riding on the beast, the angel clarified by telling John, "the woman that you saw is the great city, the one ruling over the kings of the earth" (η γυνη ην ειδες εστιν η πολις η μεγαλη η εχουσα βασιλειαν επι των βασιλεων της γης, v. 18). Since the woman "sits on seven hills" (v. 9) and "rules over the kings of the earth" (v. 18), I speculate that her corporate headquarters would likely be Rome. But as I indicated earlier, there are many cities built on seven hills in western Europe and in the Middle East which may end up being the capital city housing the activities of the prostitute who misled the world and was responsible for the deaths of millions of Christians. If the prostitute is the Roman Catholic Church, then John's astonishment would be better understood. The Vatican (officially, Vatican City State) is the world's smallest independent country with 121 acres. It would be heartbreaking to some degree if the Vatican was burned down because of its priceless artwork and architecture. But its burning would be deserved if the Church was responsible for heretical doctrine and responsible for the deaths of innocent Christians throughout the world.

REVELATION 18

Destruction of Economic Babylon

1 "After these, I saw another angel coming down out of heaven having great authority; indeed, the earth was illuminated by his glory. ² And he shouted with a loud voice, 'Fallen, fallen is Babylon the Great; she has become a dwelling place of demons and a haunt for every unclean spirit and every unclean bird and every unclean beast and that which is hated. ³ Indeed, all of the nations drank the maddening wine of her fornication and the kings of the earth fornicated with her and the merchants of the earth became rich from the power of her lustful living.' ⁴ Then I heard another voice from heaven say, 'Come out of her, My people, so that you would not associate with her sins and that you may not receive her plagues, ⁵ because her sins are piled up to heaven and God has remembered her unrighteous deeds. ⁶ Give back to her as she has given; and pay her back double what she did; and pour her out a double portion from her own cup; ⁷ and give her as much grief and torment as she gave herself in glory and lustful living. In her heart she boasts, "I sit enthroned as queen and I am not a widow, and I will never see sorrow." ⁸ Therefore, in one day her plagues will come: death, sorrow and famine; and she will be burned down by fire because the mighty Lord God has judged her.' ⁹ When the kings of the earth who fornicated

with her and shared in her sensual living, when they see the smoke of her burning, they will weep and mourn over her. [10] Terrified at her torment, they stand afar off and cry, 'Woe, woe to the great and mighty city Babylon because your punishment came in one hour.'

[11] "Then the earth's merchants weep and mourn over her because no one will buy their cargos any more: [12] cargos of gold, silver, precious stones and pearls, of fine linen, purple, silk, and scarlet cloth, of every sort of citron wood and articles made of every kind of ivory, costly wood, bronze, iron, and marble; [13] of cinnamon, spice, incense, myrrh, and frankincense, of wine, olive oil, fine flour and wheat, of cattle, sheep, horses and carriages, and bodies and lives of people. [14] And the ripe fruit of your lusting soul left you, and all of the glamorous and splendid things were lost from you; and they will never ever find them.

[15] "And her merchants made rich by her stood afar off because of fear of her torment, weeping and mourning [16] and said, 'Woe, woe to the great city clothed in fine linen, purple, and scarlet cloth and adorned with gold, precious stones, and pearls, [17] but in one hour so much wealth was destroyed.' And every ship's captain, and every sea traveler, and the sailors working on the seas stood afar off [18] and seeing the smoke of her torment cried out saying, 'Who is like the great city!' [19] And they threw dust on their heads and wailed, wept, and cried saying, 'Woe, woe to the great city where all became rich, including those who have boats on the sea; in one hour she has been brought to ruin.' [20] Now rejoice over her, heaven including the saints, apostles, and prophets because God judged her with the punishment she gave to you.

[21] "Then a mighty angel picked up a stone like a large millstone and hurled it into the sea saying, 'With sudden violence the great city Babylon will be thrown down never to be found again.' [22] Then the sound of musicians, flutists, harpists, and trumpeters will never be heard in you again. No craftsman of any trade will ever be found in you again. The sound of the millstone will never be heard in you again. [23] The light of a lamp will never shine in you again. The voice of the bride and the bride will never be heard in you again. Indeed, your merchants were the world's most important people for by your sorcery all the nations were deceived. [24] And the blood of the saints, the prophets and those slaughtered on the earth was found in her."

Destruction of Economic Babylon

As we saw in the previous chapter, possibly the Vatican or World Council of Churches align itself with the Beast. It seems that by the second half of the Tribulation Period, one of these organizations becomes opposed to anyone wanting and pursuing true relationship with the Triune God and is responsible for the martyrdom of thousands of Christians who were converted after the rapture of the Church likely by the 144,000 Jewish Christians of Revelation 7 and 14. But as mentioned previously, the Beast and political Babylon eventually destroy her (religious Babylon) probably because she was unable to deter God's wrath and His tremendous judgment against the world with the seven bowl judgments of Revelation 16.

By the beginning of chapter 13, the Beast has risen to prominence and became the world's dictator after his assassination and recovery. In Daniel 2, Daniel prophesied about the rise of the End Times Babylon and the revived Roman Empire—the ten-nation confederacy of the Beast. Daniel interpreted Nebuchadnezzar's dream of the statue made of gold, silver, bronze, iron, and clay in Daniel 2. He stated that the gold head and neck region of the statue is the original Babylon (which lasted sixty-six years); so we can surmise that the silver chest and arms was the succeeding Persian Empire (208 years); the bronze belly and thighs represented the Greek Empire (185 years) under its general and king, Alexander the Great, and the extension of the Greek Empire under his four generals; and the iron legs were the Roman Empire with its two capital cities in Rome and Constantinople (five hundred years). The ten toes of the image made of iron and clay represent the last kingdom which predicts the rise of the revived Roman Empire as depicted by the Beast with ten horns in Revelation 17:10-17 at the End Times. The statues' ten toes probably signify the ten world leaders likely spawned from the European Union led by Rome which rules the world through the administration of the Beast during the Great Tribulation Period. Some Revelation scholars feel that the political center of the world will be in Bagdad, Iraq, but I feel that Rome makes much better sense due to passages in Revelation linking the harlot (Vatican) who sits on seven hills (17: 9) to the seven headed, ten-horned Beast (17:3). The eighth king of Revelation 17:11 is the Beast and presiding president (over the ten kings and their districts) who gets assassinated and apparently resurrected. He becomes the leader of the ten countries which are identified as the ten horns of the Beast the harlot rides. Again, he is the Antichrist/Beast and is honored by the leaders/countries to whom he gave "royal authority" (17:12); his influence thrusts the revived Roman Empire to the forefront of world leadership as prophesied by Daniel in Daniel 2. How does the confederacy destroy the religious harlot? The angel in Revelation 17 told John that they burn her down with fire. Could that be a nuclear or special forces strike? By the end of chapter 17, the harlot ceases to exist leaving economic and political Babylon to fight against the forces of heaven.

The scene changes in chapter 18 with an account of the fall of economic Babylon. I think that John's reading audience was given a glimpse of the annihilation of political Babylon and the forces of the dragon at Armageddon in Revelation 14 which actually does not take place until chapter 19. But for the first time, John and his reading audience saw what the future world thought was impossible—the fall of their prosperous way of life. In the beginning of chapter 18, John saw another angel coming down out of heaven who has great authority. Maybe this was the archangel Gabriel, since he is the announcing angel, or maybe the archangel Michael. John saw two other angels in Revelation 5:2 and 10:1 who he described as mighty (ισχυρον). But here, the angel is described as having "great authority" (εχουσιαν μεγαλην) and that "the earth was illuminated by his glory" (η γη εφωτισθη εκ της δοξης αυτου, v. 1). John was indicating that God was giving this very important angel, likely an archangel, a significant announcement to make. John heard this impressive angel cry out in a mighty voice, "Fallen, fallen is Babylon the Great" (επεσεν, επεσεν Βαβυλων η μεγαλη, v. 2), which is what John heard the second angel announce in Revelation 14:8. John obviously was given insight into the two main reasons for the fall from God's perspective. The first may be the most important damning point against the economic regime of the Beast. The capital city of Babylon's economic center by this time in the Apocalypse has become the "dwelling place of demons" (κατοικητηριον δαιμονιων, v. 2) including the haunt of every unclean spirit, unclean bird, unclean beast, and "the despised/hated one" (μεμισημενου, v. 2). The citizens of this megapolis were very busy enjoying the fruits of their economic prosperity at the expense of righteous living and obedience to the commands of God. They were sinners on a mission. They even allowed the most heinous of sinners, "the hated one," to subsist and prosper in their city. Could this mean child pornographers or mass murderers? Or could the "hated one" be a reference to the Beast or even the harlot until her demise? It would seem that these sophisticated consumers also attracted Satan's demons. Of course, the dragon/the devil was behind all of what was allowed to thrive in the city as the Apostle remarked. Wherever the devil is, his demons are nearby; this "haunt" (φυλακη, v. 2) not only is the home on earth of the demons by this time in Revelation, but also the gathering place of birds and beasts which do the devil's bidding. Maybe these animals are the answer to the Lord's birds in Revelation 19:17, 21?

The second reason for the Lord's final annihilation of economic Babylon is the mesmerizing influence and power over the people of all nations of her promotion of "sensual living" (στρηνους, v. 3). Indeed, John mentioned the beguiling effects of her "maddening wine" and the "fornication" with the nations and with the kings of the earth. The Apostle characterizes Babylon's influence on the citizens of the confederacy by describing the meteoric rise to world prominence of the merchant (εμποροι) class (cf. verse 23) and the stupendous wealth they obtain. He stated, "and the merchants of the earth became rich on the power of her sensual living" (και ο εμποροι της γης εκ της δυναμεως του στρηνους αυτης επλουτησαν, v. 3). John painted the word picture of these merchants utilizing the "power" of persuasion and consumerism (cf. verses 11–14) to create an appetite for their products. This craving and conditioning for buying and selling produced unbelievable wealth for these merchants. According to the World Bank, in 2021, the gross domestic product for the United States was 25.32 trillion dollars and for China, 17.73 trillion dollars.[193] By the time the confederacy of the Beast comes to power, I would not be surprised if it was well above 25 to 30 trillion dollars or its equivalent. The Internet has become extremely influential and the major vehicle shaping economic activity and culture through business websites, the major search engines (Google, YouTube, Amazon, Facebook, Microsoft, Bing, Baidu—the dominant search engine in China—social media, and other venues). Now, mobile web traffic has accounted for at least 64 percent of all web marketing in 2021.[194] About 65.6 percent of the world's population uses the Internet, nearly five billion people. These global Internet users spend an average of almost 7 hours each day on the Internet; over 90 percent of them visit online stores, over 80 percent carry out online searches, and nearly 80 percent of them actually follow through with purchases from their searches. This all adds up to over 5.7 trillion dollars spent on ecommerce sales in 2022. China has the most Internet users who are expected to spend 1.5 trillion dollars in 2023 through ecommerce.[195] In the past few months, China has mandated a law prohibiting its elementary aged children from using the Internet for online games more than three hours per week due to an official Chinese business newspaper calling the gaming

---

193 "GDP (current US$)," The World Bank, accessed May 29, 2023, https://data.worldbank.org/indicator/NY.GDP.MKTP.CD?locations=CN.
194 "The Ultimate List of Marketing Statistics for 2022"; HubSpot, Inc., 2023, accessed May 29, 2023, https://www.hubspot.com/marketing-statistics.
195 "10 Internet Statistics Every Marketer Should Know," Oberlo, accessed September 10, 2021, https://www.oberlo.com/blog/internet-statistics#:~:text=There%20are%20currently%204.66%20billion%20active%20internet%20users,6%20hours%20and%2056%20minutes%20online%20every%20day.

industry "spiritual opium."[196] The Chinese are beginning to recognize the tremendous influence the Internet wields in shaping habits and influencing culture, politics, and mores as can be seen by *their limitation* of Internet use among its youngest citizens and by *their incursion* into America's culture and politics through TikTok.[197]

The economic influence, wealth, and power of Babylon caused the innermost thoughts and culture of the city and its leaders to think it was invulnerable to destruction despite what recently occurred to the world at the hand of God through the seven bowl judgments and what occurred to the harlot (religious Babylon). The concept of "lustful living" mediated through demons was not new to the Apostle John whose vision of the future Babylon exposes, in these verses, its pervasiveness. But the obvious influence and addiction that wealth and material comfort have on our world would and should cause us, as Christians, to reevaluate our connections to materialism. No wonder God calls the remnant of believers out and away from economic Babylon in verse 4 to clear their minds and hearts from the pollution of materialism. If they refuse, then they too are about to experience the terrible judgment coming suddenly to economic Babylon (vv. 8–17). John reported this as another voice from heaven that said, "*Come out of her, My people, so that you are not associated with her sins* and so that you do not receive her plagues; because her sins are piled up to heaven, and God has remembered her unrighteous acts" (εξελθατε ο λαος μου εξ αυτης ινα μη συγκοινωνησατε ταις αμαρτιαις αυτης, v. 4).

I think it is significant that God appeals to the remnant of believers still alive on the earth despite not joining the Beast by refusing to worship his image and refusing his chip technology. It surely must be an underground Church which has survived the terrible bowl judgments and previous trumpet and seal judgments. But God appeals to them to not give in to the materialistic pressures and attractions of the Babylon about to be destroyed in an hour. The angel made it clear to John that God would be giving her back "a double portion" (διπλωσατε τα διπλα, v. 6) of the torment and grief (βασανισμον και πενθος, v. 7) that she meted out to the

---

[196] "China limits online gaming time for children to three hours a week"; *CBS News/The Associated Press*, August 30, 2021, accessed September 10, 2021, https://www.cbsnews.com/news/china-limits-online-gaming-children-3-hours-week/.

[197] Rachel Treisman, "The FBI alleges TikTok poses national security concerns," November 17, 2022, accessed June 29, 2023, 2023, http:// www.npr.org/2022/11/17/1137155540/fbi-tiktok-national-security-concerns-china#:~:text=The%20head%20of%20the%20FBI%20says%20the%20bureau,to%20influence%20American%20users%20or%20control%20their%20devices.

people of God throughout her time of dominance in the last half of the Tribulation Period. John reported that the woman representing economic Babylon thinks and repeats a narrative that emphasizes her feeling of invulnerability, indestructability, and indomitability. She repeats these three phrases indicating this, "For she says in her heart, *'I sit enthroned as queen, I am not a widow, and I will never see sorrow'*" (καθημαι Βασιλισσα και χηρα ουκ ειμι και πενθος ου μη ιδω, **v. 7)**.

Next, John described the impending disaster that overtakes the residence of economic Babylon and the utter destruction that the city and her economic empire experiences. John was clear to report that the city is destroyed in an hour of time—remindful of the Al-Qaeda strike on the Twin Towers in New York City on September 11, 2001: "Therefore in a day her plagues will come, death, famine, and sorrow; *she will be burned down with fire since the Almighty God has judged her*" (εν πυρι κατακαυθησεται οτι ισχυρος κυριος ο θεος ο κρινας αυτην, v. 8). The city becomes a target possibly of the confederacy of ten due to some breakdown of diplomacy and trust between its civic leaders and the political leaders of Babylon; or the hour-long destruction could be the result of the effects of the megaquake destroying the nuclear power plants surrounding the city of Babylon as I suggested in Revelation 16. John nor the angel indicated *how* the hour-long firestorm occurs. But we know that the city must be near the ocean because of several passages in this chapter that I will review. John stated that "the kings of the earth who fornicated with her and shared in her lustful living, when they see the smoke of her burning they weep and mourn over her; standing afar off terrified of her torment, they cry out saying, *'Woe, woe is the great and mighty city Babylon for in one hour your punishment came*" (ουαι,ουαι η πολις η μεγαλη Βαβυλον η πολις η ισχυρα οτι μια ωρα ηλθεν η κρισις σου, v. 10). Here and in a few more verses we see the mention of the one-hour destruction of obviously a very sophisticated city certainly with resources to protect itself from outside attack. The Apostle described the shock of the merchant class supported by the wealth of the Empire: They "weep and mourn over her because no one buys their cargoes anymore" (κλαιουσιν και πενθουσιν επ αυτην οτι τον γομον αυτων ουδεις αγοραζει ουκετι, v. 11). I'm not sure why the loss of the city ended international commerce. But the shutdown of the stock market and air travel for several weeks when America was attacked on September 11, 2001, indicates how critical a city of commerce obviously means to international trade; and at the time, New York City was not destroyed—only two of its important buildings. What is of great interest is the manner in which John reported the loss of the various kinds of commerce. He basically divided all of the international commerce into eight major categories: precious stones and metals, industrial and building materials, apparel, perfume, food, agriculture, automotive, and human trafficking. The list of the top ten industries in the United States today *closely parallels* John's list of the most lucrative products managed by the merchants of the international federation of ten countries.[198] The top ten American industries (in order with the biggest first) are:

1. Information
2. Manufacturing of nondurable goods
3. Retail trade
4. Wholesale trade
5. Manufacturing of durable goods
6. Health care and social assistance
7. Finance and insurance
8. State and local government
9. Professional and business services
10. Real estate

This current list of most profitable commerce will likely be modified in the future world of the Apocalypse. But even the information, finance/insurance, and the state and local government categories which appear not to be related to the eight "cargoes" mentioned by John actually will be involved. Can you imagine the production of durable and non-durable goods of John's list *not* involving the banking and finance sector which facilitate cash flow irregularities and help enforce the tax codes of each future nation? Or what about the information sector and the advertisement function it supplies for the products on John's list through the Internet and its media outlets? No international trade would ever be possible without the cooperation of the states and regions of the Beast's confederacy following international and local export and import laws. What I think is striking and very distressing on John's list is the obvious human trafficking, "and bodies and lives of people" (και σωματων και ψυκας ανθρωπων, v. 13). This phrase utilized by John also raises the very real prospect of not just slavery and prostitution trafficking, but also the black market for body parts and organs—so called "organ trafficking."

---

[198] Norm Schriever, "Ranking the biggest industries in the US economy—with a surprise #1!" accessed September 21, 2021; https://bluewatercredit.com/ranking-biggest-industries-us-economy-surprise-1/.

Destruction of Economic Babylon

Today the global human trafficking business including sexual exploitation, forced labor, forced begging, and forced marriage is alive and well, unfortunately. Nearly twenty-five million people are presently victims of trafficking; 30 percent of victims are children with over 60 percent of victims in the United States identified as sex slaves. The top states for trafficking humans are California, Texas (not surprising due to non-existent border security at our southern border), Florida, and New York; the top countries as targets of the traffickers are Ethiopia (five million people) and Bangladesh (over 125,000 children); the top three nations engaging in the trafficking business are the United States, Mexico, and the Philippines.[199]

Organ trafficking also flourishes today. Because demand for organs exceeds supply by a wide margin, traffickers of organs thrive on this 870 million to 1.7 billion dollar-a-year industry. The most illicitly trafficked organ is the kidney with over ten thousand illegally harvested each year from the poor and then transplanted to the rich; one illegal kidney is harvested every hour with average purchase price of around sixty thousand dollars.[200]

John was seeing the world devoid of connection to the Lord dependent on acquisition of property, provisions, and people with little regard for their spiritual and emotional well-being—creature comforts of the rich and powerful. But John continued his description of the tragedy of the annihilation of economic Babylon by summarizing its terrible fate: "the ripe fruit of your lusting soul left you; and all the glamorous and splendid things were lost from you; *and they will never ever find them*" (και ουκετι ου μη αυτα ευρησουσιν, v. 14). Never again finding the wealth and

Organ Harvesting:

- ✓ **Lungs: $150,000**
- ✓ **Heart: $130,000**
- ✓ **Liver: $100,000**
- ✓ **Kidney: $60,000**
- ✓ **Cornea: $30,000**

Approximate prices paid for organs in 2022

Author created

---

199 Adriana Moskovska, 20 Horrific Human Trafficking Statistics not to Miss in 2021, July 5, 2021, accessed from the internet on September 24, 2021, https://thehighcourt.co/human-trafficking-statistics/#:~:text=Depressing%20Human%20Trafficking%20Facts%20%28Editor's%20Picks%29%201%2025,identified%20as%20sex%20trafficking%20victims.%20More%20items...%20.

200 Christina Bain and Joseph Mari, "Organ Trafficking—the Unseen Form of Human Trafficking," ACAM Today August 2018, accessed September 24, 2021, https://www.acamstoday.org/organ-trafficking-the-unseen-form-of-human-trafficking/.

influence of the city smacks of a nuclear strike or nuclear plant destruction from the megaquake and resulting tsunamis described in previous chapters and the resulting radiation poisoning of the soil and ground water of the city, not unlike the nuclear plant meltdown and destruction of Chernobyl, Russia on April 25-26, 1986. The Chernobyl nuclear reactor accident caused a kill zone of a 19-mile radius.[201] The reactors will be fully cleaned up by AD 2065,[202] but the region around the plant will be unsafe for habitation for at least three hundred years.[203]

Then John reported the one-hour collapse of the chief international business city from the perspective of the merchants and from those on the nearby seas who witnessed the nuclear disaster from their ships. John had just catalogued the loss of income from the international collapse of trade. But in the next few verses, he described the abject horror and fear of the merchant class who are watching the destruction of the source of their great wealth—the chief financial megapolis. John sets the scene by describing these merchants "standing afar off for fear of her torment weeping and mourning saying, 'Woe, woe to the great city who was clothed in fine linen, purple, and scarlet cloth and adorned in gold, precious stones and pearls; *but so much wealth was destroyed in one hour*'" (οτι μια ωρα ηρημωθη ο τουσουτος πλουτος, vv. 15-17). It's as if the merchants are watching the event on their mobile phones, computers, or tablets and become overwhelmed by what had appeared to them to be an impregnable capital city. They recounted how special the city was to them, then repeated how much economic loss their world absorbed in just one hour certainly suggestive of a nuclear disaster maybe from the megaquake as previously mentioned or from some clandestine force from the United States or from within the Confederacy Empire itself, as I have previously suggested. But remember, whatever and whomever the destruction comes by, the Lord God Almighty is the One who authorized the downfall of the city as John reported from the angel in verse 8.

---

201 Erin Blakemore, "The Chernobyl disaster: what happened, and the long-term impact," *National Geographic*, May 20, 2019, accessed May 29, 2023, https://www.nationalgeographic.co.uk/environment/2019/05/chernobyl-disaster-what-happened-and-long-term-impact.

202 "Chernobyl nuclear power plant site to be cleared by 2065," *Kyiv Post*, January 4, 2010, accessed May 29, 2023, https://web.archive.org/web/20121005150746/http:/www.kyivpost.com/content/ukraine/chornobyl-nuclear-power-plant-site-to-be-cleared-b-56391.html.

203 Raman Nijjar, Chernobyl by the numbers," *CBC News*, April 25, 2011, accessed May 29, 2023, https://www.cbc.ca/news/world/chornobyl-by-the-numbers-1.1097000.

Then the scene switches to those who can actually see the smoke of her burning rise into the sky—presumably the nuclear plume visible to sea travelers and sailors who weep and mourn over their favorite place and say, "Who is like the great city?" (τις ομοια τη πολει τη μεγαλη, v. 18). They become very emotional and in a Middle Eastern flare, throw dust on their heads and cry out again about the devastation to their world including the ship owners for whom they work (v. 19). Then the narrative switches to heaven: "Rejoice heaven and the saints, apostles, and the prophets *because God has judged her with the punishment she gave to you*" (οτι εκρινεν ο θεος το κριμα υμων εξ αυτης, v. 20).

Then John watched as a mighty angel, possibly Michael, hurls a giant boulder, as large as a millstone into the sea. Millstones in Bible times have been calculated to be upwards of 3,000 pounds and were used to grind wheat and other grains into fine powder for cooking and for sacrifices.[204] The scene with the angel is dramatic and symbolic; the millstone represented human prosperity and livelihood in the capital city. As the angel hurled the boulder into the sea, he shouted, "With sudden violence the great city Babylon is thrown down, never to be found again" (ορμηματι βληθησεται Βαβυλων η μεγαλη πολις και ου μη ευρεθη ετι, v. 21). The phrase, "with sudden violence" (ορμηματι), definitely suggests an irreversible action such as a nuclear attack and supports the narrative which follows (vv. 22–23). No activities associated with life and prosperity will ever be heard (musicians, millstones, voices of the groom and bride), found (craftsmen), or shine (lamps) in Babylon.

John concluded his vision of the fall of the great city by summarizing the reason for God's thorough judgment of the city: Babylon's merchants were the vehicle through which the whole world was *deceived* (επλανηθησαν, v. 22) into opposing the Word and purposes of God as attested by the complicity and role the agents of Babylon exhibited in the killing of God's saints and, for that matter, all innocent humans on the earth. John bluntly stated, "and the blood of the prophets and saints and all those slaughtered on the earth were found in her" (και εν αυτη αιμα προφητων και αγιων ευρεθη και παντων των εσφαγμενων επι της γης, v. 24). By this time, the Lord has had enough of Satan and his deception and influence. In chapter 19, John began to see the devil's time winding down on the earth and the demise of his Antichrist and his false prophet and their eventual sudden defeat and judgment.

---

204 Khalid Schultz, "How Much Does A Millstone Weigh In The Bible, *Receiving Helpdeak*, accessed May 29, 2023, https://receivinghelpdesk.com/ask/how-much-does-a-millstone-weigh-in-the-bible.

REVELATION 19

The Wedding of the Lamb with His Church

The Wedding Feast of the Lamb

The Fall of Political Babylon

Armageddon I

The Beast and the False Prophet Thrown into Hell

1 "After these things, I heard a loud voice from a large crowd in heaven saying, 'Hallelujah, salvation, glory and power to our God ² because His judgments are just and true and He judged the great prostitute who perverted the world with her fornication and He avenged His servants' blood on her.' ³ And again they said, 'Hallelujah, her smoke rises up forever and ever.' ⁴ Then the twenty-four elders and the four living beings fell down and worshipped God,

the One sitting on the throne, saying, 'Amen. Hallelujah.' [5] Then a voice came out of the throne saying, 'Praise to our God all His servants and those who reverently fear/worship Him, the small ones and the big ones.' [6] Then I heard the voice from a great multitude like the sound of many waters, like the sound of great thunder saying, 'Hallelujah, the Lord God reigns, God Almighty; [7] let us rejoice and be exceedingly joyful and let us give the glory to Him because the wedding of the Lamb has come and His wife has made herself ready. [8] Fine linen, clean and shining has been given to her to wear'; 'fine linen' is the righteous acts of the saints. [9] Then he said to me, 'Write, "Blessed are those having been invited to the wedding feast of the Lamb." Then he said to me, "These are the true words of God." [10] I fell down at his feet to worship him but he said, "Stop. Don't do that for I am a servant of yours and of your brothers, those having the testimony of Jesus. Worship God, for the testimony of Jesus is the Spirit of prophecy."'

[11] "Then I saw heaven opened and behold a white horse and One sitting on it faithful and true; in righteousness He judges and makes war; [12] His eyes are a flame of fire and on His head are many crowns and He has been given a written Name that no one knows except Himself, [13] And having been clothed in a robe dipped in blood and His Name was called the Word of God. [14] Then the armies of heaven dressed in clean fine, white linen followed Him on white horses. [15] And a sharp sword projects out of His mouth that with it He might strike down the nations; He will rule them with a rod of iron and He treads the winepress of the wine of the fury and of the anger of Almighty God. [16] And He has written on His robe and on His thigh a Name: 'King of kings and Lord of lords.'

[17] "And I saw one angel standing on the sun and he shouted out with a loud voice to all the birds flying in midheaven saying, 'Come here and gather for God's great banquet [18] so that you might eat the flesh of kings, and the flesh of generals, and the flesh of the powerful, and the flesh of horses and their riders, and the flesh of all freedmen and slaves both small ones and great ones. [19] Then, I saw the beast and the kings of the earth and their armies having gathered together to make war against the One sitting on the horse and against His armies. [20] But the beast was seized and with him the false prophet who performed signs before him by which he deceived those having

received the mark of the beast and those worshipping his image. The two were thrown alive into the lake of fire, the one burning with sulphur. [21] The rest were killed by the sword of the One sitting on the horse—by it projecting out of His mouth; then all the birds were gorged on their flesh."

As indicated by the Revelator in chapter 17, the harlot represents the Beast's religious organization led by his false prophet which is possibly centered in Rome. However, John was astonished by who the harlot represents: the Catholic Church or some worldwide church organization like the World Council of Churches (WCC). For reasons not entirely clear, political Babylon led by the ten leaders and the once assassinated Antichrist turn against the harlot and destroy her headquarters and influence paving the way for the Beast to totally dominate the world in religious and political matters. The harlot possibly became the scapegoat for the wrath of political Babylon against the Lord and His seven bowl judgments which nearly destroy the Beast's Empire and which the religious harlot was not able to prevent. The Beast and false prophet blame the harlot for the destruction of their property, people, and damage to their plans of world dominance because of the seven bowl judgments of Revelation 16. Chapter 18 narrates the fallout of the attack on the Empire's capital city (possibly Rome, London, New York City, etc.) near a large body of water. The destruction of the city takes an hour and could be caused by a massive earthquake with resulting tsunamis. This seventh bowl judgment caused the rest of world to mourn from a distance as they watch through the media its smoke rising. As stated, I don't favor the explanation of nuclear attack because by this time the world's powers are dominated and controlled by the Beast and his armed forces who would prevent the destruction of a nuclear attack. A much more plausible explanation of Babylon's destruction is the mega-earthquake destroying the capital city directly or spawning

Jezreel Valley, the location of the Battle of Armageddon

a giant tsunami which destroys the city and its nuclear power plants resulting in nuclear reactor malfunction and explosions. This is all speculation. What we do know about the capital city of the Beast is that the megaquake caused Babylon to split into three parts causing massive destruction and certainly the death of many of its citizens (Rev. 16:19).

John picked up the narrative in chapter 19 with a vision of an immense crowd of believers not unlike the innumerable raptured crowd in Revelation 7:9–10. He heard a loud, thunderous sound praising God with "Hallelujah, the salvation, glory, and power to our God because His judgments are true and just, *for He has judged the great prostitute*" (οτι εκρινεν την πορνην την μεγαλην, v. 2). Because of the treacheries of the religious authority in the future Babylon against the saints and against the Church of the Lamb, God declares that Babylon's days will end soon with His people proclaiming that "her [Babylon's] smoke is rising up forever and ever" (και ο καπνος αυτης αναβειναι εις τους αιωνας των αιωνων, v. 3). With this statement, the elders and seraphim bow down and worship God as He sits on His throne and confirm the crowd's statements with, "Amen, Hallelujah!" (αμην αλληλουια, v. 4). The total destruction of economic Babylon in Revelation 18 and the demise of its international trade and commerce ventures devastates the world order of the Beast and compels political Babylon and its cabinet of ten presidents (the ten horns of Rev. 17) to turn their attention and energies against the Lord God Almighty. Aided by the Beast and his false prophet, they make final preparations to go to war against the Christ and His remnant of people in and around Israel.

However, the narrative continues in heaven. John heard a voice from the throne imploring those who worship and serve the Lord to actively praise Him (v. 5), bringing to mind the many times that the kings of Israel and their prophets suggested that the nation of Israel sing praises to Yahweh right before an enemy was engaged in war (2 Chronicles 20:18-25). Next John heard a mighty roar from heaven, similar to the sound at the beginning of the chapter from likely the same massive crowd. The Apostle heard what sounded like a massive waterfall (brings to mind Niagara Falls in New York or Victoria Falls in Zimbabwe) and mighty thunder. He makes out the words of the massive crowd shouting, "Hallelujah, the Lord God Almighty reigns! Let us therefore rejoice and be exceedingly joyful and give Him the glory because *the wedding of the Lamb has come and His bride has made herself ready*" (ηλθεν ο γαμος του αρνιου και η γυνη αυτου ητοιμασεν εαυτην, v. 7). John was hearing the great roar of the bride of Christ affirming their great love for the Godhead and excitement at finally being invited into the Great Hall for the

Wedding and the Wedding Feast of the Lamb. This has been the goal of the Church/Bride of Christ since the nascent Church began at the calling of the twelve disciples and on the Day of Pentecost when the Holy Spirit indwelt the Church to launch it into the world as witness for Jesus. After several millennia, the Bride of Christ has properly prepared herself as John reported by receiving the "fine linen, clean and shining" (βυσσινον λαμπρον καθαρον, v. 8) to wear for the nuptial ceremony. As previously illustrated, the angel, who revealed the Apocalypse to John, made it clear to him that these clean, white, shining wedding garments represent "the righteous acts of the saints" (τα δικαιωματα των αγιων, v. 8). Indeed, the followers of Christ as His Body and Bride have rehearsed for this moment through their "acts of righteousness" in corporate worship, in corporate fellowship, and in corporate evangelism throughout the world and throughout time. Finally, the moment of consummation of the unity between Jesus and the Church will be made before two witnesses: God the Father and God the Holy Spirit. The angel told John that he should write a message to those invited to the wedding feast of the Lamb: "Write: 'blessed are the ones who are invited to the wedding feast of the Lamb' " (γραψον μακαριοι οι εις το δειπνον του γαμου του αρνιου κεκλημενοι, v. 9). The angel emphasized that these two events are not about individual Christians engaging or participating with their divine, heavenly Bridegroom. The angel stressed that these momentous moments were about the whole, complete Body of Christ experiencing these events with husband Jesus, Savior and Lord.

I believe that the COVID-19 pandemic and its negative impact on the Church universal has in large part been orchestrated by the devil. The damage to each local expression of the Body has been incalculable with many church closings and far fewer gatherings due to fear of the virus and due to national and local mandates limiting the number of people who attend church meetings. However, the true, vibrant Church of the Lamb continued to thrive and adapt to these constraints even if this meant meeting on-line or meeting in cars in church parking lots. Post-COVID Christianity has seen a revival of sorts of the strongest local expressions of the Body of Christ which has continued to become the bride "without spot or wrinkle" (Eph. 5:27) preparing for her moment of union with Jesus. The unity is marked eventually by God placing His name on the foreheads of each individual of His Church as the Apostle later stated in Revelation 22:4. The angel completed the vision of the wedding and wedding feast by stating that the words he just spoke to John "are the true words of God" (οι λογοι αληθινοι του θεου εισιν, v. 9).

Revelation: The Fifth Gospel

This revelation of the marriage feast is so overwhelming to John that he attempts to worship the angel facilitating the vision. But the angel stopped John from worshipping him and told him to worship God instead and to remember that the "testimony of Jesus is the spirit of the prophecy" (η μαρτυρια Ιησου εστιν το πνευμα της προφητειας v. 10). I understand this simple yet profound statement revealing the mind of God means that Jesus and His words are the center of God's world and that Jesus is the past, present, and future focus of the Kingdom of Heaven. Therefore, God's words to humans identified by the concept of "prophecy" always characterizes, reveals, and promotes Jesus to His people and to the lost. Nothing more precious or more important exists in this world or the universe than the Word of God contained in the spirit, soul, and the body of Jesus. Later, in the Apocalypse, Jesus is identified as the "Word of God" as He is throughout the New Testament (Rev. 19:13).

John's narrative shifted as the angel of the Apocalypse continued to show him the vision of the Conquering Messiah and His armies preparing for the final showdown with the Beast and his armies. John saw heaven open and a white horse standing there. Riding on the horse is Jesus with golden crowns on His head and with eyes like flames of fire. John wrote, "And behold . . . a white horse and One on it faithful and true; *in righteousness He judges and makes war; His eyes-flame of fire, and on His head are (many) crowns*" (και εν δυκαιοσυνη κρινει και πολεμει, οι δε οφθαλμοι αυτου φλοξ πυρος και επι την κεφαλην αυτου διαδαματα, vv. 11-12).

Jesus rarely reveals Himself as the Warrior General for the Kingdom of God. But here, He presents Himself with "eyes like flame of fire and wearing many crowns on His head" (v. 12); Jesus' fiery eyes reveal His inner drive to judge and His white-hot anger against the sins of the Beast, his false prophet, and their confederacy of ten presidents. John stated that He has a written name that no one knows except Himself. This name could very well be a wartime name that may be introduced around the time of the Armageddon Battle (v. 12). John also described Jesus as One about to take on the devil and his minions. John was impressed if not frightened by this sight. The Cousin he knew some seventy years before receiving this Apocalypse, who was a gentle carpenter and a rabbi, was now the most impressive General that the world has ever seen. Not only did His eyes exude anger and revenge, but the uniform He was wearing was dripping with blood: "and He is clothed in a robe dipped in blood and His name is called 'the Word of God' (και περιβεβλημενος ιματιον βεβαμμενον αιματι και κεκληται το ονομα αυτου ο λογος του θεου, v. 13). This is a graphic portrayal of the soon to be slaughtered armies of the Beast but sanctioned by the holiness and righteousness of the Word of God. God Himself authorizes His Son to slaughter the embodiment of evil who slaughtered His saints and prophets throughout the previous seven years and before. John next saw the armies of heaven all dressed in "fine linen clean and white" (νδεδυμενοι βυσσινον λευκον καθαρον, v. 14). They are following Jesus and His white horse on their white horses in a prewar parade—quite the opposite of an army's usual pre-war activities. John saw them in procession as they were gathering to fight the two hundred million soldiers of the Beast at the Valley of Megiddo/Valley of Jezreel (Rev. 9:16).

Before preceding any further with the immediate narrative build up to Armageddon, I think it necessary to discuss some of the apocalyptic statements in the Book of Daniel. Daniel was a statesman and political advisor to four kings as described in Daniel (Nebuchadnezzar, Dan. 1:1; Belshazzar, Dan. 5:1; Darius, Dan. 5:31; and Cyrus, Dan. 1:21; 6:28). But he also was a prophet par excellence—maybe the greatest of the Old Testament Apocalyptic writers. The last six chapters of Daniel (chapters 7-12) reveal as much about the End Times as any Apocalyptic literature save for what God reveals to John in Revelation. In Daniel 11, he prophesied about the military alliances and battles involving various kingdoms, including the King of the North and his allies and the king of South and his allies. As I have previously surmised, the Beast's confederacy of ten kings (the ten horns of Rev. 17) begins to unravel. One of the ten from the north (Russia?) begins to distrust and ultimately hate a king from the south (a Muslim president from Egypt or Iran?) causing strife and eventually war on the land of Israel, "the Beautiful land," that Daniel described in Daniel 11:41. But the unrest and North-South conflagration is the perfect excuse for the Antichrist and his forces to converge on Palestine to ostensibly stop the fighting. The Beast's forces conveniently occupy Israel and eventually ready themselves for the showdown against Jesus Christ and His heavenly forces. The Beast has been masterful at engineering the largest fighting force ever assembled. From earlier passages from John's Apocalypse, it can be ascertained that China (the king from the East, Rev. 9:16; 16:12) and likely others from the East (including Russia and Iran-Gog and Magog, respectively) are involved in the fight against Jesus and His armies. The prophet Ezekiel (another Old Testament writer of quality Apocalyptic literature) stated that Gog from the North (likely Russia) would be involved in a great battle decisively losing against the forces of God (Ezek. 38-39). The question is whether Ezekiel's vision was of Armageddon I reported in Revelation 19 or Armageddon II depicted in Revelation 20.

Revelation: The Fifth Gospel

It is clear that many of the ten nations of the Beast confederacy fill Megiddo Valley because of the blood loss from the slaughter filling the valley for 180 miles long and 50 miles wide as high as the horses' bridles (approximately 5 feet) as mentioned previously and John observed (Rev. 14:20). Before the actual battle, John continued to narrate the polemic intentions of Christ as He rehearses the release of His weaponized mouth-laser: "and the sharp sword projects from His mouth so that He might strike down the nations" (και εκ του στοματος αυτου εκπορευεται ρομφαια οξειαινα εν αυτη παταξη τα εθνη, v. 15). Jesus is specific in what He wears to battle. He not only wears a robe dipped in blood, but He also wears His name, "King of kings and Lord of lords," embossed on His robe and written (tattooed?) on His thigh (v. 16). Jesus wants His enemies to know who they are fighting. The angel that John saw straddling the sun cries out an invitation to the birds of prey flying in the sky overhead, "Come and gather here for the great banquet of God so that you can eat the flesh of Kings and the flesh of generals and the flesh of the powerful, and the flesh of horses and their riders and the flesh of freemen and of slaves, both small and great" (Rev. 19:17-18).

John then launched into the description of that fateful day. He saw the Beast and his Confederacy kings gathering with their armies to confront the Rider on the horse and His armies. There is no mention of actual resistance of the Antichrist's armies; I'm wondering if Jesus ever allows them to fire off even a single shot at the armies of Jesus. If they were allowed to attack, nuclear warhead detonations and nuclear holocaust would certainly result. Jerusalem would be annihilated and likely all of Palestine. Remember, Jesus' weapon appears to be laser light, far more precise and far less destructive to the environment.

John next stated that the Beast and the false prophet are apprehended: "then the beast was seized and his false prophet who performed signs before him that he might deceive those who had received the mark of the beast and who worshipped his image" (και επιασθη το θηριον και μετ αυτου ο ψυεδοπροφητης ο ποιησας τα σημεια ενωπιον αυτου εν οις επλανησεν τους λαβοντας το χαραγμα του θηριου και τους προσκυνουτσς τη εικονα αυτου, v. 20). Maybe the forces of Christ somehow send out their special forces to apprehend the Beast alive and his false prophet. Under direct orders from Jesus, one of His angels throws the Beast and his false prophet alive into the "lake of fire, the one burning with sulfur" (λιμνην του πυρος της καιομενης εν θειω, v. 20). The text never indicates *who* actually hurls these worst of sinners and God-haters into the lake of fire. I think because the lake of fire is so hot, that only angels can get close enough to throw these two into it. If any human did this, he would likely die or be severely injured from the flames and the tremendous heat generated from the lake. Because the Antichrist and his prophet who led and guided their kings and generals are gone from the scene, his armies are left powerless and disorganized to oppose Jesus and His forces.

John's vision of Armageddon I ends with the annihilation of the armies of the Confederacy. John reported that the weaponized laser device from Jesus' mouth as He attacks from His horse causes the deaths of these millions of men. The generals and their commanders and soldiers are rendered easy prey to the mop-up actions of Christ's soldiers. No enemy combatant survives. It takes seven months to bury/dispose of the bodies despite the millions of birds gorging daily on their carcasses according to Ezekiel 39:12. John states: "The rest were killed from the sword from the One sitting on the horse, by the sword projecting out of His mouth; then all the birds gorged on their flesh" (και οι λοιποι απεκτανθησαν εν τη ρομφαια του καθημενου επι του ιππου τη εξελθουση εκ του στοματος αυτου και παντα τα ορνεα εχορτασθησαν εκ των σαρκων αυτων, v. 21).

Birds are considered one of the most intelligent of animals on the earth—capable of learning, making tools, following commands, and, in the case of the parrots (greys, macaws, and parakeets), can learn languages and speak hundreds of words.[205] There are many places in Scripture where birds follow God directives (cf. I Kings 17:2-6). In Revelation 19, we see that birds are responsive to the angel and to God's will that they assist in the annihilation of the armies of the Beast by eating their flesh as they clean up the Valley of Megiddo from the dead bodies left to rot there. But after this terrible but triumphant battle and clean-up come the best years on planet earth since the Garden of Eden.

---

[205] Joan Dunayer, "The right of sentient beings: Moving beyond old and new speciesism" chapter 2 in *The Politics of Species: Reshaping our Relationships with Other Animals*, Raymond Corbey and Annette Lanjouw, eds. (New York: Cambridge University Press, 2013), 33.

REVELATION 20

Millennial Reign

1 "And I saw an angel coming down out of heaven holding the key to the Abyss and a large chain in his hand ² and he seized the dragon the ancient serpent, also called the devil and Satan, and bound him for a thousand years ³ and threw him into the Abyss and shut and sealed it above him so that he might not deceive the nations any more until the thousands years have come to an end; after these things, he must be released for a short time. ⁴ Then I saw the thrones and those sitting on them. And judging authority was given to them; these were the souls of those beheaded because of the testimony of Jesus and because of the Word of God and those not worshipping the beast or his image and not receiving the mark on their forehead or on their hands. These resurrected and reigned with Christ for one thousand years. ⁵ The rest of the dead did not come back to life until the thousand years came to an end. This is the first resurrection. ⁶ Blessed and holy are those who share in the first resurrection because the second death has no authority over them. Indeed, they will be priests of God and of his Christ and will reign with Him for a thousand years.

⁷ "Then when the thousand years come to an end, Satan will be untied from his prison ⁸ and will go out to deceive the nations, those at the four corners of the earth, including Gog and Magog, to gather them

Revelation: The Fifth Gospel

> together for battle; their numbers were like the sand of the sea. ⁹ And they marched across the breadth of the earth and surrounded the camp of the holy ones, the beloved city. But fire came down out of heaven and annihilated them; ¹⁰ then the devil, the one deceiving them, was thrown into the lake of fire and sulfur where the beast and the false prophet were; then they will be tormented day and night forever and ever.
>
> ¹¹ "Then I saw a great white throne and the One sitting on it; indeed, the earth and sky fled from His face; and no place was found for them [to hide]. ¹² Then I saw the dead both great and small standing before the throne, and the books were opened, and another book was opened, the Book of Life, and the dead were judged based on the writings in the books according to their works. ¹³ The sea gave up the dead ones in it. Death and Hades gave up the dead ones in them and each was judged according to his works. ¹⁴ Then Death and Hades were thrown into the lake of fire, which is the second death, the lake of fire. ¹⁵ And if someone was not found written in the Book of Life, he was cast into the lake of fire."

Armageddon II

Revelation 19 uncovered the reason for Christ's tremendous righteous anger and subsequent slaughter of the two hundred million soldiers depicted at the end of the chapter. But in the opening scene of chapter 20, John saw "an angel coming down out of heaven with the key to the Abyss and with a large chain in his hand" (αγγελον καταβαινοντα εκ του ουρανου εχοντα την κλειν της αβυσσου και αλυσιν μεγαλην επι την χειρα αυτου, v. 1). I would imagine that the Lord sends the archangel Michael for the task of apprehending, chaining, and imprisoning Satan because He didn't want Satan to have a chance to resist the arrest. All angels are powerful; the Archangels are the largest and most powerful of angelic beings; and remember that Lucifer used to be an archangel. Michael, the war angel, confronts and apprehends Lucifer, his arch enemy, and binds him with a great chain. Some scholars have speculated that this angel may be the same angel of Revelation 9 who opens the Abyss shaft with a key and lets the "locpions" out. However, the "star" in Revelation 9 is never identified as a holy angel and was noted by John

Millennial Reign

to have "fallen from heaven to the earth" (v. 1). He had to be given the key to the deep shaft of the Abyss; as previously mentioned, I think the "star" of Rev. 9:1 was likely a fallen angel possibly Abaddon (the death angel in charge of the Abyss, Rev. 9:11). This angel was *not* the angel seen by John in Revelation 20:1 who already had possession of the "key" to the Abyss and carried a great chain to bind Satan and throw him into the Abyss. This is what the Apostle saw: "then he seized the dragon, the ancient serpent, also known as the devil and Satan and bound him for a thousand years; then he threw him into the Abyss and shut and sealed it above him *so that he might not deceive the nations anymore until the one thousand years have come to an end; after this he must be released for a short time*" (ινα μη πλανηση ετι τα εθνη αχρι τελεσθη τα χιλια ετη μετα ταυτα δει λυθηναι αυτον μικρον χρονον, vv. 2–3). God's angel throws Lucifer into the Abyss and locks him up for one thousand years.

I wonder what the Abyss looks like. It sounds like it is confining and made of a material able to keep the great chain secure and the devil bound despite his great strength. It also must be able to keep Satan from communicating with his demons who likely are allowed to create their discord and hate for God to the vulnerable of the earth throughout the millennial reign of Christ and the governance of His once-beheaded lieutenants. The door to the Abyss appears to be in the ceiling of the structure which would be plausible if by chance the Abyss was somewhat like a shaft connected to the "lake of fire" (i.e., Hades/Hell). Remember John mentioned the Abyss in Rev. 9:1-2 (locusts come out of its smoke), Rev. 9:11 (Abaddon is king of the Abyss), Rev. 11:7 (the Beast ascends from it to kill the two Jerusalem prophets) and in this passage. Satan's millennial banishment allows the traumatized and punished earth a time of respite to recover from the seven bowl judgments of Revelation 16. His banishment also allows the Raptured Church of Revelation 7 and the saints over the ages to rest from praying for the persecuted Church still on earth during Great Tribulation Period including the Israelis for Jesus who were eventually beheaded by Revelation 14.

This period is judged by a select group either from pre-tribulation Christian martyrs (some scholars have suggested this, but it is unlikely due to the text, vv. 4-5) or more likely the martyrs of the Great Tribulation period resurrected for this task. John stated that the beheaded ones were those who refused to worship the Beast and rejected the seal or mark of the Beast and the economic security the chip afforded. Of course, this group would have to include the previously mentioned 144,000 Jews who replaced the raptured Church in Revelation 7. Without Satan, the

Revelation: The Fifth Gospel

judging may be minimal except for the disputes and sin arising from human iniquity which of course can be considerable. Jesus may actually be in Jerusalem at this time facilitating and coaching the tribulation martyrs to mediate His judgments, necessary because humans still have free will and can violate His laws.

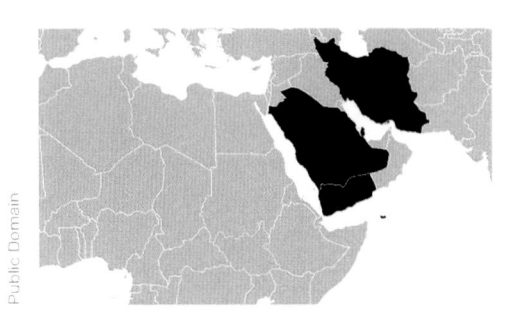

Countries with legally sanctioned decapitation practices

It is interesting to note that those martyrs resurrected for this millennial task of assisting Christ judge the earth were *beheaded* because of their Christian lifestyle and witness. Very few people groups behead others except for jihadist Muslims. I can imagine that these extremists will be beheading Christians during the Tribulation period as they are doing even today. It could be that the Antichrist makes an unholy alliance with these extremist Muslims who behead Christians at will. Remember also that John was shocked to see the prostitute of Revelation 17 drunk with the blood of the saints, possibly indicating Catholic Church complicity in the beheading martyrdom of followers of Christ. John depicted the resurrection of the beheaded in this manner: "Then I saw thrones and those sitting on them having been given judging authority; these are those souls beheaded for the word of God and testimony of Jesus who did not worship the Beast or his image and who did not receive his mark on their foreheads or on their right hand; *these resurrected and reigned with Christ for one thousand years*" *(και εζησαν και εβασιλευσαν μετα του Χριστου χιλια ετη*, v. 4). What a miracle of re-creation for the hundreds if not thousands beheaded for Christ whose resurrected bodies included fully intact heads including brains that were violated by the swords and guillotines that severed them from their saints' bodies! God will be honoring these by allowing them to help Him reign for one thousand years.

Today there are four countries with legally sanctioned decapitation: Saudi Arabia (active), Iran (suspended), Qatar (suspended), Yemen (suspended).[206] The Taliban,

---

[206] Jon Weinberg, "Sword of Justice? Beheadings Rise in Saudi Arabia," *Harvard International Review* 29, no. 4 (Winter 2008): 15, accessed May 31, 2023, https://www.proquest.com/docview/230866990?fromopenview=true&pq-origsite=gscholar.

Millennial Reign

the Islamic State of Iraq and the Levant (ISIL, also known as ISIS), al-Qaeda, and other splinter jihadists groups have been beheading "infidels" at will since 2002 (beginning with the senseless beheading of American journalist Daniel Pearl) and disseminated these horrific videos through the Internet. These groups have been using these videos not only to intimidate their enemies, but as a form of propaganda to recruit the poor and vulnerable teenagers from third world Muslim countries. Muhammed taught his followers to decapitate blasphemous Muslims, Jews, and Christians in the Quran (two citations); several other Muslim sacred books (Siras and Hadith) also encourage this practice. Muhammed hated Jews despite his marriage to one as recorded in this ancient source:

> *Then [the Jews] were made to come down, and the Messenger of God imprisoned them. . . . The Messenger of God went out into the marketplace of Medina. . . . and had them beheaded in those trenches. They were brought out to him in groups. . . . They numbered 600 or 700—the largest estimate says they were between 800 and 900. As they were being taken in groups to the Messenger of God, they said, "what do you think will be done to us? . . . By God, it is death!" The affair continued until the Messenger of God had finished with them.*[207]

No wonder the followers of Islam are so comfortable with such a barbaric way of killing the innocent and children of the Lord; as with any religion or cult, the originator of the cult or religion sets the "tone" and establishes the culture of behavior for his/her followers. Mohammed's treacherous and violent behavior as evidenced by his killing of all Jews of the Saudi Arabian Peninsula by the end of his life and "ministry" became the code of behavior of jihadists and others of his "flock."[208] Fortunately, this behavior and those who practice it will be eradicated during the millennium as far as can be ascertained from Revelation 19–22.

---

[207] *The History of al-Tabari: An Annotated Translation*, Volume VIII, *The Victory of Islam: Mohammad at Medina*, Michael Fishbein, trans. (Albany, NY: State University of New York Press, 1997) 35, accessed May 31, 2023, https://ia801706.us.archive.org/view_archive.php?archive=/4/items/history-of-islamic-kingdom-40-volumes-pdf.-7z/History%20of%20Islamic%20Kingdom-%2040%20Volumes%20PDF.7z&file=History%20of%20Al%20Tabari%20-%20Vol%2008.pdf.

[208] James Arlandson, "Muhammad's atrocity against the Qurayza Jews." *Answer Islam: A Christian/Muslim dialog*, accessed February 20, 2022, https://www.answering-islam.org/Authors/Arlandson/qurayza_jews.htm.

The governing of societies may be a challenge. But those saints from the Tribulation Period will be up to the task since they were exposed to terrible chaos and oppressive world government under the late Antichrist and his prophet. By experience, these resurrected Christians know what oppressive world governments are and what practices to avoid as they rely on the wisdom of Christ who assists them in governing the world (v. 6).

It would be interesting to know how the jihadists and other people groups fair during the millennial reign of Christ and His righteous judges. I wonder if any surviving decapitators are judged during the millennium, and if so, what their punishment is like. Would the judges who had been beheaded by these people judge their decapitators with the "eye for an eye" mentality or with a more merciful approach. I think they will judge sin with swiftness, fairness, and agape love as directed by Christ from Jerusalem. I am unsure if judging also includes supervising the day-to-day activities of the world's citizens, not all of which would necessarily be Christ followers and indwelt by the Holy Spirit. Larger significant directives would be welcomed but management of minutiae probably would not be necessary.

I can't help but think that the resurrected Christian judges would try their best to prepare the world for Satan's onslaught and treachery *after* his release from the Abyss (v. 7) with any number of educational, social, and spiritual measures. Of course, these Christian saints would know chapter 20 of John's Revelation and his description about their reign as well as John's mention of Satan being released from his prison. I wonder if Christ in Jerusalem will be actively involved in facilitating these measures to train and prepare Christians for the coming terrible years or even decades that follow the idyllic millennial reign of these saints. During this last millennium, the Christ followers of the earth had not been challenged in their Christian walks in the way the tribulation and pre-tribulation Christians have been. Satan would not be tempting the inhabitants of the earth during these one thousand years. But "Eden" is violated when the Lord allows Satan to be released to challenge and strengthen His children's faith and the world's perception of the Triune God. God allows Satan to challenge earth's citizens' autonomy and free will and how they exercise their options in life. Whatever is done to prepare the world for the return of the devil ultimately does not deter or prevent Armageddon II from taking place—the largest loss of life of any battle ever to be fought on earth.

Satan Thrown into the Lake of Fire

John stated that Satan is released after the thousand years have come to an end: "After the thousands years have come to an end, *Satan will be released from his prison and will go out to deceive the nations at the four corners of the earth, including God and Magog*" (λυθησεται ο σατανας εκ της φυλακης αυτου εξελευσεται πλανησαι τα εθνη τα εν ταις τεσσαρσιν γωνιαις της γης τον Γωγ και Μαγωγ, vv.7-8). John did not detail the specifics of the devil's release. But what Satan does immediately after his prison time expires is revealed. The devil immediately visits Gog (likely Russia) and Magog (likely Iran) and other nation states vulnerable to ultimately rejecting the rule and management of the saints of Christ. I find it hard to think that these people groups would be interested in Satan and willing to follow him. But John's words reveal resentment and hate towards the Lord and His people. Presently, the nation state which hates Israel and the Jews the most is Iran. This passage in Revelation is very believable in light of Iran's past enmity with God's chosen. Iran-Israeli relations have significantly soured since Iranian Revolution of 1979 directed by the Ayatollah Khomeini who called Israel, "The Little Satan," and the United States, "The Great Satan."[209] By the early 1990s when Iraq and its allies were defeated by coalition forces from the United States, other NATO allies, and Israel in Operation Desert Storm, Iran became markedly more antagonistic toward Israel including during the presidency of Mahmoud Ahmadinejad, a hard-liner with seething hate toward Jews and Israel. Iran became much more aggressive against Israel during his presidency by developing its nuclear capabilities and funding terrorist organizations such as Hamas and the Hezbollah to wreak havoc on Israel. These terrorist groups bombed the Israeli embassy in Buenos Aries (1992) and were responsible for the AMIA bombing also in Buenos Aries in July 1994. Other supreme ayatollahs of the ruling Shia class in Iran have continued to increase Iran's nuclear capabilities and have developed highly trained special operations forces such as "Quds" to carry out clandestine attacks and assassinations on Jewish officials around the world.[210]

---

209 "Iran to examine Holocaust evidence," *Al Jazeera*, 3 September 2006,(accessed May 31, 2023, https://www.aljazeera.com/news/2006/9/3/iran-to-examine-holocaust-evidence.
210 Peter Flinn, "Man in Iran-backed plot to kill Saudi ambassador gets 25 years," *The Washington Post*, May 30, 2012, accessed May 31, 2013, https://www.washingtonpost.com/world/national-security/man-in-iran-backed-plot-to-kill-saudi-ambassador-gets-25-years/2013/05/30/0435e7a2-c952-11e2-8da7-d274bc611a47_story.html?itid=sr_1.

Revelation: The Fifth Gospel

Russia has also hated the Jews. Josef Stalin during his thirty-year reign of terror exterminated at least hundreds of thousands of them and likely millions. Several Russian historians have suggested that he may have exterminated forty to sixty million Russians.[211] With his well-documented hate of Jews, he certainly killed many of God's chosen.[212] Vladimir Putin is the present Russian dictator with a very shady past with the Russian KGB before his selection as the Russian president in 2000. He has a reputation for human rights violations including the poisoning of those who have opposed him over his twenty-four-year reign as Russia's supreme leader. He has unlawfully imprisoned at least 380 political rivals as of 2020.[213] Putin represents some of the worst of Russian leadership aggression including his appetite for unprovoked war against the sovereign nation of Ukraine which he invaded with his troops on February 24, 2022. He is responsible for the destruction and annihilation of many towns and major cities in Ukraine and was issued a warrant by the International Criminal Court for war crimes due to his army raping and killing the innocent citizens of Ukraine and the forced evacuation of children.[214]

Vladimir Putin, Russian Dictator, 2021

After the millennial reign of Christ with His beheaded saints, I find it *very easy* to imagine Russia and Iran at the center of hostilities against the "camp of the holy ones, the beloved city" Jerusalem (v. 9) as predicted by both nations' bellicose

---

211 Palash R. Ghosh, "How Many People Did Joseph Stalin Kill?" *International Business Times*, March 5, 2013 (accessed September 25, 2022) https://www.ibtimes.com/how-many-people-did-joseph-stalin-kill-1111789.

212 Karen Dukess, "Why and How Stalin Hated Jews," *The Moscow Times*, February 1, 1995, accessed September 25, 2022, https://www.themoscowtimes.com/archive/why-and-how-stalin-hated-jews.

213 "Russia's Political Prisoners Directory: Individuals Classified ad Russia's Political Prisoners by the Memorial Human Rights Center," *American Russian-Speaking Association for Civil & Human Rights*; June 14, 2021, accessed May 31, 2023, https://amrusrights.wordpress.com/2021/06/14/russias-political-prisoners-directory/.

214 Henry Austin and Phil McCausland, "International Criminal Court issues arrest warrant for putting over alleged Ukraine war crimes," NBC News, March 17, 2023, accessed May 31, 2023, https://www.nbcnews.com/news/world/arrest-warrant-putin-international-criminal-court-ukraine-war-crimes-rcna75471.

behavior and hate of the Jews as just mentioned. Satan will have had one thousand years locked up in prison to devise a plan to organize and direct his minions of demons to assist him to align these two countries and others throughout the earth to fight against Christ and His kingdom centered in Jerusalem. The angel of Revelation did not show John or discuss with him any of the activities of the devil's hierarchical organization of demons throughout this millennium reign of Christ. But these demonic spirits have obviously been effective in planting seeds of mistrust and suspicion against the beheaded saints and against Christ ruling the world during this period. Satan would need some help to turn the world against God. Maybe his demons (who we know are organized in a hierarchical system over various nations) are still allowed to influence the world during the millennial reign but cannot orchestrate Armageddon II until their leader is released for a season. Certainly, Satan chooses to influence and recruit the most vulnerable nations to lead the fight against Jerusalem and Christ's forces. The devil, as an excellent judge of iniquitous behavior, chooses Gog (Russia) and Magog (possibly Iran) to lead his troops because of their past history of despising God's chosen as I have mentioned (v.8). Furthermore, Hades and death are still active during this millennial period as suggested by the last few verses of this chapter that sin and death still occur during this time (vv.13-14). With Armageddon II looming in the future, Satan's minions are busy orchestrating the alignment of national forces against the Christ and His kingdom on earth. As previously mentioned, Gog and Magog lead forces of the enemies of God against Jesus and the armies of heaven (the raptured Church) as we saw in Armageddon I (Revelation 19).

John continued the showdown narrative by describing the massive buildup of forces against Christ and His saints: "to gather them together for battle; there number is like the sand of the sea" (συναγαγειν αυτους εις τον πολεμον ων ο αριθμος αυτων ως η αμμος της θαλασσης, v. 8). This massive Satanic force likely dwarfed even the Beast's troupes that engaged Christ in Armageddon I. I wonder, if Satan was so smart and resourceful, why would he strike against Jerusalem if he really knew every word of Revelation and the prophecy in Revelation 20 about his demise? But remember, he was inactive and rotting in the Abyss for one thousand years. He must have lost some of his dark brilliance. He directed his armies and their nuclear arsenals against Jerusalem, as John reported: "and they marched across the breadth of the earth and surrounded the camp of the saints, the beloved city" (και ανεβησαν επι το πλατος της γης και εκυκλευσαν την παρεμβολην των αγιων και την πολιν την ηγαπημενην, v. 9). Satan's "mouth was watering" when he saw the vulnerability of Christ's earthly forces in and around Jerusalem.

He obviously had the advantage. But before his armies could destroy Jerusalem by massive nuclear strike, God the Father intervened. John depicted their sudden demise: "fire comes down out of heaven and annihilates them" (κατεβη πυρ εκ του ουρανου και κατεφαγεν αυτους, v. 9). In a moment of time, the supposed Satanic advantage, and all prospects of reversing the previous progress of Christ's millennial reign, was halted. The only being left was Satan himself. He must have known at this moment that God's purpose for his eternal life was as God's worship archangel who had the most enviable place in the whole universe. What regret and maybe remorse he felt as he was thrown into the lake of fire and sulfur. As John described it, he would now join his partners in crime. Now he would join the Beast and false prophet in pain and torment day and night forever and ever: "then the devil, the one deceiving them, was thrown into the lake of fire and sulfur where also the beast and the false prophet were, *and they will be tormented day and night forever and ever*" (και βασανισθησονται ημερας και νυκτος εις τους αιωνας των αιωνων, v. 10).

God destroys Satan's forces with "fire from heaven" similar to Armageddon I, although John does not mention by what vehicle. The "fire coming down" could be similar to the way the Lord destroyed Sodom and Gomorrah. How ever this happened, the annihilation resulted in the total collapse and destruction of Satan's forces. Satan was then thrown into hell (Lake of Fire and Sulfur) for eternity which raises the question, "Where is the Lake of Fire?" Could it be the center of the earth? Maybe Satan, the Beast, and the Prophet are thrown into the outer core of the center of the earth through a portal like the shaft of the Abyss. Temperatures in the earth's core have been estimated at the 10,000 degree Fahrenheit range; the earth's core is about 3,000 miles below the earth's surface.[215]

I think it appropriate to discuss the earth's five main layers: the crust, upper mantle, lower mantle, outer core, and inner core. These are at the following depths below the surface:

---

[215] Quentin Williams, "Why is the earth's core so hot? And how do scientists measure its temperature?" *Scientific American*, October 6, 1997, accessed May 31, 2023, https://www.scientificamerican.com/article/why-is-the-earths-core-so/.

Millennial Reign

Depth		Layer
Kilometres	**Miles**	
0–60	0–37	Lithosphere (locally varies between 5 and 200 km)
0–35	0–22	... Crust (locally varies between 5 and 70 km)
35–60	22–37	... Uppermost part of mantle
35–2,890	22–1,790	Mantle
210–270	100–200	... Upper mesosphere (upper mantle)
660–2,890	410–1,790	... Lower mesosphere (lower mantle)
2,890–5,150	1,790–3,160	Outer core (liquid of iron and nickel at 10,000 degrees F)
5,150–6,360	3,160–3,954	Inner core (solid iron/nickel in 80/20% mixture)

The devil, the Beast, his false prophet, and Christ haters will be thrown into the Lake of Fire possibly reaching the earth's outer core of liquid iron and nickel through the shaft of the Abyss. This shaft would be quite extensive and would facilitate souls passing through the earth's crust, its upper mantle, and its inner mantle before reaching the Lake. As previously indicated, angels may be responsible for throwing these beings into Hell which actually may involve escorting these condemned beings down there and making sure they have no way out (v.15).

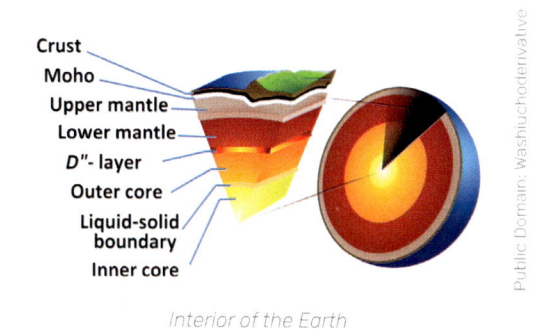

Interior of the Earth

The Judgment Seat of Christ
(2 Corinthians 5:10; Romans 14:10)

Humans face one of two great judgments after completing their lives on earth (Hebrews 9:27): the Judgment Seat of Christ or the Great White Throne Judgment. Christians who have professed their faith in Christ will face Him at their deaths in what the Apostle Paul refers to as "The Judgment Seat of Christ" as described in 2 Corinthians 5:10 and Romans 14:10. Sometime shortly after the Rapture (I Thess. 4:15–17), Christians from all ages will stand before Christ to receive our rewards based on our works of various and variable quality. Those of us executing thoughts, words, and actions in childlike faith for the Kingdom good and reflecting Kingdom principles will likely be honored with high quality position and tasks commiserate with these works. But those Christians executing thoughts, words, and actions incompatible with Kingdom principles for personal gain not promoting the Kingdom of Christ on earth will likely receive lower quality positions and tasks commensurate with these works. Many of Jesus' parables reflect this "works" evaluation and judgment at the End Times including Jesus' Parable of the Ten Talents (Mt. 25:14-30; Lk. 19: 12-27). The Judgment Seat of Christ will never strip the Christian from his/her salvation because our salvation is solely based on our faith in Christ apart from works as Paul so eloquently stated in Ephesians 2:8-9: "For by grace are you saved through faith; and this is not from you: it is the gift of God: not through works, lest any man boast." But Christ will evaluate the quality of our works whether they are gold, silver, precious stones, wood, hay, or straw (1 Cor. 3:12) and will give to each of us "according to [our] works" as He promised to the members of the church at Thyatira (Rev. 2:23). The reward will be His best judgment of each saint's character and abilities and will include utilizing gifts and proclivities for the continued preparation, construction, and upfit of New Jerusalem. Jesus will also choose our roles in ruling other beings in the universe as indicated in Revelation 22:5: "and they will reign as kings forever and ever" (και βασιλευσουσιν εις τους αιωνας των αιωνων).

But the second judgment of mankind, called the Great White Throne Judgment because of the words used by John to describe it in this passage in Revelation 20, will be a frightful experience, even for those few pagans *who are not thrown* into the Lake of Fire and Sulfur. John began this very difficult passage by discussing the fear that even "earth" and "heaven" have as He readies Himself to judge those *without* the blood of Christ redeeming their souls from lack of opportunity to hear the gospel: "Then I saw a great white throne and One sitting on it; and the earth and the heaven fled from His face and no place was found for them [to hide]" (και ειδον θρονον μεγαν λευκον και τον καθημενον επ αυτον ου απο του προσωπου εφυγεν η γη και ο ουρανος και τοπος ουχ ευρεθη αυτοις, v. 11). The earth and heaven "fleeing" from God's presence maybe signifies the dissolution and remaking of earth and heaven as we know it (see 2 Peter 3:10, 12). Or "earth" and "heaven" may actually be John utilizing two word pictures for human and other beings living in heaven and on the earth who are terrified by Father God and what is about to take place. I don't believe Christians stand before God at this judgment because this judgment determines which humans enter heaven or hell based on *works*, not on the profession of faith in Christ.

The non-Christian dead from the beginning of time and the non-Christians dying after the Judgment Seat of Christ (Rev. 14:14–20) and those pagans living and dying during the millennial reign of Christ appear before the Father; their fate ultimately determined by their names' presence or absence in the Book of Life. Because "books" of works are opened, many dead did not have the opportunity to hear the gospel for numerous reasons and are judged on the merits of their works (20:13, 15). John emphasized "works" because this is the focus and basis of the Father's judgment of non-Christians supported by other Scriptures including Romans 2:6–16. In Romans, Paul made it clear that humans who have *followed their consciences* ("the requirements of the law are written on their hearts," v. 15) despite not knowing specifically the "written law," will be given eternal life (vv. 6–7), as we see intimated in Revelation 20:13 and 15.

John continued with the Great White Throne passage: "and then I saw the dead both great and small standing before the throne" (και ειδον τους νεκρους τους μεγαλους και τους μικρους εστωτας ενωπιον του θρονου, v. 12). John did not describe *how* the *gathering* of the world's pagan population from all time occurs. But he wrote that the sea and both death and Hades give up their past dead ones to be judged at this Judgment (v. 13). Jesus shed light on *how* this *gathering* of the pagan souls occurs by telling His disciples that the angels will be tasked with gathering all peoples for the moment of eternal evaluation (Mk. 13:27; Mt. 13:49–50). But John's vision is clear about *how* the dead outside of Christ and His kingdom are *evaluated*: "*and then the books were opened and another book was opened, the Book of Life, and the dead were judged based on the writings in the books according to their works*" (και βιβλια ηνοιχθησαν και αλλο βιβλιον ηνοιχθη, ο εστιν της ζωης και εκριθησαν οι νεκροι εκ των γεγραμμενων εν τοις βιβλιος κατα τα εργα αυτων, v. 12).

I think it very perilous to base one's eternal destiny on one's works because, as a sinful being, no one is totally consistent in following the dictates of his/her conscience, God's moral law. Scripture is unclear about the standard that the Father uses to determine entrance into heaven for the pagans at His White Throne Judgment. We clearly see that only those with their names written in the Book of Life will enter heaven. But the actual criteria for evaluation of *works* and the *formula* for inclusion in the Book of Life is never given (except the passages from Paul in Romans), maybe to encourage all people to enter Heaven though the narrow "door" of Christ and faith in Him. It would seem that those who actually reject the gospel will never be allowed in heaven and face the very real prospect of living in the fire and sulfur of eternal damnation. But those ignorant of Christ who followed the dictates of their consciences will be honored with entrance into heaven because their names are written in the Book of Life. I also wonder what the chances are of pagans entering heaven based on their successful works history. I would imagine that the number will be far lower than those people who accepted Christ's blood sacrifice and enter heaven as Christ followers by faith. Another question worth exploring is the identities and the functions of the other books opened *besides* the Book of Life. Do these other books contain the accounts of each person's thoughts, words, and actions downloaded into computer-like disc, flash drive, or other solid state drive formats somewhere in heaven to minimize the space necessary for one hundred billion people over the millennia who once lived on the earth? How ever the data is stored, the books opened for this Great White Throne Judgment contain the works-based evidence necessary for God the Father to make His judgment for or against entry into heaven or entry into Hell. By the manner in which John discussed these two sets of books, the most critical one is the Book of Life because only those whose names are in it will enter heaven.

Next John reported that the sea gave up the dead ones in it, and then Death and Hades gave up the dead ones in them (v 13). I would think that if a pagan dies on land or in the sea, he/she would be under the purview and control of Death and Hades. But this passage indicates that if an unbeliever dies in the sea, his soul somehow avoids Death and Hades receiving it. I see no other place in Scripture indicating this phenomenon. But John is a faithful witness, vetted by God's angel and the Holy Spirit, and would never testify to something he never saw or heard. His reporting of the collection of every single person who ever lived on the earth was thorough. When all humans are assigned their eternal destiny, the last judgment comes—the judgment of Death and Hades. Although these names represent concepts (both action and place), remember they are both represented by actual beings identified by John in Revelation 6:8 as the principals of the fourth seal- the pale green rider and his pursuing partner. Therefore, I think Death and Hades are actually fallen angels who had been given the task of harming and tormenting humans through the ages (Ex. 12:23, Rev. 9:11). John stated that they both were thrown into the Lake of Fire never to plague the earth again. This of course means that all humans living on the earth and the soon to be New Jerusalem will never be threatened again by Death or the threat of Hell. Hell may never again receive another human after the moment that Death and Hades are banished forever: "Then Death and Hades are thrown into the Lake of Fire, which is the second death, the Lake of Fire" (και ο θανατος και ο αδης εβληθησαν εις την λιμην του πυρος ουτος ο θανατος ο δευτερος εστιν η λιμη του πυρος, v. 14).

Then John summarized the last four verses by stating, "And if anyone was not found written in the Book of Life then he was thrown into the Lake of Fire" (και ει τις ουχ ευρεθη εν τη βιβλω της ζωης γεγραμμενος εβληθη εις την λιμνην του πυρος, v. 15). This verse underlies the importance and preeminence of the Book of Life. No one entering heaven would ever do so without his or her name being written in it. I am sure that multiple angels are responsible for the cataloguing of the likely hundreds of millions of names written in this Book. I also wonder if the angels tasked with human entry into heaven utilize DNA chromosomes to verify the identity of each person standing before the throne. I think that heaven is highly organized and among its many functions has chromosome banks of every human that ever lived on the earth, so that heaven's citizens will never be mistakenly identified, or Hell's residents will never avoid eternal damnation. The United States' justice system has been noted to convict nearly 4 percent of defendants of crimes they did not commit. With nearly one million felony convictions annually in the U.S., nearly forty thousand are wrongful convictions.[216] But at the end of the Ages during the Great White Throne Judgment no mistakes are made because the Holy Spirit and the angels under His charge to catalogue human behavior from Adam and Eve until that moment have never made a mistake doing so. Their methods are without reproach. The books never have and never will lie. John next saw a new heaven and a new earth.

Should Christians feel smug about their positions in the church or parachurch organizations, we should be reminded of Jesus' comments while delivering His Sermon on the Mount as recorded in Matthew 7:21–23,

> "Not all who say to Me, 'Lord, Lord', will enter into the Kingdom of Heaven, but the one doing the will of My Father in heaven. Many will say to Me on that day, 'Lord, Lord, did we not prophecy in Your Name and exorcise demons in Your Name, and perform many miracles in Your Name?' And then I will say to them, 'I never knew you; depart from Me you lawless ones (evil doers)!'"

In this passage, Jesus warned His disciples of substituting the busyness of personal religious career for true relationship with God through intimacy with Jesus. The

---

216   Mathew Clarke, "Racism and Wrongful Convictions," *Criminal Legal News*, May 15, 2020, accessed November 11, 2021, https://www.criminallegalnews.org/news/2020/may/15/racism-and-wrongful-convictions/

Revelation: The Fifth Gospel

Pharisees, Sadducees, and lawyers were infamous for their show of piety and religiosity without true heart connection to the God of Israel. While promoting their religious activities before the public, they would deny their personal responsibility to pursue the will of God. Jesus trained His disciples to deny their own hunger for personal promotion and success by putting His Father's and others' agendas first, so eloquently illustrated by His Parable of the Good Samaritan (Lk. 10:30-37). If the lure of success, power, and prestige overtakes our desire for intimacy with God through Jesus, then Jesus' admonitions in Matthew 7 and 22:11-14 warn us of the *possibility* of not being accepted into heaven and having to face the Great White Throne Judgment as pagans-being unknown by Christ despite our belief to the contrary. The Holy Spirit is the only Being capable of knowing our innermost thoughts and motives. Jesus would never allow His true children to experience the uncertainty of the Great White Throne Judgment and the tenuousness of works-based salvation, particularly when Jesus' blood is so free and available to all.

REVELATION 21

New Jerusalem

The Bride of Christ

1 "And I saw a new heaven and a new earth; for the first heaven and the first earth passed and the sea is no longer. ² Then I saw the holy city New Jerusalem coming down out of heaven from God having been prepared as a bride adorned for her husband. ³ And then I heard a loud voice from the throne say, 'Behold, the Tabernacle of God is with men, and He will tabernacle with them and they themselves will be His people and God Himself will be with them; ⁴ and He will wipe every tear from out of their eyes and there will be no longer any more death nor sorrow nor weeping nor pain because the first order of things is passed.' ⁵ Then the One sitting on the throne said, 'Behold, I make all things new.' Then He says, 'Write, for these words are faithful and true.' ⁶ Then He said to me, 'It is finished. I am the alpha and the omega, the beginning and the end; to the thirsty one I will freely give out of the Fountain of the Water of Life. ⁷ The overcomer will inherit these things; and I will be God to Him and he will be son to Me. ⁸ But the cowardly, the unbelievers, the vile, the murderers, the fornicators, the sorcerers, the idolaters, and all liars will have a share in the burning lake of fire and sulfur, which is the second death.'

⁹ "Then one of the seven angels with the seven bowls filled with the seven last plagues came and spoke with me, 'Come, and I will show you the bride, the wife of the Lamb.' ¹¹ And he carried me away in the Spirit to a great and high mountain and showed me the holy city Jerusalem coming down out of heaven from God ¹¹ having the glory of God. Its light (radiance) was like a very precious stone, like a jasper, shining like crystal; ¹² and having a great and high wall, and having twelve gates with twelve angels at the gates and on the gates were written the names of the twelve tribes of the sons of Israel: ¹³ three gates on the East, three gates on the North, three gates on the South and three gates on the West. ¹⁴ And the wall had twelve foundations and on them the twelve names of the Lamb's twelve apostles.

¹⁵ "Now (the angel) the one speaking with me had a golden measuring rod with which to measure the city, its gates and its wall. ¹⁶ The city was laid out like a square as long as it was wide. And he measured the city with the rod and found it to be 12,000 stadia—its length, breadth, and height are equal. ¹⁷ And he measured the wall—144 cubits by man's measurement which the angel was using. ¹⁸ The material of the wall was jasper and the city was pure gold like pure crystal. ¹⁹ And the foundations of the city wall were adorned with every precious stone: the first foundation jasper, the second sapphire, the third agate, the fourth emerald, ²⁰ the fifth onyx, the sixth ruby, the seventh chrysolite, the eighth beryl, the ninth topaz, the tenth turquoise, the eleventh jacinth, and the twelfth amethyst. ²¹ The twelve gates [of the city] are twelve pearls—each gate is made of a single pearl; the main street of the city was pure gold, like transparent glass.

²² "And I did not see a Temple in the city because the Lord God Almighty and the Lamb are its Temple. ²³ The city does not need the sun nor the moon to shine on it because the glory of God gives it light and the Lamb is its Lamp. ²⁴ And the nations will walk about by its light; and the kings of the earth will bring their glory into it. ²⁵ The gates of the city will never be shut in a day because night will never be there. ²⁶ And they will bring the glory and the honor of the nations into it. ²⁷ And nothing profane will ever enter it, neither those making abominations nor liars except those having been written in the Lamb's Book of Life."

New Jerusalem

John's vision of the End Times winds down with his description of Armageddon 1 resulting in over two hundred million troops dead and the total annihilation of the Beast's forces in Revelation 19. The Apostle saw the Beast and the false prophet thrown alive into the lake of fire and sulfur, possibly into the liquid outer core of the earth. The destruction and loss of life from Jesus' weaponized mouth-laser results in seven months of clean up. In chapter 20, John described the idyllic millennial reign of Christ and the persecuted/beheaded judges of the Tribulation Period who assist Jesus in establishing world peace. But Satan knew that he would be released to instigate Armageddon II as he foments worldwide rebellion among the descendants of Gog (Russia) and Magog (Iran). The earth becomes polarized again with the saints being attacked by even more of Satan's forces than in Armageddon I, one thousand years before. But just as Armageddon I resulted in the slaughter of the opposing armies, so too, the devil's pagan forces are vaporized from the "fire coming down from heaven and annihilating them" (Rev. 20:9). As a consequence of his thoughts, words, and actions through the eons, Satan is thrown into Hell to remain forever where the Antichrist and the false prophet had already been banished.

Then John saw the Great White Throne Judgment where God the Father decides which non-Christians enter into heaven and which are thrown into the lake of fire and sulfur. This decision is ultimately based on whether each person's name has been written in the Book of Life. The Book of Life not only contains the names of all Christians, but also those without exposure to the gospel who lived their lives in accordance with their consciences reflecting awareness of God's moral law (Rev. 20:12–15; cf. Romans 2:6–16).

As chapter 21 opens, John described the *remaking* of heaven and the earth with a simple observation: "Then I saw a new heaven and a new earth; for the first heaven and the first earth have passed and the sea is no longer" (και ειδον ουρανον καινον και γην καινην ο γαρ πρωτος ουρανος και η πρωτη γη απαλθην και η θαλασσα ουκ εστιν ετι, v. 1). The Greek word translated "new" (καινος) means newness of *quality* not newness *with respect to time*. The earth is upgraded to its perfect Garden of Eden state

The Apocalypse Revealed

Painting by Pattie Sheets

after it is cleansed by fire as Peter related (2 Peter 3:10–12); καινος is the same Greek term used by Paul to describe the newness of our life in Christ when we are changed by the Holy Spirit as new believers at salvation (2 Cor.5:17). This newness probably means that all catastrophic weather patterns, earthquakes, volcanos, tornados, hurricanes, and tsunamis cease which may mean no polar caps. John saw no sea which may mean no Mediterranean Sea. I wonder if maybe the Lord directs the Mediterranean Sea water through the shaft of the Abyss into the iron-nickel core of the earth (outer core) to cool it down to a more manageable "sizzle" creating "the burning lake of fire and sulfur." The present temperature of the outer core (below the crust and mantle of the earth) is roughly ten thousand degrees Fahrenheit which would cause water to vaporize and not be a lake at all but a collection of plasma. As I will discuss below, the Mediterranean Sea basin may be the site for the New Jerusalem.

John then continued his vision of the newness of the earth by describing the arrival of the New Jerusalem as it comes to the earth. Remember that in the beginning of his vision in Revelation 3:12, when describing the reward to the church in Philadelphia, John told his reading audience that the New Jerusalem will come down from heaven onto the earth. This is exactly what he saw and described in these next few verses. But to describe the descent of the city onto the earth's surface, John used the language of a bride meeting her groom at her wedding: "And I saw the holy city New Jerusalem coming down out of heaven from God prepared as a bride adorned for her husband" (και την πολιν την αγιαν Ιερουσαλημ καινην ειδον καταβαινουσαν εκ του ουρανου απο του θεου ητοιμασμενην ως νυμφην κεκοσμημενην τω ανδρι αυτης, v. 2). This metaphor for the description of this unbelievable scene reminds the reader that the city structure is surely not the bride. John confirmed that it is *not* the *city* but the *individuals* making up the city which are the focus of the Godhead when the New Jerusalem appears—despite the city's breathtaking beauty. The bride is really the church occupying the city as the bride "adorned for her husband" (v. 2). John then explained the very intimate and touching details of the Church meeting her husband, Jesus of Nazareth, the Father, and the Holy Spirit over the next few verses: "Then I heard a loud voice out of the throne say, *'Behold, the tabernacle of God is with men, and He will tabernacle with them, and they will be His people, and God Himself will be with them'*" (ιδου, η σκηνη του θεου μετα των ανθρωπων και σκηνωσει μετ αυτων και αυτοι λαοι αυτοι εσονται και αυτος ο θεος μετ αυτων εσται, v. 3). With these words, John indicated that God seeks to be extremely intimate with His Church, with the individuals who make it up. The Father knows and loves us so much that He will not allow any reason for tears of regret, shame, or sorrow as the Bride of Christ in the New Jerusalem.

John used the Greek word "σκηνη" (tabernacle, v. 3) to not only describe the New Jerusalem as His vehicle to dwell with/tabernacle with blood-brought humans, but also to describe the manner in which He engages His people. The Tabernacle of the Lord in the Sinai wilderness was the touchpoint that God used to fellowship with and communicate with His servant Moses, who was the only human to see God (albeit His backside, Ex. 33:18-23) besides Jesus, of course. The tabernacle brings back those very intimate Old Testament memories of divine encounter. But this term tabernacle "σκηνη" also brings to mind Peter's desire to build three tabernacles to capture the intimate moment he, James, and John had with the transfigured Jesus, Moses, and Elijah (Mt. 17:1-8; 2 Pet. 1:16-18). When John was writing his Gospel, he began his account of Jesus' life with the words, "and He tabernacled among us" (και εσκηνωσεν εν ημιν, Jn. 1:14), using the verb form of the word, "tabernacle." But nothing is as intimate as the "tabernacling" that the Holy Spirit enjoys with each Christian who gives his/her heart to Jesus, particularly those with release of the Holy Spirit in their lives through the baptism of the Holy Spirit (1 Cor. 3:16).

John described the benefits of this spiritual and physical intimacy with God in the following verse: *"And He will wipe every tear from out of their eyes; and there will be no more death, nor sorrow, nor weeping, nor pain, because the first things have passed; and the One sitting on the throne says, 'Behold, I have made all things new'"* (και εξαλειψει παν δακρυον εκ των οφθαλμων αυτων και ο θανατος ουκ εσται ετι ουτε πενθος ουτε κραυγη ουτε πονος ουκ εσται ετι" (vv. 4-5). Certainly, without Satan and his minions, the threat of sin dominating is gone from the lives of those who have survived the earth's misfortunes over the past seven years and during both Armageddons. With the Beast, the false prophet, and the ten kings of the Beast's Confederacy all in Hell, Christ followers have very little negative to have to contend with. Their time can now be spent enjoying their new existence with God and the rest of humanity either redeemed to God by Jesus' death on the cross or with the rare souls entering heaven through the Great White Throne Judgment as previously mentioned. The Triune God has thoroughly engaged in and enjoyed the wedding of His Son to His Church and presided over the wedding feast of the Lamb. But now God is relocating the heavenly residence of the Bride and her Groom, His Son, to the surface of the earth.

As John visualized this residence relocation, God told him, "Write, for these words are faithful and true" (γραψον, οτι ουτοι οι λογοι πιστοι και αληθινοι εισιν, v. 5). As previously noted, John in his brilliance had a tendency to rely on his memory and not write "things down." But this situation involving the New Jerusalem was getting intense because the Father was about to reveal *many* details concerning the new holy city. The Father wanted John to record these details accurately. Then God told John, "It is finished; I am the alpha and the omega, the beginning and the end" (γεγονα, εγω ειμι το αλφα και το ω η αρχη και το τελος, v. 6). God reminded John that all human time from the old order on the former earth was finished, including humanity's former role. God was about to reveal the new order with the Godhead at the center of the universe residing in the holy city. But He wanted John to know that the Godhead wanted His subjects to be whole and fully nourished in all aspects of their being.

The Father continued His discussion of the new order with John by telling him, "To the thirsty one, I will freely give from the fountain of water of life; the overcomer will inherit these things; and I will be God to him and he will be son/daughter to Me" (εγω τω διψωντι δωσω εκ της πηγης του υδατος της ζωης δωρεαν, ο νικων κληρονομησει ταυτα και εσομαι αυτω θεος και αυτος εσται μοι υιος, vv. 6–7). One of the most basic nutrients of life is water and our ability to drink water sustains our physical lives. Without the "water of life" (υδατος της ζωης, v. 6), humans would die within three days. But the Father discussed "the water" of the Holy Spirit equally critical in the survival of resurrected humans in the new world. God assured John that all people in the new city will not only survive but will *flourish* because of the inheritance they will receive through their relationship restored with the Father through the work of the New Adam Jesus (Rom. 5:12–21). This inheritance includes access to the "water of life" (which sparkles like crystal as it flows as a river from the throne down the middle of the main street of New Jerusalem (Rev. 22:1). As I have previously mentioned, the Holy Spirit energizes these Christians as they drink this "water." The Holy Spirit throughout the Church Age is represented as the "living water" introduced by Jesus as He taught His disciples and the religious elite about the role of the Holy Spirit in their lives (cf. Jn. 4: 13–14; 7:37–38). John also reported that the Father is very clear about those who are overcomers in their previous lives on earth. He told John that they will not only receive the "water" of the Holy Spirit and always have their thirst for God quenched, but they will also be called sons and daughters of God. God also told John that He will consider each individual His very own child and each will reciprocate His boundless love by being devoted to God for eternity.

New Jerusalem

Unfortunately, the other side of God's great mercy and grace is His great wrath and ultimate judgment against those rejecting Him while living out their lives on earth. He stated, "But the cowardly, the unbelievers, the vile, the murderers, the fornicators, the sorcerers, the idolaters, and all liars will have a portion/part in the burning lake of fire and sulfur, which is the second death" (τοις δε δειλοις και απιστοις και εβδελυγμενοις και φονευσιν και πορνοις και φαρμακοις και ειδωλολατραις και πασιν τοις ψευδεσιν το μερος αυτων εν τη λιμνη τη καιομενη πυρι και θειω ο εστιν ο θανατος ο δευτερος, v. 8). God made it perfectly clear that those rejecting His love and purpose for every human's life have only Hell to look forward to. I find it interesting that God elaborated on the types of sinners that will populate the Lake of Fire; He describes eight habitual sinner types who *will not* be allowed to enter the City and live with Him for eternity. These may be the most common sins then and even today. He begins His list with the "cowardly" (δειλοις)—I guess it takes a fair amount of courage to leave a life of sin, repent, and accept Jesus as Savior and Lord. It is the essence of faith to make a leap into the unknown spirit realm and believe that Jesus came to reconnect us with the Trinity as we had once enjoyed in the Garden of Eden.

Those who don't have the courage to respond to the wooing of the Holy Spirit become identified by God as "unbelievers" (απιστοις) some of which become "the vile ones" (εβδελυγμενοις) which in various New Testament passages intimate the sexually perverse (i.e., homosexuals, cf. Rom. 1:24-28). The list continues with murderers (φονευσιν) and fornicators (πορνοις) both of which are blatantly evident in the United States today, particularly during the COVID pandemic and the stress that shutdown of the economy generated for the population. The murder rate in the United States has risen to an all-time high, particularly in the larger cities across our country who defunded the police. According to the CDC's National Center for Health Statistics the murder rate went from 6:100,000 in 2019 to 7.8:100,000 in 2020, a nearly 30 percent increase in one year. This marks the highest annual rate of increase in murder in over one hundred years.[217] The fornication rate marked by the rate of divorce because of infidelity is increasing. The rate of extramarital affairs among married couples in 2023 is nearing 50 percent with no prospect of this ever going down.[218] The next Greek term (φαρμακοις) is the root word for our English

---

217   Jacqueline Howard, "US records highest increase in nation's homicide rate in modern history, CDC says," October 6, 2021, accessed November 17, 2021, https://www.cnn.com/2021/10/06/health/us-homicide-rate-increase-nchs-study/index.html.
218   Paul Brian, "Infidelity Statistics (2023): How Much Cheating is Going On?" April 14, 2023, accessed June 9, 2023, https://hackspirit.com/infidelity-statistics/.

word "pharmacy," but translated in this context as "sorcerers" indicating that many at this time on the earth have been engaging in the occult and in demon worship as we saw in Revelation 9:20–21. I would suspect that by the time of the descent of the New Jerusalem onto the new earth, that the banished devil and his angels would not have the control or connection to their followers. But because all humans on the earth at that time, just as in the present, have free will, they could venerate whomever or whatever they desire to worship, including religions from the past (as Satanism would be by this future time). But I suspect that the list of eight repeat offenders refers to the earth *before* the Great White Throne Judgment because of the Father's words that these types of sinners would "have a share in the burning Lake of Fire and Sulfur" (v. 8) which by chapter 21 has been closed to anymore souls as far as can be ascertained.

There are no objective measures of the number of "idolaters" (ειδωλολατραις) in America; but I venture to speculate that most pagans and a majority of Christians could be classified as "idolaters" simply because of the prevalence of sports enthusiasts venerating numerous favorite sports stars and because of food and Internet purchasing addictions. In 2021, most Americans spent at least 2 hours each day in various social media platforms including Facebook, YouTube, Twitter, TikTok, Instagram, and LinkedIn. The worldwide user number for all of these platforms is now over 4.2 billion people. This is included with the 4.66 billion people using the Internet and 5.22 billion using mobile devices.[219] All of this access to social media solidifies consumerism and idolatry of Mammon (wealth and material avarice) and what it can purchase along with the worship of entertainment stars in numerous venues as John related in Revelation 18. The last chronic sin condition mentioned is "and all liars" (και πασιν τοις ψευδεσιν, v. 8) which pretty much characterizes not just pagans, but some Christians as well. But I suppose in this passage the Lord is referring to those lying continuously, habitual lying, causing the conscience to be seared and resulting in an inability to stop this sin (cf. 1 Tim. 4:2).

John then next had another angel encounter. One of the seven angels with the responsibility of disseminating one of the seven bowl judgments of Revelation 16 came to John and spoke with him about joining him to see a close-up view

---

[219] Milos Djordjevic, Global Social Media Usage Statistics: How Much Time Do People Spend on Social Media?", *The Oklahoma Eagle*, October 5, 2021, accessed November 17, 2021, https://theokeagle.com/2021/10/05/global-social-media-usage-statistics-how-much-time-do-people-spend-on-social-media/.

of the New Jerusalem and those Christ followers within its walls—the city and its inhabitants that he had been seeing from the earth's surface. John described his angel encounter this way, "one of the seven angels with the seven bowls filled with the seven *last* plagues came and spoke to me, 'Come here I will show you the bride, the wife of the Lamb.'" It is easy to overlook the adjective "last" (εσχατων, v. 9) in this verse. This word signifies that this angel was involved in the "last" of the three series of seven judgments. It would appear from this adjective that the three series of judgments were *not* the same events as some theologians have posited but were correctly reported as successive events from the first seal judgment (Rev. 6:2) to the last bowl judgment (Rev. 16:17–21). As John was levitated, he must have had his "heart in his mouth" with excitement. As the angel took him "away in the Spirit to a great and high mountain" (και απηνεγκεν με εν πνευματι επι ορος μεγα και υψηλον, v. 10), John saw the overwhelming brilliance and beauty of the New Jerusalem.

He described, "And he showed me the holy city Jerusalem coming down out of heaven from God having the glory of God, its light was like a very valuable stone, like a jasper stone shining like crystal" (και εδειξεν μοι την πολιν την αγιαν Ιερουσαλημ καταβανουσαν εκ του ουρανου απο του θεου εχουσαν την δοξαν του θεου ο φωστηρ αυτης ομοιος λιθω τιμιωτατω ως λιθω ιασπιδι κρυσταλλιζοντι, v. 10). At the beginning of the chapter, John saw the first appearance of the holy city and its introduction to the earth presumably from the Father's voice while He was sitting on His throne. But here, John reported the continuation of the city's descent onto the surface of the earth and how brilliant it looked. He noticed that it was shining like a brilliant green jasper stone. John saw the spewing of the light of the holy city into the surrounding sky which he describes as breathtaking. As I discuss later, I believe that the brilliant green light comes from one of at least twelve types of laser lights generated from the light sources of the city (the Father and the Son which are the "sun" and "the lamp"). But more on this phenomenon later.

Then the angel showed the Apostle the high walls of the city, its twelve gates, and the twelve angels guarding its gates: "having a great and high wall and having twelve gates with twelve angels at the gates and written on the gates the names of the twelve tribes of the sons of Israel" (εχουσα τειχος μεγα και υψηλον εχουσα πυλωνας δωδεκα και επι τοις αγγωτους δωδεκα και ονοματα επιγεγραμμενα α εστιν {τα ονοματα} των δωδεκα φυλων υιων Ισραηλ, v. 12). John later indicates that the city is a perfect cube with three gates on each side of the city (v. 16). Above each entrance is the name of each of the sons of Israel (v. 12). I would not be surprised if the names of the twelve tribes mentioned in Revelation 7 are the names used for each of these entrances. This may mean that the tribes of Dan and Ephraim are not honored due to their Old Testament idolatry and tendency to displease the Lord.

An angel standing guard at each of the twelve doors would be quite an effective security system for the holy city. Since the dimensions of the city are 12,000 stadia (approximately 1,400 miles) for its length, width, and height (v. 16), the gates/doors of the city are 350 miles apart with three gates per side (v. 13). We learn from John later in this chapter that these angels only allow those to enter the city whose names are written in the Book of Life (v. 21). I wonder how the angels at the gates know who is sealed for eternity for Kingdom living and who is not? I think a clue to this is the seal of God discussed on the foreheads of not only the Jewish Christian evangelists in Rev. 7:4–8; 14:1; and 22:14, but John also described God's Church as those who "will worship Him indeed they will see His face and also His name [will be] on their foreheads" (λατρευσουσιν αυτω και οψονται το προσωπον αυτου και το ονομα αυτου επι των μετωπων αυτων, v. 4). The angels must be able to "see" the stamp or seal of God (Eph. 1:13) by seeing the resurrected spirit after conversion that occurs within each Christian.

John then noticed that the high wall has twelve foundations supporting it with "the twelve names of the Lamb's twelve apostles on them" (επ αυτων δωδεκα ονοματα των δωδεκα αποστολων του αρνιου, v. 14). Of course, Judas' name is not one of them; I would suspect that Matthias' name or possibly Paul's may be the twelfth apostle's name on one of those foundations. Remember that all of the original Apostles including Matthias and Paul died martyrs' deaths, save for the Apostle John. I also wonder if the angel showing John the city was showing him its foundations from outside the city. However, I would think that foundations of such a large structure would have to be underneath the earth's surface in order to properly stabilize its immense structure. If that is the case, then the angel would have had to show John the underground foundations through an elevator system *inside* the city or by letting him see the twelve basement floors from inside.

Another interesting observation is the Apostle John obviously saw *his own* name written on one of the twelve city foundations. I wonder what thoughts went through his mind as he observed a great tribute to his contribution to Christendom. Surely, John had much to be proud of; but at the end of his life, I'm sure he was humble and maybe not even thinking about the honor of his name placed on one of the foundations of the New Jerusalem.

Now a word on the massiveness of the holy city. John was allowed to see the measurement calculations of the dimensions of the city because he watched the angel measure it with a "golden measuring rod" (μετρον καλαμον χρυσουν, v. 15). I wonder if the measuring instrument was really a laser with a golden handle and/or with a "golden" light emitted. John saw that the city was 12,000 stadia long, high, and wide. One stadion is anywhere from 600 feet to 687 feet depending on the source consulted. Twelve thousand stadia calculate to around fourteen hundred miles and is the distance between New York City and Dallas. It appears from John's description that New Jerusalem is a perfect cube. The length and breadth of this cube would be like the distance between Minneapolis, Minnesota, at the Northeast corner, Seattle, Washington, at the Northwest corner, San Diego, California, at the Southwest corner and Little Rock, Arkansas. at the Southeast corner. If you flew in a commercial jet around the outside of the city walls, it would take 10 to 12 hours to completely encircle New Jerusalem! A fourteen hundred mile high, wide, and long city would contain 2.744 billion cubic miles within its boundaries assuming that this city has floors at 1-mile intervals with fourteen hundred floors. If this was the case, each floor would have almost 2 million square miles of living/working space. If only ten billion believers live in the City[220], then each would have about .28 square miles or about 15,000 square feet of living space; this would be unlikely because New Jerusalem would obviously have more than living quarters in it including space for commercial uses, agricultural farms, industrial complexes, and infrastructure.

Earth presently has 60 million square miles of land surface and 140 million square miles of water surface, equaling 200 million square miles of total surface. The surface area of the New Jerusalem would be fifteen times greater than the surface area of the earth if fourteen hundred floors at 1-mile intervals are assumed. The sun and photosynthesis likely will persist on the earth's *surface* including the dark reaction of photosynthesis at night (when the sugars are made from carbon dioxide of man and animals and from the photons from the sun). I think that the earth's atmosphere will mimic the Garden of Eden with no temperature variations except slightly cooler during the evenings/night hours. Of course, in the New Jerusalem there is no night but likely lower light periods for our rest dominated by Jesus' Lamp (21:23-25). I still feel that the oceans will be present since John wrote, "and the *sea* is no longer" (η θαλασσα ουκ εστιν ετι, v. 1) probably indicating the loss of the

---

220   George Barna, "Release #6: What Does It Mean When People Say They Are "Christian' "? *American Worldview Inventory 2021*, Cultural Research Center, Arizona Christian University, August 31, 2021, accessed November 26, 2021, https://www.arizonachristian.edu/wp-content/uploads/2021/08/CRC_AWVI2021_Release06_Digital_01_20210831.pdf.

Mediterranean Sea in order for the dry seabed to receive the New Jerusalem—but I may be wrong about this. I can't imagine not having sea life on the earth from the lack of oceans.

The angel continued to measure the city and allows John to see that its walls are 144 cubits or about 216 feet thick.[221] If the New Jerusalem was scaled down to about 12½ feet high (an inch equivalent to 10 miles), the ozone layer would be one inch from the base (ten miles high), the dust belt 5 inches from the base (50 miles high), meteors at 10 inches (100 miles high), and satellites 12½ feet from the base (1500 miles high). Likely the jasper stone gives this thick wall more tensile strength than any substance we know of today, because the over 200 foot wide wall composed of concrete or even the strongest metal known today would be too thin to support the 1,400-mile cubed structure.[222]

Some scholars feel the New Jerusalem will not touch earth but will hover over the earth in the stratosphere.[223] Passages in both Revelation 21 and 22 would seem to contradict this with people entering and leaving, indicating land location of the city. As previously noted, my best guess is that the Mediterranean Sea basin is the location for the city since John mentions that he sees no more sea in Revelation 21:1. He could be referring to the oceans but I think he is looking at the Middle East from a high elevation and sees no more Mediterranean Sea which roughly fits the dimensions of the New Jerusalem (the Mediterranean Sea dimensions are 2,400 miles by 1000 miles). The main building material of the four walls is jasper but interspersed between the sheets of this substance are collections of twelve "precious stones" (λιθω τιμιω, v. 19) including jasper. Interestingly, the twelve precious stones mentioned by John were also found in the ephod breast-piece worn by the high priest as he performed his duties in the Temple (Ex. 39:10-13). The twelve stones of his breast-piece represented the twelve tribes of the sons of Israel.

Each of the rare stones possesses colors and physical characteristics which complement the beauty of New Jerusalem, and which probably add some practical benefit to the city. These stones could possibly balance gravitational forces/factors

---

221   One cubit is about 18 inches; therefore, 144 cubits equal about 2,592 inches or about 216 feet.
222   "R404.1.5 Foundation Wall Thickness Based on Walls Supported," Colorado Residential Code 2021, accessed November 26, 2021, https://up.codes/s/foundation-wall-thickness-based-on-walls-supported.
223   Dan Greenup, "Revelation 21:1-27: New Jerusalem," accessed February 26, 2022, https://dangreenup.com/revelation-211-27-new-jerusalem/.

which otherwise might be altered on the earth from the massiveness of the New Jerusalem. Each foundation stone has a crystal type that could serve as laser generators when the light from Jesus and the Father pass into the foundation walls. As the light photons pass through the precious stone material, they become collimated, coherent, and monochromatic and then reflect off the mirror-like walls and transparent gold floors of New Jerusalem. Each monochromatic, coherent, collimated laser light beam from each of the foundation crystals could be harnessed to generate power for New Jerusalem and the universe and could be used to cut, punch, abrade, shape, vaporize—whatever task is necessary to perform. The generated laser light could also act as the power source for other generators and could generate the power for other energy sources including electricity and nuclear power. For that matter, the light from the Father and the Son along with the foundation crystals would allow for the production of the whole electromagnetic spectrum including the production of and industries associated with gamma waves, X-rays, radio and television waves, Internet, and technologies yet undiscovered or not utilized. It might also be possible to harness the specific light energies from these stones to create human light travel to distant locations in the universe to expand God's Kingdom. More on this in the next chapter.

The precious stones adorning the twelve foundations of New Jerusalem.

The Apostle next described the material of each of the twelve gates: "And the twelve gates [are] twelve pearls—each gate composed of a single pearl" (και οι δωδεκα πυλωνες δωδεκα μαργαριται ανα εις εκαστος των πυλωνων ην εξ ενος μαργαριτου, v. 21). Pearls are very beautiful but also very hard materials—fitting for the entrances/exits of the City. The gates are guarded by one angel per entrance; no wonder there is no need for the entrances to be closed at night on earth; each angel would have unheard of intelligence, strength, and connection with his fellow angels that would make the New Jerusalem the safest place in the literal universe. I think each entrance could be supervised by one of the patriarchs whose name graces each entrance. The city is composed of pure gold—purer than we are familiar with because it is transparent (v. 18); its walls are composed of brilliant red or green jasper (v. 18). Its main street also is composed of transparent gold which could act as perfect mirrors to enhance and reflect the laser light energy not unlike the mirrors contained in laser boxes today which assist in collimating the laser light beams before they are released on the target. The Father's light radiation incredibly satisfies the energy requirements for the City. Jesus gives enough light for the "evening and night" time because His light is called the "lamp" of the City. Even though John stated that there is no night in the city, there could be less light when Jesus' Lamp light takes over during nighttime hours, giving our pineal glands the ability to produce melatonin and maintaining our circadian rhythm. Remember there is still time as we know it because of comments about the Tree of Life bearing its fruit *every month* (Rev. 22:2). Maybe the Father's light allows no dependence on the sun which could mean that the City is contained in a bubble-like membrane or covering material. Remember that the structure of New Jerusalem is around 1,400 miles high which would mean that as one goes into the higher elevations of the city weightlessness is encountered; unless the city is self-contained and has some gravity generating mechanisms in place at higher elevations. It may be that the Lord in His wisdom constructed the New Jerusalem to be *without* gravity in its upper levels which would enhance our ability to not wear out our joints and cardiovascular systems and more easily live for eternity. As previously suggested, each foundation level could be responsible for the specific laser energy necessary as power sources for the city and even the universe.

Water comes from His throne and satisfies water requirements for the city and for each human. The rehabilitation of each traumatized Christian and citizen of New Jerusalem involves the satiation of his/her thirst with the "fountain of the water of life" (v. 6) which the Father makes available to the thirsty who overcame the difficulties of life to be faithful throughout their life to Christ. I believe that all of the deficiencies within our lives on earth resulting from our sinful nature, iniquities, and from negative life experiences and the memories these produce are rehabilitated by the environment of the New Jerusalem, including the thirst quenching we get from the River of Life that John sees flowing out of the Father and the Lamb's thrones (Rev. 22:1). Throughout the Scriptures, water has been associated with the Holy Spirit as we see in the following: Zechariah 14:8, John 14:10, Hebrews 10:22, 1 Peter 3:21, Revelation 7:17; 21:6: 22:1.

Now about the citizens in the city. At least 100 billion humans have existed from prehistoric times to present.[224] New Jerusalem's first few floors could contain all of these humans combined in comfortable quarters; Jesus states that He is preparing many mansions for us (John 14:2) which means ample space and great comforts. Christians live in the city. But humans who never knew Jesus judged by the Father at the Great White Throne Judgment worthy for heaven (20:12-15) might live in or outside the city or both? It seems that the world's population will always have choice/free will and may even be able to sin because John states that sinners will not be able to enter the City (Rev. 21:27; 22:14) because very intelligent and very powerful angels guard the gates 24/7. Assuming that only 10 percent of the population living on the earth ever become Christians (Jesus said that few would enter by the "narrow door," Mt. 7:14) then maybe only 10 billion believers live in the City. If this was the case, then each person would have nearly one-third of a square mile of living space assuming fourteen hundred floors of living space. Of course, every human would have sanitation needs; our gastrointestinal tracts still work because we will still be eating as we see in Revelation 19:9 at the Wedding Feast of the Lamb. Of course, the resurrected Jesus demonstrated an active and working GI tract with His disciples on at least three different post-resurrection occasions (Lk. 24:41-43; Jn.21:4-13; Acts 1:4). This brings up the issue of a sewage system and waste disposal system. I am certain that Father God and Jesus are working on this issue now and will reveal the absolute best waste management system ever devised—one that will recapture lost energy without polluting the environment.

Despite all the glorious details of the magnificent and palatial New Jerusalem throughout Revelation 21 and the first portion of Revelation 22, John delivered an astounding picture of who the New Jerusalem structure contains—the true Bride of Christ. We see the individuals of the Body/Bride of Christ identified in Rev. 21:2-9 as:

- Those adorned for her husband (v. 2)
- He will tabernacle with them (v. 3)
- They will be His people (v. 3)
- He Himself will be with them (v. 3)
- He will wipe every tear from out of their eyes (v. 4)

---

224 Toshiko Kaneda and Carl Haub, "How Many People Have Ever Lived on Earth?" Population Reference Bureau, November 15, 2022, accessed June 1, 2023, https://www.prb.org/articles/how-many-people-have-ever-lived-on-earth/

- No more death, sorrow, weeping, nor pain (v. 4)
- Spiritual and physical thirst will be satiated from the fountain/river of the water of life (v. 6)

These passages from the first portion of chapter 21 reveal the tenderness and the completeness with which God rehabilitates His people after their trauma of experiencing the events of the Tribulation Period and before. These passages make it very clear that the Lord has unlimited love and connection with every individual making up the Church, the Bride of His Son. The future of every believer will have the intimate experience with the Father, lacking on this earth where each receives "a glimpse or two" of their heavenly Father in a lifetime. But in heaven, by comparison, each Christ follower will be inundated and initially overwhelmed with the purest of love and the attention given to each believer, even down to the wiping away of every tear from previous difficult memories of the past. In chapter 22, John affirms God's intimate connection to His children by describing God's Church as "worshipping Him, and they will see His face, and His name will be on their foreheads" (και οι δουλοι αυτου λατρευσουσιν αυτω και οψονται το προσωπων αυτου και το ονομα αυτου επι των μετωπων αυτων, vv. 3-4). These verses suggest that God's work of rehabilitation mentioned here in chapter 21 recreates newness in His disciples with lives brimming with the desire to worship Him. God reciprocates by giving them unlimited access to His presence and writing His name on their foreheads. Forehead writing occurred in Revelation 7 and reiterated in Revelation 14 when the Jewish Billy Grahams were "stamped" with the seal of God but also occurred when the false prophet forced the followers of the Beast to receive an identification number (RFID, Rev. 13:16) on their forehead or right-hand. The tephillin (Gk, φυλακτήριον [phylacteries]) of the orthodox Jews as discussed in the Pentateuch (Exod. 13:9, 16; Deut. 6:8 and 11:18) were metaphors of the identification of God's people with His ways and with His rulership just as we see here in Revelation 21-22.

The next section, Rev. 21:22-27, demonstrates the amenities of the Bride including the spiritual, practical, and the protective attributes of those members of Christ's Church living in the New Jerusalem:

- No Temple in the city "because the Lord God Almighty and the Lamb are its Temple" (ο γαρ κυριος ο θεος ο παντοκρατωρ ναος αυτης εστιν και το αρνιον, v. 22)

- The light of the glory of God and the lamp of the Lamb gives the city light instead of the sun and moon (v. 23)
- The gates will never close because night will never be there and each gate guarded by an angel (vv. 12, 25)
- No active sinners including any making abominations(sins) and liars will ever be allowed to enter the city (v. 27)
- The only people allowed to enter have their "names written in the Lamb's Book of Life" (οι γεγραμμενοι εν τω βιβλιω της ζωης του αρνιου, v. 27)

The comments in these last few verses of chapter 21 indicate that some of those living outside of the New Jerusalem on the earth may choose to do so even though they have free access into the city. Their names *have* been written in the Lamb's Book of Life and have been faithful Christians with the task of resettling the earth which has recently been destroyed by fire (2 Peter 3:10–15, Rev. 20:11). However, not all seems to be rosy on the earth. It seems that free will continues to be very much a part of homo sapiens and some elect over eternity to challenge the Trinity and New Jerusalem. Thus, the mention of angels guarding each gate and the comments that "abomination makers and liars" cannot enter the city (v. 27). The mention of unsavory individuals even in eternity is very consistent with the Father's idea of creating humans in His image including with the *same free will* that He and the other members of the Godhead have as well as His angels.

REVELATION 22

The River of the Water of Life

The Tree of Life

We Are Kings Forever

The Blessing and the Curses (Adding/Subtracting)

> 1 "And he [the angel] showed me the River of the Water of Life sparkling like crystal flowing out of the throne of God and of the Lamb 2 down the middle of the great street; and on either side of the River, the Tree of Life producing fruit for twelve months, bearing its fruit each month; and the leaves of the tree are for the healing of the nations. 3 No longer will there be any curse; indeed, the throne of God and of the Lamb will be in it [the city] and His servants will worship Him; 4 and they will see His face and His Name will be on their foreheads. 5 Night will not be there anymore; indeed, they will not need the light of a lamp or the light of the sun because the Lord God will shine on them and they will reign as kings forever and ever.

Revelation: The Fifth Gospel

⁶ "Then he said to me, 'These words are faithful and true. The Lord God of the spirits of the prophets sent his angel to show His servants what must soon take place. ⁷ Pay attention, Behold! I am coming soon. Blessed is the one who obeys the words of the prophecy of this book.' ⁸ I, John, was the one seeing and hearing these things and when I heard and saw, I fell down to prostrate myself at the feet of the angel, the one showing me these things. ⁹ But he said to me, 'Don't do that because I am a fellow servant of you and of your brothers the prophets and those who obey the words of this book. Worship God.' ¹⁰ Then he says to me, 'Do not seal the words of the prophecy of this book, for the time is near. ¹¹ So let the unrighteous one, still be unrighteous, let the vile one still be vile, let the righteous one, still be righteous, let the holy one still be holy.'

¹² "'Behold I am coming soon and I have My reward with Me to give to each according to what his work is. ¹³ I am the alpha and the omega, the first and the last, the beginning and the end. ¹⁴ Blessed are those washing their long robes that they may have right to the Tree of Life and may go through the gates into the city. ¹⁵ Outside are the perverts the sorcerers, the fornicators, the murderers, the idolaters, and all those who love and practice the lie. ¹⁶ I, Jesus, sent My angel to give you this testimony for the churches. I am the root and offspring of David, the bright, morning star.'

¹⁷ "Now let the Spirit and the Bride say, 'Come'; let the one hearing say, 'Come'; let the thirsty one come and let the one desiring freely receive the water of life. ¹⁸ I warn everyone hearing the words of the prophecy of this Book, if anyone adds to them, God will add to him the plagues having been written in this Book; ¹⁹ and if anyone takes away from the words of the prophecy of this Book, God will take away his share in the Tree of Life and in the Holy City, the things written in this Book." ²⁰ The One testifying to these things says, 'Yes, I am coming soon.' Amen; Come Lord Jesus. ²¹ May the grace of the Lord Jesus be with all."

The River of the Water of Life

John began the last chapter of Revelation by discussing the City River teeming with energy and life-promoting effects from the Holy Spirit: "and then he [the angel] showed me the river of the water of life sparkling like crystal flowing out from the throne of God and from the Lamb down the middle of its great street" (και εδειξεν μοι ποταμον υδατος ζωης λαμπρον ως κρυσταλλον εκπορευομενον εκ θρονου του θεου και του αρνιου εν μεσω της πλατειας αυτης, vv. 1-2). The angel showed John a waterfall of the purest water in the universe cascading down from the elevated throne room eventually onto the main street of the city that he had earlier described as being made of pure gold like transparent glass (Rev. 21:21). The waterfall is called "the River of the Water of Life" and has healing properties and the ability to quench more than thirst (Rev. 21:6). It flows from God's throne in the middle of the city and supplies the water needs of New Jerusalem. As previously indicated, I think that the Holy Spirit literally flows into the water and energizes the citizens and the plant life of the city. One very important River function is to nourish and energize the Tree of Life which John states is on both sides of the River of Life: "and on either side of the river is the Tree of Life producing fruit for twelve months bearing fruit each month" (και του ποταμου εντευθεν και εκειθεν ξυλον ζωης ποιουν καρπους δωδεκα κατα μηνα εκαστον αποδιδουν τον καρπον αυτου, v. 2). Even though verse 2 only mentions a single tree, I think John intimates that the Tree of Life is the type of tree on *both* sides of the River of Life. Unfortunately, John's Greek is very rough and probably should have been more explicit about identifying many trees on either side of the great main street. His point is well-taken, though. The Tree of Life played a major role in the Garden of Eden—at first being the centerpiece of creation for the blessings of life and security that God gave to Adam and Eve. But eventually the Tree became the main reason why God removed Adam and Eve from the Garden. The eternal longevity gained from its fruit would have caused eternal misery due to the sin that both Eve and Adam acquired and became vulnerable to by eating the forbidden fruit of the Tree of Knowledge of Good and Evil (cf. Gen. 3:22-24). God felt compelled to keep His new sinners from eating the fruit of the Tree of Life because He knew death was best for His first family newly introduced to sin and its degrading effects. He longed for the day, as we see through John's eyes here in Rev. 22, when the Tree of Life would again play an important role in promoting quality eternal life with redeemed New Jerusalem citizens.

I am not sure from the Greek if the tree produces twelve *different* types of fruit harvested each month or the *same* type of fruit each month. But knowing the Lord and His penchant for variety, I could easily imagine different fruit crops each month. John states that, "the leaves of the tree are for the healing of the nations" (και τα φυλλα του ξυλου εις θεραπειαν των εθνων, v. 2). Of course, tree leaves produce chlorophyll, sugars, and oxygen by utilizing carbon dioxide and light energy. But here in the New Jerusalem, it would appear from John's words that this unbelievable tree is to play a central role in the medical practice of "healing the nations" (θεραπειαν των εθνων, v. 2). This passage suggests that some beings in the universe, human and non-human, or humans outside the city on the new earth might need to be healed of their diseases. It may also imply that the New Jerusalem residents also may need to experience occasional rejuvenation by ingesting the leaves from the Tree of Life. This brings up the possibility of sin and the negative effects of free will outside the Kingdom of God and the Holy City. Time is still present in the universe as we can see by the mention of months (v.2) and "day" and the prospect of "night" outside of the New Jerusalem on the earth (21:25) and likely lesser light in New Jerusalem for rest times (Jesus being the "lamp" or lesser light for those times-21:23). But to His Church/Bride, time has no negative effects. "Will we still age?" is a question that Revelation does not answer.

John then discussed us, God's servants, who reign for eternity. Our occupations or roles in the New Jerusalem economy remain to be seen. But the statements concerning "reigning forever" (v. 5) indicate that we will have work to do as emissaries of the King maybe outside New Jerusalem on the earth and possibly in other places in the universe with subjects under our reigns. John's statements in Revelation 21:24-26 indicate that many New Jerusalem citizens have assignments on the earth maybe as judges (as in the millennial period) and as kings and in other roles not mentioned. It is interesting to note that there is no mention of any menial roles or of physical labor in chapter 21 or 22. The only clue to our roles in heaven on earth and beyond is that we "will reign as kings forever and ever" (βασιλευσουσιν εις τους αιωνας των αιωνων, v. 5). It is hard to imagine not working up a sweat and not serving others through physical labor particularly when we have bodies that appear to be indestructible (vis-à-vis Jesus' resurrected body as a pattern or "first fruit" of our resurrected bodies, 1 Cor. 15:52-54).

John stated that the curse (sin, aging, death) will no longer be present in the city because the Source of all life and health, the Godhead, has taken up residence there: "And there will be no more curse because the throne of God and of the Lamb are in it" (και παν καταθεμα ουκ εσται ετι και ο θρονος του θεου και του αρνιου εν αυτη εσται, v. 3). Ten to fifteen years before he received his Revelation, the Apostle John wrote in his Gospel that "the light shone in the darkness, but the darkness did not overcome it," Jn.1:5, author's translation). I think this indicates that the power and holiness of God overwhelms the curse of sin, aging, and death and all of their accoutrements (e.g. sorrow, weeping, and pain, Rev. 21:4), particularly in the New Jerusalem. John followed the observation of the banishment of the "curse" by noticing that the residents of this blessed city will be constantly worshipping God, will also be in close contact with Him, and will wear His name on their foreheads: "and His servants will worship Him and will see His face and His Name will be on their foreheads" (και ο δουλοι αυτοι λατρευσουσιν αυτω και οψονται το προσωπον αυτου και το ονομα αυτου επι των μετωπων αυτων, vv. 3-4). One of the practical effects of the Godhead living in New Jerusalem is the constant light power source generated by the Father: "And there will be no more night; indeed they will not need the light of a lamp nor the light of the sun because the Lord God shines on them" (και νυξ ουκ εσται ετι και ουκ εχουσιν χρειαν φωτος λυχνου και φωτος ηλιου οτι κυριος ο θεος φωτισει επ αυτους, v. 5). Since the plant life in the New Jerusalem will no longer need the sunlight to survive, as previously discussed, the New Jerusalem may have a self-contained environment, a bubble of sorts surrounding the city.

One of the major negatives of our present world which accelerates human aging is the force of gravity over a lifetime. Gravity benefits the development of humans in utero and during childhood years because of the needed muscle development and hypertrophy that it assists in. However, as we enter our sixth and seventh decades, we begin to experience gravity's negative impact on our spines, joints, and cardiovascular systems. Our vertebral columns lose height on average about 2½ to 4 inches if we live to eighty years of age. The joints become less mobile over a lifetime due to lack of joint synovial cell production of lubricant (synovial fluid) exacerbated by the force of gravity. The heart beats over three billion times in an eighty-year lifetime; it loses its ability to pump blood through the body and back to the heart in later life partly because it must pump against gravity. It is more difficult as we grow older to accommodate gravity and get the blood from the legs to the inferior vena cava then back to the heart; thus, the tendency for swelling around the ankles in the elderly (venous insufficiency with stasis dermatitis). It would not surprise me if the Father in His wisdom created a very controlled, graduated gravity environment for His redeemed humans to survive for eternity within the walls of New Jerusalem.

The next phrase from John's pen describes the activities of the redeemed for eternity: "and they will reign as kings forever and ever" (και βασιλευσουσιν εις

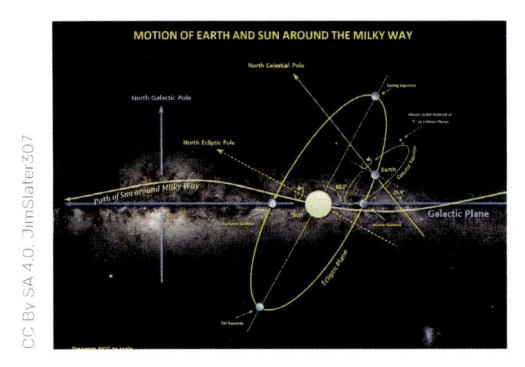

Illustration of Motion of Earth, Moon and Sun around the Milky Way

τους αιωνας των αιωνων, v. 5). Eternity is a long time, longer than anyone could imagine. But here in John's last chapter of His vision, he clearly stated that we who are admitted to the Holy City, who have citizenship there, who worship the Father and see His face, and who have His name on our foreheads will be *very productive* for the rest of eternity. The question is, "What will believers be doing for eternity?" It would appear from the verse 5 that we will be assisting the Father in organizing, developing, and maintaining the influence and blessing of the Kingdom of God in all parts of the universe.

The universe is immensely huge and possibly infinite in volume.[225] The region visible from Earth (the observable universe) is a sphere with a radius of about 46 billion light years or around 93 billion light years in diameter, based on where the expansion of space has taken the most distant objects observed. For comparison, the diameter of a typical galaxy is only 30,000 light-years, and the typical distance between two neighboring galaxies is only 3 million light-years. Our Milky Way Galaxy is roughly 100,000 light years in diameter and about 1,000 light years thick. Our nearest sister galaxy, the Andromeda Galaxy, is located roughly 2.5 million light years away. Our Solar System is about 8.3 light hours in diameter or about 7.5 billion miles (80 astronomical units). The diameter of the Milky Way in comparison to our Solar System would be comparing the length of the United States to the diameter of a quarter.

There are at least two hundred billion galaxies to as many as ten trillion galaxies in the observable universe. Typical galaxies range from dwarfs with as few as ten million stars up to giants with one trillion stars, all orbiting the galaxy's center of mass. Using the Milky Way Galaxy's estimated 100 billion stars, a very rough estimate would suggest there are around one septillion (1 followed by 24 zeros) stars in the

---

[225] All information about the planets, stars, and galaxies is from the website, The Planets, accessed 4/24/23, https://theplanets.org/.

observable universe.[226] The Milky Way Galaxy is estimated to have at least fifty billion planets, five hundred million (one out of every 100) of which could be located in the "habitable zone" (able to maintain liquid water and support earthlike life) of their parent star. New data suggests there may be up to twice as many free-floating planets in the Milky Way as there are stars which would mean that there may be 400 billion planets in the Milky Way and around four billion habitable planets. In 2017, the Kepler Space Observatory Mission team released a list of 2,335 extrasolar planet candidates, including sixty-four that may be in the "habitable zone."[227] Based on these Kepler findings, astronomer Seth Shostak estimated that "within a thousand light-years of Earth . . . there are at least 30,000 of these habitable worlds."[228]

Interstellar Neighborhood

It could be very possible that some of these one hundred billion stars could have multiple habitable planets for us to begin building societies for the Kingdom and require our attention and expertise in guiding and nurturing these worlds along the path of Christ centeredness. If ten billion Christians live in New Jerusalem, then each could at one point or another rule over a habitable planet.

An interesting thought might be that the Lord could allow individuals, families, communities, societies, and cultures to develop on these habitable planets disparate from our own but within the limits of His will and providence. The words

---

226   Alisa Harvey and Elizabeth Howell, "How Many Stars Are In The Universe?" Space.com, February 11, 2002, accessed June 2, 2023, https://www.space.com/26078-how-many-stars-are-there.html.
227   "New Kepler Planet Candidates," Rick Chen, ed., NASA, June 19, 2017, accessed June 2, 2023, https://www.nasa.gov/image-feature/ames/kepler/new-kepler-planet-candidates.
228   Seth Shostak, "A Bucketful of Worlds," HuffPost, February 3, 2022, accessed June 2, 2023, https://www.huffpost.com/entry/a-bucketful-of-worlds_b_817921.

of Revelation 22:5 make it clear that we will be reigning over "subjects" possibly from other worlds and very likely of non-human origin according to the latest from Area 51 and the "All-domain Anomaly Resolution Office" (AARO) of the Department of Defense formed in July, 2022. Its findings suggest that the United States government is in possession of at least a dozen extraterrestrial flying spacecraft and their non-human pilots.[229] All of this will likely involve evangelizing, teaching, preaching, and utilizing the other gifts developed while fulfilling our God-given callings on earth. Of course, we will be maturing these skills and gifts while living for eternity because an innate characteristic of "humanness" is to grow in intellect and giftings as we see in our lives on earth. Our New Jerusalem reigning might also require servant-like leadership to many in other worlds since "reigning" will surely require subjugating our will to the Father's.

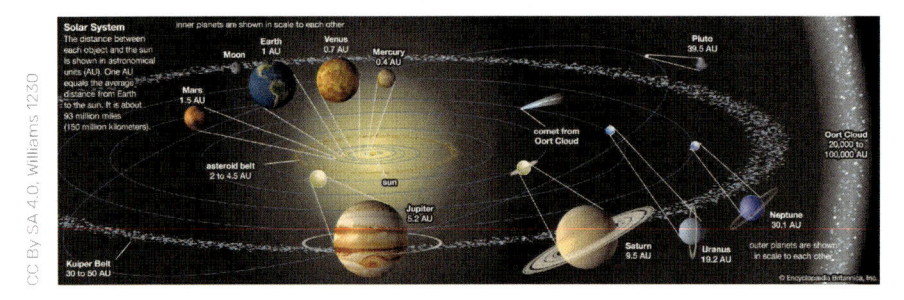

The orbits of the planets and other bodies of the solar system.

Many other questions arise from the phrase "and they will reign as kings forever and ever" (v. 5). The idea of the gospel influencers going to all parts of the universe is particularly intriguing but challenging since the Milky Way Galaxy is so vast, let alone the rest of the universe (93 billion light years in diameter, as previously indicated). But the Creator of the universe by the time of Revelation 22 would have already developed a solution or solutions. Maybe this would include a system of wormholes and faster-than-light travelling capabilities which spirit beings obviously have no difficulty doing. It also may be mediated through the system of laser light production mentioned in chapter 21. I could imagine the saints being transported through tracks of laser light through wormholes whose entrance and exit points are nearby due to wormhole folding by the command of the Father and faster than

---

229   Jesse Waters Prime Time, Fox News, June 7, 2023.

light travel within the hole.[230] This would allow for travelling to distant worlds with minimal time lost. Another possibility would be transfer of beings through "mind-transfer"—a sort of "think-travel" through the Holy Spirit who is ubiquitous anyway. Many other questions arise.

What about the possibility of non-human intelligent beings as previously mentioned and their introduction to the Triune God? And what about the possibility of other situations different from earth's concerning sin and atonement for it? Would we ever have to give our life up as Jesus did for us? The later question, I would think not. Hebrews 10:12-18 tells us that Jesus already has paid for the cost of sin throughout time through His sinless life and propitious death on the cross two thousand years ago on planet earth. I cannot imagine our lives being considered "sinless sacrifices" for the sins of beings from other worlds when Jesus' perfect life and selfless sacrifice is considered by God to be acceptable for *our* world's human shortcomings and sinful acts.

John continued his dialogue with the angel. The angel reminded him again, as did Father God (Rev. 21:5), that "these words are faithful and true" (ουτοι οι λογοι πιστοι και αληθινοι, v. 5). Both times when these words were communicated to John, he had *just* seen and heard about heavenly matters hardly imaginable. Here it was the cataract, the Tree of Life, and the believers' future as kings; in Revelation 21, John had *just* been introduced to the New Jerusalem and the bride of Christ living in the holy city. The angel was reiterating that everything John was hearing and seeing was straight from the mind of God and there was no need to question the truthfulness of the experience. John also heard the angel tell him what he had heard in the first verse of the Book of Revelation: "the Lord God of the spirits of the prophets *sent His angel to show His servants what must soon take place*" (απεστειλεν τον αγγελον αυτου δειξαι τοις δουλοις αυτου α δει γενεσθει εν ταχει, v. 6). Time in heaven is far different than on earth. It would seem that hundreds of years on earth could be minutes or days in heaven; which prompted the next statement, "Behold I am coming soon; blessed are the ones obeying the words of the prophecy of this book" (και ιδου ερχομαι ταχυ ο μακαριος τηρων τους λογους της προφητειας του βιβλιου τουτου, v. 7). Jesus speaking directly to John told him that in heaven-time, He will be returning soon despite being away

---

230   Michael S. Morris, Kip S. Thorne, Ulvi Yurtsever, "Wormholes, Time Machines, and the Weak Energy Condition," *Physical Review Letters* 61, no. 13, September 26, 1988: 1446-1449, accessed June 2, 2023, http://authors.library.caltech.edu/9262/1/MORprl88.pdf.

Revelation: The Fifth Gospel

from the earth for over sixty-five years since His resurrection and ascension. Jesus reminded John that despite the Apocalypse being a prophecy giving the Church and pagans insight into End-Time events, Jesus considers this book no less than the Word of God. He reminded John, just like He did in the second verse of chapter 1, that those obeying the words from God in this book will be blessed and happy in their lives.

John knew from his discussion of the End Times with Jesus on Mount Olivet (Mt. 24) that during the latter half of the first century and the first part of the second century (through the insight of the Holy Spirit) that many would-be prophets tried to predict what would happen to the earth in Jesus' absence and what would have to happen before His coming. Many pseudepigrapha apocalyptic works littered the Christian world including the Apocalypses of Peter, Stephen, and Thomas to name just a few of the spurious works not received or written by these saints but by authors coveting the influence of Christians curious about their futures.[231] The authors of these visions would often "borrow" the names of the great first century saints to somehow add veracity to their presumptive, misleading prophecies. Maybe this is why the Holy Spirit prompted John to tell his reading audience that he was "the one who saw and heard these things" (ο ακουων και βλεπων ταυτα και οτε ηκουσα και εβλεψα, v. 8). Most of the first century church knew about the twelve apostles and would certainly have been introduced to John from the Synoptics but also by his own widely popular Gospel as the "disciple whom Jesus loved." But John positively identified himself by telling his reading audience that he was about to worship the angel responsible for giving him the Revelation which he also attempted to do in Revelation 19:10. In chapter 22, the angel again told John to desist from bowing down and worshipping him: "Stop! Don't do it because I am a servant of yours and of your brothers the prophets and those who obey the words of this book; worship God" (ορα μη σουνδουλος σου ειμι και των αδελφων σου των προφητων και των τηρουντων τους λογους του βιβλιου τουτου τω θεω προσκυνησον, v. 9). John must have had a tendency to want to honor angels. He obviously held them in high esteem. But as in the previous case of *almost* angel worship, the angel was quick to prevent idol worship—which is what John would have done in his exuberance to honor the angel.

---

[231] Robert Henry Charles, "Apocalyptic Literature, *Encyclopaedia Britannica*, Vol. 2, 11th edition, Hugh Chisholm, ed., (Cambridge, England, Cambridge University Press, 1922), 169–175, accessed June 2, 2023, https://archive.org/details/encyclopaediabri02chisrich/page/170/mode/2up.

Then John heard the angel tell him, "Do not to seal up the words of the prophecy of this book, *for the time is near*" (ο καιρος γαρ εγγυς εστιν, v. 10). Again, we see the urging to John and his reading audience about the necessity to anticipate the events of the end of the Church Age. But also necessary is the urging to be focused on Kingdom building for the present, and surprisingly, to not be overly concerned about the unrighteous and the vile since the time is near: "therefore let the unrighteous still be unrighteous let the vile still be vile, but let the righteous still be righteous and let the holy one still be holy" (v. 11). This verse strongly supports the Calvinistic theological perspective that each person is predestined to fulfill his/her personal path to heaven or hell. This verse is sandwiched between two verses suggesting that the time for fulfillment of this Revelation Apocalypse is very near; therefore, the urging for the believer to get his/her house in order to insure readiness for Christ's coming.

In verse 12, Jesus stated, "Behold, I am coming soon and I have My reward with Me to give to each according what his work is" (ιδου ερχομαι ταχυ και ο μισθος μου μετ εμου αποδουναι εκαστω ως το εργον εστιν αυτου, v. 12). Jesus told John—and us—that He is coming soon no less than three times in this last chapter of Revelation (vv. 7, 12, 20). He emphasized what He wants us to concentrate on—His coming back is imminent, and he wants us ready to receive Him. Indeed, He gauges readiness by the kind of works each believer executes throughout his/her life and emphasizes a "works-based" reward system as Paul wrote (cf. 1 Cor. 3:13–15). After three "I am" statements ("I am the alpha and the omega, the first and the last, the beginning and the end," v. 13), Jesus told John that those who are rewarded "have washed their long robes" (οι πλυνοντες τας στολας αυτων) and are "blessed." The Greek word "μαρκαριοι" can be translated as blessed, happy, and fortunate—so all Christians should look forward to the moment in which each of us stand before Jesus and experience His unbelievable love. We have no idea how much He wants to reward us (cf. Isaiah 64:4, 1 Cor. 2:9), but John stated in Revelation 7:14 that the saints are blessed who "wash their long robes and make them white in the blood of the Lamb"; he also stated in Revelation 19:8 that the "fine linen" are "the righteous acts of the saints." John used the same metaphor here to characterize the saints' behavior as sanctified by the blood of the Lamb and their belief in the salvatory work of Jesus in their lives. The "blessedness" of the faith and works of their salvation play out in the New Jerusalem by the invitation and privilege to enter through the gates of the city and eat from the Tree of Life. In other words, the access that Adam and Eve lost to the Tree of Life and the Garden of Eden has now been reestablished and reinstated to all those taking on the New Adam nature of Jesus Christ. But

John warned the saints and pagans alike that those who practice various types of sin including those outside the city—"outside are the perverts, the sorcerers, the fornicators, the murderers, the idolaters, and all those who love and practice the lie" (εξω οι κυνες και οι φαρμακοι και οι πορνοι και οι φονεις και οι ειδωλολατραι και πας φιλων και ποιων ψευδος, v. 15)—are considered persona non grata and not allowed past the gates, through the city walls, and into the city.

The Trinity shuns worship from beings *without* freewill and *without* the choice to refuse to worship and obey the God of the universe. The same God who freely chose to plan for our salvation and execute that plan through His Son and His Holy Spirit also made sure that the angels had free wills including Lucifer who opted out of Kingdom living for his own path. I have doubt about whether sin would exist on the earth after New Jerusalem came down onto it. But nowhere in Revelation 21-22 does it indicate that beings will not have free will and nowhere does it suggest that humans will no longer make wrong choices. However, as previously mentioned, the curse of death with its accompanying sorrow, weeping, and pain will no longer exist (Rev. 22:3) which would mean that sin will not be present in the lives of those believers who occupy the holy city. But likely *some* humans or even non-humans from other parts of the universe who choose to live outside the New Jerusalem walls on earth will be engaging in at least these six sins; hence, the Greek word "εξω" (outside) before the list of sinful behavior. Besides, it would not be necessary for twelve angels to stand guard at each of the twelve city gates if sinful behavior was not present on the earth or beyond after the new heaven and the new earth are established (Rev. 21:12). Also, the comments at the end of Revelation 21 make it clear that sinners are not allowed into the city: "Nothing profane will enter it neither those making abominations nor liars, except those written in the Lamb's Book of Life" (v. 27). The mention of those doing "παν κοινον" (defiling things), "ποιων βδελυγμα" (making abominations), and "ψευδος" (liars) surely indicates that those choosing to reject Kingdom living even during this idyllic time may continue to persist in their sins on the earth. Maybe that is one of the reasons why the leaves of the Tree of Life in the New Jerusalem is for "the healing of the nations" (θεραπειαν των εθνων, v. 2). Persistent sin produces a negative hormonal milieu of activated stress genes and their protein products eventually contributing to negative physical consequences (e.g. diabetes, obesity, hypertension, and cancer).[232]

---

[232] David Spencer, "The Effects of Sin and Righteousness on Aging," Doctoral Dissertation for DMin, Assemblies of God Theological Seminary, Springfield, MO, 2008.

Then the Apostle began to close out the Revelation with a few verses about the purpose of the Apocalypse. He recorded for the reading audience, including the members of the seven Lycus Valley churches, what Jesus said. Jesus was sending this testimony to the churches through His angel (v. 16). The angel made sure that the vision, its events, and the words witnessed and heard by John were reported correctly and, as much as humanly possible, understood by John for maximum transmission effectiveness (Rev. 1:1). Jesus also reiterated that He is the "root and offspring of David, the bright morning star" (η ριζα και το γενος Δανιδ ο αστηρ ο λαμπρος ο πρωινος, v. 16) indicating His fulfillment of the covenant to Abraham and his descendants including David and his lineage as prophesied throughout Scripture. The Revelation of Jesus Christ as the fifth Gospel is meant to encourage, educate, and prepare the body of Christ for life as we enter the End Times and make each believer shine like the morning star Venus as a witness to the pagans of the world (cf. Rev. 2:28). It's a compelling metaphor.

John then mentioned that the Holy Spirit and the Church invite the one hearing and thirsting for the Water/Word of Life to drink in the life of Jesus. Here, the Apostle was connecting desire for a fuller experience by ingesting the freely given Life of the Spirit of Jesus, "Now the Spirit and the bride say, 'Come'; and the one hearing says, 'Come'; and the thirsty one, let him come *and let the one desiring freely receive from the water of life*" (ο θελων λαβετω υδωρ ζωης δωρεαν, v. 17). This brings to mind Jesus' statement to His followers, the Feast crowd, and to the religious elite when He stood up on the last day of the Feast of Tabernacles and proclaimed, "If any man thirsts, let him come to Me and let him drink, the one believing in Me, out of his innermost being will flow streams of living water, as the Scriptures say" (Jn. 7:37–38).

The Apostle gave many warnings throughout the Book of Revelation. But in the last few verses, he warned the reader and the hearer of these passages to take care of how he/she handles this epic, Apocalyptic vision of the future. He alerts anyone who adds or subtracts from the words of this Book: he/she will experience consequences that will far outweigh their mishandling of any other Book of the New Testament. The angel says, "I warn everyone hearing the words of the prophecy of this book, if anyone adds to them, God will add to him the plagues written in this book" (μαρτυρω εγω παντι τω ακουοντι τους λογους της προφητειας του βιβλιου τουτου εαν τις επιθη επ αυτα επιθησει ο θεος επ αυτον τας πληγας τας γεγραμμενας εν τω βιβλιω τουτω, v. 18). John reported the angel infers that God is very jealous concerning the words and substance of His words about the End

Revelation: The Fifth Gospel

Times, His mercy toward believers, and His judgment of sin and sinners particularly during the last days of planet earth as we know it. He is so adamant about the faithful and respectful treatment of Revelation that He will punish the perpetrators of altering by *adding* to the Word of Revelation by *adding* to their lives the same plagues mentioned throughout its chapters—presumably any of the twenty-one seal, trumpet, or bowl judgments mentioned in the Apocalypse. I'm not sure how God could add the threat of violence (second seal: red horse), inflation (third seal: black horse), or a mega-earthquake (sixth seal) *only to an individual perpetrator* and not those associated with him and with his sin of unauthorized addition(s) to the Revelation message. Equally egregious to the Lord would be the unauthorized *subtraction* from the words of this book which would trigger two devastating consequences- maybe more catastrophic than the "addition" punishments. This is how John reported the *subtraction* consequences: "and if anyone takes away from the words of the prophecy of this book, then God will take away his part from the Tree of Life and from the holy city, the things written about in this book" (και εαν τις αφελη απο των λογων του βιβλιου της προφητειας ταυτης αφελει ο θεος το μερος αυτου απο του ξυλου της ζωης και εκ της πολεως της αγιας των γεγραμμενων εν τω βιβλιω τουτω, v. 19). Jesus made it clear that taking away from the truths of this prophecy will trigger a citizen exclusion from the New Jerusalem and will deny the perpetrator any access to the Tree of Life and its healing and nourishment—maybe two curses difficult to carry on throughout eternity. By these addition and subtraction warnings, Jesus indicated that His wrath against those who would try to alter His vision of the future given to the Apostle John is complete and unrelenting. Hopefully, any who attempt to do so would have read these warnings or at least have been told about them. Nonetheless, those who add or subtract from the Book of Revelation in ignorance, unaware of these two prohibitions, appear not to be spared from the consequences of their actions. I would hope very few would ever violate the sanctity of these prohibitions.

The Apostle reported that Jesus is very much wanting to return to collect His Church and mediate the events of the End Times: "The One who testifies to these things says, 'Yes, I am coming soon'" (λεγει ο μαρτυρων ταυτα, ναι ερχομαι ταχυ, v. 20). Of all the words that Jesus could say at the end of the most extensive apocalypse ever given to humans and at the very end of His Word to humans (the Bible), I find it revealing that Jesus again emphasized how short a time exists before the events of Revelation unfold. This surely indicates that heaven time is different from ours. But Jesus' response may indicate how much we humans procrastinate from responsibility and underestimate the preciousness of time. Jesus warned His followers multiple times throughout the Gospels about how little time they have on this earth before He returns to the earth (cf. Mt. 25:1–13). But the Greek word translated "soon" (ταχυ) can also mean "suddenly" which then would point to a rapidity of Jesus' actual return to the earth once the time is right. But whether "ταχυ" refers to the *shortness* of earth time before He returns or to the *rapidity* of the actual events of His return, His followers should never underestimate the imminence of His Parousia. I would hope we as believers would live out each day as if each day was our last on this earth.

The last sentence captures the blessedness of our lives in Christ with John stating, "May the grace of the Lord Jesus [be] with all" (η χαρις του κυριου Ιησου μετα παντων, v. 21). Without the grace or unmerited favor of the Godhead, the individual's prospect of taking part in the blessings of the New Jerusalem would not be possible. The grace (χαρις) of God is really the center of the believer's universe. Jesus is the source of the grace that John identified here and throughout the Revelation. Jesus' love for His Church enables grace to permeate our lives; through His grace we become conquerors and assist others to be the same.

Summary

The Revelation of Jesus Christ began with a political prisoner on a small island in the Aegean Sea far from the churches under his influence. The Apostle John was the perfect person to experience and report the words and events of the Apocalypse—he was a nonagenarian with an ability to remember everything he heard and saw. He wrote his Gospel ten to fifteen years before he received the Revelation. Despite writing his Gospel at least fifty years after walking the shores of Galilee with Jesus and His companions, John remembered the essential dialogues of Jesus with His disciples and with the religious elite including Jesus' "I am" sermons delivered during the Feasts over the three years of Jesus' public ministry in the Jerusalem Temple. Matthew and the other two evangelists did not record these complicated sermons and interactions with the Sanhedrin officials and with the Jews curious about and interested in His ministry. But John the Apostle, first cousin of Jesus, came from a genetic line that was brilliant and accentuated by early boyhood contact with the Savior of the world. The Holy Spirit preserved John even through the frightful boiling vat of oil in the coliseum in Rome ordered by Emperor Domitian. Jesus wanted John to receive the "words of the prophecy of this book" so that His Church would not lose hope through time as concerning the inevitability of the New Jerusalem or their futures in it. John did not disappoint.

The Apocalypse began with the assurance to five of the seven church of the Lycus Valley that, despite weaknesses and shortcomings demonstrated in the past, those overcoming in these congregations will receive rewards in the near or far future.

The two churches persecuted for their unwavering commitment to the Triune God and refusal to worship the Roman Emperor—Smyrna and Philadelphia—were encouraged to hold on to their faith and not deny their Lord. If they remained staunch and not shrink from their identity in Him, then Jesus would reward them with entrance into the Holy City, sustenance and rejuvenation from Him, and no harm from the second death.

The vision of the future started in chapter 4 with John being invited into heaven to see "what must soon take place" (Rev. 1:1; Rev. 4:1). John observed the throne room of God including the Father sitting on the throne, the seven spirits of God and the sea of glass before the throne as well as the twenty-four elders dressed in white with golden crowns on their heads. He saw the four living creatures/seraphim surrounding the throne and their incessant worship with the elders and angels of the Father and the Lamb. John saw both the conquering Messiah (the lion of Judah) and the suffering Messiah (the recently slaughtered lamb) in chapter 5. In chapter 6, he then observed the Lamb opening the Father's scroll of six seals and their effects on the earth, on the Church, and on the sun, moon, and stars (the earth's atmosphere), including World War III from the fourth seal judgment. Chapter 7 introduces the 144,000 Israeli Christians who appear to take the place of the raptured Church. Chapter 8 marks the opening of the seventh seal which ushers in the seven angels with the seven trumpet judgments. The first four judgments likely demonstrate the effects of the comet Wormwood and its tail and large meteorite breaking off from it striking the earth, and its radioactive impact plume obscuring the sun, moon, and stars and possibly creating a nuclear winter (trumpet judgments 1 through 4). In chapter 9, John reported trumpet judgments 5 (first woe) and 6 (the second woe) beginning with the "weaponized" locusts which act more like scorpions due to their stings to pagans over five months. John told his reading audience that the pain from the scorpion inoculations cause men to want to seek death and die. However, something about the stings and God's desire for men to survive for more chances to hear the gospel, cause death to flee from them and not be found (v. 6). The sixth trumpet judgment results in World War IV with a third of earth dying from nuclear holocaust presumably between East and West (maybe China against the United States). John received the command from another mighty angel in chapter 10 to prophecy about the future particularly in regard to Jerusalem and its place in the End-Times account.

In chapter 11, John saw the vision of the two Jerusalem prophets, presumably two of the 144,000 Jewish Christian evangelists, causing frustration and havoc to the

Summary

Beast and his forces for 1,260 days. When their prophecies about Jesus and the Kingdom are completed at the end of three and a half years, the Beast is allowed by the Lord to murder the two prophets. But after three days, the Spirit of God raises them from the dead in full view of the world presumably via the media, cell phones, and Internet services. Within the hour, an earthquake destroys one tenth of the city and kills seven thousand residents. The seventh angel blows his trumpet and John saw a vision of the Temple open in heaven signifying the beginning of the last half of the End Times with the ascendance of the Beast and his worldwide political system. However, Jesus interjected a quasi-historical account in chapter 12 of the development of the salvation story and its relationship to Israel and the Church. Also mentioned in this chapter is the struggle between Satan, his angels, and the Beast against the archangel Michael and the angels of God. Chapter 12 ends with the Beast being frustrated by the earth assisting the woman (the Church) fleeing and resisting the harm and destruction to it from the dragon (Satan), who stands on the seashore apparently waiting for his protégé, the Beast, to formally join him in the fight against the Lion of Judah.

Revelation 13 opens with the assassination of the Beast and his miraculous recovery from death solidifying his preeminence in the political world dominated by ten world leaders who give him their allegiance. The Church of Christ on the earth is severely persecuted by the Beast and these world leaders by not just being "killed by the sword" (v. 10), but by being forced to do business in a command economy and forced to worship his image. The Beast is joined by the false prophet who immediately establishes his boss' artificial intelligence image in the rebuilt Jerusalem Temple and requires all to worship that image, marking the abomination of desolation prophesied by Daniel in Daniel 11:31 and 12:11, and by Jesus in Matthew 24:15–16 and Luke 21:20–21. Those refusing to worship the image of the Beast are at risk of being killed (Rev. 15); those who refuse his identification (RFID) chip are excluded from commerce (vv. 16–17).

Revelation 14 describes the entrance into heaven of the 144,000 Jewish Christian evangelists who appear to be slaughtered for their faith after planting the seeds of the Word into the hearts of pagans after the Church was raptured. John described the first angel appearing after their deaths as continuing their evangelistic efforts to harvest souls for Jesus; the second angel proclaims abject and stringent judgment against the Beast and his political system in the near future; then Jesus, the Son of Man, harvests the souls of these recently converted Christians after their deaths at the hands of the Beast. This is followed by a third angel who gave John a glimpse of the judgment of the Beast and his kings' armed forces at the Battle of Armageddon in the Valley of Megiddo outside Jerusalem. John saw that the level of blood from this Battle fills the length of the Valley (900 stadia or about 170 miles) as high as the horses' bridles (about 5 feet).

Chapter 15 sets the stage for the execution of the seven bowl judgments which marks the final seven judgments against the Beast and the pagans who follow him. John saw one of the four seraphs filling the bowls of each of seven angels with terrible plagues of God's wrath—more destructive than the previous seven seal and seven trumpet judgments. Of note, "the smoke of the glory of God filled the Temple" and "no one could enter the Temple until the seven plagues" are executed (v. 8).

Chapter 16 chronicles the execution of the seven bowl plagues beginning with the first on the worshippers and followers of the Beast who contract painful sores, possibly from infections caused by their subcutaneous chips used to align them with the Beast. The second bowl judgment angel injects a toxic, blood-like material into the salt water of the oceans resulting in destruction of the sea life. Not surprisingly, the third plague involves this blood-like substance polluting fresh water sources as well. The fourth plague angel is given authority to strike the sun causing solar flares of radiation from coronal mass ejections onto the earth. These extreme, sun-induced radiation storms cause severe skin burns to those still on earth and accentuate the dehydration already severe due to the loss of fresh water from the third bowl judgment. They also cause the electrical brown- and blackouts of the Beast's capital city which are initiated by the fifth angel and his bowl judgment. John described this city's residents as biting their tongues due to the severe dehydration from the lack of available water caused by the blackouts. The residents' extreme reactions are also caused by the inability to heal their skin sores from the first bowl judgment due to their severe dehydration and possibly decreased health care services because of lack of electricity. John also stated that the residents of the city and citizens of the world experiencing the skin burns still don't repent from their rejection of God and worship of the Beast—quite astounding but indicating a true hate for the Lord and of Kingdom matters. The sixth plague is triggered by the sixth angel pouring out his bowl onto the Great Euphrates River causing it to dry up as the army from the East marches up its riverbed to position itself in the Valley of Megiddo for the Battle of Armageddon. The Apostle then saw three frog-like evil spirits coming out of the mouths of the unholy trinity of the devil, the Beast, and his false prophet which enable the three to convince the nations of the world to align with the ten nations of the Beast and unite to fight against the

Summary

"rider of the white horse" and His forces (Rev. 19:11-19). The seventh angel ends the bowl judgments by pouring out his bowl on the atmosphere causing a megaquake which is the worst ever to strike the earth since the beginning of man's history. The quake is so terrible and destructive that the major cities of the world collapse, including the capital city (splits into three parts), mountain ranges, and islands. Giant meteor-like "hail" of 90 to 100 pounds fall onto the earth presumably because of volcanic eruptions of the fault-line shift that produced the megaquake. Another possibility is that tsunamis spawned by the megaquake knock out control of the 18,000 satellites orbiting the earth causing their collision and free-fall to the earth.

Chapter 17 opens with one of the bowl angels showing John the scarlet Beast with ten horns on seven heads with the drunken prostitute who has become inebriated on the blood of the martyrs for Jesus. She lives in the city on seven hills, presumably Rome. According to John, she "sits on many waters" (v. 1) which is a metaphor for the nations which worship the Beast and have rejected the Triune God (v. 15). The seven heads of the best are previous leaders of state with an eighth king coming from this group—the text infers that he is the Antichrist from the revived Roman Empire (v. 11). The ten horns are the ten leaders of the ten districts under the Antichrist's leadership who are ruled by him from the capital city (presumably from the one established on seven hills (Rome?). From the vision in this chapter, it appears that the prostitute represents the Beast's church alliance which ultimately is rejected and decimated by these ten kings who "hate the prostitute and will make her desolate, and naked, and they will eat her flesh and will burn her down with fire" (v. 16). Thus marks the end of religious Babylon.

John next saw the destruction of economic Babylon and the capital city in chapter 18. This attack is initiated by a mighty angel (perhaps the Archangel Michael or Gabriel) who discusses the city's merchants who have mesmerized the pagan world with its lust for wealth and commercialism. John saw the destruction of international trade due to what appears to be a nuclear strike against it. Maybe economic Babylon is destroyed by the 7th bowl judgment's megaquake from the tsunami it produced, as previously iterated. Remember, John mentioned that the capital city of Babylon was split into thirds in Revelation 16:19 by the megaquake which may actually be what John's audience read in chapter 18. John discusses the destruction of the city and the loss of worldwide commerce and wealth. He even mentioned the type of products and activities lost by the interruption of international trade: precious stones and metals, industrial and building materials, apparel, perfume, food, agriculture, automotive, and human trafficking. This destruction of worldwide wealth marks the end of economic Babylon.

Revelation: The Fifth Gospel

This sets the stage for the last battle that the Beast and his forces wage against the Lamb and His heavenly forces as witnessed by John in chapter 19. He began by describing the official Marriage and Wedding Feast of the Lamb. Then John saw Jesus riding a white horse leading His armies of horsemen as they take their stance against the kings of the Beast and their forces. As I have noted, it appears that the Beast's forces don't get to fire a shot due to Jesus' weaponized mouth-laser destroying at least two hundred million troops maybe in just a few seconds. The Beast and the false prophet are hurled into Hell and the birds of prey gorge themselves on the totally destroyed armies' flesh as a clean-up crew takes seven months to dispose of what the birds leave behind (cf. Ezek. 39:12).

The Apostle then witnessed the millennial reign of those martyred for Christ during the End Times and possibly throughout the Church Age in chapter 20. Before their rule begins, however, an angel (maybe the archangel Michael) grabs Satan, chains him up, then throws him into the Abyss, and shuts and seals the door above him which keeps him imprisoned for a millennium unable to deceive the nations. John stated that those who sit on thrones and rule with Christ on the earth during these one thousand years have been beheaded, which suggests more recent martyrs by the hands of the Muslims. Perhaps their deaths are at the hands of jihadist states which have arisen in the past fifty years. Satan is released from the Abyss after the thousand years have come to an end. He immediately gathers those most vulnerable to being deceived: Gog (Russia) and Magog (Iran) and others. They "march across the breadth of the earth" (v. 9), an innumerable army, and surround Jerusalem and ready themselves to destroy it. But before they have opportunity to do so, just as with Armageddon I, they are annihilated by "fire [that] came down out of heaven" (v. 9). The devil is thrown into Hell and he along with the Beast and the false prophet are tormented forever by its flames. The chapter ends with the Great White Throne judgment of all pagan souls from all time. Those written in the Book of Life, who followed their God-given consciences and did not violate moral law, will be admitted to heaven/the New Jerusalem and those whose names are not found in the Book of Life, who sinned against their consciences and violated moral law, will be thrown into Hell.

Revelation 21 begins with an amazing statement, "Then I saw a new heaven and a new earth; for the first heaven and the first earth have passed; and the sea is no longer." Between the Great White Throne Judgment and this verse, the Father recreated His universe after destroying it with fire as per the Apostle Peter's words in 2 Peter 3:7-11. But here, John likely saw the Mediterranean Sea basin drained to decrease the upper inner core of the earth's temperature to allow for painful, but not annihilating heat as it is today (around 10,000 F). Then John saw the New Jerusalem coming down out of heaven maybe through a wormhole onto the earth. I think the holy city could actually fill the emptied sea basin of the Mediterranean Sea which has about the same length and width dimensions of this perfect cube of 1,400 miles. One of the seven bowl angels takes John to a very high mountain to inspect the city. John recorded that every 350 miles the city wall has an entrance made of a single giant pearl and that an angel guards each entrance. John observes that each entrance has one of the twelve patriarch's names on it and that the wall is made of high-grade jasper. It appears that the angel takes John inside the city after measuring its dimensions outside with "a golden measuring rod," which actually might be a laser. As previously mentioned, John heard that the city is 12,000 stadia long, wide, and high and that its walls are 144 cubits or around 200 feet thick. John is allowed to see the twelve foundation levels of the city which are named after each of the twelve apostles (is the twelfth apostle the Apostle Matthias or the Apostle Paul?) and he sees that these are adorned with very precious gems/stones. I think that each foundation has the ability to transmit a certain electromagnetic wavelength producing laser light for use in the city and for energy production around the universe. John noticed that the city is primarily composed of jasper and that the city streets, particularly the main street of the city, is composed of pure gold of a quality maybe not known to us today. The city has no Temple because the Father and the Lamb who have taken up full-time residence are its Temple. John also reported that the light sources of the city are the radiances from the Father (during the day) and from the Lamb (during the evening hours) and that the city's gates are never shut because no night exists in the city. Could this mean that sleeping is not necessary? Despite the twelve gates always open, the residents don't have to fear that sinners and those wishing to harm would want to enter the city. Remember, the security angels at each gate insure that only those with their names written in the Lamb's Book of Life enter the gates of the city.

In the last chapter of Revelation, chapter 22, the angel showed John the "river of the water of life," likely a metaphor for the Holy Spirit coursing through the city from the throne of God. Also noted was the Tree of Life probably duplicated as multiple trees on both sides of the river. The tree produces fruit throughout the year each month and the leaves of the tree are used for healing whoever needs to be rejuvenated or healed outside of the city. The residents will no longer experience death, illness, or sorrow because the curse will no longer be in the city nor in the residents' lives.

Revelation: The Fifth Gospel

The citizens of New Jerusalem will continuously worship God. They will have intimacy (i.e., "they will see His face") with the Lord not experienced to this degree before and will have the Godhead's name written on their foreheads. The apocalyptic vision ends with John being told that the citizens of the holy city will "reign as kings forever and ever"—quite a statement. This raises the likely prospect that maybe millions even billions of habitable worlds exist throughout the universe accessible through the Spirit through wormholes or mind-travel to these places.

Then the angel verified the truthfulness of these words and told John not to worship him because he also is a fellow servant. Then Jesus explained to John that the time of His return is soon and encourages the listener to remain faithfully dedicated to serving the Lord and longing for His return. He also encourages those hearing this prophecy never to add or subtract from the Apocalypse or risk the Book's plagues being added to his life or the Tree of Life and citizenship in the Holy City being excluded from his life. Jesus affirmed the truthfulness of this book and again mentioned that He will be coming back for His Church soon.

As the fifth Gospel, the Book of Revelation reveals Jesus as the slaughtered Lamb who becomes judge against the enemies of His Church, the Godhead, and His Kingdom. The spirit of antichrist (Satan)—which had his way against Jesus when He became a death target of the Sanhedrin and when He was convicted by Pilate and crucified on the cross at Golgotha—was opposed, adjudicated, and put to rest forever by the Lion of Judah after a series of judgments and events designed for maximum aversion to the Evil of the world and attraction to the Godhead. Let us press forward into our world of challenge and great potential for truly the harvest is ripe but the workers are few (Mt. 9:36-38). What a wonderful life and what a wonderful Jesus.

"Amen. Come Lord Jesus!"

Index

Symbols

1,260 days
155, 160, 162, 163, 169, 176, 178, 180, 183, 235, 311

144,000
111, 113, 115, 118, 119, 141, 161, 176, 178, 180, 182, 195, 197, 198, 207, 209, 231, 239, 261, 310, 311

666
182, 191, 192

A

Abaddon
136, 137, 141, 142, 261

abomination of desolation
92, 120, 190, 193, 311

Abyss
135, 136, 137, 139, 141, 145, 155, 163, 227, 259, 260, 261, 264, 267, 268, 269, 278, 314

acidification
166

adultery
146

Aegean Sea
8, 16, 17, 40, 45, 309

African tectonic plate
164

Ahmadinejad
265

airlift
178, 183, 198

Alexander
16, 41, 73, 78, 174, 233, 239

Alexander the Great
13, 41, 112, 119, 120, 136, 153, 159, 164, 174, 177, 184, 187, 196, 199, 212, 224, 227, 230, 233, 235, 237, 239, 240, 252, 261, 269, 270, 271, 273, 274, 277, 279, 282, 289, 312, 314

All-domain Anomaly Resolution
300

Allegorists
12

Alzheimer's disease
18, 104

amillennialism
95

Antichrist
25, 93, 94, 98, 99, 125, 142, 144, 156, 158, 160, 161, 163, 167, 180, 182, 183, 184, 185, 188, 189, 191, 192, 193, 197, 198, 200, 220, 221, 229, 230, 233, 234, 239, 247, 251, 255, 256, 257, 262, 264, 277, 313

Antipater
174

Apollyon
136, 137, 141, 142

apostles
14, 30, 31, 75, 105, 114, 120, 238, 247, 276, 284, 302, 315

Area 51
76, 178, 179, 180, 198, 300

Aristobulus
174

Ark of the Covenant
156, 166

Armageddon I
13, 52, 122, 151, 177, 200, 203, 223, 255, 257, 267, 268, 277, 314

Armageddon II
52, 200, 255, 260, 264, 267, 277

artificial intelligence
189, 190, 311

Asher
112, 116

assassinated
161, 163, 165, 184, 187, 230, 232, 239, 251

asteroid
127, 129, 130, 131, 132, 133, 137

Ataturk Dam
220

autotrophs
215

Ayatollah Khomeini
265

B

Babylonian Captivity
35

Baidu
241

Balaam
32, 47

Balak
32, 46

Barna
69, 285

Basilica
35

bazaar
43

bear
146, 181, 184

beast
104, 160, 181, 182, 184, 188, 190, 191, 192, 193, 196, 200, 205, 211, 217, 218, 227, 228, 229, 230, 232, 233, 235, 237, 240, 250, 256, 259, 260, 268

Beast
25, 27, 29, 47, 52, 92, 94, 100, 119, 131, 153, 155, 160, 161, 162, 163, 164, 165, 166, 183, 184, 185, 187, 188, 189, 191, 192, 193, 194, 197, 198, 199, 200, 201, 202, 207, 213, 217, 218, 220, 221, 225, 229, 230, 232, 233, 234, 235, 239, 240, 241, 242, 244, 251, 252, 254, 255, 256, 257, 261, 262, 267, 268, 269, 277, 279, 290, 311, 312, 313, 314

Beast's Confederacy
279

Benjamin
112, 118

Bethlehem
174

big ones
156, 182, 250

birth pains
91, 169, 171

black horse
96, 100, 306

blackout
218

blood
19, 21, 25, 29, 47, 84, 87, 89, 96, 105, 106, 107, 112, 113, 121, 123, 126, 129, 155, 162, 170, 177, 196, 199, 202, 205, 211, 213, 214, 215, 227, 231, 232, 238, 247, 249, 250, 254, 256, 262, 270, 272, 274, 278, 297, 303, 312, 313

Book of Life
55, 60, 119, 182, 187, 201, 228, 232, 260, 271, 273, 276, 277, 284, 291, 304, 314, 315

bride
238, 247, 252, 253, 275, 276, 278, 282, 301, 305

bridegroom
238

C

Cahill
58

Caicus River
45

Caligula
16, 34, 41

Calvin
89, 187

camp of the saints
267

cataract
29, 197, 301

cattle
157, 238

Cayster
37

center of the earth
268

Ceres
129, 132

chavrutas
14

Chernobyl
246

Chicxulub asteroid
133

Chinese Communist Party
144, 191

Chinese Liberation Air Force
143

chromosomes
273

circular letter
17, 51

circum-Pacific seismic belt
225

citron wood
238

close encounter
28

codex
26, 85

comet
126, 127, 128, 129, 131, 132, 133, 137, 138, 310

Commiphora
40

Comte
36

Conquering Messiah
25, 52, 90, 165, 167, 175, 234, 254

Copenhagen criteria
186

coronal mass ejections
216, 218, 312

Corsica
183

council of governments
229

COVID-19
69, 146, 192, 253

craftsmen
247

crimson worm
158

Croesus
57

crystal
71, 76, 122, 276, 280, 283, 287, 293, 295

curse
130, 293, 296, 304, 315

Cyrus
233, 255

D

Dan
10, 11, 75, 92, 93, 94, 118, 120, 160, 189, 255, 283, 286

death angel
141, 261

Decius
12, 34

deep pit
135, 137

Dehydration
215

desert
176, 178, 180, 183

despised
240

diatoms
215

dinoflagellates
215

Diocletian
12, 34

dipped
250, 254, 256

dispensationalists
35, 60, 64

divorce
146, 281

DNA
273

Index

Dome of the Rock
156, 157, 158, 159

Domitian
8, 16, 17, 26, 34, 37, 41, 43, 105, 233, 309

double portion
237, 242

dragon
25, 52, 86, 145, 169, 170, 171, 172, 174, 175, 176, 177, 178, 179, 180, 181, 182, 183, 185, 188, 200, 207, 212, 229, 240, 259, 261, 311

drunk
227, 229, 231, 262

E

earth time
23, 167, 307

economic Babylon
193, 235, 240, 241, 242, 243, 245, 252, 313

Egypt
104, 118, 141, 155, 172, 183, 221, 230, 233, 255

Elijah
28, 53, 160, 279

Emperor Constantine
34

emperor worship
17, 62

Ephesus
8, 12, 15, 17, 18, 22, 23, 26, 27, 31, 37, 38, 39, 40, 41, 46, 48, 65

Ephraim
116, 118, 283

eschatology
91

Euphrates River
142, 144, 219, 220, 312

Eurasia Tectonic Plates
164

European Economic Community
183, 185

European Union
99, 184, 185, 186, 191, 230, 234, 239

eutrophication
166

extinction level event
133

eye ointment
68

Ezekiel
10, 11, 76, 78, 80, 118, 150, 152, 153, 172, 202, 221, 255, 257

F

Feuerbach
36

Fifth Bowl Judgment
217

Fifth Seal
105

Fifth Trumpet Judgment
136

fire from heaven
268

first bowl judgment
219, 312

First Seal
97

first trumpet judgment
129, 131

first woe
136, 142, 310

forced labor
245

foreign body response
213

forty-two months
155, 160, 176, 181, 187, 235

Foundation Stone
157, 159

fourth bowl judgment
122, 216, 217

Fourth Seal
101

fourth trumpet judgment
134

four winds
111, 112

frankincense
125, 238

fruit
39, 40, 43, 105, 145, 167, 197, 201, 238, 245, 288, 293, 295, 296, 315

G

Gabriel
23, 85, 148, 149, 150, 157, 198, 240, 313

Gad
111, 115

galaxy
298

gematria
192

geomagnetic storm
218

global Internet
184, 241

Gnostic philosophers
33, 38

gold
56, 57, 65, 67, 136, 145, 158, 227, 230, 238, 239, 246, 270, 276, 287, 288, 295, 315

golden censer
123, 125

golden goblet
230

gorged
251, 257

grapevines
201

grasshoppers
140

gravity
86, 288, 297

great eagle
170, 176, 178, 180

Great Rift-Dead Sea fault
164

Great Rift Valley
164

Great Tribulation Period
10, 109, 150, 153, 177, 184, 187, 233, 239, 261

great white throne
260, 270

gross domestic product
241

guild prostitutes
50, 51

Gunshot
184, 185

H

Halley's Comet
127

Hamas
265

harpists
195, 197, 238

haunt
237, 240

Hawking
132, 190

heaven time
23, 306

Heinrich Zwingli
9

Hezbollah
265

honey
148, 152

Hoover Dam
178

horse-drawn chariots
136, 140

horse's bridle
202

human trafficking
244, 245, 313

hurricanes
113, 218, 277

Hybrid Locusts
136

I

idol
32, 33, 39, 46, 50, 145, 160, 189, 193, 229, 302

impact plume
132, 134, 137, 310

incense offerings
42, 125

International Criminal Court
266

International Monetary Fund
98

Iran
97, 144, 191, 221, 255, 262, 265, 266, 277, 314

Iraq
97, 218, 221, 230, 239, 263, 265

Iron Beam
29

iron oxide crystals
129

Islam
157, 171, 263

Israeli Temple Movement
158

Issachar
112, 117

J

jasper
71, 75, 172, 276, 283, 286, 288, 315

Jews sealed for Christ
115

Jezebel
33, 36, 50, 51, 52

jihadist
184, 262, 314

John
7, 8, 9, 10, 11, 12, 13, 14, 15, 16, 17, 18, 21, 22, 23, 24, 25, 26, 27, 28, 29, 30, 33, 35, 37, 38, 39, 40, 41, 42, 45, 46, 47, 49, 51, 57, 58, 59, 62, 64, 65, 67, 68, 72, 73, 74, 76, 77, 78, 79, 80, 84, 86, 87, 89, 94, 97, 98, 99, 100, 101, 105, 106, 107, 108, 109, 112, 114, 115, 119, 120, 121, 122, 124, 125, 126, 129, 130, 131, 132, 136, 137, 139, 141, 142, 144, 145, 148, 149, 150, 151, 152, 153, 158, 159, 160, 161, 162, 163, 164, 165, 166, 167, 170, 172, 174, 175, 176, 177, 178, 179, 183, 184, 185, 187, 188, 189, 191, 192, 193, 194, 197, 198, 199, 200, 201, 206, 207, 208, 212, 214, 215, 216, 217, 218, 219, 220, 221, 224, 229, 230, 231, 232, 233, 234, 235, 239, 240, 241, 242, 243, 244, 245, 246, 247, 251, 252, 253, 254, 255, 256, 257, 260, 261, 262, 264, 265, 267, 268, 270, 271, 272, 273, 277, 278, 279, 280, 282, 283, 284, 285, 286, 288, 289, 290, 294, 295, 296, 297, 301, 302, 303, 305, 307, 309, 310, 311, 312, 313, 314, 315, 316

Joseph
112, 115, 116, 118, 245, 266

Judah
78, 79, 83, 86, 104, 111, 115, 117, 125, 234, 310, 311, 316

K

Kaaba
157

Kant
36, 60

key of David
56, 62

King Eumenes
41

King of the North
255

King of Tyre
172, 173

kosher dye
158

Krakatoa
63

L

lamb
23, 26, 85, 87, 182, 188, 310

Index

Laodicea
13, 22, 27, 56, 65, 66, 68

laser
19, 29, 47, 52, 159, 173, 202, 221, 256, 257, 277, 283, 285, 287, 288, 300, 314, 315

leaves
40, 75, 158, 188, 293, 296, 304, 315

leopard
181, 184

leukotrienes
138

Levi
112, 117, 118, 157

Lion
83, 84, 86, 87, 104, 234, 311, 316

liquid iron
269

Lisbon Treaty
186

Literal futurists
13

locpions
138, 139, 260

Lucifer
79, 145, 149, 167, 172, 173, 174, 175, 260, 304

Lukewarm
65

Lycus Valley
8, 16, 17, 24, 29, 30, 38, 40, 48, 60, 62, 74, 85, 305, 309

Lydia
49, 58, 61

M

Mammon
282

Manasseh
79, 112, 116, 118

manna
32, 47, 48, 166

Mao Tse Tung
191

Mariamne
174

Martin Luther
9, 35, 228

martyrdom
13, 106, 176, 231, 239, 262

Mary
7, 14, 15, 23, 150, 159, 167, 171

materialism
242

Mediterranean Sea
214, 277, 286, 314

merchants
237, 238, 241, 244, 246, 247, 313

meteor
127, 128, 129, 130, 131, 132, 313

meteorite
129, 130, 131, 310

methyl isocyanate
128, 129, 131

midheaven
124, 198, 250

mid-tribulationists
93

mighty angel
83, 85, 137, 147, 148, 150, 152, 165, 238, 247, 310, 313

Milky Way
298, 300

Millennialism
94

millstone
108, 238, 247

moon
28, 96, 107, 113, 124, 132, 134, 169, 170, 171, 276, 291, 310

mother
7, 14, 15, 159

mountain
57, 96, 123, 126, 129, 130, 222, 276, 283, 313, 315

Mount Zion
197

Mt. Moriah
197

Muhammed
157, 263

murder
48, 145, 146, 152, 185, 281, 311

myrrh
40, 125, 238

mystery
22, 74, 103, 147, 152, 165, 218, 227

N

Naphtali
112, 116

National Center for Health Statistics
281

near death experiences
23, 72

Nebuchadnezzar
233, 239, 255

Nero
12, 16, 34, 41, 46, 105, 192

Neuralink
190

neuraminidase
138

new
8, 32, 46, 47, 56, 64, 69, 83, 87, 98, 132, 145, 167, 195, 206, 230, 242, 257, 273, 275, 277, 279, 280, 281, 286, 295, 296, 299, 304, 314

New Jerusalem
13, 28, 39, 40, 56, 64, 68, 74, 75, 76, 77, 118, 121, 122, 125, 152, 159, 167, 177, 223, 231, 270, 272, 275, 278, 279, 280, 281, 282, 284, 285, 286, 287, 288, 289, 290, 291, 295, 296, 297, 299, 300, 301, 303, 304, 306, 307, 309, 314, 315, 316

nickel
269, 278

Nicolaitans
31, 32, 39, 40, 46, 48

Northern Hemisphere
129, 131

Index

Nostradamus
192

nuclear reactor
246, 252

nuclear reactors
223

Nuclear Warfare
142

nuclear winter
113, 130, 310

O

oath
147, 151, 152

Operation Israelis for Jesus
178

organ trafficking
244

outer core
268, 269, 277, 278

ozone depletion
121

P

pale green horse
96, 101

papyrus
26, 27, 84

parchment
26, 27, 85

parrots
257

Parthians
97

Patmos
8, 16, 17, 18, 22, 25

pearl
276, 287, 315

pebble
32, 47, 48, 127, 130

perfect cube
283, 285, 315

Pergamum
12, 22, 27, 32, 35, 41, 45, 46, 47, 48, 51, 62

Peter
8, 15, 17, 28, 35, 94, 151, 152, 190, 192, 199, 265, 270, 277, 279, 289, 291, 302, 314

Pharaoh Thutmose III
233

phenotypic plasticity
140

Philadelphia
13, 16, 17, 22, 26, 27, 42, 44, 56, 61, 62, 63, 64, 65, 278, 310

phytoplankton
215

plagues
10, 74, 102, 103, 136, 143, 162, 205, 206, 208, 211, 212, 228, 237, 242, 243, 276, 282, 294, 305, 312, 316

political Babylon
193, 221, 239, 240, 251, 252

Polycarp
45

Pope Leo X
35

Postmillennialists
95

Post-tribulationists
94

pregnant
124, 169, 171, 206

Premillennialists
94

presidents
185, 229, 252, 254

Preterists
11

pre-tribulationists
93, 109

Prion disease
104

projects
22, 35, 40, 98, 250, 256

prophecy
10, 21, 41, 52, 93, 148, 153, 155, 162, 170, 173, 193, 250, 254, 267, 273, 294, 301, 303, 305, 309, 310, 316

prophets
13, 27, 40, 79, 91, 92, 118, 147, 152, 153, 156, 160, 161, 162, 163, 164, 165, 166, 167, 176, 182, 184, 197, 211, 215, 221, 238, 247, 252, 255, 261, 294, 301, 302, 310

Prophet's Mosque
157

prostanoids
138

Put
221

Putin
266

R

radiation storms
216, 312

rainbow
75, 147, 148

Ramsey
48, 49

rapture
73, 94, 239

recursive self-improvement
190

Red Heifer program
157

red horse
306

religio illicita
34, 40

religio licita
42

Reuben
111, 115

Reverse fault shifts
222

revived Roman Empire
230, 239, 313

Ring
72, 73

Index

River of Life
288, 295

roar
147, 151, 252

Robert Estienne
27

rod
33, 52, 155, 159, 166, 169, 175, 250, 276, 285, 315

Roman Catholic Church
35, 231, 235

S

sackcloth
96, 107, 155, 160, 162

Salome
7, 14, 159

Sardinia
183

Sardis
12, 22, 27, 45, 50, 55, 57, 58, 59, 61

Sartre
36

scarlet
158, 227, 229, 230, 238, 246, 313

scorching heat
121

scorpion
135, 137, 141, 310

scroll
22, 26, 83, 84, 85, 87, 88, 90, 96, 97, 108, 147, 148, 150, 152, 310

Scroll
84, 85, 159

Second Bowl Judgment
214

second death
32, 44, 259, 260, 272, 275, 280, 310

Second Seal
99

second trumpet judgment
129, 130

sensual living
238, 241

Seraphim

seraph
73, 78

seven angels
10, 28, 80, 123, 124, 126, 205, 206, 208, 211, 213, 227, 235, 276, 282, 310, 312

seven burning lamps
71, 76, 151

seven heads
169, 172, 181, 183, 188, 218, 227, 228, 229, 232, 313

seven hills
183, 218, 228, 233, 235, 239, 313

Seven Seals
85

Seventh Bowl Judgment
222

seven thousand
92, 156, 164, 311

Seventh Seal
94, 124, 201

Seventh Trumpet Judgment
165

seven thunders
147, 151, 152

seven trumpets
123, 124, 125

seventy weeks of years
11, 91

shaft of the Abyss
138, 261

sheep
26, 27, 85, 104, 238

sickle
196, 201

sign
94, 149, 169, 170, 172, 205, 206

signet ring
113

Simeon
112, 117

Sixth Bowl Judgment
219

Sixth Seal
96, 106

Sixth Trumpet Judgment
142

small ones
156, 182, 250

Smyrna
12, 17, 22, 26, 27, 32, 34, 40, 41, 42, 43, 44, 45, 46, 62, 64, 310

Solar System
127, 128, 132, 298

soon
21, 23, 32, 47, 56, 125, 151, 152, 164, 174, 252, 254, 272, 294, 301, 303, 306, 310, 316

sorcery
136, 146, 238

sore
211, 213

soteriology
88

sour
148, 150, 152, 201

stadia
196, 276, 284, 285, 312, 315

Stalin
266

stars
22, 29, 30, 31, 52, 55, 74, 96, 107, 108, 124, 132, 134, 169, 170, 172, 173, 174, 282, 298, 299, 310

stealing
145, 146, 175

Stephen Langton
27

stomach
148, 150, 152

Strabo
61

Suffering Messiah
87

suicide
73, 138, 139

Index

sulfur
131, 133, 134, 136, 143, 200, 256, 260, 268, 272, 275, 277, 278, 280

sunblocks
217

sunburns
217

Synagogue of Satan
32, 43, 56

T

tabernacle
112, 121, 275, 278, 289

Taliban
262

tear

tears
112, 122, 275, 279, 290

technological singularity
190

Temple of Artemis
37, 38, 58

ten archangels
149

ten horns
169, 172, 181, 183, 185, 188, 227, 228, 229, 233, 235, 239, 252, 255, 313

ten kings' confederacy
221, 234

tephillin
290

Tertullian
8, 17, 35, 106

testimony
21, 22, 42, 76, 96, 119, 155, 162, 167, 170, 177, 179, 208, 250, 254, 259, 262, 294, 305

the chosen
228, 234

The Great Satan
265

Theodosius I
34

The Vatican
235

think-travel
301

Third Bowl Judgment
215

Third Seal
100

Third Trumpet Judgment
130

three and a half days
155, 161, 163

three archangels
145, 149, 172

Thyatira
12, 22, 27, 33, 36, 45, 48, 49, 50, 51, 52, 57, 59, 62, 270

Tiberius
41, 58

Tiglath-Pileser
233

TikTok
242, 282

Time of Sorrows
10, 79, 97, 109, 113, 117, 120, 165, 177, 183, 233

Titus
15, 16, 42, 104, 156, 160, 189

torment
135, 136, 137, 140, 141, 142, 196, 237, 238, 242, 243, 246, 268

tornadoes
113

torrent
86, 170, 178

trade guilds
43, 49, 52

Transfiguration
28

Tree of Life
32, 39, 40, 173, 288, 293, 294, 295, 296, 301, 303, 304, 306, 315, 316

trisagion
77, 80

Tunguska River
129

two lampstands
27, 155, 160

two olive trees
155, 160

U

Ukraine
266

unclean bird
237, 240

underground reservoirs
179

unholy trinity
25, 180, 193, 200, 220, 225, 229, 234, 312

United States
99, 102, 121, 134, 138, 145, 146, 176, 178, 179, 180, 183, 185, 186, 198, 221, 233, 234, 241, 244, 245, 246, 265, 273, 281, 298, 300, 310

United States Air Force
178, 180, 198

universe
36, 77, 84, 85, 90, 109, 148, 152, 172, 173, 175, 233, 254, 268, 270, 280, 287, 288, 295, 296, 298, 300, 304, 307, 314, 316

unmanned computer directed assault devices
138

unpotable water
131

V

Valley of Jezreel
255

Valley of Megiddo
144, 202, 203, 221, 229, 255, 257, 312

vellum
26, 27, 85

Victorinus
9, 78

virgins
119, 195, 197

Index

Vulgate
27

W

water of life
76, 122, 280, 288, 290, 294, 295, 305, 315

web
118, 132, 191, 241, 246

wedding feast
106, 250, 253, 279

wedding of the Lamb
250, 252

Wesleyan Quadrilateral
26

white horse
96, 97, 98, 202, 250, 254, 255, 313, 314

widow
25, 237, 243

wine
40, 46, 96, 100, 196, 199, 212, 224, 227, 229, 237, 238, 241, 250

winepress
196, 201, 250

World Bank
98, 223, 233, 241

World Council of Churches
231, 232, 239, 251

wormholes
300, 316

Wormwood
124, 126, 127, 129, 130, 131, 132, 133, 134, 137, 138, 310

Wycliffe Bible
27

Y

Yeshiva
14

Yucatan Peninsula
133

Z

Zebedee
14

Zebulon
112, 117

Zeus
41

Made in the USA
Columbia, SC
10 August 2024

f31baccf-bdae-4413-835d-50b9166c1fbeR07